Making Standards Useful IN THE CLASSROOM

Making Standards Useful

Standards

Useful IN THE CLASSROOM

ROBERT J.
MARZANO

MARK W.
HAYSTEAD

**Association for Supervision and
Curriculum Development**

Alexandria, Virginia USA

Association for Supervision and Curriculum Development
1703 N. Beauregard St. • Alexandria, VA 22311-1714 USA
Phone: 800-933-2723 or 703-578-9600 • Fax: 703-575-5400
Web site: www.ascd.org • E-mail: member@ascd.org
Author guidelines: www.ascd.org/write

Gene R. Carter, *Executive Director;* Nancy Modrak, *Publisher;* Julie Houtz, *Director of Book Editing &
Production;* Darcie Russell, *Project Manager;* Reece Quiñones, *Senior Graphic Designer;* Valerie Younkin,
Desktop Publishing Specialist; Dina Murray Seamon, *Production Specialist/Team Lead*

All Web links in this book are correct as of the publication date below but may have become inac-
tive or otherwise modified since that time. If you notice a deactivated or changed link, please e-mail
books@ascd.org with the words "Link Update" in the subject line. In your message, please specify the
Web link, the book title, and the page number on which the link appears.

PAGEBACK ISBN: 978-1-4166-0648-2   ASCD product #108006   s3/08
PAPERBACK ISBN: 978-1-4166-0648-2   ASCD product #108006   s3/08
Also available as an e-book through ebrary, netLibrary, and many online booksellers (see Books in
Print for the ISBNs).

Quantity discounts for the paperback edition only: 10–49 copies, 10%; 50+ copies, 15%; for 1,000 or
more copies, call 800-933-2723, ext. 5634, or 703-575-5634. For desk copies: member@ascd.org.

Library of Congress Cataloging-in-Publication Data
Marzano, Robert J.
     Making standards useful in the classroom / Robert J. Marzano and Mark W. Haystead.
          p.   cm.
     Includes bibliographical references.
     ISBN 978-1-4166-0648-2 (pbk. : alk. paper) 1. Education—Standards—United States.   2. Educational
evaluation—United States.   3. Grading and marking (Students)—United States.   I. Haystead, Mark W.,
1969–   II. Association for Supervision and Curriculum Development.   III. Title.

     LB3060.83.M379 2008
     379.1'59—dc22

                                                                                        2007042402

18 17 16 15 14 13 12 11 10 09 08   1 2 3 4 5 6 7 8 9 10 11 12

To my family—Jana, Todd and Whitney, Christine and Mark, Carmen and Tomi, Ashley, Cecilia, Aida, and Jacob

—Robert J. Marzano

To my family—Christine, my wife and best friend, you are truly the wind beneath my wings. Cecilia and Aida, I am so proud to be your dad; keep reaching for the stars.

—Mark W. Haystead

Making Standards Useful

IN THE CLASSROOM

PART I

Using Standards
and Measurement Topics

1

Standards in Education

The standards movement in the United States has a long and interesting history. Many trace its genesis back to the publication of *A Nation at Risk*, which sounded the following alarm: "The education foundations of our society are presently being eroded by a rising tide of mediocrity that threatens our very future as a nation and a people. . . . We have, in effect, been committing an act of unthinking, unilateral educational disarmament" (National Commission on Excellence in Education, 1983, p. 5). These ominous words sparked a flood of impassioned pleas to upgrade the K–12 educational system in the United States.

In September 1989, President George H. W. Bush convened the nation's governors at an Education Summit in Charlottesville, Virginia. The summit identified six broad national goals that were to be reached by the year 2000. In general terms, those goals called for U.S. students to master complex academic content in English, mathematics, science, history, and geography. The goals were showcased in the 1990 State of the Union address.

That same year, the National Education Goals Panel (NEGP) was established; the following year, the National Council on Education Standards and Testing (NCEST) was established. Together these two groups were to deal with such implementation issues as which standards would be addressed, the performance levels that would be expected for these standards, and the types of assessments that would be used. Subject matter organizations were called upon to identify the knowledge that all students would be expected to learn within their domains. The National Council of Teachers of Mathematics (NCTM) took the lead in these efforts by publishing its *Curriculum and Evaluation Standards for School Mathematics* in 1989. Other subject matter organizations followed suit. Figure 1.1 outlines the major events in the design of standards documents in the subject areas from 1989 through 2000, at which time the major national and state-level standards documents were in place.

Figure 1.1 Major Events in the Development of Subject Matter Standards, 1989–2000

Year	Event
1989	The 50 governors and President George H. W. Bush identify English, mathematics, science, history, and geography as subjects in need of challenging national achievement standards in National Education Goals for the year 2000.
1989	The National Council of Teachers of Mathematics publishes *Curriculum and Evaluation Standards for School Mathematics*.
1989	Project 2061 of the American Association for the Advancement of Science (AAAS) publishes *Science for All Americans*, outlining which "understandings and habits of mind are essential for all citizens of a scientifically literate society."
1990	President Bush announces the National Education Goals for the year 2000 and works with Congress to establish a National Education Goals Panel (NEGP).
1990	To determine the skills young people need for success in the working world, the U.S. secretary of labor appoints the Secretary's Commission on Achieving Necessary Skills (SCANS).
1990	The National Center on Education and the Economy and the Learning Research and Development Center create the New Standards Project to define standards for student achievement in a number of areas.
1991	The knowledge and skills essential for the working world are described in a SCANS document titled *What Work Requires of Schools*.
1992	The U.S. Department of Education teams up with the National Endowment for the Humanities to provide funding for the National History Standards Project.
1992	The National Association for Sport and Physical Education develops *Outcomes for Quality Physical Education Programs*, setting a foundation for physical education standards.
1992	The U.S. Department of Education teams up with the National Endowment for the Arts and the National Endowment for the Humanities to fund the writing of standards for the arts through the Consortium of National Arts Education Associations.
1992	Standards for civics and government are written by the Center for Civic Education with financial help from the U.S. Department of Education and the Pew Charitable Trusts.
1992	The Geography Standards Education Project writes the first standards for geography.
1992	The American Cancer Society funds the Committee for National Health Education.
1992	The federal government provides funds to the National Council of Teachers of English, the International Reading Association, and the Center for the Study of Reading at the University of Illinois to create English language arts standards.
1993	Foreign language standards are formed with federal funding through the National Standards in Foreign Language Project.
1993	AAAS's Project 2061 publishes *Benchmarks for Science Literacy*.
1993	"The Malcolm Report," also known as *Promises to Keep: Creating High Standards for American Students*, is released. The document is compiled by the NEGP and recommends creating a National Education Standards and Improvement Council (NESIC) whose presence would enable voluntary national standards to exist.
1993	Standards development, teaching, and assessment are overseen by the National Committee on Science Education Standards and Assessment (NCSESA) with funding from the U.S. Department of Education, the National Research Council, and the National Science Foundation.

Figure 1.1 *(continued)*	

Year	Event
1994	The *Incomplete Work of the Task Forces of the Standards Project for English Language Arts* is published by the Center for the Study of Reading, the International Reading Association, and the National Council of Teachers of English.
1994	Foreign languages, the arts, economics, and civics and government are added to the list of areas for which students should demonstrate "competency over subject matters," bringing the total number of subjects covered to nine. Two new goals are added to the National Education Goals, and the National Education Standards and Improvement Council (NESIC) is created by President Clinton in his Goals 2000: Educate America Act for the purpose of certifying national and state content and performance standards, state assessments, and opportunity to learn standards.
1994	Funding for the Standards Project for the English Language Arts is cut by the U.S. Department of Education.
1994	Arts standards (dance, theater, visual arts, and music) are published through the Consortium of National Arts Education Associations. This effort is funded by the U.S. Department of Education, the National Endowment for the Arts, and the National Endowment for the Humanities.
1994	*Curriculum Standards for the Social Studies: Expectations for Excellence* is published by the National Council for the Social Studies.
1994	U.S. history standards, world history standards, and K–4 history standards are released.
1994	*Geography for Life: National Geography Standards* is published by the Geography Education Standards Project.
1994	Standards for civics and government education are published by the Center for Civic Education, a project funded by the U.S. Department of Education and the Pew Charitable Trusts.
1995	The U.S. Department of Education withdraws funding from a project by the National Council on Economic Education to create standards in economics.
1995	*National Health Education Standards: Achieving Health Literacy* is published by the Joint Committee on National Health Education Standards.
1995	*Moving into the Future: National Standards for Physical Education* is released, a product of the National Association for Sport and Physical Education.
1995	The National Council on Economic Education sets a goal of publishing standards in the winter of 1996.
1995	*Performance Standards* for English language arts, science, mathematics, and "applied learning" are released in three volumes, a product of the New Standards Project.
1995	*National Standards for Business Education: What America's Students Should Know and Be Able to Do in Business* is released, a product of the National Business Education Association.
1996	*Foreign Language Learning: Preparing for the 21st Century* is released, the product of the National Standards in Foreign Language Project.
1996	*National Science Education Standards* is released, a product of the National Research Council.
1996	Forty state governors and 45 business leaders attend the National Education Summit, pledging to support efforts toward creating academic standards in the core subject areas at both the state and local levels; business leaders recognize a need to consider these standards when opening or relocating facilities.

Year	Event
	Figure 1.1 *(continued)*
1996	*Standards for the English Language Arts* is released, a product of the National Council of Teachers of English and the International Reading Association.
1996	A new draft of history standards is released.
1996	A document designed to help create technology standards is released by the International Technology Education Association, a project in cooperation with the National Science Foundation and the National Aeronautics and Space Administration.
1997	President Clinton declares a need for every state to adopt national standards and implement statewide testing for 4th graders in reading and 8th graders in math by 1999 in order to monitor progress.
1997	*Voluntary National Content Standards* is published by EconomicsAmerica. This document is also available on CD-ROM.
1997	*ESL Standards for Pre-K-12 Students* is released, a product of Teachers of English to Speakers of Other Languages.
1997	*Performance Standards: English Language Arts, Mathematics, Science, Applied Learning* is released by the National Center on Education and the Economy.
1998	*Competent Communicators: K–12 Speaking, Listening, and Media Literacy Standards and Competency Statements* is released, a product of the Council for Basic Education.
1998	Nine encompassing literacy standards are included in *Information Power: Building Partnerships for Learning*, a product of the American Library Association.
1999	Improving educator quality, helping all students reach high standards, and increasing accountability are named as three major areas in need of improvement by governors, educators, and business leaders at the National Education Summit. The meeting concludes with a goal of specifying how each state will accomplish the tasks.
1999	Specific standards for Chinese, classical languages, French, German, Italian, Japanese, Portuguese, Russian, and Spanish are added to the original standards and republished as *Standards for Foreign Language Learning in the 21st Century*, a product of the National Standards in Foreign Language Education Project.
2000	*Standards for Technological Literacy: Content for the Study of Technology* is published, a product of the International Technology Association.
2000	*National Educational Technology Standards for Students: Connecting Curriculum and Technology* is published, a product of the International Society for Technology in Education.
2000	*Principles and Standards for School Mathematics* is released, a product of the National Council of Teachers of Mathematics.

Figure 1.1 adds some detail to the rich history of the modern standards movement and attests to the prominence of the movement in the 1980s and 1990s. Discussing the movement's impact, Robert Glaser and Robert Linn (1993) explain:

> In the recounting of our nation's drive toward educational reform, the last decade of this century will undoubtedly be identified as the time when a

concentrated press for national educational standards emerged. The press for standards was evidenced by the efforts of federal and state legislators, presidential and gubernatorial candidates, teachers and subject-matter specialists, councils, governmental agencies, and private foundations. (p. xiii)

Glaser and Linn made their comments at the end of the 20th century. There is no indication that the standards movement has lost any momentum at the beginning of the 21st century.

Flaws in the Standards

Given the power of the standards movement, one might assume that national standards and state standards have enhanced the daily practice of K–12 education. Although it is true that in many states teachers are aware of the content of their state standards because school districts have aligned grade-level curriculums with state and national standards, it is not necessarily true that the standards movement has enhanced the life of the classroom teacher. In fact, a case can be made that state and national standards, as currently designed, detract from a teacher's ability to teach effectively. At least two reasons account for this unfortunate situation: the standards articulate too much content, and they lack unidimensionality.

Too Much Content

State and national standards articulate far too much content. To illustrate, researchers at Mid-continent Research for Education and Learning (McREL) identified some 200 standards and 3,093 benchmarks in national and state-level documents across 14 subject areas (Kendall & Marzano, 2000). They then asked classroom teachers how long it would take to address the content in those standards and benchmarks. When the researchers compared the estimated amount of time it would take to teach the content in the standards documents with the amount of time that is available for classroom instruction, they found that addressing the mandated content would require 71 percent more instructional time than is now available (Marzano, Kendall, & Gaddy, 1999). Looking at this situation in another way, schooling, as currently configured, would have to be extended from kindergarten to grade 21 or 22 to accommodate all the standards and benchmarks in the national documents. Certainly this is not possible.

What, then, do busy classroom teachers do when asked to teach 71 percent more content than time allows for? Probably one of two things. They simply pick and choose from among the vast array of information and skills articulated in the standards, or they race through all the content in an attempt at complete "coverage." To dramatize this situation, Figure 1.2 contains 5 statements out of more than 120 similar statements related to content that 5th grade language arts teachers in one state are expected to teach in a single year of school. (To avoid denigrating any particular state standards document, we

---

Figure 1.2   Sample Competency Statements for 5th Grade Language Arts from a State Document

1. Apply prior knowledge and experience to make inferences and respond to new information presented in text.

2. Draw inferences and conclusions about text and support them with textual evidence and prior knowledge.

3. Describe elements of character development in written works (e.g., differences between main and minor characters; stereotypical characters as opposed to fully developed characters; changes that characters undergo; the importance of character's actions, motives, and appearance to plot and theme).

4. Make inferences or draw conclusions about characters' qualities and actions (e.g., based on knowledge of plot, setting, characters' motives, characters' appearances, other characters' responses to a character).

5. Participate in creative response to text (e.g., art, drama, and oral presentation).

---

have not identified the state. In fact, just about any state document could have been used to make the same point.)

Given that the state document has more than 120 statements like those in Figure 1.2 and that the school year comprises only 180 days, a teacher would have to teach and assess the content in one statement every one-and-one-half days to address all the statements in one year. This situation is troublesome for classroom teachers. Even though their schools or districts might have organized the content in the state standards into a set of learning objectives for students and perhaps even sequenced those objectives, teachers have little option other than to select the content they will actually teach, leaving the rest untaught; or they must attempt the impossible task of covering all the content while effectively teaching none of it.

Lack of Unidimensionality

Even if state and national standards did not have too much content, they still suffer from a major flaw as written: they typically mix multiple dimensions in a single statement. Multiple dimensions make it almost impossible to effectively assess the content in standards, particularly if teachers use formative assessment (we discuss formative assessment in more depth shortly).

A basic principle underlying measurement theory is that a single score on a test should represent a single dimension or trait that has been assessed; this is referred to as the principle of unidimensionality (Hattie, 1984, 1985; Lord, 1959). Unfortunately, standards documents are not written with unidimensionality or effective assessment in mind. To illustrate, consider the following benchmark statement from the mathematics standards document published by the National Council of Teachers of Mathematics (2000), which articulates what students should know and be able to do by the end of the 5th grade:

• Develop fluency in adding, subtracting, multiplying, and dividing whole numbers. (p. 392)

The information and skills in the benchmark are certainly related—they all involve computation with whole numbers. However, the underlying processes are not the same and, in fact, might be quite different (Anderson, 1983). This single benchmark most probably addresses four separate dimensions:

• The process of adding whole numbers
• The process of subtracting whole numbers
• The process of multiplying whole numbers
• The process of dividing whole numbers

This "unpacking" is informative in itself because it demonstrates how much subject matter content might be embedded in standards documents. Specifically, the NCTM standards document contains only 241 benchmarks that span grades K through 12. One might assume that the NCTM document therefore addresses 241 dimensions. However, when the benchmarks in the document were unpacked as demonstrated here, more than 741 unique elements were revealed (Marzano, 2002).

In addition to making effective assessment difficult for the classroom teacher, the lack of unidimensionality of standards in state and national documents causes problems for classroom instruction. Consider again the single NCTM benchmark that includes addition, subtraction, multiplication, and division. Obviously these four operations are not to be taught simultaneously. In effect, districts, schools, or individual teachers must unpack this single benchmark statement to determine the scope and sequence of instruction for the content embedded within it.

In summary, national and state standards documents, as written, pose serious barriers to effective instruction and effective assessment for classroom teachers. This book provides a viable way of overcoming those barriers and rendering standards a vital, positive force in the work of classroom teachers. Although our recommended solution will positively affect instruction, our main emphasis in this book is a particular form of classroom assessment: formative assessment.

The Benefits of Formative Assessment

The benefits of formative assessment are becoming more and more obvious. In their meta-analysis of some 250 studies, Black and Wiliam (1998) concluded that formative assessment, when used properly, has the potential to dramatically enhance academic achievement in the United States and the United Kingdom (see page 61 of Black and Wiliam's article). In *Classroom Assessment and Grading That Work*, Marzano (2006) has identified some defining features of effective formative assessment and translated those characteristics into concrete application. *Classroom Assessment and Grading That Work* makes the point that the ultimate goal of a formative assessment system is to collect and report data on every student for specific areas of knowledge and skill that are referred to as "measurement topics." Figure 1.3 depicts how data might be displayed for one measurement topic for a specific student.

Figure 1.3 displays six formative assessment scores for a student named Jana on a specific language arts measurement topic, Language Conventions. (In Chapter 4, we consider how these scores are obtained and used.) The benefits of a system like this are many. First, the visual display itself will most

---

Figure 1.3   Sample Display of Formative Assessment Scores

Keeping Track of My Learning

Name: Jana

Measurement Topic: Language Conventions

My score at the beginning: 1.5   My goal is to be at 3   by May 30

Specific things I am going to do to improve: Work 15 minutes three times a week

Measurement Topic: Language Conventions

a	b	c	d	e	f	g	h	i	j

a April 5   f May 26

b April 12   g

c April 20   h

d April 30   i

e May 12   j

likely enhance both the teacher's interpretation of formative data and the student's ability to see her progress (Fuchs & Fuchs, 1986). Second, a display like this allows for tracking and celebrating knowledge gain. That is, a student who has advanced from a score of 1.0 to a score of 2.5 on a measurement topic has gained 1.5 scale points. Likewise, a student who began with a score of 2.0 and advanced to a score of 3.5 has gained 1.5 scale points. We can celebrate knowledge gain for both students. This is not to say that we should not acknowledge and also celebrate "status." That is, we should recognize those students who have obtained high scores of 4.0 and 3.0 on a scale of 0 through 4.0. However, it is equally important to acknowledge those students who have demonstrated gains in knowledge regardless of where they began.

A system of classroom formative assessment like that described in *Classroom Assessment and Grading That Work* (and in Chapter 4 of this book) allows for a type of report card that provides specific information to parents and students regarding areas where students are progressing well versus areas where additional help must be provided. We discuss such report cards in Chapter 5.

Reconstituting Standards Documents

As formidable as these barriers to the usefulness of standards documents might seem, they can be overcome if a district or school is willing to reconstitute the knowledge in their standards documents. The need to reconstitute state standards and benchmarks has been addressed by many researchers, theorists, and consultants who work with districts and schools to implement standards-based education (see Ainsworth, 2003a, 2003b; Reeves, 2002; Wiggins & McTighe, 2005). In this book we present a system that translates standards documents into a format that is designed to make standards useful for formative assessment and to guide classroom instruction.

Summary

The standards movement has played an important role in K–12 education in the United States. Two major problems have emerged: standards documents identify more content than can actually be taught, and standards documents are not written in a way that enhances classroom instruction and assessment. The proposed solution to these problems is to reconstitute standards documents to make them more useful to classroom teachers.

2

Unpacking Standards and Designing Measurement Topics

The first step in reconstituting standards documents is to unpack the benchmarks with the intent of designing measurement topics. Unpacking benchmarks simply involves identifying the unique elements of information and skill in each benchmark statement. We have found that subject matter specialists are quite skilled and efficient at doing this task. Consequently, a district need only assemble its expert mathematics teachers and curriculum specialists to unpack the mathematics standards, assemble the expert science teachers and curriculum specialists to unpack the science standards, and so on.

To illustrate, consider the following 5th grade benchmark for the Measurement standard from the Ohio state standards document titled *Academic Content Standards: K–12 Mathematics* (Ohio Department of Education, 2001):

1. Identify and select appropriate units to measure angles; i.e., degrees.
2. Identify paths between points on a grid or coordinate plane and compare the lengths of the paths; e.g., shortest path, paths of equal length.
3. Demonstrate and describe the differences between covering the faces (surface area) and filling the interior (volume) of three-dimensional objects.
4. Demonstrate understanding of the differences among linear units, square units and cubic units.
5. Make conversions within the same measurement system while performing computations.
6. Use strategies to develop formulas for determining perimeter and area of triangles, rectangles and parallelograms, and volume of rectangular prisms.
7. Use benchmark angles (e.g., 45°, 90°, 120°) to estimate the measure of angles, and use a tool to measure and draw angles. (pp. 72–73)

This single benchmark includes seven statements. One might assume, then, that this benchmark contains seven unique dimensions. Although a case might be made for this assumption, unpacking benchmarks provides subject matter experts with an opportunity to delete content that is not considered essential, delete content that is not amenable to classroom assessment, and combine content that is highly related. Following these guidelines, a district's mathematics teachers and curriculum specialists might restate the seven elements as follows:

1. Demonstrate a basic understanding of degrees and use of benchmark angles (i.e., 45°, 90°, and 120°) to estimate and draw angles.
2. Demonstrate an understanding of various types of units of measure (e.g., linear units, square units) and convert between units within the same measurement.
3. Identify and compare paths between points on a grid or a coordinate plane.
4. Demonstrate an understanding of the difference between covering the faces (surface area) and filling the interior (volume) of three-dimensional objects.
5. Develop formulas for determining perimeter and area of triangles, rectangles, and parallelograms, and volume of rectangular prisms.

This listing of benchmark elements is somewhat more condensed than the previous listing. The original Statements 1 and 7 have been combined (see new Statement 1) because they both address degrees and angles—concepts that would probably be taught together. Original Statements 4 and 5 have been combined (see new Statement 2) because they both address units of measure. As we shall see in subsequent chapters, these new statements can be pared further when levels of complexity are considered.

One common convention not illustrated in this example is that often statements are dropped when benchmarks are reconstituted. To illustrate, consider the following examples, which are representative of statements found in state and national documents:

- Explore the use of mathematical patterns.
- Demonstrate an interest in reading a variety of genres.
- Make observations of scientific interest.
- Participate in discussions regarding issues of social interest.

These statements are simply too general to be amenable to effective measurement or instruction. In effect, we have found that the process of rewriting benchmark statements commonly results in trimming the amount of content in standards documents considerably.

Finally, we should note that many times curriculum specialists and subject matter teachers find benchmark statements perfectly useful as stated. To illustrate, consider the following 8th grade science statements regarding motions and forces from the Oklahoma state standards:

1. The motion of an object can be measured. The position of an object, its speed and direction can be represented on a graph.
2. An object that is not being subject to a net force will continue to move at a constant velocity (in a straight line and a constant speed). (Oklahoma State Department of Education, 2005, p. 34)

These statements are clear and focused and consequently quite useful for assessment and instruction as written.

It is hard to overemphasize the importance of dramatically decreasing the number of benchmark statements explicit and implicit in standards documents. Recall from Chapter 1 that unpacking the 241 benchmark statements from the national NCTM standards document led to the identification of 741 dimensions. This massive array of content must be pared substantially to fit into the time available for instruction. Again, this can be done fairly efficiently by using expert teachers and curriculum specialists.

To illustrate, consider the aforementioned study regarding mathematics (Marzano, 2002). Specifically, 10 mathematics educators were shown the 741 mathematics dimensions drawn from the national mathematics standards (National Council of Teachers of Mathematics, 2000) and asked to identify those that were essential for all students to learn. Each educator independently rated each of the 741 dimensions. Combining the ratings produced a list of 404 essential dimensions—a reduction of 46 percent. Following this same basic process, a district or school might convene its subject matter specialists and give them the task of dramatically paring the content as they unpack and rewrite the standards.

Forming Measurement Topics

Once benchmark statements have been restated and their number dramatically reduced, the next step is to organize the statements identified as essential into categories of related elements referred to as "measurement topics." Of course, the critical aspect of this step is clarity about what we mean when we say that dimensions are "related." The concept of "covariance" clarifies this issue nicely.

Covariance means that as ability in one dimension increases, so does that in another. (For a more technical discussion of covariance, see Marzano, 2006.) One thing to keep in mind regarding the covariance of dimensions is that it is partly a function of instruction. To illustrate, reconsider the dimensions that were embedded in the NCTM benchmark:

- The process of adding whole numbers
- The process of subtracting whole numbers
- The process of multiplying whole numbers
- The process of dividing whole numbers

One can make a case that these dimensions are somewhat independent in that a student might be fairly proficient at adding whole numbers but not at subtracting whole numbers. On the other hand, one can make a case that addition and subtraction of whole numbers have overlapping steps and, perhaps more important, are typically taught in tandem. The fact that they overlap and are taught together implies that they covary. As skill in one goes up, so does skill in the other. "Related" dimensions, then, which would be combined to form a measurement topic, overlap in their component parts and are commonly taught together or are taught in relationship to one another.

To get a sense of a measurement topic composed of covarying dimensions, consider Figure 2.1, which lists the covarying dimensions for the measurement topic Reading for Main Idea. (It is important to note that Figure 2.1 does not represent the final format for a measurement topic. Chapter 3 presents a preferred, rubric-based format.) For grade 8, the measurement topic states that while engaged in grade-appropriate reading tasks, the student demonstrates an ability to do the following:

• identify complex causal relationships (*e.g., observing that the plight of Anne Frank in* The Diary of Anne Frank *is the result of causes ranging from the policies of the Nazis in Amsterdam to the childhood of Adolph Hitler*);

• identify and react to textual arguments (*e.g., summarizing the argument presented and explaining why he was persuaded or not*);

• identify problems that cannot or will not be solved in the text (*e.g., observing that a story about the fate of Native Americans will not include a solution to the problem of the U.S. government taking their lands*); and

• identify complex plots with multiple story lines (*e.g., observing that understanding a story following people in different social classes during a specific time involves understanding not only the stories of those specific people, but how their stories interact*).

At the heart of this measurement topic is the ability to identify patterns of information in texts. One might say that this dynamic operationally defines "reading for main idea." For example, if an 8th grade student reads *The Red Badge of Courage*, an important part of understanding the main idea of the book is identifying the various aspects of the plot and discerning the various story lines (i.e., *identify complex plots with multiple story lines*). If a student reads an editorial on the benefits of strictly enforced laws regarding the environment, understanding the main idea of the editorial is synonymous with discerning the basic aspects of the implicit and explicit arguments laid out by the author of the editorial (i.e., *identify and react to textual arguments*).

Including these dimensions in the same measurement topic asserts that as a student's ability to identify patterns of information involving complex plots with multiple story lines increases, so too does her ability to identify patterns of information involving textual arguments, as does her ability to identify patterns of information involving complex causal relationships, and so on.

As we shall see in subsequent chapters, articulating measurement topics as depicted in Figure 2.1 makes it easier to develop formative classroom assessments. It also clearly delineates what teachers are to address from one grade level to the next. Consider the progression of covarying elements from grades 1 through 8. At grade 8, four elements are listed. The same is true at grade 7. On the surface, one of the four elements looks identical—the first element at both grade levels reads "*identify complex causal relationships*." However, the stem for both grade levels (see the first row of Figure 2.1)

Figure 2.1 Measurement Topic: Reading for the Main Idea	
Stem	While engaged in grade-appropriate reading tasks, the student demonstrates an ability to . . .
Grade 8	• identify complex causal relationships (*e.g., observing that the plight of Anne Frank in* The Diary of Anne Frank *is the result of causes ranging from the policies of the Nazis in Amsterdam to the childhood of Adolph Hitler*); • identify and react to textual arguments (*e.g., summarizing the argument presented and explaining why he was persuaded or not*); • identify problems that cannot or will not be solved in the text (*e.g., observing that a story about the fate of Native Americans will not include a solution to the problem of the U.S. government taking their lands*); and • identify complex plots with multiple story lines (*e.g., observing that understanding a story following people in different social classes during a specific time involves understanding not only the stories of the specific people, but how their stories interact*).
Grade 7	• identify complex causal relationships (*e.g., when reading about the Japanese internment camps in the United States during World War II, identifying the Japanese attack on Pearl Harbor and the subsequent propaganda against Japanese Americans as causal factors*); • identify and react to basic textual arguments (*e.g., observing specific reasons why she was or was not persuaded by the argument*); • identify problems with complex solutions (*e.g., observing while reading about the civil rights movement that achieving racial equality has been a long and difficult process*); and • identify plots with multiple story lines (*e.g., observing that although* The Sisterhood of the Traveling Pants *follows the stories of four very different girls, in each story the traveling pants help them resolve a difficult issue*).
Grade 6	• identify complex causal relationships (*e.g., observing all the ways Old Dan and Little Ann in* Where the Red Fern Grows *affect Billy's family*); • identify complex chronologies (*e.g., recounting the events in a book such as* The Lion, the Witch, and the Wardrobe); • identify problems that only an outside source or person can solve (*e.g., observing that Helen Keller's problem of communication could not have been solved without her teacher*); and • identify plots with two parallel story lines (*e.g., observing that* Seabiscuit *follows the life of both a man and a horse and that these story lines both represent the growth, courage, and change central to the story's plot*).
Grade 5	• identify complex causal relationships (*e.g., observing that many events in* Harry Potter and the Sorcerer's Stone *seem strange until the book reveals their causes*); • identify complex chronologies (*e.g., observing that many of the events affecting Harry in* Harry Potter and the Sorcerer's Stone *happened before the story takes place*); • identify problems that only a character can solve (*e.g., observing that Malfoy will always bully Harry in* Harry Potter and the Sorcerer's Stone *unless Harry stands up to him*); and • identify plots with single story lines (*e.g., observing that a biography or an autobiography follows the story of one person's life and explains the important details of that person's life*).
Grade 4	• identify basic cause and effect (*e.g., observing that Charlie in* Charlie and the Chocolate Factory *wins the contest because he behaves well while the other children behave badly*); • identify simple chronologies (*e.g., recalling the order and cause of each child's exit from the story in* Charlie and the Chocolate Factory); • identify problems with simple solutions (*e.g., observing that the problem of poverty within Charlie's family in* Charlie and the Chocolate Factory *is only solved by having more money*); and • identify plots with single story lines (*e.g., observing that the plot of* Charlie and the Chocolate factory *involves Charlie's ability to save both his poor family and a lonely man, and the story line follows the boy's strange journey through the factory*).

Figure 2.1 *(continued)*	
Grade 3	• identify basic cause and effect (*e.g., observing that in* Because of Winn-Dixie, *the entrance of a dog into a young girl's life causes many changes that help the girl grow*); • identify simple chronologies (*e.g., recalling the correct order of the people Opal meets in* Because of Winn-Dixie); • identify problems with basic solutions (*e.g., observing that Gloria Dump's problem of blindness is solved by seeing with her heart in* Because of Winn-Dixie); *and* • identify plots with single story lines (*e.g., observing that the story line of* Because of Winn-Dixie *follows the adventures of a young girl and her dog and that the plot involves her growth throughout the story and her coming to peace with her mother's absence*).
Grade 2	• identify basic cause and effect (*e.g., observing that Amelia Bedelia does not produce the right effects at her job as a maid*); *and* • identify simple story lines *(e.g., observing that* Mike Mulligan and His Steam Shovel *follows a man trying to find out what he is supposed to do).*
Grade 1	• identify simple story lines (*e.g., observing that the story line of* Are You My Mother? *follows a baby bird who is searching for his mother*).
Grade K	Not applicable.

begins, "while engaged in grade-appropriate reading tasks, the student demonstrates an ability to . . .". Thus the assumption is that identifying complex causal relationships and complex plots with multiple story lines is done with more sophistication at 8th grade than it is at 7th. These differing expectations should be spelled out for teachers in the examples that are provided for each covarying element as depicted in Figure 2.1.

To illustrate, the 8th grade example for identifying complex causal relationships involves students linking the plight of Anne Frank not only to the behavior of the Nazis but also to the childhood of Adolf Hitler—a diverse and complex set of causal factors. At 7th grade, the expectation is less. Here students are expected to identify the Japanese attack on Pearl Harbor and the resulting propaganda against Japanese Americans as being causally related to Japanese internment camps during World War II—a much less subtle causal pattern than that in the 8th grade example. Thus when bulleted items are identical at two grade levels, the examples provided for teachers should demonstrate the differing expectations regarding students' knowledge and skill.

The remaining three elements at 7th and 8th grade in Figure 2.1 are slightly different. At 8th grade, students are expected to identify and react to textual arguments; at 7th grade, students are expected to identify and react to *basic* textual arguments. Also at 8th grade, students must summarize the argument presented and explain why they are or are not persuaded; at 7th grade, students are not expected to summarize the basic argument, only to explain why they are or are not persuaded.

From one grade level to another, then, the covarying dimensions within a measurement topic become more sophisticated and more complex. Teachers should receive specific guidance regarding how expectations differ from grade level to grade level.

Guidelines for Designing a System of Measurement Topics

The process for identifying measurement topics and covarying elements within those topics is fairly straightforward. Over years of working with districts and schools, we have identified the following general guidelines for designing measurement topics:

- Limit the number of measurement topics to 20 or fewer per subject area, per grade level.
  - Limit the number of bulleted elements within each measurement topic.
  - Include measurement topics for life skills.
  - Change the structure of measurement topics at the high school level.
  - Possibly allow for a "teacher's choice" measurement topic.

Let's consider each of these in succession.

Limiting the Number of Measurement Topics

Given that one of the main barriers to implementing standards is that they contain too much content, it would be counterproductive to identify too many measurement topics. We recommend no more than 20 measurement topics per subject, per grade level—ideally, about 15. To illustrate, Figure 2.2 provides a list of sample K–8 measurement topics for language arts, mathematics, science, and social studies found in the scoring scales in Part II of the book. It is important to note that the list in Figure 2.2 is a sample only. Districts must articulate their own topics to reflect the content in their state standards and the priorities of their teachers and the community.

Notice that the list has 15 topics for language arts, 13 for mathematics, 12 for science, and 10 for social studies. Although not shown in Figure 2.2, all measurement topics do not span all grade levels. For example, the measurement topics in mathematics of basic addition and subtraction and basic multiplication and division begin in kindergarten and end at grade 6. Also note that the topics are grouped under categories. In language arts, the first five measurement topics are organized under the category "Writing." Districts and schools use different terms to refer to these categories, such as *strands*, *themes*, and even *standards*. For reporting purposes, districts and schools might use strands (themes or standards), measurement topics, or both.

If the number of topics is few enough at a particular grade level, a teacher can address some of them multiple times within a given year. Some topics might be addressed during one quarter only, whereas others might be addressed every quarter. For example, at the 3rd grade, mathematics

Figure 2.2   Sample Measurement Topics

Language Arts

Writing

1. Research and Information Organization
2. Drafting and Revising
3. Format
4. Audience and Purpose
5. Word Processing

Language

6. Spelling
7. Language Mechanics
8. Language Conventions

Reading

9. Reading for the Main Idea
10. Word Recognition and Vocabulary
11. Literary Analysis
12. Genre

Listening and Speaking

13. Oral Comprehension
14. Analysis and Evaluation of Oral Media
15. Speaking Applications

Mathematics

Numbers and Operations

1. Number Sense and Number Systems
2. Basic Addition and Subtraction
3. Basic Multiplication and Division
4. Operations, Computation, and Estimation

Algebra

5. Basic Patterns
6. Functions and Equations
7. Algebraic Representations and Mathematical Models

Geometry

8. Lines, Angles, and Geometric Objects
9. Transformations, Congruency, and Similarity

Measurement

10. Measurement Systems
11. Perimeter, Area, and Volume

Data Analysis and Probability

12. Data Organization and Interpretation
13. Probability

Science

Earth and Space Sciences

1. Atmospheric Processes and the Water Cycle
2. Composition and Structure of the Earth
3. Composition and Structure of the Universe and the Earth's Place in It

Life Sciences

4. Principles of Heredity and Related Concepts
5. Structure and Function of Cells and Organisms
6. Relationships Between Organisms and Their Physical Environment

Physical Sciences

7. Structure and Properties of Matter
8. Sources and Properties of Energy
9. Forces and Motion

Nature of Science

10. Nature of Scientific Inquiry
11. Scientific Enterprise

Figure 2.2 *(continued)*

Social Studies

Citizenship, Government, and Democracy

1. Rights, Responsibilities, and Participation in the Political Process
2. The U.S. and State Constitutions
3. The Civil and Criminal Legal Systems

Culture and Cultural Diversity

4. The Nature and Influence of Culture

Economics

5. The Nature and Function of Economic Systems
6. Economics Throughout the World
7. Personal Economics

History

8. Significant Individuals and Events
9. Current Events and the Modern World

Geography

10. Spatial Thinking and the Use of Charts, Maps, and Graphs

---

measurement topics Basic Addition and Subtraction and Basic Multiplication and Division might be addressed each quarter, whereas the topic Lines, Angles, and Geometric Objects might be addressed in one quarter only. We consider this issue in more depth in Chapter 3.

Limiting the Number of Bulleted Elements

The benefits gained by keeping the number of measurement topics small can be undone if the number of bulleted items for each measurement topic becomes too large. Figure 2.3 depicts the number of bulleted elements per grade level, per measurement topic, for the sample measurement topics in the scoring scales in Part II.

We recommend about three or four elements per grade level. Figure 2.3 indicates that this is typically the case—with notable exceptions. For example, the language arts measurement topics of Language Conventions and Spelling commonly have more elements, particularly at lower grades. In these cases, it is typical for specific elements to be taught during different grading periods. To illustrate, consider Language Conventions at 3rd grade. It has seven elements, two of which might be taught in the first quarter, two in the second quarter, two in the third quarter, and one in the fourth quarter.

A well-articulated set of measurement topics goes a long way toward implementing what Marzano has referred to as elsewhere as "a guaranteed and viable curriculum." This concept is described in depth in the book *What Works in Schools* (Marzano, 2003). Briefly, a district that has such a curriculum can *guarantee* that no matter who teaches a given course or grade level, certain topics will be adequately addressed. Obviously, requiring teachers to keep track of specific measurement topics fulfills this requirement. For such a guarantee to be *viable*, the district must have few enough measurement topics to ensure that the process of keeping track of the topics is possible in the time available. This is why it is necessary to limit the number of measurement topics and the bulleted elements within each topic.

Including Measurement Topics for Life Skills

One area that has not been mentioned in the discussion thus far is "life skills"—information and skills that are not specific to traditional academic subject areas (such as mathematics, science, and language arts) but are important to success in a variety of situations. The importance of these skill areas has been affirmed by several studies and reports over the last few decades, such as the 1991 report by the Secretary's Commission on Achieving Necessary Skills (SCANS) titled *What Work Requires of Schools: A SCANS Report for America 2000* (1991), *Workplace Basics: The Essential Skills Employers Want* (Carnevale, Gainer, & Meltzer, 1990), and *First Things First: What Americans Expect from Public Schools* (Farkas, Friedman, Boese, & Shaw, 1994), sponsored by the polling firm Public Agenda. Additionally, in a general survey of adults in the United States conducted by the Gallup Corporation under the direction of McREL researchers, respondents rated life skills higher than 13 academic subject areas (including mathematics, science, history, language arts, and physical education) as definitely required for all students to learn before high school graduation (Marzano, Kendall, & Cicchinelli, 1998).

Given the perceived importance of life skills and the apparently solid mandate from the world of work to teach and reinforce them in schools, we recommend the design of measurement topics to address selected life skills. The following are life skills topics that districts commonly identify as important:

> • **Participation** refers to the extent to which students make an effort to be engaged in class and respond to the tasks presented to them.
> • **Work completion** involves the extent to which students adhere to the requirements regarding the tasks assigned to them. Work completion involves students turning in assignments in a timely fashion and following the conventions that have been established by the teacher (e.g., format considerations for a report).
> • **Behavior** involves the extent to which students adhere to the rules for conduct and behavior. This includes rules set by individual teachers and those established schoolwide.
> • **Working in groups** addresses the extent to which students actively participate in the accomplishment of group goals. It should be noted that this category does not include student behavior within a group, since that is addressed by the category of "behavior." Rather, working in groups is focused on the extent to which students participate in the accomplishment of group goals as opposed to focusing only on their own goals. (Marzano, 2006, p. 26)

As with academic measurement topics, covarying dimensions should be articulated for each life skills measurement topic at different grade levels. However, the life skills measurement topics will probably have more overlap

Figure 2.3 Number of Elements per Grade Level, per Measurement Topic

	Grade									Total by Measurement Topic
	8	7	6	5	4	3	2	1	K	
Language Arts										
Writing										
Research and Information Organization	3	3	2	2	2	2	1	1	n/a	16
Drafting and Revising	3	2	3	3	2	2	2	1	1	19
Format	2	3	2	2	2	2	2	2	1	18
Audience and Purpose	2	2	2	2	2	2	n/a	n/a	n/a	12
Word Processing	1	1	1	1	1	1	1	n/a	n/a	7
Language										
Spelling	1	2	4	4	6	6	4	4	4	35
Language Mechanics	1	1	1	3	4	3	3	2	3	21
Language Conventions	3	4	4	4	4	7	6	5	2	39
Reading										
Reading for the Main Idea	4	4	4	4	4	4	2	1	n/a	27
Word Recognition and Vocabulary	3	3	3	3	2	3	2	2	1	22
Literary Analysis	3	2	4	3	3	2	2	1	n/a	20
Genre	1	1	1	1	1	1	1	1	1	9
Listening and Speaking										
Oral Comprehension	3	3	3	2	2	2	1	1	1	18
Analysis and Evaluation of Oral Media	4	3	1	n/a	n/a	n/a	n/a	n/a	n/a	8
Speaking Applications	3	3	3	3	2	2	2	2	1	21
Total by Grade Level	**37**	**37**	**38**	**37**	**37**	**39**	**29**	**23**	**15**	**292**
Mathematics										
Numbers and Operations										
Number Sense and Number Systems	3	3	3	3	3	2	2	3	3	25
Basic Addition and Subtraction	n/a	n/a	1	3	3	2	3	3	2	17
Basic Multiplication and Division	n/a	n/a	2	2	3	3	3	2	2	17
Operations, Computation, and Estimation	3	4	4	4	2	1	1	n/a	n/a	19

Figure 2.3 *(continued)*

	Grade									Total by Measurement Topic
	8	**7**	**6**	**5**	**4**	**3**	**2**	**1**	**K**	
Algebra										
Basic Patterns	n/a	n/a	n/a	n/a	2	2	2	2	2	10
Functions and Equations	3	2	2	3	n/a	n/a	n/a	n/a	n/a	10
Algebraic Representations and Mathematical Models	4	3	2	3	3	3	n/a	n/a	n/a	18
Geometry										
Lines, Angles, and Geometric Objects	4	3	3	3	4	2	4	3	2	28
Transformations, Congruency, and Similarity	3	3	4	2	3	3	3	3	3	27
Measurement										
Measurement Systems	3	3	3	4	4	3	4	4	3	31
Perimeter, Area, and Volume	4	3	3	4	3	3	n/a	n/a	n/a	20
Data Analysis and Probability										
Data Organization and Interpretation	2	3	2	3	3	2	3	3	1	22
Probability	4	2	2	3	3	2	2	1	1	20
Total by Grade Level	**33**	**29**	**31**	**37**	**36**	**28**	**27**	**24**	**19**	**264**
Science										
Earth and Space Sciences										
Atmospheric Processes and the Water Cycle	2	4	3	2	2	2	2	3	2	22
Composition and Structure of the Earth	3	2	2	2	2	2	2	1	n/a	16
Composition and Structure of the Universe and the Earth's Place in It	4	2	1	1	2	1	1	2	1	15
Life Sciences										
Principles of Heredity and Related Concepts	2	2	2	2	1	1	1	1	n/a	12
Structure and Function of Cells and Organisms	3	4	2	3	4	2	2	2	2	24
Relationships Among Organisms and Their Physical Environment	3	2	2	3	2	4	2	2	3	23
Biological Evolution and Diversity of Life	2	2	2	3	2	3	3	2	2	21

continued on next page

Figure 2.3   *(continued)*

	Grade									Total by Measurement Topic
	8	**7**	**6**	**5**	**4**	**3**	**2**	**1**	**K**	
Physical Sciences										
Structure and Properties of Matter	3	2	2	2	2	2	2	2	1	18
Sources and Properties of Energy	3	2	3	3	4	3	3	2	2	25
Forces and Motion	3	3	4	3	2	2	2	2	2	23
Nature of Science										
Nature of Scientific Inquiry	1	1	1	1	1	1	1	1	1	9
Scientific Enterprise	2	2	2	3	1	1	1	1	1	14
Total by Grade Level	**31**	**28**	**26**	**28**	**25**	**24**	**22**	**21**	**17**	**222**
Social Studies										
Citizenship, Government, and Democracy										
Rights, Responsibilities, and Participation in the Political Process	3	2	2	2	2	2	1	2	n/a	16
The U.S. and State Constitutions	3	3	1	n/a	n/a	n/a	n/a	n/a	n/a	7
The Civil and Criminal Legal Systems	2	4	2	2	3	4	3	3	3	26
Culture and Cultural Diversity										
The Nature and Influence of Culture	3	3	2	3	2	2	3	3	2	23
Economics										
The Nature and Function of Economic Systems	2	2	1	1	1	n/a	n/a	n/a	n/a	7
Economics Throughout the World	3	2	3	3	3	2	2	n/a	n/a	18
Personal Economics	4	2	2	n/a	n/a	n/a	n/a	n/a	n/a	8
History										
Significant Individuals and Events	2	2	3	3	2	3	1	1	n/a	17
Current Events and the Modern World	4	4	4	4	4	4	n/a	n/a	n/a	24
Geography										
Spatial Thinking and the Use of Charts, Maps, and Graphs	1	2	3	2	3	1	2	2	3	19
Total by Grade Level	**27**	**26**	**23**	**20**	**20**	**18**	**12**	**11**	**8**	**165**

of dimensions from one grade level to the next. To illustrate, a district might identify the following elements for the life skills topic of Participation at the middle school level:

 • offering ideas without waiting for a question to be asked (*e.g., taking an active role in a classroom discussion by volunteering opinions for consideration*);

 • staying focused during whole-class activities (*e.g., attending to whole-class activities by taking notes*); and

 • staying focused during individual activities (*e.g., actively engaging in assigned seatwork*).

Instead of listing different elements for each grade level, these might be identified as important to all middle school grade levels.

Changing the Structure of Measurement Topics for High School

The approach to measurement topics described thus far works well for kindergarten through grade 8. That is, it makes sense to have measurement topics that become progressively more complex in terms of the covarying elements from grade level to grade level. However, this approach does not work well in the course structure used by most high schools. Consequently, at the high school level, measurement topics are articulated for each course that is offered. For example, measurement topics would be articulated for Algebra I, Geometry, Algebra II, and so on. For example, Township High School District 211 in Palatine, Illinois, developed measurement topics for Algebra I, Geometry, and Algebra II similar to those in Figure 2.4.

At the high school level, then, teachers in each department would gather to develop measurement topics for courses within their departments, taking heed to follow the general guidelines discussed previously (that is, not too many measurement topics, not too many bulleted elements within a measurement topic, and so on).

Allowing a Teacher's Choice Measurement Topic

The final suggestion we typically make to districts and schools is to allow for a "teacher's choice" measurement topic for every subject area at every grade level. If a district or school has been truly efficient in designing its measurement topics, there should be room to allow for this option. As its name implies, a teacher's choice topic involves content considered important by a teacher but not reflected in the measurement topics articulated by the district or school. In effect, this "residual" topic allows teachers to supplement the district or school curriculum. A teacher might wish to supplement the curriculum because she brings a unique set of experiences and background to the subject matter. For example, an English teacher at the 10th grade level might have an extensive background in journalism, but her district or school has nothing in its measurement topics that reflect journalism skills. She may add a measurement topic on journalism, such as the following:

**Figure 2.4   Sample Measurement Topics
for Algebra I, Geometry, and Algebra II**

Algebra I
Formulas
Polynomial operations
Solving equations and inequalities in one variable
Radicals and factoring
Solving quadratic equations
Solving systems of linear equations
Rational expressions
Ratios, proportions, and percents
Graphing linear equations and inequalities
Word problems involving algebraic equations

Geometry
Applying the concept of deductive reasoning and proof
Applying the properties of points, segments, angles, lines, and their relationships
Polygon congruence and similarity
Triangle calculations: Pythagorean theorem, right triangle trigonometry
Polygon and circle measures
Perimeter, area, surface area, volume
Transformational geometry
Probability

Algebra II
Radicals and exponents operations
Function operations
Systems of equations and matrices
Equation solving
Complex number operations
Modeling with equations/data analysis
Conic sections
Function graphing and transformations
Logarithmic and exponential equations

• being objective when reporting on an incident;
• keeping the focus on the story, not the reporter; and
• validating eyewitness accounts.

It makes sense that a district or a school might want to provide enough flexibility in its system of measurement topics to accommodate the individual strengths of teachers they have hired.

Summary

Unpacking standards and designing measurement topics involves a number of steps. Benchmark statements in standards documents should be unpacked and rewritten to combine like content. Some content statements should be dropped because they are not easy to translate into instructional or assessment practices. Other content should be dropped because it is not considered essential for all students. Remaining statements should then be organized into measurement topics that are composed of covarying elements. In general, about 15 measurement topics should be identified for each subject matter at each grade level, kindergarten through grade 8. At the high school level, measurement topics should be identified for each course. Measurement topics for life skills should be identified for kindergarten through grade 12.

3

A Scale Format for
Measurement Topics

Once measurement topics and accompanying elements have been identified for grade levels and courses, the next step is to state them in the format of a scale. Some educators like to use the term *rubric*. We prefer the term *scale* for reasons articulated in the book *Classroom Assessment and Grading That Work* (Marzano, 2006). The scale we recommend appears in Figure 3.1.

Figure 3.1 is a 0-through-4 scale with half-point scores that are set off to the right to signify that they describe student-response patterns between the whole-point scores. To understand the scale, it is best to begin with the score value of 3.0.

• A score of 3.0 indicates that a student has correctly answered all items or performed all tasks that involve simpler details and processes *as well as* all items or tasks that involve more complex ideas and processes that were explicitly taught. In effect, the score of 3.0 is the fulcrum of the scale. It represents the instructional goal for a measurement topic.

• A score of 2.0 indicates that a student has correctly answered all items or performed all tasks that involve simpler details and processes but has missed all items or tasks that involve more complex ideas and processes (score 3.0 items and tasks).

• If a student has correctly answered all items or performed all tasks regarding simpler details and processes (score 2.0 items and tasks) and has correctly answered *some* items or performed *some* tasks involving more complex ideas and processes (score 3.0 items and tasks) or has received *partial credit* on those items or tasks, a score of 2.5 is assigned.

• A score of 1.5 is assigned if a student receives partial credit on the score 2.0 items or tasks but misses all other types of items.

• A score of 1.0 is assigned if a student misses all items or tasks but with help from the teacher demonstrates partial credit on the score 2.0 and score 3.0 items or tasks.

Figure 3.1 Scale for Measurement Topics

Score 4.0: In addition to score 3.0 performance, in-depth inferences and applications that go beyond what was taught.

Score 3.5: In addition to score 3.0 performance, partial success at inferences and applications that go beyond what was taught.

Score 3.0: No major errors or omissions regarding any of the information and/or processes (simple or complex) that were explicitly taught.

Score 2.5: No major errors or omissions regarding the simpler details and processes and partial knowledge of the more complex ideas and processes.

Score 2.0: No major errors or omissions regarding the simpler details and processes but major errors or omissions regarding the more complex ideas and processes.

Score 1.5: Partial knowledge of the simpler details and processes but major errors or omissions regarding the more complex ideas and processes.

Score 1.0: With help, a partial understanding of some of the simpler details and processes and some of the more complex ideas and processes.

Score 0.5: With help, a partial understanding of some of the simpler details and processes but not the more complex ideas and processes.

Score 0.0: Even with help, no understanding or skill demonstrated.

• A score of 0.5 is assigned if the student misses all items or tasks but with help demonstrates partial credit on the score 2.0 items or tasks but not on the score 3.0 items or tasks.

• A score of 0.0 indicates that, even with help, the student cannot answer any items or perform any tasks correctly.

• At the top end of the scale, a score of 4.0 indicates a student has answered all items or performed all tasks correctly (score 4.0 items or tasks, score 3.0 items or tasks, and score 2.0 items or tasks).

• A score of 3.5 is assigned if a student correctly answers or performs score 2.0 and score 3.0 items or tasks and receives partial credit on score 4.0 items or tasks.

Of course, the success of the scale in Figure 3.1 rests on the ability of the teacher to design items for scores 4.0, 3.0, and 2.0. To facilitate this, all measurement topics at each grade level and in each course should be written in scale form. To illustrate, consider Figure 3.2. This scale provides specific guidance to teachers as to expectations at 3rd grade for the measurement topic Number Sense and Number Systems. The sample measurement topics in the scoring scales in Part II are all in the format depicted in Figure 3.2. To exemplify the score values in the scale, we begin again with the score 3.0 elements because they are the fulcrum of the scale.

It is important to note that score 3.0 elements all begin with a stem. In Figure 3.2 the stem is, "While engaged in grade-appropriate tasks, the student demonstrates an understanding of numbers and number systems by . . .". This stem provides a context in which the bulleted information or skill is to be demonstrated. Score 3.0 bullets are the covarying elements that are identified as a result of unpacking and reconstituting state standards documents (as

Figure 3.2	Scale for 3rd Grade Measurement Topic: Number Sense and Number Systems
Score 4.0	**In addition to score 3.0 performance, the student demonstrates in-depth inferences and applications that go beyond what was taught.**
Score 3.5	In addition to score 3.0 performance, the student demonstrates in-depth inferences and applications with partial success.
Score 3.0	**While engaged in grade-appropriate tasks, the student demonstrates an understanding of numbers and number systems by . . .** • using mathematical language and symbols to compare and order whole numbers (up to 9,999), decimals (hundredths), and commonly used fractions and mixed numbers (*e.g., explaining and exemplifying the difference between < and ≤*); and • generating equivalent forms of whole numbers (*e.g., explaining and exemplifying how different forms of a whole number are the same*). **The student exhibits no major errors or omissions.**
Score 2.5	The student exhibits no major errors or omissions regarding the score 2.0 elements and partial knowledge of the score 3.0 elements.

Score 2.0	**The student exhibits no major errors or omissions regarding the simpler details and processes, such as . . .**
	• recognizing and recalling specific terminology (*e.g., less than, greater than, mixed number*); and
	• recognizing and recalling the accuracy of basic solutions and information, such as . . .
	  ○ < is a symbol that means "less than"; > is a symbol that means "greater than"; and
	  ○ 15 + 10 is the same as 25.
	However, the student exhibits major errors or omissions with score 3.0 elements.

Score 1.5	The student demonstrates partial knowledge of the score 2.0 elements but major errors or omissions regarding the score 3.0 elements.
Score 1.0	**With help, the student demonstrates partial understanding of some of the score 2.0 elements and some of the score 3.0 elements.**
Score 0.5	With help, the student demonstrates partial understanding of some of the score 2.0 elements but not the score 3.0 elements.
Score 0.0	**Even with help, the student demonstrates no understanding or skill.**

discussed in Chapter 2). Thus, by definition, the process of reconstituting benchmark statements and organizing them into measurement topics identifies the score 3.0 elements.

Whereas score 3.0 elements are identified as a natural consequence of reconstituting state standards documents, score 2.0 elements are usually derived from the score 3.0 elements. This noted, sometimes when educators are unpacking standards documents, they find that some of the content is better assigned to score 2.0. As the generic scale in Figure 3.1 indicates, score 2.0 elements are simpler details and processes associated with the score 3.0 elements. Many times these are identified right in the standards documents. That is, some of the statements taken from standards documents are score 3.0 elements and some are score 2.0 elements.

One aspect of score 2.0 elements is basic terminology associated with score 3.0 elements. Marzano (2006) describes vocabulary terms used as score 2.0 elements in the following way:

> Vocabulary terms are a common type of basic detail [score 2.0 elements]. Whether or not information qualifies as a vocabulary term is a function of how it is approached instructionally. For example, *heredity, offspring, sexual reproduction, asexual reproduction*, and *gene* all involve complex information, but each can be approached as a vocabulary term. When this is the case, the expectation is not that students can demonstrate in-depth knowledge, but rather that they have an accurate but somewhat surface-level understanding. (p. 66)

Another aspect of score 2.0 elements is basic or simple solutions for complex processes. For example, in Figure 3.2, the first bulleted element at score 3.0 addresses comparing and ordering whole numbers (up to 9,999), decimals (hundredths), and commonly used fractions and mixed numbers. It has the following associated score 2.0 element: < is a symbol meaning 'less than' and > is a symbol meaning 'greater than.' The score 2.0 element, then, is a simple but necessary piece of information that would be required to complete a score 3.0 task, such as the following:

> Determine if the following statement is true or false:
> 9,878 > 9,432 < 9432.78 > 9432 3/4

The second bulleted element for score 3.0 addresses generating equivalent forms of whole numbers. The associated score 2.0 element is the following: 15 + 10 is the same as 25. This is a simplified version of what is required for a score value of 3.0. Specifically, to receive a score of 3.0, students might be expected to demonstrate that 5,250 can be represented as 5 units of 1,000, 2 units of 100, and 5 units of 10. In this case, the score 2.0 element is a simpler version of what is expected for a score value of 3.0. In general, then, score values of 2.0 either identify necessary components of what is required for a score value of 3.0, or they identify simpler versions of what is expected for a score value of 3.0.

Although it is quite feasible for districts and schools to identify explicit score 4.0 elements, we have found that a common practice is to provide general guidance but leave the identification of specific score 4.0 elements to teachers. Note that in the generic scale represented in Figure 3.1, score 4.0 addresses inferences and applications that go beyond what was explicitly taught. To provide more concrete guidance, a district might suggest specific types of tasks. Marzano (2006) notes that the following cognitive processes are commonly used to design score 4.0 items and tasks:

Comparing is the process of identifying similarities and differences among or between things or ideas. Technically speaking, *comparing* refers to identifying similarities, and *contrasting* refers to identifying differences. However, many educators use the term *comparing* to refer to both.

Classifying is the process of grouping things that are alike into categories based on their characteristics.

Creating metaphors is the process of identifying a general or basic pattern that connects information that is not related at the surface or literal level.

Creating analogies is the process of identifying the relationship between two sets of items—in other words, identifying the relationship between relationships.

Analyzing errors is the process of identifying and correcting errors in the way information is presented or applied. (p. 68)

To illustrate how these cognitive processes might be used to design score 4.0 items and tasks, consider the following task designed for the measurement topic Number Sense and Number Systems as depicted in Figure 3.2.

Classify the following quantities into two or more categories, and then explain the rule for being assigned to a category. Do not use "whole numbers," "decimals," "fractions," or "mixed numbers" as any of your categories:

9,728	4,001	250.62
1/3	750 1/4	35.8
7/22	40	300
55	1025	5000
25 1/5	0.25	0.75

This is an open-ended task that requires students to make inferences and applications that go beyond what was actually taught in class. For a more detailed discussion of how to construct tasks for a score value of 4.0, see Marzano (2006).

Finally, for score values of 1.0 and 0.0, no specifics have to be provided in the scale because those values do not address new content per se. Rather, they signify the extent to which students can demonstrate, with help, knowledge of content at score values 3.0 or 2.0.

In summary, all measurement topics at each grade level should be written in scale format using the generic scale in Figure 3.1. Specific academic content must be identified for score values 3.0 and 2.0 only, and possibly for score value 4.0 if a district or school so desires. If not, teachers should be provided general guidance as to how to construct items and tasks for score value 4.0.

Part II contains examples of measurement topics for language arts, mathematics, science, social studies, and life skills for kindergarten through 8th grade. Elements for score values 3.0 and 2.0 are provided for each measurement topic.

Measurement Topics and Sequencing Content

A district or school can use a well-articulated set of measurement topics with score 3.0 and score 2.0 elements stated in scale format to provide scope-and-sequence guidance for its teachers. As mentioned previously, one of the intended consequences of a system of measurement topics is to ensure that teachers have a clear set of instructional targets that are few and concise enough to be adequately taught in a school year.

In general, U.S. teachers have a 180-day (or 36-week) school year. Teachers typically organize their content into units of instruction. Although these units vary in length (Bloom, 1976), let's assume that they average 3 weeks. Thus in a 36-week year, a teacher will have about 12 units. For discussion's sake, we will assume that a subject area has 15 measurement topics. If the bulleted elements in each measurement topic truly represent covarying elements, a teacher need have only three units that address two topics in a given year and other units that address a single measurement topic only. This, of course, is an ideal and is probably unrealistic for some districts or schools.

The reason why the ideal is not always achieved is that districts and schools sometimes create measurement topics with elements that are not as highly related as they should be; that is, not all measurement topics have elements that truly covary. Recall that whether items covary or not is greatly dependent on how they are taught; if theoretically covarying elements are not taught in tandem, then they might be learned as somewhat independent elements by students. Consider, for example, the score 3.0 elements for the 7th grade science measurement topic Biological Evolution and Diversity of Life, found in the scoring scales for science in Part II:

- distinctions between how life is thought to have begun (scientific theories, religious theories) (*e.g., explaining the key points of different explanations for how life is thought to have begun—for example, describing basic differences between common scientific and religious theories that attempt to explain how life is thought to have begun*); and
- basic implications of natural selection (diversity of past life, unity of past life) (*e.g., explaining the basic impact of natural selection on past life—for example, describing basic effects of natural selection on the unity that can be found in past life*).

Distinctions between how life is thought to have begun (Element 1) and basic implications of natural selection (Element 2) are obviously related and could be taught within the same unit or units of instruction. In this case, scores on the two elements would probably covary—as a student's scores on the first element increase, so would his scores on the second element. However, these two elements could be taught in isolation during different units of instruction. In this case, scores on the two elements probably would not covary.

To maximize the guidance provided to teachers, a district or school should explicitly identify which elements within a measurement topic should be taught during the same grading period or units of instruction. To illustrate, consider Figure 3.3, which represents a fairly typical way that districts and schools treat measurement topics and their covarying elements. First consider the last row of Figure 3.3. It indicates that the first grading period (i.e., first quarter) should address 9 measurement topics; the second quarter, 9 measurement topics; the third quarter, 10 measurement topics; and the fourth quarter, 9 measurement topics. Again, if we assume three-week units of instruction and nine-week quarters, then each quarter is composed of three units, each of which addresses three measurement topics. The only exception to this is the third quarter, when one of the three units must address four measurement topics.

Now we consider how the elements within measurement topics are addressed. The first measurement topic in Figure 3.3, Research and Information Organization, is addressed during the third and fourth quarters. Because each of the two elements is addressed each quarter, the measurement topic truly involves covarying elements. Both elements are taught and assessed as related elements. The same is true for the following measurement topics—every time they are addressed, all elements are taught and assessed as related:

- Drafting and Revising
- Audience and Purpose
- Word Processing
- Literary Analysis
- Genre
- Oral Comprehension
- Speaking Applications

This convergence and resulting covariance of elements is not the case for the measurement topic Reading for Main Idea. The first two elements are taught during the first and second quarters; the third and fourth elements are taught during the third and fourth quarters. In effect, this measurement topic is being treated as two topics, each with two elements. It might have been better for the district or school to give different names to these topics, but this is not necessary as long as the district or school is aware of how the topic is treated in the first and second quarters versus the third and fourth quarters. The most extreme example in Figure 3.3 of a topic that has been subdivided is Language Conventions. Here, the first and second elements are addressed in the first quarter, the third and fourth in the second quarter, the fifth and sixth in the third quarter, and the seventh in the fourth quarter. Again, as long as the district or school is aware of which elements are addressed during each quarter, there is no need to give the topic a different name for each quarter.

Figure 3.3	Scope and Sequence for 3rd Grade Language Arts				
Measurement Topic	**Number of Score 3.0 Elements**	**Elements Addressed 1st Grading Period**	**Elements Addressed 2nd Grading Period**	**Elements Addressed 3rd Grading Period**	**Elements Addressed 4th Grading Period**
Writing					
Research and Information Organization	2			1st, 2nd	1st, 2nd
Drafting and Revising	2	1st, 2nd	1st, 2nd	1st, 2nd	
Format	2	1st	1st	2nd	2nd
Audience and Purpose	2		1st, 2nd		1st, 2nd
Word Processing	1				1st
Language					
Spelling	6	1st, 2nd	3rd, 4th	5th, 6th	
Language Mechanics	3	1st, 2nd	3rd		
Language Conventions	7	1st, 2nd	3rd, 4th	5th, 6th	7th
Reading					
Reading for Main Idea	4	1st, 2nd	1st, 2nd	3rd, 4th	3rd, 4th
Word Recognition and Vocabulary	3	1st	2nd	3rd	
Literary Analysis	2	1st, 2nd		1st, 2nd	
Genre	1		1st		1st
Listening and Speaking					
Oral Comprehension	2	1st, 2nd		1st, 2nd	1st, 2nd
Analysis and Evaluation of Oral Media	n/a	n/a	n/a	n/a	n/a
Speaking Applications	2			1st, 2nd	1st, 2nd
Number of Topics Addressed		9	9	10	9

Summary

A scale should be used to articulate all measurement topics at each grade level and in each course. Each scale should include score 3.0 and 2.0 elements, as well as explicit guidance for score 4.0 elements. Districts and schools should provide explicit guidance on the sequencing of measurement topics and the elements within them.

4

A Formative Assessment System Using Measurement Topics

———

Once teachers have a well-developed set of measurement topics written in scale format, they can design and use formative classroom assessments. In fact, classroom teachers should be able to construct formative assessments right from the scales provided them.

To illustrate, consider the scale for the 6th grade social studies measurement topic, the Nature and Influence of Culture, depicted in Figure 4.1. Assume that a 6th grade teacher wished to design a formative assessment for this topic. Again, it is useful to begin with the score 3.0 elements. The scale provides fairly explicit guidance. The example for the first bulleted element suggests that students should explain and exemplify how ancient civilizations affect society today, with special emphasis on ancient Egyptian architecture. Based on this, the teacher might construct the following item:

> We have been studying ancient Egypt and theories about how they constructed the pyramids and why they used this particular structure. We have also seen that the pyramid structure is used today. Identify a structure in our city that we have studied and explain how it follows the same principles as those used in the pyramids.

The second bulleted element suggests that students should explain and exemplify how classical civilization affected later civilizations, with special emphasis on the influence of Greek culture and customs on Roman civilization. Based on this suggestion, the teacher might construct the following item:

> We have also been studying Greek architecture and how it affected Roman architecture. Identify one of the structures we have studied from the Roman Empire and explain how it was probably influenced by Greek architecture.

The elements for score 2.0 also provide guidance for item construction. Based on the examples provided in the scale, score 2.0 should involve basic terminology such as *philosophy*, *ethnic art*, and *cultural heritage*. This list is not

Figure 4.1	Scale for 6th Grade Measurement Topic: The Nature and Influence of Culture
Score 4.0	**In addition to score 3.0 performance, the student demonstrates in-depth inferences and applications that go beyond what was taught.**
Score 3.5	In addition to score 3.0 performance, the student demonstrates in-depth inferences and applications with partial success.
Score 3.0	**While engaged in tasks that address the nature and influence of culture, the student demonstrates an understanding of important information, such as . . .** • how ancient civilizations influence the modern world (technology, music, art, religion) (*e.g., explaining and exemplifying how ancient civilizations impact society today—for example, discussing the influence of ancient Egyptian architecture on buildings constructed today*); and • how classical civilizations influence later civilizations and modern society (technology, beliefs, customs, language) (*e.g., explaining and exemplifying how classical civilizations impacted later civilizations—for example, describing the influence of Greek beliefs and customs on the Roman civilization*). **The student exhibits no major errors or omissions.**
Score 2.5	The student exhibits no major errors or omissions regarding the score 2.0 elements and partial knowledge of the score 3.0 elements.

Score 2.0	**The student exhibits no major errors or omissions regarding the simpler details and processes, such as . . .**
	• recognizing and recalling specific terminology, events, people, and locations (*e.g., philosophy, ethnic art, cultural heritage*); and
	• recognizing and recalling isolated details, such as . . .
	  ○ the Parthenon was a model used to design some of the buildings in Washington D.C.; and
	  ○ Plato's writings had a major influence on modern philosophers.
	However, the student exhibits major errors or omissions with score 3.0 elements.

Score 1.5	The student demonstrates partial knowledge of the score 2.0 elements but major errors or omissions regarding the score 3.0 elements.
Score 1.0	**With help, the student demonstrates partial understanding of some of the score 2.0 elements and some of the score 3.0 elements.**
Score 0.5	With help, the student demonstrates partial understanding of some of the score 2.0 elements but not the score 3.0 elements.
Score 0.0	**Even with help, the student demonstrates no understanding or skill.**

intended to be exhaustive; rather, it is an example of the type of terminology that teachers might consider to be score 2.0 elements. Based on this guidance, the teacher might design the following score 2.0 questions:

Briefly describe the basic meaning of each of the following five terms:

1. philosophy
2. ethnic art
3. cultural heritage
4. theocracy
5. romance language

The scale also recommends that score 2.0 should involve recognizing or recalling isolated details, and it provides two examples. Again, this is not an exhaustive list. Based on this guidance, the teacher might construct the following items.

Identify each of the following statements as true or false:

• One of Plato's influential writings was *Republic*.
• The Parthenon was a model used to design some of the buildings in Washington, D.C.
• Aristotle wrote *Phaedo*.
• The Pyramid of Menkaure is the third-largest pyramid in Egypt.
• Aristotle was a student of Socrates.

Finally, the scale provides general guidance for score 4.0 items and tasks. It simply states that students are expected to make inferences and applications that go beyond what was explicitly taught. However, knowing that score 4.0 items and tasks frequently involve comparing, classifying, designing analogies, and designing metaphors, the teacher might construct the following score 4.0 task:

We have seen that classical civilizations such as Greece commonly influence later civilizations such as Rome. Based on your understanding of how Greece influenced Rome, complete the following analogy and explain your answer:

Greece is to Rome as _____ is to _____.

With the items constructed, the teacher can now combine them into a single assessment (Figure 4.2). Note that the assessment is organized into three sections, cueing students as to the type of items and tasks in each section. In general, score 2.0 items tend to follow a forced-choice or short-answer format, whereas the score 3.0 and 4.0 items tend to follow a longer, constructed-response format. For a more detailed discussion see Marzano (2006).

The Use of Common Items as Opposed to Common Assessments

Common assessments are becoming quite popular among districts and schools attempting to implement formative assessment (Ainsworth & Viegut, 2006). The general approach to common assessments is to develop a number of formative assessments that all teachers are to use for each measurement topic. Although this endeavor is noteworthy, we recommend a slightly different approach. Rather than develop common assessments, per se, we recommend the use of "common items and tasks" for each measurement topic. For example, reconsider Figure 4.2 and the items constructed for score values 4.0, 3.0, and 2.0. Over time the district or school should construct common items at score values 4.0, 3.0, and 2.0 for each measurement topic, at each grade level, and for each course. With such an item bank available, classroom teachers could easily design formative assessments that address what they have taught.

**Figure 4.2   Assessment for 6th Grade Measurement Topic:
The Nature and Influence of Culture**

Section I. Answer the following questions on a separate sheet of paper.

Briefly describe the basic meaning of each of the following five terms:

  1. philosophy
  2. ethnic art
  3. cultural heritage
  4. theocracy
  5. romance language

Identify if each of the following statements is true or false:

  6. One of Plato's influential writings was *Republic*.
  7. The Parthenon was a model used to design some of the buildings in Washington, D.C.
  8. Aristotle wrote *Phaedo*.
  9. The Pyramid of Menkaure is the third-largest pyramid in Egypt.
 10. Aristotle was a student of Socrates.

Section II: Answer the following questions on a separate sheet of paper.

 11. We have been studying ancient Egypt and theories about how they constructed the pyramids and why they used this particular structure. We have also seen that the pyramid structure is used today. Identify a structure in our city that we have studied and explain how it follows the same principles as those used in the pyramids.

 12. We have also been studying Greek architecture and how it affected Roman architecture. Identify one of the structures we have studied from the Roman Empire and explain how it was probably influenced by Greek architecture.

Section III. Answer the following question on a separate sheet of paper. We didn't address this specific analogy in class, so you will have to think of some examples on your own to answer this.

 13. We have seen that classical civilizations such as Greece commonly influence later civilizations such as Rome. Based on your understanding of how Greece influenced Rome, complete the following analogy and explain your answer:

Greece is to Rome as _____ is to _____.

Using a Formative Approach
to Assigning Final Topic Scores

In addition to designing assessments for each measurement topic, a system should be in place to assign final topic scores using a formative approach. In a formative approach, the teacher considers learning over time as opposed to simply averaging scores. To illustrate, assume that a teacher has administered five formative assessments for a specific measurement topic. Figure 4.3 shows the scores for one student on these five assessments. The student received scores of 1.0 on the first and second assessments, 2.5 on the third assessment, 2.0 on the fourth assessment, and 3.5 on the fifth assessment. At the end of a grading period, some type of summary score or final score is needed for the student on this topic. One obvious way to determine such a score is to compute the average of the five assessments, or 2.0 (see Figure 4.4). However, as the line depicting the average in Figure 4.4 illustrates, the average does not seem to represent the student's true learning at the end of the grading period. Granted, the student started with two low scores of 1.0, but he achieved a score of 2.5 on the third assessment and a score of 3.5 on the final assessment. The average of 2.0 indicates that the student has mastered only the simple details and processes. This does not reflect his performance on the third and fifth assessments during the later part of the grading period.

The reason the average doesn't make intuitive sense as a summary score or final score is that averaging scores is not appropriate for formative assessments. In fact, averaging assumes that no learning has occurred from assessment to assessment (for a discussion, see Marzano, 2006). Obviously, formative assessments are designed to capture student learning over time.

One approach to this challenge is to use computer software that is designed to measure student learning across formative assessments on specific measurement topics. One such program is the Pinnacle Plus System by Excelsior Software (http://excelsiorsoftware.com). It uses a mathematical algorithm to estimate each student's learning across assessments. This estimate is depicted in Figure 4.5. The diagonal line in Figure 4.5 depicts the

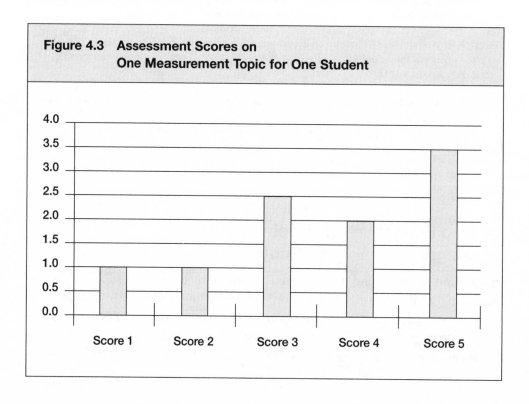

Figure 4.3   Assessment Scores on One Measurement Topic for One Student

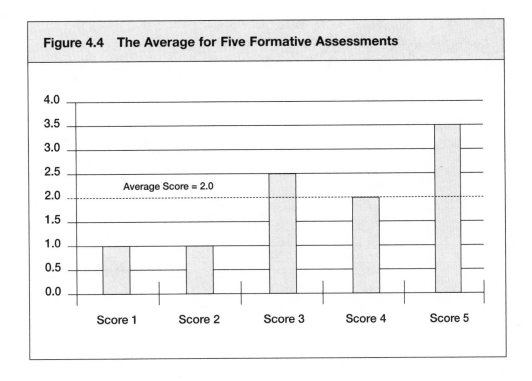

Figure 4.4   The Average for Five Formative Assessments

student's learning as computed by the "learning trend" formula in the Pinnacle Plus System. As indicated, when the learning trend is computed, the student's final score for the grading period is 3.07 as opposed to the average of 2.00. The teacher would most likely round this score of 3.07 to a 3.0.

An alternative to using computer software such as Pinnacle Plus is to use what Marzano (2006) refers to as the "low-tech" approach or the "method of mounting evidence," depicted in Figure 4.6. Here we briefly describe the "low-tech" method. For a more detailed discussion, see Marzano (2006).

One obvious difference between the grade book shown in Figure 4.6 and the traditional grade book is that this version requires more space for a single student. Whereas records for about 25 students can fit on a single page in a traditional grade book, only about five can fit on a single page in this type of grade book. The columns in Figure 4.6 show the various measurement topics that the teacher is addressing over a given grading period. In this case, the teacher has addressed five science topics: Structure and Properties of Matter, Forces and Motion, Sources and Properties of Energy, Nature of Scientific Inquiry, and Scientific Enterprise. The teacher has also kept track of three life skills topics: Behavior, Work Completion, and Class Participation.

In each cell of the grade book, the scores are listed in order of assignment, going from the top left to the bottom and the top right to the bottom. Thus, for Structure and Properties of Matter, Aida received six scores, in the following order: 1.5, 2.0, 2.0, 2.0, 2.5, and 2.5. Also note that the second score of 2.0 has a circle around it. This represents a situation in which the teacher gave Aida an opportunity to raise her score on a given assessment. In this case, she raised her score from 1.5 to 2.0.

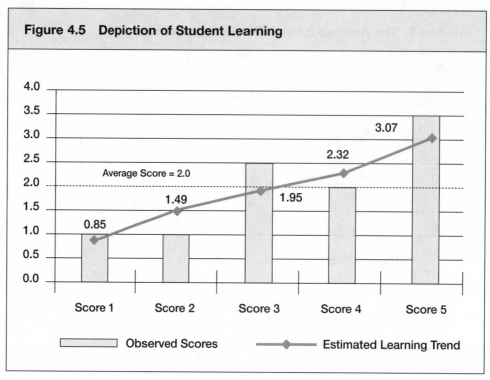

Figure 4.5 Depiction of Student Learning

Source: Adapted from *Classroom Assessment and Grading That Work* (p. 98), by Robert J. Marzano, 2006, Alexandria, VA: Association for Supervision and Curriculum Development. Copyright 2006 by ASCD. Adapted with permission.

Another convention to note in Figure 4.6 is that some scores—such as Aida's fourth score of 2.0—are enclosed in a box. When a teacher uses this convention, it means that she has seen enough evidence to conclude that a student has reached a certain point on the scale. By the time the teacher entered the fourth score for Aida, she was convinced that Aida had attained a score of 2.0. From that assessment on, the teacher examined Aida's responses for evidence that she had *exceeded* this score.

The low-tech method is powerful but more labor intensive than using computer software such as Pinnacle Plus. We typically recommend the low-tech method when individual teachers wish to try out formative record keeping. Once they decide to make a full-scale transition, computer software is a more viable option.

	Structure & Properties of Matter	Forces & Motion	Sources & Properties of Energy	Nature of Scientific Inquiry	Scientific Enterprise	Behavior		Work Completion		Class Participation	
Aida	1.5 [2.5]	2.0	1.0 [2.5]	2.0 [3.0]	3.0	3.0 3.5		4.0 3.5		2.5 3.5	
	(2.0)	[2.0]	[1.5]	2.0	[3.0]	[3.0] 3.0		4.0 4.0		[3.0] 3.5	
	2.0	2.0	2.0	2.0	3.5	2.5 [3.5]		4.0 3.5		3.5 3.5	
	[2.0]	(2.5)	(2.5)	(2.5)	[3.5]	[3.0] [3.5]		3.5 [4.0]		3.0 [4.0]	
	2.5	[2.5]	[2.5]	3.0	[3.5]	3.5		[4.0]		[3.5]	

Note: A circle indicates that the teacher gave the student an opportunity to raise her score from the previous assessment. A box indicates that the student is judged to have reached a specific score level from that point on.

Source: From *Classroom Assessment and Grading That Work* (p. 100), by Robert J. Marzano, 2006, Alexandria, VA: Association for Supervision and Curriculum Development. Copyright 2006 by ASCD. Adapted with permission.

Summary

Measurement topics can be used to design a system of formative assessments. The scales for each measurement topic should provide teachers with explicit guidance regarding the design of score 4.0, 3.0, and 2.0 items and tasks. A district or school might also design a bank of common items for these score values. To compute final topic scores, teachers should not use averaging in a formative assessment system. Rather, we recommend computer software that computes a learning trend. Teachers can also use a low-tech solution that relies on demonstrated competence at a specific score.

5

Grades and Report Cards
Using Measurement Topics

Given that teachers have kept track of student progress on measurement topics, they can assign grades using this information. To illustrate, assume that at the end of a grading period a student received the following scores on seven mathematics topics and three life skills measurement topics:

Number Sense and Number Systems: 3.5
Operations, Computation, and Estimation: 2.5
Functions and Equations: 2.5
Lines, Angles, and Geometric Objects: 1.5
Transformations, Congruency, and Similarity: 3.0
Data Organization and Interpretation: 2.0
Probability: 2.5
Work Completion: 2.5
Participation: 2.5
Behavior: 3.5

The teacher may have addressed the seven mathematics measurement topics in three units of instruction during the grading period. She would have computed the final scores on these measurement topics using one of the methods briefly described in Chapter 4 (i.e., using computer software designed to measure learning trend or using the low-tech approach). To summarize the scores across measurement topics, the teacher could compute a simple average. Although averaging is not appropriate to summarize learning *within* a measurement topic, it is appropriate when trying to capture the tendency *between* measurement topics. In this case, the average across measurement topics is 2.6. The teacher could then translate this average score into a traditional grade using a system like the following:

3.00 – 4.00 = A	2.00 – 2.49 = C	1.49 and below = F
2.50 – 2.99 = B	1.50 – 1.99 = D	

Thus the average score across measurement topics for the grading period would be translated to an overall grade of B. Of course, the teacher could have used a weighted average that gave more mathematical weight to some measurement topics. Other options for combining final topic scores to compute a grade have also been devised (for a discussion, see Marzano, 2006).

Figure 5.1 shows a report card that reports overall scores as well as individual topic scores. The top of the report card looks very traditional in that grades are reported for each course or subject area, and those grades are composed of scores on academic topics and life skills topics. In general, including both of these types of knowledge (academic and life skills) is a frequent practice in classrooms where overall grades are assigned. However, the bottom portion of the report card is anything but traditional. It reports scores and bar graphs on individual measurement topics (academic and life skills), thus allowing students and parents to see the student's status on each topic addressed during the grading period. Such information could be used to identify areas where students need help.

Reporting on individual topics gives the district or school great flexibility in terms of report cards. To illustrate, consider the report card shown in Figure 5.2. The top portion is nontraditional in the sense that it separates academic measurement topics from life skills topics. Whereas the overall grade for language arts in Figure 5.1 was made up of scores on language arts measurement topics and life skills topics, the overall grade for language arts in Figure 5.2 is composed of language arts topics only. Although each teacher has assessed the student in the life skills measurement topics, these scores are combined across teachers to form an overall grade for each life skills measurement topic, thus focusing grades for a specific subject area on subject matter content only.

The two report cards depicted in Figures 5.1 and 5.2 are only two of many options for reporting when scores are computed for individual measurement topics using a formatively based system of assessment.

Conclusion

In this book we have described the rationale for and specifics of designing measurement topics for academic information and skills and for life skills. Such a process necessarily involves reconstituting state and national standards documents. Part II of this book is a series of *sample* measurement topics for language arts, mathematics, science, and social studies in kindergarten through 8th grade, and measurement topics for life skills in kindergarten through 12th grade.

For each topic, the scoring scale presents the complete 0.0 through 4.0 scale for grade 8 only (or the highest grade level represented in the measurement topic). For grades 7 and below, the scoring scales provide only score values 3.0 and 2.0. As described and illustrated in previous chapters, the wording of each scale at each grade level for all other score values would be

Figure 5.1   Report Card with Overall Grade

Name:	Aida Haystead	**Subject Areas:**	
Address:	123 Some Street	Language Arts	B
City:	Anytown, CO 80000	Mathematics	B
Grade Level:	5	Science	D
Homeroom:	Ms. Becker	Social Studies	A
		Art	B

Language Arts
Writing:

Drafting and Revising	3.0
Format	2.5

Language:

Language Mechanics	3.5
Language Conventions	2.0

Reading:

Reading for the Main Idea	1.0
Genre	1.5

Listening and Speaking:

Analysis and Evaluation of Oral Media	2.5

Life Skills:

Participation	4.0
Work Completion	3.0
Behavior	4.0
Working in Groups	2.5

Mathematics
Numbers and Operations:

Number Sense and Number Systems	4.0
Basic Addition and Subtraction	3.5
Basic Multiplication and Division	3.0

Algebra:

Functions and Equations	4.0

Figure 5.1 *(continued)*

Measurement:		
Measurement Systems	3.5	
Perimeter, Area, and Volume	2.5	
Data Analysis and Probability:		
Data Organization and Interpretation	0.5	
Life Skills:		
Participation	4.0	
Work Completion	2.5	
Behavior	3.0	
Working in Groups	2.0	

Science		
Earth and Space Sciences:		
Atmospheric Processes and the Water Cycle	1.5	
Composition and Structure of the Earth	2.5	
Life Sciences:		
Principles of Heredity and Related Concepts	1.0	
Structure and Function of Cells and Organisms	2.0	
Physical Sciences:		
Structure and Properties of Matter	1.0	
Sources and Properties of Energy	1.5	
Nature of Science:		
Scientific Enterprise	2.5	
Life Skills:		
Participation	1.5	
Work Completion	2.0	
Behavior	3.0	
Working in Groups	1.0	

continued on next page

Figure 5.1   *(continued)*

Social Studies
Citizenship, Government, and Democracy:
The Civil and Criminal Legal Systems   3.5

Culture and Cultural Diversity:
The Nature and Influence of Culture   3.0

Economics:
The Nature and Function of Economic   3.5
Systems

Economics Throughout the World   3.5

History:
Significant Individuals and Events   3.0

Current Events and the Modern World   1.0

Life Skills:
Participation   4.0

Work Completion   4.0

Behavior   4.0

Working in Groups   3.5

Art
Purposes of Art   1.5

Art Skills   2.5

Art and Culture   3.0

Life Skills:
Participation   2.5

Work Completion   2.0

Behavior   4.0

Working in Groups   3.0

identical from grade level to grade level. We have not included elements for score value 4.0 because, in our experience, this approach seems to be the preference of districts and schools with whom we have worked, although we believe it would be quite useful for a district or school to provide guidance for score value 4.0 at each grade level by listing specific examples. We have also not included examples of measurement topics for high school courses. Measurement topics for high school courses would be stated in exactly the same format as shown in the scoring scales in Part II. However, different topics would be constructed for each course, as opposed to common topics from grade level to grade level.

We caution the reader to note that the measurement topics listed in the scoring scales in Part II are examples of the recommended *format* for measurement topics, not the recommended *content*. Indeed, what is deemed appropriate to teach at 3rd grade in one school district in a particular state or province might be more appropriate for the 4th grade in another school district in another state or province. Ideally, districts and schools throughout the United States and elsewhere will use the information in this book and in *Classroom Assessment and Grading That Work* (Marzano, 2006) to design their own measurement topics that are then used to develop a system of formatively based assessment, record keeping, and grading for the enhancement of student learning.

Figure 5.2   Report Card with Academic and Life Skills Grades

Name: Aida Haystead
Address: 123 Some Street
City: Anytown, CO 80000
Grade Level: 5
Homeroom: Ms. Becker

Language Arts	2.29	C	Participation	3.20	A
Mathematics	3.00	A	Work Completion	2.70	B
Science	1.71	D	Behavior	3.60	A
Social Studies	2.92	B	Working in Groups	2.40	C
Art	2.33	C			

Language Arts
Writing:

Drafting and Revising	3.0
Format	2.5

Language:

Language Mechanics	3.5
Language Conventions	2.0

Reading:

Reading for the Main Idea	1.0
Genre	1.5

Listening and Speaking:

Analysis and Evaluation of Oral Media	2.5

Life Skills:

Participation	4.0
Work Completion	3.0
Behavior	4.0
Working in Groups	2.5
Average for Language Arts	2.29

Mathematics
Numbers and Operations:

Number Sense and Number Systems	4.0
Basic Addition and Subtraction	3.5
Basic Multiplication and Division	3.0

Algebra:

Functions and Equations	4.0

Measurement:

Measurement Systems	3.5

Figure 5.2   *(continued)*

Perimeter, Area, and Volume	2.5	
Data Analysis and Probability: Data Organization and Interpretation	0.5	
Life Skills: Participation	4.0	
Work Completion	2.5	
Behavior	3.0	
Working in Groups	2.0	
Average for Mathematics	3.00	

Science
Earth and Space Sciences:

Atmospheric Processes and the Water Cycle	1.5	
Composition and Structure of the Earth	2.5	
Life Sciences: Principles of Heredity and Related Concepts	1.0	
Structure and Function of Cells and Organisms	2.0	
Physical Sciences: Structure and Properties of Matter	1.0	
Sources and Properties of Energy	1.5	
Nature of Science: Scientific Enterprise	2.5	
Life Skills: Participation	1.5	
Work Completion	2.0	
Behavior	3.0	
Working in Groups	1.0	
Average for Science	1.71	

continued on next page

Figure 5.2 *(continued)*		
Social Studies		
Citizenship, Government, and Democracy:		
The Civil and Criminal Legal Systems	3.5	
Culture and Cultural Diversity:		
The Nature and Influence of Culture	3.0	
Economics:		
The Nature and Function of Economic Systems	3.5	
Economics Throughout the World	3.5	
History:		
Significant Individuals and Events	3.0	
Current Events and the Modern World	1.0	
Life Skills:		
Participation	4.0	
Work Completion	4.0	
Behavior	4.0	
Working in Groups	3.5	
Average for Social Studies	2.92	
Art		
Purposes of Art	1.5	
Art Skills	2.5	
Art and Culture	3.0	
Life Skills:		
Participation	2.5	
Work Completion	2.0	
Behavior	4.0	
Working in Groups	3.0	
Average for Art	2.33	

PART II

Scoring Scales

Scoring Scales for
Language Arts

Language Arts

Note: For each measurement topic, the scale for the first grade level (the highest grade level to which the topic extends) shows all scores, including half-point scores. For all other grade levels, the scale shows scores 3.0 and 2.0 only, because the descriptors for the other scores on the scale do not change from grade level to grade level.

Writing

Research and Information Organization

Grade 8		
Score 4.0	**In addition to score 3.0 performance, the student demonstrates in-depth inferences and applications that go beyond what was taught.**	
	Score 3.5	In addition to score 3.0 performance, the student demonstrates in-depth inferences and applications with partial success.
Score 3.0	**While engaged in grade-appropriate writing tasks, the student demonstrates an understanding of and skill at research and information organization by . . .** • conducting detailed Internet searches for information that might be used in a composition (*e.g., when writing about a current political event, finding sites that cover the event from different viewpoints*); • generating multilevel formal or informal outlines (*e.g., including a draft of the introduction and conclusion to the composition in the outline*); and • using interviewing techniques to gather information, such as asking thought-provoking questions, remaining flexible with interview questions, and avoiding interruptions (*e.g., planning for and asking different types of questions during an interview*). **The student exhibits no major errors or omissions.**	
	Score 2.5	The student exhibits no major errors or omissions regarding the score 2.0 elements and partial knowledge of the score 3.0 elements.

Score 2.0	**The student exhibits no major errors or omissions regarding the simpler details and processes, such as . . .**
	• recognizing and recalling specific terminology (*e.g., relevant information, accurate information, reputable information versus irreputable information*); and
	• performing basic processes, such as . . .
	  ○ identifying Internet sites that provide reliable and accurate information;
	  ○ generating an outline but not including drafts of key parts such as the introduction and conclusion; and
	  ○ identifying well-constructed questions that can be used to gather information during an interview.
	However, the student exhibits major errors or omissions with score 3.0 elements.	

	Score 1.5	The student demonstrates partial knowledge of the score 2.0 elements but major errors or omissions regarding the score 3.0 elements.
Score 1.0	**With help, the student demonstrates partial understanding of some of the score 2.0 elements and some of the score 3.0 elements.**	
	Score 0.5	With help, the student demonstrates partial understanding of some of the score 2.0 elements but not the score 3.0 elements.
Score 0.0	**Even with help, the student demonstrates no understanding or skill.**	

Grade 7	
Score 3.0	**While engaged in grade-appropriate writing tasks, the student demonstrates an understanding of and skill at research and information organization by . . .** • conducting Internet searches for information that might be used in a composition (*e.g., using http://scholar.google.com to find useful information about an academic topic*); • generating multilevel formal or informal outlines (*e.g., outlining the order in which each fact might be presented, including the details of each fact*); and • using basic interviewing techniques to gather information, such as researching the person or subject ahead of time, preparing written questions, and taking notes (*e.g., developing a comprehensive set of interview questions for a specific interview*). **The student exhibits no major errors or omissions.**

Score 2.0	**The student exhibits no major errors or omissions regarding the simpler details and processes, such as . . .**
	• recognizing and recalling specific terminology (*e.g., multilevel formal outline, multilevel informal outline*); and
	• performing basic processes, such as . . .
	  ○ identifying multiple Internet sites that might be useful;
	  ○ generating an outline but not including the details for each fact; and
	  ○ developing a basic set of interview questions for a specific interview.
	However, the student exhibits major errors or omissions with score 3.0 elements.

Grade 6	
Score 3.0	**While engaged in grade-appropriate writing tasks, the student demonstrates an understanding of and skill at research and information organization by . . .** • conducting basic Internet searches for information that might be used in a composition (*e.g., using http://google.com to find relevant information*); and • generating a basic outline and changing the outline when necessary to produce the most effective composition (*e.g., changing an original outline that covered the entire life of an influential person to a new outline that covers only the relevant portion of the person's life*). **The student exhibits no major errors or omissions.**

Score 2.0	**The student exhibits no major errors or omissions regarding the simpler details and processes, such as . . .**
	• recognizing and recalling specific terminology (*e.g., notes, Internet research, database*); and
	• performing basic processes, such as . . .
	  ○ downloading information from Internet sites; and
	  ○ identifying portions of an outline that might be changed to make the composition more effective.
	However, the student exhibits major errors or omissions with score 3.0 elements.

Grade 5	
Score 3.0	**While engaged in grade-appropriate writing tasks, the student demonstrates an understanding of and skill at research and information organization by . . .** • using standard reference books to gather information that might be used in a composition (*e.g., using encyclopedias, atlases, and biographies to gather information about a specific event*); and • generating a basic outline (*e.g., when writing about an event, generating a basic outline of the order of events; when writing about a person, generating a basic chronological outline of the person's life*). **The student exhibits no major errors or omissions.**
Score 2.0	**The student exhibits no major errors or omissions regarding the simpler details and processes, such as . . .**

Score 2.0 *(continued)*	• recognizing and recalling specific terminology (*e.g., outline, order of events/chronology*); and • performing basic processes, such as . . . ◦ identifying the appropriate reference source to gather information for a composition; and ◦ recording ideas about what might be included in a composition. **However, the student exhibits major errors or omissions with score 3.0 elements.**
Grade 4	
Score 3.0	**While engaged in grade-appropriate writing tasks, the student demonstrates an understanding of and skill at research and information organization by . . .** • using encyclopedias to gather information that might be used in a composition (*e.g., using an encyclopedia to gather information about a specific person*); and • organizing information into categories of ideas that might be used in the beginning, middle, and end of a composition (*e.g., when writing about a process, such as making a sandwich, the beginning of the composition involves preparation, the middle involves assembly or completion, and the end involves what happens after the completion of the process*). **The student exhibits no major errors or omissions.**
Score 2.0	**The student exhibits no major errors or omissions regarding the simpler details and processes, such as . . .** • recognizing and recalling specific terminology (*e.g., encyclopedia, reference book*); and • performing basic processes, such as . . . ◦ locating a specific person in an encyclopedia when asked to do so by the teacher; and ◦ identifying potential categories for ideas. **However, the student exhibits major errors or omissions with score 3.0 elements.**
Grade 3	
Score 3.0	**While engaged in grade-appropriate writing tasks, the student demonstrates an understanding of and skill at research and information organization by . . .** • organizing information that might be used for a composition into categories of like ideas (*e.g., organizing a book report by first summarizing the events of the story and then giving opinions about the story*); and • using class discussion to gather information that might be used in a composition (*e.g., when writing about the seasons, recording information from a class discussion about winter sports and activities*). **The student exhibits no major errors or omissions.**
Score 2.0	**The student exhibits no major errors or omissions regarding the simpler details and processes, such as . . .** • recognizing and recalling specific terminology (*e.g., opinion, formal writing, informal writing*); and • performing basic processes, such as . . . ◦ identifying potential categories for ideas; and ◦ recognizing when a particular class discussion might be relevant for a given composition. **However, the student exhibits major errors or omissions with score 3.0 elements.**
Grade 2	
Score 3.0	**While engaged in grade-appropriate writing tasks, the student demonstrates an understanding of and skill at research and information organization by . . .** • organizing information that might be used for a composition into categories of like ideas (*e.g., when writing about cars, creating one group of ideas for the good things about cars and one group for the bad things about cars*). **The student exhibits no major errors or omissions.**

Score 2.0	The student exhibits no major errors or omissions regarding the simpler details and processes, such as . . . • recognizing and recalling specific terminology (*e.g., grouping, clumping, webbing, category*); and • performing basic processes, such as . . . ○ identifying the like ideas in a composition. However, the student exhibits major errors or omissions with score 3.0 elements.
Grade 1	
Score 3.0	While engaged in grade-appropriate writing tasks, the student demonstrates an understanding of and skill at research and information organization by . . . • recording ideas or information that might be used in a composition (*e.g., drawing a picture of a zebra to help recall information for later use in a composition on animals*). The student exhibits no major errors or omissions.
Score 2.0	The student exhibits no major errors or omissions regarding the simpler details and processes, such as . . . • recognizing and recalling specific terminology (*e.g., idea/writing idea, keeping a list*); and • recognizing and recalling isolated details, such as . . . ○ recognizing that only some ideas and information are relevant to a composition. However, the student exhibits major errors or omissions with score 3.0 elements.
Grade K	
Score 3.0	Not applicable.
Score 2.0	Not applicable.

Drafting and Revising

	Grade 8	
Score 4.0	**In addition to score 3.0 performance, the student demonstrates in-depth inferences and applications that go beyond what was taught.**	
	Score 3.5	In addition to score 3.0 performance, the student demonstrates in-depth inferences and applications with partial success.
Score 3.0	**While engaged in grade-appropriate writing tasks, the student demonstrates an understanding of and skill at drafting and revising by . . .** • proofreading for tense, voice, and point of view with an emphasis on purposeful tense shifts, consistent voice, and appropriate point of view (*e.g., finding voice errors and correcting them by asking if a consistent emotion is being communicated*); • using revision tools when revising (*e.g., using spell check and grammar check as a way of checking if any errors were overlooked*); and • checking for clarity (*e.g., asking others to read a composition to determine if they found any part of it confusing*). **The student exhibits no major errors or omissions.**	
	Score 2.5	The student exhibits no major errors or omissions regarding the score 2.0 elements and partial knowledge of the score 3.0 elements.

Score 2.0	**The student exhibits no major errors or omissions regarding the simpler details and processes, such as . . .**
	 • recognizing and recalling specific terminology (*e.g., tense shift, clarity*); and
	 • performing basic processes, such as . . .
	    ○ identifying possible tense, voice, and point-of-view errors in a written sample provided by the teacher;
	    ○ identifying potential tools that can be used to check for grammar errors; and
	    ○ identifying potentially confusing passages in a written sample provided by the teacher.
	 However, the student exhibits major errors or omissions with score 3.0 elements.	

	Score 1.5	The student demonstrates partial knowledge of the score 2.0 elements but major errors or omissions regarding the score 3.0 elements.
Score 1.0	**With help, the student demonstrates partial understanding of some of the score 2.0 elements and some of the score 3.0 elements.**	
	Score 0.5	With help, the student demonstrates partial understanding of some of the score 2.0 elements but not the score 3.0 elements.
Score 0.0	**Even with help, the student demonstrates no understanding or skill.**	
	Grade 7	
Score 3.0	**While engaged in grade-appropriate writing tasks, the student demonstrates an understanding of and skill at drafting and revising by . . .** • proofreading for tense and point of view with an emphasis on tense consistency, active versus passive voice, and first versus third person (*e.g., finding and correcting voice errors by reading each sentence and determining its voice*); and • adding transition words/sentences and deleting extraneous information (*e.g., finding extraneous information by reading every sentence and asking if it is necessary*). **The student exhibits no major errors or omissions.**	
Score 2.0	**The student exhibits no major errors or omissions regarding the simpler details and processes, such as . . .**	

Score 2.0 (continued)	• recognizing and recalling specific terminology (*e.g., tense, voice, point of view, extraneous information*); and
	• performing basic processes, such as . . .
	   ◦ identifying incorrect use of first and third person in a written composition provided by the teacher; and
	   ◦ identifying extraneous information in a written sample provided by the teacher.
	However, the student exhibits major errors or omissions with score 3.0 elements.

Grade 6	
Score 3.0	**While engaged in grade-appropriate writing tasks, the student demonstrates an understanding of and skill at drafting and revising by . . .** • proofreading for spelling, punctuation, and grammar with an emphasis on correct use of modifiers (*e.g., finding and correcting modifier errors by identifying nouns and verbs and examining their modifiers*); • consulting Internet sources or a style manual when revising (*e.g., using a style manual to find guidelines for when use of slang is and is not appropriate in writing*); and • elaborating on ideas and adding transitional words/sentences (*e.g., rereading each paragraph of a research paper to ensure that it includes a topic sentence*). **The student exhibits no major errors or omissions.**

Score 2.0	**The student exhibits no major errors or omissions regarding the simpler details and processes, such as . . .**
	• recognizing and recalling specific terminology (*e.g., transition, final draft*); and
	• performing basic processes, such as . . .
	   ◦ identifying modifier errors in a written sample provided by the teacher;
	   ◦ identifying which style manual or Internet source is the most appropriate in a given situation; and
	   ◦ identifying potential transition sentences that might be used in a specific situation.
	However, the student exhibits major errors or omissions with score 3.0 elements.

Grade 5	
Score 3.0	**While engaged in grade-appropriate writing tasks, the student demonstrates an understanding of and skill at drafting and revising by . . .** • proofreading for spelling, punctuation and grammar with an emphasis on subject-verb agreement and pronoun-antecedent agreement (*e.g., finding and correcting subject-verb agreement and pronoun-antecedent agreement errors by rereading each sentence and determining the subject and the predicate*); • consulting Internet sources or a style manual when revising (*e.g., looking up different sentence forms in an attempt to find variety*); and • adding descriptive words and details and verifying correct order of information (*e.g., rereading portions of a book being reported on to be sure the events of the story have been recounted in correct order*). **The student exhibits no major errors or omissions.**

Score 2.0	**The student exhibits no major errors or omissions regarding the simpler details and processes, such as . . .**
	• recognizing and recalling specific terminology (*e.g., elaboration of ideas, style manual*); and
	• performing basic processes, such as . . .
	   ◦ identifying errors in subject-verb agreement and pronoun-antecedent agreement in a written sample provided by the teacher;
	   ◦ identifying potential Internet sources that might be used when revising; and
	   ◦ identifying information out of sequence in a written sample provided by the teacher.
	However, the student exhibits major errors or omissions with score 3.0 elements.

Grade 4	
Score 3.0	**While engaged in grade-appropriate writing tasks, the student demonstrates an understanding of and skill at drafting and revising by . . .** • proofreading for spelling, basic punctuation, and grammar, with an emphasis on capitalization and correct sentence form (*e.g., rereading each sentence to ensure it begins with a capital letter*); and • using a dictionary and a thesaurus when revising (*e.g., looking up words in a dictionary and a thesaurus to generate ideas for revision*). **The student exhibits no major errors or omissions.**

Score 2.0	**The student exhibits no major errors or omissions regarding the simpler details and processes, such as . . .**
	• recognizing and recalling specific terminology (*e.g., spell check, correct order of information*); and
	• recognizing and recalling isolated details, such as . . .
	  ◦ capitalization and sentence forms follow certain rules; and
	  ◦ if a word is marked either by a teacher or by a computer program, the word is misspelled, used incorrectly, or not the best choice.
	However, the student exhibits major errors or omissions with score 3.0 elements.

Grade 3	
Score 3.0	**While engaged in grade-appropriate writing tasks, the student demonstrates an understanding of and skill at drafting and revising by . . .** • proofreading for spelling (*e.g., rereading a composition to identify words that might be misspelled*); and • using a thesaurus when revising (*e.g., when describing something very cold, using a thesaurus to find words such as* chilly, freezing, *and* frigid). **The student exhibits no major errors or omissions.**

Score 2.0	**The student exhibits no major errors or omissions regarding the simpler details and processes, such as . . .**
	• recognizing and recalling specific terminology (*e.g., proofreading, thesaurus*); and
	• recognizing and recalling isolated details, such as . . .
	  ◦ words that are obviously misspelled need to be corrected, and any word the student is unsure of should be checked; and
	  ◦ a dictionary and a thesaurus provide different types of information.
	However, the student exhibits major errors or omissions with score 3.0 elements.

Grade 2	
Score 3.0	**While engaged in grade-appropriate writing tasks, the student demonstrates an understanding of and skill at drafting and revising by . . .** • using a dictionary when revising (*e.g., looking up words in the dictionary to obtain ideas for revising*); and • correcting obvious errors before turning in an assignment (*e.g., correcting any proper names that are not capitalized*). **The student exhibits no major errors or omissions.**
Score 2.0	**The student exhibits no major errors or omissions regarding the simpler details and processes, such as . . .** • recognizing and recalling specific terminology (*e.g., description, detail*); and • recognizing and recalling isolated details, such as . . . ◦ if a student is unsure of the spelling of any word in an assignment, the word should be looked up in a dictionary; and

Score 2.0 (continued)	○ assignments should be free of errors in spelling, grammar, and punctuation before they are turned in. **However, the student exhibits major errors or omissions with score 3.0 elements.**
Grade 1	
Score 3.0	**While engaged in grade-appropriate writing tasks, the student demonstrates an understanding of and skill at drafting and revising by . . .** • rereading an assignment before handing it in (*e.g., ensuring that no obvious errors are made*). **The student exhibits no major errors or omissions.**
Score 2.0	**The student exhibits no major errors or omissions regarding the simpler details and processes, such as . . .** • recognizing and recalling specific terminology (*e.g., dictionary, error*); and • recognizing and recalling isolated details, such as . . . 　○ errors in an assignment can be found by rereading it. **However, the student exhibits major errors or omissions with score 3.0 elements.**
Grade K	
Score 3.0	**While engaged in grade-appropriate writing tasks, the student demonstrates an understanding of and skill at drafting and revising by . . .** • writing an assignment legibly in pencil before handing it in. **The student exhibits no major errors or omissions.**
Score 2.0	**The student exhibits no major errors or omissions regarding the simpler details and processes, such as . . .** • recognizing and recalling specific terminology (*e.g., revision pencil, neat versus messy*); and • recognizing and recalling isolated details, such as . . . 　○ sometimes one letter of the alphabet can look like another if not written clearly and neatly. **However, the student exhibits major errors or omissions with score 3.0 elements.**

Format

Grade 8		
Score 4.0	**In addition to score 3.0 performance, the student demonstrates in-depth inferences and applications that go beyond what was taught.**	
	Score 3.5	In addition to score 3.0 performance, the student demonstrates in-depth inferences and applications with partial success.
Score 3.0	**While engaged in grade-appropriate writing tasks, the student demonstrates competence in a variety of formats by . . .** • writing complex persuasive compositions (*e.g., writing persuasive compositions that use clear claims, backing, warrants, and qualifiers*); and • writing letters of response and letters of request (*e.g., writing business letters of request and response*). **The student exhibits no major errors or omissions.**	
	Score 2.5	The student exhibits no major errors or omissions regarding the score 2.0 elements and partial knowledge of the score 3.0 elements.

Score 2.0	**The student exhibits no major errors or omissions regarding the simpler details and processes, such as . . .**
	• recognizing and recalling specific terminology (*e.g., claim, qualifier, persuasive technique, formal letter*); and
	• recognizing and recalling isolated details, such as . . .
	  ○ the defining features of persuasive compositions; and
	  ○ the defining features of business letters.
	However, the student exhibits major errors or omissions with score 3.0 elements.	

	Score 1.5	The student demonstrates partial knowledge of the score 2.0 elements but major errors or omissions regarding the score 3.0 elements.
Score 1.0	**With help, the student demonstrates partial understanding of some of the score 2.0 elements and some of the score 3.0 elements.**	
	Score 0.5	With help, the student demonstrates partial understanding of some of the score 2.0 elements but not the score 3.0 elements.
Score 0.0	**Even with help, the student demonstrates no understanding or skill.**	
Grade 7		
Score 3.0	**While engaged in grade-appropriate writing tasks, the student demonstrates competence in a variety of formats by . . .** • writing narrative stories that focus on tone and mood (*e.g., using setting to create tone and mood*); • writing basic persuasive compositions (*e.g., writing a clear claim with supporting details*); and • writing letters of response and letters of request (*e.g., writing personal letters of request and response*). **The student exhibits no major errors or omissions.**	
Score 2.0	**The student exhibits no major errors or omissions regarding the simpler details and processes, such as . . .** • recognizing and recalling specific terminology (*e.g., tone, mood, persuade, respond*); and • recognizing and recalling isolated details, such as . . . ○ specific characteristics of setting;	

Score 2.0 (continued)	○ the basic features of persuasive compositions; and ○ the defining features of personal letters. **However, the student exhibits major errors or omissions with score 3.0 elements.**

Grade 6	
Score 3.0	**While engaged in grade-appropriate writing tasks, the student demonstrates competence in a variety of formats by . . .** • writing narrative stories that focus on voice (*e.g., using specific word choices to create voice*); and • writing expository compositions that focus on problem/solution (*e.g., clearly describing a problem and the possible solution that might be used*). **The student exhibits no major errors or omissions.**
Score 2.0	**The student exhibits no major errors or omissions regarding the simpler details and processes, such as . . .** • recognizing and recalling specific terminology (*e.g., voice, problem, solution, research*); and • recognizing and recalling isolated details, such as . . . ○ specific characteristics of voice; and ○ the defining characteristics of problem/solution compositions. **However, the student exhibits major errors or omissions with score 3.0 elements.**

Grade 5	
Score 3.0	**While engaged in grade-appropriate writing tasks, the student demonstrates competence in a variety of formats by . . .** • writing narratives that focus on point of view (*e.g., using statements of personal opinion to create point of view*); and • writing expository compositions that focus on comparison/contrast (*e.g., clearly identifying the elements that are being compared and the criteria used to compare them*). **The student exhibits no major errors or omissions.**
Score 2.0	**The student exhibits no major errors or omissions regarding the simpler details and processes, such as . . .** • recognizing and recalling specific terminology (*e.g., point of view, compare, contrast*); and • recognizing and recalling isolated details, such as . . . ○ a narrative can look very different from different points of view; and ○ comparison/contrast involves a discussion of two or more subjects and how they are alike and how they are different. **However, the student exhibits major errors or omissions with score 3.0 elements.**

Grade 4	
Score 3.0	**While engaged in grade-appropriate writing tasks, the student demonstrates competence in a variety of formats by . . .** • writing narrative stories (*e.g., providing a clear plot or process*); and • writing expository compositions that focus on classification (*e.g., explaining the features of a category and listed related elements*). **The student exhibits no major errors or omissions.**
Score 2.0	**The student exhibits no major errors or omissions regarding the simpler details and processes, such as . . .** • recognizing and recalling specific terminology (*e.g., category, classification*); and • recognizing and recalling isolated details, such as . . . ○ a process depicted in a story includes each step along the way, whereas the plot of a story includes what happened, how it happened, and why it happened; and

Score 2.0 (*continued*)	○ classification is used in expository compositions and involves grouping ideas, information, people, objects, or events according to chosen similarities. **However, the student exhibits major errors or omissions with score 3.0 elements.**

Grade 3	
Score 3.0	**While engaged in grade-appropriate writing tasks, the student demonstrates competence in a variety of formats by . . .** • writing simple narrative stories (*e.g., providing a basic but discernable plot or process*); and • writing basic expository compositions (*e.g., providing a generalization with supporting detail*). **The student exhibits no major errors or omissions.**
Score 2.0	**The student exhibits no major errors or omissions regarding the simpler details and processes, such as . . .** • recognizing and recalling specific terminology (*e.g., plot, generalization, support*); and • recognizing and recalling isolated details, such as . . . 　○ a successful narrative story has either a process or a plot as its focus; and 　○ expository compositions usually include generalizations that need support. **However, the student exhibits major errors or omissions with score 3.0 elements.**

Grade 2	
Score 3.0	**While engaged in grade-appropriate writing tasks, the student demonstrates competence in a variety of formats by . . .** • writing simple narrative stories (*e.g., describing events or processes in correct order*); and • writing sensory descriptions (*e.g., providing basic descriptions of people, places, or things*). **The student exhibits no major errors or omissions.**
Score 2.0	**The student exhibits no major errors or omissions regarding the simpler details and processes, such as . . .** • recognizing and recalling specific terminology (*e.g., event, process, order of information, description*); and • recognizing and recalling isolated details, such as . . . 　○ narrative stories often center around events or processes described in order; and 　○ sensory descriptions can be centered around people, places, and things. **However, the student exhibits major errors or omissions with score 3.0 elements.**

Grade 1	
Score 3.0	**While engaged in grade-appropriate writing tasks, the student demonstrates competence in a variety of formats by . . .** • writing brief explanations of personal experiences (*e.g., writing a description of a family vacation*); and • writing brief, sensory descriptions of a concrete object (*e.g., describing what it is like to take a walk in the woods*). **The student exhibits no major errors or omissions.**
Score 2.0	**The student exhibits no major errors or omissions regarding the simpler details and processes, such as . . .** • recognizing and recalling specific terminology (*e.g., taste, touch, concrete object, story*); and • recognizing and recalling isolated details, such as . . . 　○ written stories and explanations are often based on personal experiences; and 　○ sensory descriptions often focus on a concrete object. **However, the student exhibits major errors or omissions with score 3.0 elements.**

Grade K	
Score 3.0	**While engaged in grade-appropriate writing tasks, the student demonstrates competence in a variety of formats by . . .** • describing personal experiences by telling and dictating (*e.g., describing an event that happened at home*). **The student exhibits no major errors or omissions.**
Score 2.0	**The student exhibits no major errors or omissions regarding the simpler details and processes, such as . . .** • recognizing and recalling specific terminology (*e.g., reading, writing, pictures, personal experience*); and • recognizing and recalling isolated details, such as . . . ◦ describing personal experiences helps people understand you. **However, the student exhibits major errors or omissions with score 3.0 elements.**

Audience and Purpose

	Grade 8	
Score 4.0	**In addition to score 3.0 performance, the student demonstrates in-depth inferences and applications that go beyond what was taught.**	
	Score 3.5	In addition to score 3.0 performance, the student demonstrates in-depth inferences and applications with partial success.
Score 3.0	**While engaged in grade-appropriate writing tasks, the student demonstrates an understanding of audience and purpose by . . .** • discriminating among multiple possible purposes for a given composition and combining purposes if necessary or effective (*e.g., attempting not only to inspire in a given composition but also to enhance inspiration with entertainment*); and • discriminating among multiple possible audiences in a given composition and selecting the most useful (*e.g., when writing in favor of animal rights, tailoring the composition to fur manufacturers because they are one of the largest violators of animal rights*). **The student exhibits no major errors or omissions.**	
	Score 2.5	The student exhibits no major errors or omissions regarding the score 2.0 elements and partial knowledge of the score 3.0 elements.

Score 2.0	**The student exhibits no major errors or omissions regarding the simpler details and processes, such as . . .**
	• recognizing and recalling specific terminology (*e.g., ethos, logos, pathos*); and
	• performing basic processes, such as . . .
	  ○ exemplifying how multiple purposes are often present in compositions; and
	  ○ exemplifying how any given composition can be tailored to one of a variety of audiences.
	However, the student exhibits major errors or omissions with score 3.0 elements.	

	Score 1.5	The student demonstrates partial knowledge of the score 2.0 elements but major errors or omissions regarding the score 3.0 elements.
Score 1.0	**With help, the student demonstrates partial understanding of some of the score 2.0 elements and some of the score 3.0 elements.**	
	Score 0.5	With help, the student demonstrates partial understanding of some of the score 2.0 elements but not the score 3.0 elements.
Score 0.0	**Even with help, the student demonstrates no understanding or skill.**	
	Grade 7	
Score 3.0	**While engaged in grade-appropriate writing tasks, the student demonstrates an understanding of audience and purpose by . . .** • discriminating among multiple possible purposes for a given composition and selecting the most useful (*e.g., when writing about peer pressure and drugs, determining that the best purpose would be to illustrate what happens with prolonged drug use, because most people are more affected by a story than by a list of facts*); and • discriminating among multiple possible audiences in a given composition and selecting the most useful (*e.g., when writing a composition about peer pressure and drugs, determining that the best audience is the specific age range the composition concerns*). **The student exhibits no major errors or omissions.**	
Score 2.0	**The student exhibits no major errors or omissions regarding the simpler details and processes, such as . . .**	

Score 2.0 (*continued*)	• recognizing and recalling specific terminology (*e.g., selective choosing, shades of meaning*); and
	• performing basic processes, such as . . .
	  ○ exemplifying how when writing about a specific issue (an endangered species) the approach taken can be informative (informing the public about this species), persuasive (appealing to those who endanger the species to change), or entertaining (telling the story of a particular member of this species); and
	  ○ exemplifying how only some audiences would find any particular writing composition useful.
	However, the student exhibits major errors or omissions with score 3.0 elements.

Grade 6	
Score 3.0	**While engaged in grade-appropriate writing tasks, the student demonstrates an understanding of audience and purpose by . . .** • selecting and defending a clear purpose for a given composition (*e.g., selecting an investigative purpose when writing about the deterioration of the rain forest*); and • selecting and defending a specific audience within a given format for composition (*e.g., when writing business letters of inquiry, choosing a person or organization of particular interest*). **The student exhibits no major errors or omissions.**

Score 2.0	**The student exhibits no major errors or omissions regarding the simpler details and processes, such as . . .**
	• recognizing and recalling specific terminology (*e.g., investigation, sensory detail*); and
	• performing basic processes, such as . . .
	  ○ exemplifying how a clear purpose can be defined in many different ways; and
	  ○ exemplifying how different audiences can exist within one given format.
	However, the student exhibits major errors or omissions with score 3.0 elements.

Grade 5	
Score 3.0	**While engaged in grade-appropriate writing tasks, the student demonstrates an understanding of audience and purpose by . . .** • maintaining a clear purpose for a given composition (*e.g., selecting a specific purpose, such as critiquing a book, and maintaining that purpose throughout a composition*); and • adhering to the selection of a specific audience for a given composition (*e.g., selecting a specific audience, such as parents, and maintaining that audience throughout a composition*). **The student exhibits no major errors or omissions.**

Score 2.0	**The student exhibits no major errors or omissions regarding the simpler details and processes, such as . . .**
	• recognizing and recalling specific terminology (*e.g., specific purpose, specific audience, inquiry, critique*); and
	• performing basic processes, such as . . .
	  ○ exemplifying specific purposes, including inquiry, critique, inspiration, illustration, and advertisement; and
	  ○ exemplifying specific audiences, including particular individuals, particular companies or groups, people of a particular age or gender, and people or organizations with particular beliefs.
	However, the student exhibits major errors or omissions with score 3.0 elements.

Grade 4	
Score 3.0	**While engaged in grade-appropriate writing tasks, the student demonstrates an understanding of audience and purpose by . . .** • using a general purpose for a given composition (*e.g., selecting a general informative purpose and maintaining that focus throughout a composition*); and

Score 3.0 (*continued*)	• writing to a general audience (formal versus informal) for a given composition (*e.g., selecting a general informal audience and maintaining that audience throughout a composition*). **The student exhibits no major errors or omissions.**

Score 2.0	**The student exhibits no major errors or omissions regarding the simpler details and processes, such as . . .**
	• recognizing and recalling specific terminology (*e.g., formal language, informal language*); and
	• recognizing and recalling isolated details, such as . . .
	  ◦ formal compositions (book reports, class writing assignments) generally serve informative or persuasive purposes, whereas informal compositions (letters to friends) generally serve communication or entertainment purposes; and
	  ◦ audience selection can make the overall composition either more or less effective.
	However, the student exhibits major errors or omissions with score 3.0 elements.

Grade 3	
Score 3.0	**While engaged in grade-appropriate writing tasks, the student demonstrates an understanding of audience and purpose by . . .** • appropriately writing for an assigned purpose (*e.g., in a composition about summer vacation, writing the true events in order so as to appropriately inform*); and • distinguishing between a formal and an informal audience (*e.g., explaining why the audience in a given composition is formal or informal*). **The student exhibits no major errors or omissions.**

Score 2.0	**The student exhibits no major errors or omissions regarding the simpler details and processes, such as . . .**
	• recognizing and recalling specific terminology (*e.g., informal audience, formal audience*); and
	• recognizing and recalling isolated details, such as . . .
	  ◦ in a book report assignment, the composition should inform someone about the book; and
	  ◦ notes to friends or letters to family members do not need to look like class assignments need to look.
	However, the student exhibits major errors or omissions with score 3.0 elements.

Grade 2	
Score 3.0	Not applicable.
Score 2.0	Not applicable.
Grade 1	
Score 3.0	Not applicable.
Score 2.0	Not applicable.
Grade K	
Score 3.0	Not applicable.
Score 2.0	Not applicable.

Word Processing

Grade 8		
Score 4.0	**In addition to score 3.0 performance, the student demonstrates in-depth inferences and applications that go beyond what was taught.**	
	Score 3.5	In addition to score 3.0 performance, the student demonstrates in-depth inferences and applications with partial success.
Score 3.0	**While engaged in grade-appropriate writing tasks, the student demonstrates an understanding of word processing by . . .** • using various computer software programs to enhance writing projects (*e.g., using Microsoft Excel for complex tables and charts and Microsoft PowerPoint for visual presentations*). **The student exhibits no major errors or omissions.**	
	Score 2.5	The student exhibits no major errors or omissions regarding the score 2.0 elements and partial knowledge of the score 3.0 elements.
Score 2.0	**The student exhibits no major errors or omissions regarding the simpler details and processes, such as . . .** • recognizing and recalling specific terminology (*e.g., Microsoft Excel, Microsoft PowerPoint*); and • performing basic processes, such as . . . ◦ performing simple data entry using Microsoft Excel and creating basic slides using Microsoft PowerPoint. **However, the student exhibits major errors or omissions with score 3.0 elements.**	
	Score 1.5	The student demonstrates partial knowledge of the score 2.0 elements but major errors or omissions regarding the score 3.0 elements.
Score 1.0	**With help, the student demonstrates partial understanding of some of the score 2.0 elements and some of the score 3.0 elements.**	
	Score 0.5	With help, the student demonstrates partial understanding of some of the score 2.0 elements but not the score 3.0 elements.
Score 0.0	**Even with help, the student demonstrates no understanding or skill.**	
Grade 7		
Score 3.0	**While engaged in grade-appropriate writing tasks, the student demonstrates an understanding of word processing by . . .** • using a word processor to create charts, tables, or graphs (*e.g., using the "Table" menu in Microsoft Word to create a table with multiple rows and columns and to modify its properties to depict information in the best way possible*). **The student exhibits no major errors or omissions.**	
Score 2.0	**The student exhibits no major errors or omissions regarding the simpler details and processes, such as . . .** • recognizing and recalling specific terminology (*e.g., chart, table, graph*); and • performing basic processes, such as . . . ◦ creating basic charts, tables, and graphs on a word processor (*e.g., keeping Microsoft Word's default formatting when inserting a chart into the document*). **However, the student exhibits major errors or omissions with score 3.0 elements.**	

Grade 6	
Score 3.0	**While engaged in grade-appropriate writing tasks, the student demonstrates an understanding of word processing by . . .** • using a word processor to combine documents and keep track of sources (*e.g., creating different sections of a composition in different files and then combining all files into a single document*). **The student exhibits no major errors or omissions.**
Score 2.0	**The student exhibits no major errors or omissions regarding the simpler details and processes, such as . . .** • recognizing and recalling specific terminology (*e.g., source, bibliography*); and • performing basic processes, such as . . . ◦ generating a plan for keeping track of various files to be combined into a single document. **However, the student exhibits major errors or omissions with score 3.0 elements.**
Grade 5	
Score 3.0	**While engaged in grade-appropriate writing tasks, the student demonstrates an understanding of word processing by . . .** • using a word processor to create specific assignment formats (*e.g., when writing a formal letter, using a formatting guide provided by Microsoft Word*). **The student exhibits no major errors or omissions.**
Score 2.0	**The student exhibits no major errors or omissions regarding the simpler details and processes, such as . . .** • recognizing and recalling specific terminology (*e.g., computer program, computer formatting*); and • recognizing and recalling isolated details, such as . . . ◦ the characteristics of specific templates included in a word processing program. **However, the student exhibits major errors or omissions with score 3.0 elements.**
Grade 4	
Score 3.0	**While engaged in grade-appropriate writing tasks, the student demonstrates an understanding of word processing by . . .** • using a word processor to cut and paste a document for correct organization (*e.g., moving paragraphs that originally described an event out of order by highlighting the appropriate area and using the cut and paste features*). **The student exhibits no major errors or omissions.**
Score 2.0	**The student exhibits no major errors or omissions regarding the simpler details and processes, such as . . .** • recognizing and recalling specific terminology (*e.g., correct order of information, cut and paste*); and • recognizing and recalling isolated details, such as . . . ◦ large portions of text can be moved or deleted on a word processor. **However, the student exhibits major errors or omissions with score 3.0 elements.**
Grade 3	
Score 3.0	**While engaged in grade-appropriate writing tasks, the student demonstrates an understanding of word processing by . . .** • using a word processor to make basic editorial changes (*e.g., correcting misspellings and grammatical errors by placing the cursor on the error, deleting, and replacing*). **The student exhibits no major errors or omissions.**

Score 2.0	The student exhibits no major errors or omissions regarding the simpler details and processes, such as . . . • recognizing and recalling specific terminology (*e.g., draft/drafting, edit/editing*); and • recognizing and recalling isolated details, such as . . . ○ misspellings and grammatical errors can be corrected on a word processor. However, the student exhibits major errors or omissions with score 3.0 elements.
Grade 2	
Score 3.0	While engaged in grade-appropriate writing tasks, the student demonstrates an understanding of word processing by . . . • using a word processor to generate basic text (*e.g., writing a class assignment on a computer and saving it on the hard drive*). The student exhibits no major errors or omissions.
Score 2.0	The student exhibits no major errors or omissions regarding the simpler details and processes, such as . . . • recognizing and recalling specific terminology (*e.g., word processor/computer, text*); and • performing basic processes, such as . . . ○ creating a new file on a word processor and saving that file to the hard drive. However, the student exhibits major errors or omissions with score 3.0 elements.
Grade 1	
Score 3.0	Not applicable.
Score 2.0	Not applicable.
Grade K	
Score 3.0	Not applicable.
Score 2.0	Not applicable.

Language

Spelling

Grade 8		
Score 4.0	**In addition to score 3.0 performance, the student demonstrates in-depth inferences and applications that go beyond what was taught.**	
	Score 3.5	In addition to score 3.0 performance, the student demonstrates in-depth inferences and applications with partial success.
Score 3.0	**While engaged in grade-appropriate tasks, the student demonstrates an ability to . . .** • analyze unfamiliar words using spelling conventions (*e.g., using the awareness that a suffix often begins with a vowel to analyze unfamiliar words*). **The student exhibits no major errors or omissions.**	
	Score 2.5	The student exhibits no major errors or omissions regarding the score 2.0 elements and partial knowledge of the score 3.0 elements.
Score 2.0	**The student exhibits no major errors or omissions regarding the simpler details and processes, such as . . .** • recognizing and recalling specific terminology (*e.g., regular structural changes, irregular structural changes*); and • performing basic processes, such as . . . ○ identifying basic parts of unfamiliar words. **However, the student exhibits major errors or omissions with score 3.0 elements.**	
	Score 1.5	The student demonstrates partial knowledge of the score 2.0 elements but major errors or omissions regarding the score 3.0 elements.
Score 1.0	**With help, the student demonstrates partial understanding of some of the score 2.0 elements and some of the score 3.0 elements.**	
	Score 0.5	With help, the student demonstrates partial understanding of some of the score 2.0 elements but not the score 3.0 elements.
Score 0.0	**Even with help, the student demonstrates no understanding or skill.**	
Grade 7		
Score 3.0	**While engaged in grade-appropriate tasks, the student demonstrates an ability to . . .** • spell derivatives correctly using bases and affixes (*e.g., using "apply" to spell "application"*); and • correctly spell low-frequency, commonly misspelled words (*e.g., spelling "accelerate"*). **The student exhibits no major errors or omissions.**	
Score 2.0	**The student exhibits no major errors or omissions regarding the simpler details and processes, such as . . .** • recognizing and recalling specific terminology (*e.g., derivative, base*); and • performing basic processes, such as . . .	

Score 2.0 (continued)	○ identifying the base word in a derivative; and ○ recognizing when commonly misspelled words are spelled correctly. **However, the student exhibits major errors or omissions with score 3.0 elements.**
Grade 6	
Score 3.0	**While engaged in grade-appropriate tasks, the student demonstrates an ability to . . .** • correctly spell high-frequency but commonly misspelled words (*e.g., spelling "judgment"*); • use less common roots to spell words (*e.g., using the root "ann" to spell "annual"*); • use less common suffixes to spell words (*e.g., using "des" and "ment"*); and • use less common prefixes to spell words (*e.g., using "dis" and "ad"*). **The student exhibits no major errors or omissions.**
Score 2.0	**The student exhibits no major errors or omissions regarding the simpler details and processes, such as . . .** • recognizing and recalling specific terminology (*e.g., affix, appositive*); and • performing basic processes, such as . . . ○ identifying when commonly misspelled words are spelled correctly; ○ identifying less common roots; ○ identifying less common suffixes; and ○ identifying less common prefixes. **However, the student exhibits major errors or omissions with score 3.0 elements.**
Grade 5	
Score 3.0	**While engaged in grade-appropriate tasks, the student demonstrates an ability to . . .** • use roots to spell words (*e.g., using "uni" to spell "unify," "unit," and "unilateral"*); • use suffixes to spell words (*e.g., using "er," "ly," and "tion"*); • use prefixes to spell words (*e.g., using "ex" and "pre"*); and • use syllable constructions to spell words (*e.g., spelling "recognize" by splitting the word into the syllables re/cog/nize*). **The student exhibits no major errors or omissions.**
Score 2.0	**The student exhibits no major errors or omissions regarding the simpler details and processes, such as . . .** • recognizing and recalling specific terminology (*e.g., syllable construction, syllable splitting*); and • performing basic processes, such as . . . ○ identifying roots within words; ○ identifying suffixes; ○ identifying prefixes; and ○ successfully breaking words into syllables. **However, the student exhibits major errors or omissions with score 3.0 elements.**
Grade 4	
Score 3.0	**While engaged in grade-appropriate tasks, the student demonstrates an ability to . . .** • use common roots to spell words (*e.g., using "tele" to spell "telephone" and "telepathy"*); • use common suffixes to spell words (*e.g., using "ing," "ed," and "tion"*); • use common prefixes to spell words (*e.g., using "a," "ex," "in," and "un"*); • use syllable constructions to spell words (*e.g., spelling "recognize" by splitting the word into the syllables cus/tom*); • use vowel combinations to spell words (*e.g., using "igh" to spell "high," "freight," and "weigh"*); and • use initial consonant substitutions to spell words (*e.g., changing the word "sigh" to "high"*). **The student exhibits no major errors or omissions.**

Score 2.0	The student exhibits no major errors or omissions regarding the simpler details and processes, such as . . .
	• recognizing and recalling specific terminology (*e.g., homophone, word roots, suffix, prefix*); and
	• performing basic processes, such as . . .
	   ○ identifying roots within words;
	   ○ identifying basic suffixes;
	   ○ identifying common prefixes;
	   ○ breaking words into syllables;
	   ○ identifying basic vowel combinations in words; and
	   ○ identifying consonant substitution in a list of words.
	However, the student exhibits major errors or omissions with score 3.0 elements.

Grade 3	
Score 3.0	**While engaged in grade-appropriate tasks, the student demonstrates an ability to . . .** • spell common compound words (*e.g., spelling "doghouse" and "butterfly"*); • spell basic contractions (*e.g., spelling "can't," "isn't," and "it's"*); • spell words beginning with the "qu" combination (*e.g., spelling "quiet" and "queen"*); • spell words with double consonants (*e.g., spelling "berry" and "butter"*); • spell "ies" as the plural ending for words ending with a "y" in singular form (*e.g., spelling "cherries" as the plural form of "cherry"*); and • spell basic homophones (*e.g., spelling "pale" and "pail"*). **The student exhibits no major errors or omissions.**

Score 2.0	The student exhibits no major errors or omissions regarding the simpler details and processes, such as . . .
	• recognizing and recalling specific terminology (*e.g., contractions, syllable*); and
	• performing basic processes, such as . . .
	   ○ recognizing correctly spelled compound words;
	   ○ recognizing correctly spelled basic contractions;
	   ○ recognizing correctly spelled words beginning with the "qu" combination;
	   ○ recognizing correctly spelled words with double consonants;
	   ○ recognizing correctly spelled words with a plural "ies" ending; and
	   ○ recognizing correctly spelled basic homophones in context.
	However, the student exhibits major errors or omissions with score 3.0 elements.

Grade 2	
Score 3.0	**While engaged in grade-appropriate tasks, the student demonstrates an ability to . . .** • arrange words in alphabetical order (*e.g., placing "baby" before "gate" in an alphabetical list*); • spell frequently used, irregular words (*e.g., spelling words such as "was," "were," "says," "said," "who," "what," and "why"*); • spell words with the "ight" ending (*e.g., spelling words such as "sight," "fright," and "flight"*); and • spell basic compound words (*e.g., spelling words such as "sailboat" and "grandfather"*). **The student exhibits no major errors or omissions.**

Score 2.0	The student exhibits no major errors or omissions regarding the simpler details and processes, such as . . .
	• recognizing and recalling specific terminology (*e.g., alphabetical order, irregular word, compound word*); and
	• performing basic processes, such as . . .
	   ○ recognizing correct alphabetical order;
	   ○ recognizing correctly spelled frequently used, irregular words;

Score 2.0 (continued)	◦ recognizing correctly spelled words with the "ight" ending; and ◦ recognizing correctly spelled basic compound words. **However, the student exhibits major errors or omissions with score 3.0 elements.**
Grade 1	
Score 3.0	**While engaged in grade-appropriate tasks, the student demonstrates an ability to . . .** • spell basic r-controlled patterns (*e.g., spelling words such as "her," "burn," "pour," and "alarm"*); • spell basic consonant-blend patterns (*e.g., spelling and pronouncing words such as "front," "trip," "crow," and "sleep"*); • spell basic long-vowel patterns (*e.g., spelling and pronouncing words such as "apron," "evil," "iron," "open," and "bugle"*); and • spell basic short-vowel patterns (*e.g., spelling and pronouncing words such as "smack," "hem," "pick," "hop," and "cup"*). **The student exhibits no major errors or omissions.**
Score 2.0	**The student exhibits no major errors or omissions regarding the simpler details and processes, such as . . .** • recognizing and recalling specific terminology (*e.g., consonants/consonant blends, vowels [long vowel and short vowel]*); • performing basic processes, such as . . . ◦ recognizing correctly spelled basic *r*-controlled patterns; ◦ recognizing correctly spelled basic consonant-blend patterns; ◦ recognizing correctly spelled basic long-vowel patterns; and ◦ recognizing correctly spelled basic short-vowel patterns. **However, the student exhibits major errors or omissions with score 3.0 elements.**
Grade K	
Score 3.0	**While engaged in grade-appropriate tasks, the student demonstrates an ability to . . .** • spell basic two-letter words (*e.g., spelling words such as "as," "be," "at," and "am"*); • spell basic three-letter, consonant-vowel-consonant words (*e.g., spelling words such as "mom," "dad," "cat," and "dog"*); • spell basic words ending in a silent "e" (*e.g., spelling words such as "hope," "rope," "rove," and "have"*); and • spell basic words with a double "e" and double "o" (*e.g., spelling words such as "beet," "heel," "book," and "soot"*). **The student exhibits no major errors or omissions.**
Score 2.0	**The student exhibits no major errors or omissions regarding the simpler details and processes, such as . . .** • recognizing and recalling specific terminology (*e.g., sight word, alphabet, letter*); and • performing basic processes, such as . . . ◦ recognizing correctly spelled basic two-letter words; ◦ recognizing correctly spelled basic three-letter, consonant-vowel-consonant words; ◦ recognizing correctly spelled basic words ending in a silent "e"; and ◦ recognizing correctly spelled basic words with a double "e" and double "o." **However, the student exhibits major errors or omissions with score 3.0 elements.**

Language Mechanics

	Grade 8	
Score 4.0	**In addition to score 3.0 performance, the student demonstrates in-depth inferences and applications that go beyond what was taught.**	
	Score 3.5	In addition to score 3.0 performance, the student demonstrates in-depth inferences and applications with partial success.
Score 3.0	**While engaged in grade-appropriate tasks, the student demonstrates an understanding of standard English mechanics by . . .** • correctly using italics and underlining (*e.g., putting the titles of books in italics*). **The student exhibits no major errors or omissions.**	
	Score 2.5	The student exhibits no major errors or omissions regarding the score 2.0 elements and partial knowledge of the score 3.0 elements.
Score 2.0	**The student exhibits no major errors or omissions regarding the simpler details and processes, such as . . .** • recognizing and recalling specific terminology (*e.g., underline, italics*); and • performing basic processes, such as . . . ◦ recognizing correct use of italics and underlining. **However, the student exhibits major errors or omissions with score 3.0 elements.**	
	Score 1.5	The student demonstrates partial knowledge of the score 2.0 elements but major errors or omissions regarding the score 3.0 elements.
Score 1.0	**With help, the student demonstrates partial understanding of some of the score 2.0 elements and some of the score 3.0 elements.**	
	Score 0.5	With help, the student demonstrates partial understanding of some of the score 2.0 elements but not the score 3.0 elements.
Score 0.0	**Even with help, the student demonstrates no understanding or skill.**	
	Grade 7	
Score 3.0	**While engaged in grade-appropriate tasks, the student demonstrates an understanding of standard English mechanics by . . .** • appropriately using hyphens, dashes, and brackets (*e.g., using hyphens to break a word into syllables or to avoid confusion, as in "re-sign" versus "resign"*). **The student exhibits no major errors or omissions.**	
Score 2.0	**The student exhibits no major errors or omissions regarding the simpler details and processes, such as . . .** • recognizing and recalling specific terminology (*e.g., hyphens, brackets*); and • performing basic processes, such as . . . ◦ recognizing correct use of hyphens, dashes, and brackets. **However, the student exhibits major errors or omissions with score 3.0 elements.**	
	Grade 6	
Score 3.0	**While engaged in grade-appropriate tasks, the student demonstrates an understanding of standard English mechanics by . . .** • correctly using the semicolon and colon (*e.g., connecting two complete sentences with a semicolon and preceding a list with a colon*). **The student exhibits no major errors or omissions.**	

Score 2.0	The student exhibits no major errors or omissions regarding the simpler details and processes, such as . . . • recognizing and recalling specific terminology (*e.g., semicolon, colon*); and • performing basic processes, such as . . . 　○ recognizing correct use of the semicolon and the colon. **However, the student exhibits major errors or omissions with score 3.0 elements.**

Grade 5	
Score 3.0	While engaged in grade-appropriate tasks, the student demonstrates an understanding of standard English mechanics by . . . • correctly using apostrophes in cases of plural possessives (*e.g., using "teacher's" to describe an object belonging to one teacher and "teachers'" to describe something belonging to a group of teachers*); • correctly using parentheses in less common situations (*e.g., using parentheses to provide an opinion about information contained in a sentence*); and • correctly using commas as interrupters (*e.g., using commas to set off phrases that express contrast in a sentence*). **The student exhibits no major errors or omissions.**
Score 2.0	The student exhibits no major errors or omissions regarding the simpler details and processes, such as . . . • recognizing and recalling specific terminology (*e.g., plural possessive, interrupter*); and • performing basic processes, such as . . . 　○ recognizing correct use of apostrophes in cases of plural possessives; 　○ recognizing correct use of parentheses in less common situations; and 　○ recognizing correct use of commas as interrupters. **However, the student exhibits major errors or omissions with score 3.0 elements.**

Grade 4	
Score 3.0	While engaged in grade-appropriate tasks, the student demonstrates an understanding of standard English mechanics by . . . • correctly using direct quotations (*e.g., using quotation marks to indicate when someone is speaking: Charlie said, "I like you."*); • correctly using commas in direct quotations and with conjunctions (*e.g., using commas correctly in the following sentence: "Leave me alone," he said.*); • correctly using apostrophes in cases of possessives and contractions (*e.g., using apostrophes correctly in the following sentence: "Jenny's cat hasn't come home today."*); and • correctly using parentheses in common situations (*e.g., using parentheses to encapsulate supplementary information in a sentence*). **The student exhibits no major errors or omissions.**
Score 2.0	The student exhibits no major errors or omissions regarding the simpler details and processes, such as . . . • recognizing and recalling specific terminology (*e.g., possessive, contraction, parentheses*); and • performing basic processes, such as . . . 　○ recognizing when someone is directly speaking in a text; 　○ recognizing correct use of commas in a direct quotation; 　○ recognizing correct use of apostrophes in cases of possessives and contractions; and 　○ recognizing correct use of parentheses in common situations. **However, the student exhibits major errors or omissions with score 3.0 elements.**

Grade 3	
Score 3.0	While engaged in grade-appropriate tasks, the student demonstrates an understanding of standard English mechanics by . . .

Score 3.0 (continued)	• using commas with cities, states, dates, and addresses (*e.g., correctly inserting commas when writing a full address*); • correctly using capitalization for holidays and historical periods (*e.g., capitalizing specific holidays such as Christmas but not capitalizing general references such as "the holidays"*); and • correctly using abbreviations (*e.g., correctly abbreviating "et cetera" as "etc."*). **The student exhibits no major errors or omissions.**

Score 2.0	**The student exhibits no major errors or omissions regarding the simpler details and processes, such as . . .**
	• recognizing and recalling specific terminology (*e.g., city, state, and date*); and
	• performing basic processes, such as . . .
	  ○ recognizing correctly punctuated cities, states, dates, and addresses;
	  ○ recognizing correct capitalization involving holidays and historical periods; and
	  ○ recognizing correct common abbreviations.
	However, the student exhibits major errors or omissions with score 3.0 elements.

Grade 2

Score 3.0	**While engaged in grade-appropriate tasks, the student demonstrates an understanding of standard English mechanics by . . .** • correctly using commas in a series (*e.g., correctly inserting commas in the following sentence: "On my trip I'm going to bring a book, a camera, a cell phone, and my glasses."*); • correctly using capitalization in cases of proper nouns, months, days of the week, titles, and initials (*e.g., capitalizing titles of organizations and their initials: General Motors Corporation—GMC, Major League Baseball—MLB, National Football League—NFL, etc.*); and • correctly using common abbreviations (*e.g., using CO as an abbreviation for Colorado*). **The student exhibits no major errors or omissions.**

Score 2.0	**The student exhibits no major errors or omissions regarding the simpler details and processes, such as . . .**
	• recognizing and recalling specific terminology (*e.g., commas, series, proper noun*); and
	• performing basic processes, such as . . .
	  ○ recognizing correct use of commas in a series;
	  ○ recognizing correct use of capitalization; and
	  ○ recognizing correct common abbreviations.
	However, the student exhibits major errors or omissions with score 3.0 elements.

Grade 1

Score 3.0	**While engaged in grade-appropriate tasks, the student demonstrates an understanding of standard English mechanics by . . .** • concluding sentences using proper punctuation (*e.g., ending questions with question marks*); and • using basic capitalization, including first word in a sentence, proper names, and the pronoun I (*e.g., capitalizing names of people, such as Jane, Jim*). **The student exhibits no major errors or omissions.**

Score 2.0	**The student exhibits no major errors or omissions regarding the simpler details and processes, such as . . .**
	• recognizing and recalling specific terminology (*e.g., sentence, punctuation, period*); and
	• performing basic processes, such as . . .
	  ○ recognizing correct sentence-ending punctuation; and
	  ○ recognizing correct basic capitalization.
	However, the student exhibits major errors or omissions with score 3.0 elements.

Grade K	
Score 3.0	**While engaged in grade-appropriate tasks, the student demonstrates an understanding of standard English mechanics by . . .** • using correct letter formation to write uppercase letters (*e.g., demonstrating proper letter formation by tracing given uppercase letters and mimicking the form in the space provided*); • using correct letter formation to write lowercase letters (*e.g., demonstrating proper letter formation by tracing given lowercase letters and mimicking the form in the space provided*); and • spacing words appropriately (*e.g., demonstrating proper spacing of words by mimicking the spacing of a given sentence in the space provided*). **The student exhibits no major errors or omissions.**

Score 2.0	**The student exhibits no major errors or omissions regarding the simpler details and processes, such as . . .**
	• recognizing and recalling specific terminology (*e.g., uppercase letter, lowercase letter, word*); and
	• performing basic processes, such as . . .
	  ○ recognizing correctly formed uppercase letters;
	  ○ recognizing correctly formed lowercase letters; and
	  ○ recognizing correctly spaced grade-appropriate words.
	However, the student exhibits major errors or omissions with score 3.0 elements.

Language Conventions

Grade 8		
Score 4.0	**In addition to score 3.0 performance, the student demonstrates in-depth inferences and applications that go beyond what was taught.**	
	Score 3.5	In addition to score 3.0 performance, the student demonstrates in-depth inferences and applications with partial success.
Score 3.0	**While engaged in grade-appropriate tasks, the student demonstrates an understanding of standard English conventions by . . .** • exemplifying effective use of voice (*e.g., explaining and exemplifying when it is appropriate to shift from active to passive voice*); • demonstrating fluid use of all tense forms (*e.g., explaining and exemplifying when it is appropriate to change tense*); and • varying sentence forms in writing (*e.g., explaining and exemplifying when it is appropriate to change sentence forms*). **The student exhibits no major errors or omissions.**	
	Score 2.5	The student exhibits no major errors or omissions regarding the score 2.0 elements and partial knowledge of the score 3.0 elements.

Score 2.0	**The student exhibits no major errors or omissions regarding the simpler details and processes, such as . . .**
	• recognizing and recalling specific terminology (*e.g., active voice, passive voice*); and
	• performing basic processes, such as . . .
	  ○ recognizing effective and ineffective uses of voice in text;
	  ○ recognizing consistent and inconsistent use of tense in text; and
	  ○ recognizing use of varied sentences in text.
	However, the student exhibits major errors or omissions with score 3.0 elements.	

	Score 1.5	The student demonstrates partial knowledge of the score 2.0 elements but major errors or omissions regarding the score 3.0 elements.
Score 1.0	**With help, the student demonstrates partial understanding of some of the score 2.0 elements and some of the score 3.0 elements.**	
	Score 0.5	With help, the student demonstrates partial understanding of some of the score 2.0 elements but not the score 3.0 elements.
Score 0.0	**Even with help, the student demonstrates no understanding or skill.**	
Grade 7		
Score 3.0	**While engaged in grade-appropriate tasks, the student demonstrates an understanding of standard English conventions by . . .** • correcting run-on sentences, fragments, and comma splices (*e.g., correcting sentences with commas used to separate two independent clauses without a conjunction*); • correctly changing tense when necessary (*e.g., explaining and exemplifying that it is appropriate to change from present tense to past tense when writing a flashback in a story*); • correctly using commonly confused words (*e.g., correctly using beside/besides, between/among, can/may, fewer/less, formerly/formally, if/whether, leave/let, lose/loose*); and • using compound-complex sentences (*e.g., constructing sentences with two or more main clauses and two or more subordinate clauses*). **The student exhibits no major errors or omissions.**	

Score 2.0	**The student exhibits no major errors or omissions regarding the simpler details and processes, such as . . .**
	• recognizing and recalling specific terminology (*e.g., comma splice, flashback*); and
	• performing basic processes, such as . . .
	  ◦ recognizing run-on sentences, fragments, and comma splices in text;
	  ◦ recognizing correct and incorrect shift in tense in text;
	  ◦ recognizing misuse of commonly confused words in text; and
	  ◦ recognizing correct use of compound-complex sentences in text.
	However, the student exhibits major errors or omissions with score 3.0 elements.

Grade 6

Score 3.0	**While engaged in grade-appropriate tasks, the student demonstrates an understanding of standard English conventions by . . .** • correcting run-ons and fragments (*e.g., correcting a sentence fragment such as "going inside soon" to read "I will be going inside soon"*); • using one tense consistently throughout a piece (*e.g., explaining and exemplifying when it is appropriate to stay in one tense*); • correctly using commonly misused words (*e.g., correctly using its/it's, there/their/they're, your/you're, to/too/two, can/may, bring/take, rise/raise, learn/teach, stationary/stationery, who's/whose*); and • using common compound-complex sentences (*e.g., constructing sentences with two main clauses and one subordinate clause*). **The student exhibits no major errors or omissions.**

Score 2.0	**The student exhibits no major errors or omissions regarding the simpler details and processes, such as . . .**
	• recognizing and recalling specific terminology (*e.g., run-on sentence, sentence fragment, compound-complex sentence*); and
	• performing basic processes, such as . . .
	  ◦ recognizing run-ons and fragments in text;
	  ◦ recognizing inconsistent use of tense in text;
	  ◦ recognizing misuse of commonly confused words in text; and
	  ◦ recognizing correct use of common compound-complex sentences in text.
	However, the student exhibits major errors or omissions with score 3.0 elements.

Grade 5

Score 3.0	**While engaged in grade-appropriate tasks, the student demonstrates an understanding of standard English conventions by . . .** • applying all major tense forms (*e.g., constructing sentences exemplifying the major tense forms*); • appropriately using commonly misused verbs (*e.g., using "laid" when writing about setting a book down and using "lie" to describe a person's repose*); • correcting dangling modifiers (*e.g., identifying and correcting dangling modifiers in text*); and • using complex sentences (*e.g., writing sentences with one main clause and more than one subordinate clause*). **The student exhibits no major errors or omissions.**

Score 2.0	**The student exhibits no major errors or omissions regarding the simpler details and processes, such as . . .**
	• recognizing and recalling specific terminology (*e.g., dangling modifier, tense forms*); and
	• performing basic processes, such as . . .
	  ◦ recognizing correct use of all tense forms;
	  ◦ recognizing a misused verb;
	  ◦ recognizing a dangling modifier in text; and

Score 2.0 (continued)	◦ recognizing correct use of complex sentences. **However, the student exhibits major errors or omissions with score 3.0 elements.**

Grade 4	
Score 3.0	**While engaged in grade-appropriate tasks, the student demonstrates an understanding of standard English conventions by . . .** • using progressive forms of past, present, and future tenses (*e.g., constructing text in each tense*); • identifying subject-verb agreement with intervening phrases (*e.g., identifying subject-verb agreement in sentences designed to have intervening phrases*); • correcting double negatives (*e.g., correcting sentences specifically designed with double negatives*); and • using common forms of complex sentences (*e.g., writing sentences with one main clause and one subordinate clause*). **The student exhibits no major errors or omissions.**

Score 2.0	**The student exhibits no major errors or omissions regarding the simpler details and processes, such as . . .**
	• recognizing and recalling specific terminology (*e.g., phrase, clause, double negative, complex sentence*); and
	• performing basic processes, such as . . .
	  ◦ recognizing correct use of progressive forms of past, present, and future tenses;
	  ◦ recognizing sentences that have intervening phrases between the subject and verb;
	  ◦ recognizing double negatives in text; and
	  ◦ recognizing complex sentences in text.
	However, the student exhibits major errors or omissions with score 3.0 elements.

Grade 3	
Score 3.0	**While engaged in grade-appropriate tasks, the student demonstrates an understanding of standard English conventions by . . .** • using less common and specific types of adjectives (*e.g., constructing sentences with indefinite and numerical adjectives*); • using less common and specific types of adverbs (*e.g., constructing sentences with positive, comparative, and superlative adverbs*); • using prepositional phrases and other word groups (*e.g., constructing sentences with phrases such as "down the stairs" or "due to the fire"*); • using subordinating conjunctions and other word groups (*e.g., creating subordinating clauses such as "until he gets well" or "now that the mail had arrived"*); • identifying subject-verb agreement when there are no intervening phrases or clauses (*e.g., identifying subject-verb agreement or lack of agreement in sentences with subject and verb next to each other*); • using perfect forms of past, present, and future tenses (*e.g., constructing sentences that use past perfect, present perfect, and future perfect tenses*); and • using compound sentences (*e.g., constructing compound sentences*). **The student exhibits no major errors or omissions.**

Score 2.0	**The student exhibits no major errors or omissions regarding the simpler details and processes, such as . . .**
	• recognizing and recalling specific terminology (*e.g., subject-verb agreement, compound sentence, tense*); and
	• performing basic processes, such as . . .
	  ◦ recognizing correct use of less common and specific types of adjectives in text;
	  ◦ recognizing correct use of less common and specific types of adverbs in text;
	  ◦ recognizing correct use of prepositional phrases in text;

Score 2.0 (*continued*)	◦ recognizing correct use of subordinating conjunctions in text; ◦ recognizing subjects and verbs in sentences; ◦ recognizing perfect forms of past, present, and future tenses in text; and ◦ recognizing compound sentences in text. **However, the student exhibits major errors or omissions with score 3.0 elements.**
Grade 2	
Score 3.0	**While engaged in grade-appropriate tasks, the student demonstrates an understanding of standard English conventions by . . .** • using helping verbs (*e.g., constructing sentences that use "can," "have to," "should," and "will" in conjunction with a main verb*); • using common adverbs correctly to modify verbs (*e.g., constructing sentences that modify the verb "walk" with the adverb "quickly"*); • using common adjectives correctly to modify nouns (*e.g., constructing sentences that modify the noun "car" with the adjective "new"*); • using common prepositions correctly (*e.g., constructing sentences that use "under" to describe the relationship between the noun "dog" and the noun "table"*); • using simple forms of past, present, and future tense (*e.g., constructing sentences demonstrating past, present, and future tense*); and • using less common pronouns (*e.g., constructing sentences that use indefinite, relative, interrogative, demonstrative, intensive, and reflexive pronouns*). **The student exhibits no major errors or omissions.**

Score 2.0	**The student exhibits no major errors or omissions regarding the simpler details and processes, such as . . .**
	 • recognizing and recalling specific terminology (*e.g., helping verb, adjective, adverb, preposition*); and
	 • performing basic processes, such as . . .
	   ◦ recognizing helping verbs in context;
	   ◦ recognizing adverbs in text;
	   ◦ recognizing adjectives in text;
	   ◦ recognizing prepositions in text;
	   ◦ recognizing simple forms of past, present, and future tense; and
	   ◦ recognizing less common pronouns in text.
	 However, the student exhibits major errors or omissions with score 3.0 elements.

Grade 1	
Score 3.0	**While engaged in grade-appropriate tasks, the student demonstrates an understanding of standard English conventions by . . .** • using regular and irregular verbs (*e.g., constructing sentences that use regular and irregular verbs*); • using basic pronouns (*e.g., using "I," "you," "he," and "they" in sentences*); • using basic (coordinating and correlative) conjunctions (*e.g., using "and" and "but" in sentences*); • writing in past, present, and future tense (*e.g., constructing sentences in past, present, and future tenses*); and • naming and identifying the basic parts of a simple sentence (*e.g., identifying the subject and predicate*). **The student exhibits no major errors or omissions.**
Score 2.0	**The student exhibits no major errors or omissions regarding the simpler details and processes, such as . . .** • recognizing and recalling specific terminology (*e.g., complete sentence, subject, predicate*); and

Score 2.0 (*continued*)	• performing basic processes, such as . . .
	  ◦ recognizing regular and irregular verbs in text;
	  ◦ recognizing which noun a pronoun refers to in a text;
	  ◦ recognizing basic conjunctions;
	  ◦ recognizing past, present, and future tenses; and
	  ◦ naming basic parts of a sentence when identified by the teacher.
	However, the student exhibits major errors or omissions with score 3.0 elements.

Grade K	
Score 3.0	**While engaged in grade-appropriate tasks, the student demonstrates an understanding of standard English conventions by . . .** • using verbs as action words (*e.g., using "walking," "walks," "running," "runs," "skipping," and "skips" as action words describing different ways people can be mobile*); and • using nouns for simple objects, family members, and community workers (*e.g., using nouns to accurately describe the objects found on the playground*). **The student exhibits no major errors or omissions.**

Score 2.0	**The student exhibits no major errors or omissions regarding the simpler details and processes, such as . . .**
	• recognizing and recalling specific terminology (*e.g., verbs, nouns*); and
	• performing basic processes, such as . . .
	  ◦ recognizing basic action verbs when identified by the teacher; and
	  ◦ recognizing basic nouns when identified by the teacher.
	However, the student exhibits major errors or omissions with score 3.0 elements.

Reading

Reading for the Main Idea

Grade 8		
Score 4.0	**In addition to score 3.0 performance, the student demonstrates in-depth inferences and applications that go beyond what was taught.**	
	Score 3.5	In addition to score 3.0 performance, the student demonstrates in-depth inferences and applications with partial success.
Score 3.0	**While engaged in grade-appropriate reading tasks, the student demonstrates an ability to . . .** • identify complex causal relationships (*e.g., observing that the plight of Anne Frank in* The Diary of Anne Frank *is the result of causes ranging from the policies of the Nazis in Amsterdam to the childhood of Adolph Hitler*); • identify and react to textual arguments (*e.g., summarizing the argument presented and explaining why he was persuaded or not*); • identify problems that cannot or will not be solved in the text (*e.g., observing that a story about the fate of Native Americans will not include a solution to the problem of the U.S. government taking their lands*); and • identify complex plots with multiple story lines (*e.g., observing that understanding a story following people in different social classes during a specific time involves understanding not only the stories of those specific people but how their stories interact*). **The student exhibits no major errors or omissions.**	
	Score 2.5	The student exhibits no major errors or omissions regarding the score 2.0 elements and partial knowledge of the score 3.0 elements.

Score 2.0	**The student exhibits no major errors or omissions regarding the simpler details and processes, such as . . .**
	• recognizing and recalling specific terminology (*e.g., counterargument, explicit, implicit*); and
	• performing basic processes, such as . . .
	   ○ recognizing that certain genres of literature often contain complex causal relationships;
	   ○ recognizing claims with support and qualifiers;
	   ○ recognizing textual clues that indicate a problem that cannot or will not be solved in a text; and
	   ○ recognizing textual clues across multiple story lines that indicate a complex plot.
	However, the student exhibits major errors or omissions with score 3.0 elements.	

	Score 1.5	The student demonstrates partial knowledge of the score 2.0 elements but major errors or omissions regarding the score 3.0 elements.
Score 1.0	**With help, the student demonstrates partial understanding of some of the score 2.0 elements and some of the score 3.0 elements.**	
	Score 0.5	With help, the student demonstrates partial understanding of some of the score 2.0 elements but not the score 3.0 elements.

Score 0.0	**Even with help, the student demonstrates no understanding or skill.**

Grade 7	
Score 3.0	**While engaged in grade-appropriate reading tasks, the student demonstrates an ability to . . .** • identify complex causal relationships (*e.g., when reading about the Japanese internment camps in the United States during World War II, identifying the Japanese attack on Pearl Harbor and the subsequent propaganda against Japanese Americans as causal factors*); • identify and react to basic textual arguments (*e.g., observing specific reasons why she was or was not persuaded by the argument*); • identify problems with complex solutions (*e.g., observing while reading about the civil rights movement that achieving racial equality has been a long and difficult process*); and • identify plots with multiple story lines (*e.g., observing that although* The Sisterhood of the Traveling Pants *follows the stories of four very different girls, in each story the traveling pants help them resolve a difficult issue*). **The student exhibits no major errors or omissions.**

Score 2.0	**The student exhibits no major errors or omissions regarding the simpler details and processes, such as . . .**
	• recognizing and recalling specific terminology (*e.g., character efficacy, argument*); and
	• performing basic processes, such as . . .
	  ◦ recognizing textual clues that indicate complex causal relationships;
	  ◦ recognizing the basic textual indicators of an argument being made;
	  ◦ recognizing textual clues that indicate a problem with a complex solution; and
	  ◦ recognizing textual clues within each of the multiple story lines in a text that indicate the nature of the plot.
	However, the student exhibits major errors or omissions with score 3.0 elements.

Grade 6	
Score 3.0	**While engaged in grade-appropriate reading tasks, the student demonstrates an ability to . . .** • identify complex causal relationships (*e.g., observing all the ways Old Dan and Little Ann in* Where the Red Fern Grows *affect Billy's family*); • identify complex chronologies (*e.g., recounting the events in a book such as* The Lion, the Witch, and the Wardrobe); • identify problems that only an outside source or person can solve (*e.g., observing that Helen Keller's problem of communication could not have been solved without her teacher*); and • identify plots with two parallel story lines (*e.g., observing that* Seabiscuit *follows the life of both a man and a horse and that these story lines both represent the growth, courage, and change central to the story's plot*). **The student exhibits no major errors or omissions.**

Score 2.0	**The student exhibits no major errors or omissions regarding the simpler details and processes, such as . . .**
	• recognizing and recalling specific terminology (*e.g., parallel story lines, complex versus simple relationships, complex versus simple chronology*); and
	• performing basic processes, such as . . .
	  ◦ recognizing textual clues that indicate complex causal relationships;
	  ◦ recognizing textual clues that indicate complex chronologies;
	  ◦ recognizing vulnerable or helpless characters in a text; and
	  ◦ recognizing that more than one story is occurring in a text.
	However, the student exhibits major errors or omissions with score 3.0 elements.

Grade 5	
Score 3.0	**While engaged in grade-appropriate reading tasks, the student demonstrates an ability to . . .** • identify complex causal relationships (*e.g., observing that many events in* Harry Potter and the Sorcerer's Stone *seem strange until the book reveals their causes*); • identify complex chronologies (*e.g., observing that many of the events affecting Harry in* Harry Potter and the Sorcerer's Stone *happened before the story takes place*); • identify problems that only a character can solve (*e.g., observing that Malfoy will always bully Harry in* Harry Potter and the Sorcerer's Stone *unless Harry stands up to him*); and • identify plots with single story lines (*e.g., observing that a biography or an autobiography follows the story of one person's life and explains the important details of that person's life*). **The student exhibits no major errors or omissions.**

Score 2.0	**The student exhibits no major errors or omissions regarding the simpler details and processes, such as . . .**
	• recognizing and recalling specific terminology (*e.g., causal relationship, internal struggle, external struggle*); and
	• performing basic processes, such as . . .
	   ◦ recognizing words or groups of words that indicate complex cause and effect;
	   ◦ recognizing textual clues that indicate complex chronologies;
	   ◦ recognizing words, phrases, or textual clues that indicate a problem that only a character can solve; and
	   ◦ recognizing the parts of a text that convey information about the story line.
	However, the student exhibits major errors or omissions with score 3.0 elements.

Grade 4	
Score 3.0	**While engaged in grade-appropriate reading tasks, the student demonstrates an ability to . . .** • identify basic cause and effect (*e.g., observing that Charlie in* Charlie and the Chocolate Factory *wins the contest because he behaves well while the other children behave badly*); • identify simple chronologies (*e.g., recalling the order and cause of each child's exit from the story in* Charlie and the Chocolate Factory); • identify problems with simple solutions (*e.g., observing that the problem of poverty within Charlie's family in* Charlie and the Chocolate Factory *is solved only by having more money*); and • identify plots with single story lines (*e.g., observing that the plot of* Charlie and the Chocolate Factory *involves Charlie's ability to save both his poor family and a lonely man, and the story line follows the boy's strange journey through the factory*). **The student exhibits no major errors or omissions.**

Score 2.0	**The student exhibits no major errors or omissions regarding the simpler details and processes, such as . . .**
	• recognizing and recalling specific terminology (*e.g., chronology, cue words/signal words*); and
	• performing basic processes, such as . . .
	   ◦ recognizing words or groups of words that indicate cause and effect;
	   ◦ recognizing words or groups of words that indicate an order of events;
	   ◦ recognizing words or groups of words that indicate when someone might be having a problem and when someone might have reached a solution; and
	   ◦ recognizing words or groups of words that indicate information about the story line.
	However, the student exhibits major errors or omissions with score 3.0 elements.

Grade 3	
Score 3.0	**While engaged in grade-appropriate reading tasks, the student demonstrates an ability to . . .** • identify basic cause and effect (*e.g., observing that in* Because of Winn-Dixie, *the entrance of a dog into a young girl's life causes many changes that help the girl grow*); • identify simple chronologies (*e.g., recalling the correct order of the people Opal meets in* Because of Winn-Dixie); • identify problems with basic solutions (*e.g., observing that Gloria Dump's problem of blindness is solved by seeing with her heart in* Because of Winn-Dixie); and • identify plots with single story lines (*e.g., observing that the story line of* Because of Winn-Dixie *follows the adventures of a young girl and her dog and that the plot involves her growth throughout the story and her coming to peace with her mother's absence*). **The student exhibits no major errors or omissions.**

Score 2.0	**The student exhibits no major errors or omissions regarding the simpler details and processes, such as . . .**
	• recognizing and recalling specific terminology (*e.g., order of events, problem, solution, plot*); and
	• recognizing and recalling isolated details and performing basic processes, such as . . .
	  ◦ recognizing words or groups of words that indicate cause and effect;
	  ◦ recognizing words or groups of words that indicate an order of events;
	  ◦ recognizing words or groups of words that indicate when someone might be having a problem; and
	  ◦ recognizing that a story line is occurring in a text.
	However, the student exhibits major errors or omissions with score 3.0 elements.

Grade 2	
Score 3.0	**While engaged in grade-appropriate reading tasks, the student demonstrates an ability to . . .** • identify basic cause and effect (*e.g., observing that Amelia Bedelia does not produce the right effects at her job as a maid*); and • identify simple story lines (*e.g., observing that* Mike Mulligan and His Steam Shovel *follows a man trying to find out what he is supposed to do*). **The student exhibits no major errors or omissions.**

Score 2.0	**The student exhibits no major errors or omissions regarding the simpler details and processes, such as . . .**
	• recognizing and recalling specific terminology (*e.g., cause, effect, story line*); and
	• performing basic processes, such as . . .
	  ◦ recognizing words or groups of words that indicate cause and effect; and
	  ◦ recognizing the parts of a text that will most likely provide information about the beginning, the middle, and the end of a story.
	However, the student exhibits major errors or omissions with score 3.0 elements.

Grade 1	
Score 3.0	**While engaged in grade-appropriate reading tasks, the student demonstrates an ability to . . .** • identify simple story lines (*e.g., observing that the story line of* Are You My Mother? *follows a baby bird who is searching for his mother*). **The student exhibits no major errors or omissions.**

Score 2.0	**The student exhibits no major errors or omissions regarding the simpler details and processes, such as . . .** • recognizing and recalling specific terminology (*e.g., story, information*); and • performing basic processes, such as . . . 　○ recognizing certain parts of a story that provide different information about the story. **However, the student exhibits major errors or omissions with score 3.0 elements.**
Grade K	
Score 3.0	Not applicable.
Score 2.0	Not applicable.

Word Recognition and Vocabulary

Grade 8		
Score 4.0	**In addition to score 3.0 performance, the student demonstrates in-depth inferences and applications that go beyond what was taught.**	
	Score 3.5	In addition to score 3.0 performance, the student demonstrates in-depth inferences and applications with partial success.
Score 3.0	**While reading grade-appropriate materials, the student enriches her word recognition and vocabulary by . . .** • analyzing a variety of idioms and comparisons to infer the literal and figurative meanings of phrases (*e.g., understanding that the idiom "kicking the bucket" literally means just what the action implies but that the essence of the phrase's meaning is death*); • explaining the influence of current events on the meaning of English words and vocabulary expansion (*e.g., understanding that the term "going postal" is a relatively new phrase invented in light of recent events*); and • verifying the meaning of a word in its context through the use of definition or example (*e.g., understanding what "malevolence" means by providing examples of people the word is used to describe in the text*). **The student exhibits no major errors or omissions.**	
	Score 2.5	The student exhibits no major errors or omissions regarding the score 2.0 elements and partial knowledge of the score 3.0 elements.

Score 2.0	**The student exhibits no major errors or omissions regarding the simpler details and processes, such as . . .**
	• recognizing and recalling specific terminology (*e.g., idiom, alternative meaning*);
	• performing basic processes, such as . . .
	  ○ identifying complex similes and metaphors;
	  ○ describing basic changes that have occurred in the English language; and
	  ○ using general context to decipher meanings of unknown words.
	However, the student exhibits major errors or omissions with score 3.0 elements.	

	Score 1.5	The student demonstrates partial knowledge of the score 2.0 elements but major errors or omissions regarding the score 3.0 elements.
Score 1.0	**With help, the student demonstrates partial understanding of some of the score 2.0 elements and some of the score 3.0 elements.**	
	Score 0.5	With help, the student demonstrates partial understanding of some of the score 2.0 elements but not the score 3.0 elements.
Score 0.0	**Even with help, the student demonstrates no understanding or skill.**	
Grade 7		
Score 3.0	**While reading grade-appropriate materials, the student enriches his word recognition and vocabulary by . . .** • analyzing metaphors and similes to infer the literal and figurative meanings of phrases (*e.g., while reading Robert Frost's poem "The Road Not Taken," recognizing both the literal dilemma of the narrator [which actual road to take] and the figurative dilemma [which direction to take in life]*); • explaining the influence of historical events on the meanings of words in English and vocabulary expansion (*e.g., understanding that historical events such as the invention of the car led to phrases in the English language such as "backseat driver"*); and	

Score 3.0 (continued)	• verifying the meaning of a word in its context through the use of restatement or comparison/contrast (*e.g., restating the word "notorious" as "infamous" or "famous in a bad way" after reading the word in reference to Billy the Kid*). **The student exhibits no major errors or omissions.**

Score 2.0	**The student exhibits no major errors or omissions regarding the simpler details and processes, such as . . .**
	• recognizing and recalling specific terminology (*e.g., literal meaning, figurative meaning, comparison, contrast*); and
	• performing basic processes, such as . . .
	  ○ identifying basic similes and metaphors;
	  ○ describing how the English language changes as time goes on; and
	  ○ using basic context to decipher the meanings of unknown words.
	However, the student exhibits major errors or omissions with score 3.0 elements.

Grade 6	
Score 3.0	**While reading grade-appropriate materials, the student enriches her word recognition and vocabulary by . . .** • interpreting figurative language (including similes, metaphors, and implied comparisons) and words with multiple meanings (*e.g., understanding the statement "she was a fortress" to be a metaphor illustrating the subject's emotional state*); • verifying the origins and meanings of foreign words and phrases that are often used in English and using them accurately in speaking and writing (*e.g., using and understanding the phrase "je ne sais quoi"*); and • explaining slight differences in meaning in related words (*e.g., understanding that "ecstatic" is a stronger form of the similar word "happy"*). **The student exhibits no major errors or omissions.**

Score 2.0	**The student exhibits no major errors or omissions regarding the simpler details and processes, such as . . .**
	• recognizing and recalling specific terminology (*e.g., poems, narrative text*); and
	• performing basic processes, such as . . .
	  ○ identifying figurative language;
	  ○ identifying frequently used foreign words or phrases; and
	  ○ describing why it is important to be aware of slight differences in meaning.
	However, the student exhibits major errors or omissions with score 3.0 elements.

Grade 5	
Score 3.0	**While reading grade-appropriate materials, the student enriches his word recognition and vocabulary by . . .** • using basic context clues to determine the meanings of unknown words (*e.g., determining that if a sentence is about a woman who rules over many people, the word "matriarch" might have a similar meaning*); • using less common roots and word parts to analyze the meanings of complex words (*e.g., recognizing the meaning of the root "mono" and using this knowledge to decipher words such as "monotony" and "monogamous"*); and • explaining the figurative use of words in similes and metaphors (*e.g., explaining the meaning of a simile such as "his heart was as big as a house" by saying the comparison shows the reader how large the subject's heart is and therefore how loving and generous he must be*). **The student exhibits no major errors or omissions.**
Score 2.0	**The student exhibits no major errors or omissions regarding the simpler details and processes, such as . . .** • recognizing and recalling specific terminology (*e.g., figurative language, similes, metaphors*); and

Score 2.0 (continued)	• performing basic processes, such as . . .
	   ◦ identifying the general topic of the context surrounding an unknown word;
	   ◦ identifying less common word roots; and
	   ◦ describing the general characteristics of similes and metaphors.
	However, the student exhibits major errors or omissions with score 3.0 elements.

	Grade 4
Score 3.0	**While reading grade-appropriate materials, the student enriches her word recognition and vocabulary by . . .** • reading and using idioms (*e.g., explaining what "apple of my eye" and "break a leg" mean*); and • using basic word roots to analyze the meaning of complex words (*e.g., using knowledge of the root "migr" to analyze the meaning of words such as "immigrant" and "migratory"*). **The student exhibits no major errors or omissions.**

Score 2.0	**The student exhibits no major errors or omissions regarding the simpler details and processes, such as . . .**
	• recognizing and recalling specific terminology (*e.g., idiom, word root*); and
	• performing basic processes, such as . . .
	   ◦ describing general characteristics of idioms; and
	   ◦ identifying basic word roots.
	However, the student exhibits major errors or omissions with score 3.0 elements.

	Grade 3
Score 3.0	**While reading grade-appropriate materials, the student enriches his word recognition and vocabulary by . . .** • reading and using more difficult word families and multisyllable words (*e.g., reading and using the "ology" and "cide" word families*); • reading and using basic homophones and homographs (*e.g., observing the meanings and spellings of "die" and "dye" as well as the different meanings of "arms"*); and • reading words using basic prefixes and suffixes (*e.g., reading prefixes such as "pre" and "in" as well as suffixes such as "ful" and "ship"*). **The student exhibits no major errors or omissions.**

Score 2.0	**The student exhibits no major errors or omissions regarding the simpler details and processes, such as . . .**
	• recognizing and recalling specific terminology (*e.g., word families, homophones, homographs*); and
	• performing basic processes, such as . . .
	   ◦ identifying more difficult word families and multisyllable words;
	   ◦ describing characteristics of basic homophones and homographs; and
	   ◦ identifying basic prefixes and suffixes.
	However, the student exhibits major errors or omissions with score 3.0 elements.

	Grade 2
Score 3.0	**While reading grade-appropriate materials, the student enriches her word recognition and vocabulary by . . .** • reading words using knowledge of basic spelling patterns (*e.g., recognizing that a word ending in an "e" is read with a long-vowel sound preceding it in words such as "make" and "hide"*); and • reading and using basic synonyms and antonyms (*e.g., recognizing that "large" is an antonym for "small" and that "tiny" is a synonym for "small"*). **The student exhibits no major errors or omissions.**

Score 2.0	The student exhibits no major errors or omissions regarding the simpler details and processes, such as . . .
	• recognizing and recalling specific terminology (*e.g., synonym, antonym*); and
	• performing basic processes, such as . . .
	  ◦ identifying basic spelling patterns; and
	  ◦ describing characteristics of basic synonyms and antonyms.
	However, the student exhibits major errors or omissions with score 3.0 elements.

Grade 1

Score 3.0	While reading grade-appropriate materials, the student enriches his word recognition and vocabulary by . . . • decoding unknown words by using knowledge of vowel digraphs and of how vowel sounds change when followed by the letter *r* (*e.g., correctly pronouncing "far" and "bare"*); and • reading and using simple compound words and contractions (*e.g., using "butterfly" and "can't"*). **The student exhibits no major errors or omissions.**

Score 2.0	The student exhibits no major errors or omissions regarding the simpler details and processes, such as . . .
	• recognizing and recalling specific terminology (*e.g., compound words, contractions*); and
	• performing basic processes, such as . . .
	  ◦ describing the general rules regarding *r*-controlled vowels; and
	  ◦ identifying that a word is a compound or a contraction.
	However, the student exhibits major errors or omissions with score 3.0 elements.

Grade K

Score 3.0	While reading grade-appropriate materials, the student enriches her word recognition and vocabulary by . . . • using basic elements of phonetic analysis to decode unknown words (*e.g., using common letter-sound relationships, beginning and ending consonants, vowel sounds, blends, word patterns*). **The student exhibits no major errors or omissions.**
Score 2.0	The student exhibits no major errors or omissions regarding the simpler details and processes, such as . . . • recognizing and recalling specific terminology (*e.g., vowel, consonant*); and • performing basic processes, such as . . . ◦ stopping at unrecognized words and attempting to decode them. **However, the student exhibits major errors or omissions with score 3.0 elements.**

Literary Analysis

Grade 8		
Score 4.0	**In addition to score 3.0 performance, the student demonstrates in-depth inferences and applications that go beyond what was taught.**	
	Score 3.5	In addition to score 3.0 performance, the student demonstrates in-depth inferences and applications with partial success.
Score 3.0	**While reading grade-appropriate texts, the student demonstrates an ability to analyze and respond to literature by performing tasks such as . . .** • analyzing the importance of the setting to the mood and tone of the text (*e.g., explaining how the harsh climate in a specific story adds to the impression that certain characters are harsh and unyielding*); • comparing and contrasting recurring themes that appear frequently across traditional and contemporary works (*e.g., identifying recurring themes such as coming of age, love and loss, war and politics, and friendship/family*); and • analyzing significant literary devices that define a writer's style to interpret the work (*e.g., observing that a writer may use particular literary devices across different works and that understanding this device is a key to interpretation*). **The student exhibits no major errors or omissions.**	
	Score 2.5	The student exhibits no major errors or omissions regarding the score 2.0 elements and partial knowledge of the score 3.0 elements.

Score 2.0	**The student exhibits no major errors or omissions regarding the simpler details and processes, such as . . .**
	• recognizing and recalling specific terminology (*e.g., significant literary device, traditional, contemporary*); and
	• performing basic processes, such as . . .
	  ○ identifying parts of a text that might reflect setting, mood, or tone;
	  ○ identifying recurring themes that appear frequently across traditional and contemporary works; and
	  ○ identifying literary devices within an author's work.
	However, the student exhibits major errors or omissions with score 3.0 elements.	

	Score 1.5	The student demonstrates partial knowledge of the score 2.0 elements but major errors or omissions regarding the score 3.0 elements.
Score 1.0	**With help, the student demonstrates partial understanding of some of the score 2.0 elements and some of the score 3.0 elements.**	
	Score 0.5	With help, the student demonstrates partial understanding of some of the score 2.0 elements but not the score 3.0 elements.
Score 0.0	**Even with help, the student demonstrates no understanding or skill.**	
Grade 7		
Score 3.0	**While reading grade-appropriate texts, the student demonstrates an ability to analyze and respond to literature by performing tasks such as . . .** • identifying the importance of the setting to the mood and tone of the text (*e.g., observing that a story set in a harsh climate, where the characters are indoors, will be different in tone than a story set in a warm, tropical climate where the characters are outdoors*); and	

Score 3.0 (continued)	• analyzing a work of literature, showing how it reflects the heritage, traditions, attitudes, and beliefs of its author (*e.g., observing that a nonfiction story about surviving the Holocaust will likely give the reader insight into the author's heritage, traditions, attitudes, and beliefs*). **The student exhibits no major errors or omissions.**
Score 2.0	**The student exhibits no major errors or omissions regarding the simpler details and processes, such as . . .** • recognizing and recalling specific terminology (*e.g., mood, heritage, style*); and • performing basic processes, such as . . . ◦ identifying parts of the text that might reflect setting, mood, or tone; and ◦ identifying parts of the text that might reflect heritages, traditions, and attitudes. **However, the student exhibits major errors or omissions with score 3.0 elements.**

Grade 6

Score 3.0	**While reading grade-appropriate texts, the student demonstrates an ability to analyze and respond to literature by performing tasks such as . . .** • analyzing the effects of characters' traits on the plot and the resolution of the conflict (*e.g., understanding that a noble character will likely behave with nobility and that this will probably affect the resolution of the plot in a positive way*); • explaining how tone and meaning are conveyed in poetry through word choice, figurative language, sentence structure, line length, punctuation, rhythm, alliteration, or rhyme (*e.g., understanding how use of a word such as "devastating" instead of a word such as "disappointing" changes the tone and entire effect of a poem*); • determining the speaker and the point of view (*e.g., identifying first person, third person*); and • explaining the effects of common literary devices, such as symbolism, imagery, or metaphor (*e.g., observing that symbolism can serve to tell a reader about larger issues than the basic plot, such as the politics of the time, or smaller issues than the plot, such as the emotional state of a particular character*). **The student exhibits no major errors or omissions.**
Score 2.0	**The student exhibits no major errors or omissions regarding the simpler details and processes, such as . . .** • recognizing and recalling specific terminology (*e.g., tone, word choice, point of view*); and • recognizing and recalling isolated details and performing basic processes, such as . . . ◦ identifying characters' traits and the resolution of the plot; ◦ identifying the basic tone of a poem; ◦ identifying the point of view in a text; and ◦ identifying basic literary devices. **However, the student exhibits major errors or omissions with score 3.0 elements.**

Grade 5

Score 3.0	**While reading grade-appropriate texts, the student demonstrates an ability to analyze and respond to literature by performing tasks such as . . .** • identifying themes, whether they are implied or stated directly (*e.g., observing that an implied theme in "The Emperor's New Clothes" is the ability to resist peer pressure*); • describing the function and effect of common literary devices, such as imagery, metaphor, and symbolism (*e.g., observing that the purpose of imagery is to put a vivid image in a reader's head and interest the reader as a result*); and • evaluating the author's use of various techniques to influence readers' perspectives (*e.g., observing that a testimonial approach might be better in certain circumstances than a bandwagon approach*). **The student exhibits no major errors or omissions.**

Score 2.0	The student exhibits no major errors or omissions regarding the simpler details and processes, such as . . .
	• recognizing and recalling specific terminology (*e.g., theme, imagery, symbolism, influence*); and
	• performing basic processes, such as . . .
	   ◦ identifying parts of a text that might convey information about its themes;
	   ◦ identifying literary devices in a text; and
	   ◦ identifying portions of a text where the author is trying to persuade.
	However, the student exhibits major errors or omissions with score 3.0 elements.

Grade 4	
Score 3.0	While reading grade-appropriate texts, the student demonstrates an ability to analyze and respond to literature by performing tasks such as . . . • determining character traits and their effect on the characters' actions (*e.g., observing that a character who is noble will most likely perform noble actions*); • identifying and explaining figurative language (*e.g., defining a simile as a comparison using "like" or "as" and using these textual clues to identify and interpret similes in a text*); and • determining the speaker or narrator (*e.g., understanding that a narrator, as opposed to a character, is telling the story in "The Tortoise and the Hare"*). **The student exhibits no major errors or omissions.**

Score 2.0	The student exhibits no major errors or omissions regarding the simpler details and processes, such as . . .
	• recognizing and recalling specific terminology (*e.g., figurative language, simile, metaphor*); and
	• performing basic processes, such as . . .
	   ◦ identifying character traits and character actions;
	   ◦ identifying figurative language; and
	   ◦ identifying the speaker or narrator from a list of options.
	However, the student exhibits major errors or omissions with score 3.0 elements.

Grade 3	
Score 3.0	While reading grade-appropriate texts, the student demonstrates an ability to analyze and respond to literature by performing tasks such as . . . • determining and explaining basic character traits (*e.g., determining from the text that a character is kind, noble, and brave*); and • determining and explaining an author's basic message (*e.g., understanding that the author's message in "The Tortoise and the Hare" is that it is better to be slow and consistent than fast and inconsistent*). **The student exhibits no major errors or omissions.**

Score 2.0	The student exhibits no major errors or omissions regarding the simpler details and processes, such as . . .
	• recognizing and recalling specific terminology (*e.g., character traits, character actions, author's message*); and
	• performing basic processes, such as . . .
	   ◦ identifying a specific character's traits; and
	   ◦ identifying the author's message from a list of options.
	However, the student exhibits major errors or omissions with score 3.0 elements.

Grade 2	
Score 3.0	While reading grade-appropriate texts, the student demonstrates an ability to analyze and respond to literature by performing tasks such as . . . • identifying the use of basic rhythm, rhyme, and alliterations in basic text (*e.g., recognizing nursery rhymes and alliterations such as "Sally sold seashells by the seashore"*); and

Score 3.0 (continued)	• understanding the impact of different endings to a story (*e.g., observing that a sad ending makes a reader sad and a happy ending makes a reader happy*). **The student exhibits no major errors or omissions.**
Score 2.0	**The student exhibits no major errors or omissions regarding the simpler details and processes, such as . . .** • recognizing and recalling specific terminology (*e.g., rhythm, rhyme. alliteration*); and • performing basic processes, such as . . . 　○ recognizing that passages using rhythm, rhyme, and alliteration have a certain common "sound" when read aloud; and 　○ recognizing her own reaction to different endings. **However, the student exhibits major errors or omissions with score 3.0 elements.**

Grade 1	
Score 3.0	**While reading grade-appropriate texts, the student demonstrates an ability to analyze and respond to literature by performing tasks such as . . .** • understanding the roles of authors and illustrators (*e.g., observing that authors write the stories and illustrators draw the pictures*). **The student exhibits no major errors or omissions.**
Score 2.0	**The student exhibits no major errors or omissions regarding the simpler details and processes, such as . . .** • recognizing and recalling specific terminology (*e.g., author, illustrator*); and • performing basic processes, such as . . . 　○ identifying the author and illustrator from the text cover. **However, the student exhibits major errors or omissions with score 3.0 elements.**

Grade K	
Score 3.0	Not applicable.
Score 2.0	Not applicable.

Genre

	Grade 8	
Score 4.0	**In addition to score 3.0 performance, the student demonstrates in-depth inferences and applications that go beyond what was taught.**	
	Score 3.5	In addition to score 3.0 performance, the student demonstrates in-depth inferences and applications with partial success.
Score 3.0	**While engaged in grade-appropriate tasks, the student demonstrates an ability to identify and analyze literary genre by . . .** • evaluating the relationship between the purposes and characteristics of various forms of poetry (*e.g., observing that some poetry uses specific forms to convey a sense of order within humanity, whereas some poetry breaks form to convey the opposite message*). **The student exhibits no major errors or omissions.**	
	Score 2.5	The student exhibits no major errors or omissions regarding the score 2.0 elements and partial knowledge of the score 3.0 elements.
Score 2.0	**The student exhibits no major errors or omissions regarding the simpler details and processes, such as . . .** • recognizing and recalling specific terminology (*e.g., blank verse, free verse*); and • recognizing and recalling isolated details, such as . . . 　○ the purposes of various forms of poetry. **However, the student exhibits major errors or omissions with score 3.0 elements.**	
	Score 1.5	The student demonstrates partial knowledge of the score 2.0 elements but major errors or omissions regarding the score 3.0 elements.
Score 1.0	**With help, the student demonstrates partial understanding of some of the score 2.0 elements and some of the score 3.0 elements.**	
	Score 0.5	With help, the student demonstrates partial understanding of some of the score 2.0 elements but not the score 3.0 elements.
Score 0.0	**Even with help, the student demonstrates no understanding or skill.**	
	Grade 7	
Score 3.0	**While engaged in grade-appropriate tasks, the student demonstrates an ability to identify and analyze literary genre by . . .** • comparing and contrasting the purposes of different forms of poetry (*e.g., observing that an epic poem uses specific language techniques to tell a story, whereas a sonnet uses a specific poetic form to illustrate an emotion*). **The student exhibits no major errors or omissions.**	
Score 2.0	**The student exhibits no major errors or omissions regarding the simpler details and processes, such as . . .** • recognizing and recalling specific terminology (*e.g., epic poem, haiku*); and • recognizing and recalling isolated details, such as . . . 　○ characteristics of various forms of poetry. **However, the student exhibits major errors or omissions with score 3.0 elements.**	
	Grade 6	
Score 3.0	**While engaged in grade-appropriate tasks, the student demonstrates an ability to identify and analyze literary genre by . . .**	

Score 3.0 (*continued*)	• comparing and contrasting different types of nonfiction (*e.g., biography, autobiography, magazine article, historical essay*). **The student exhibits no major errors or omissions.**
Score 2.0	**The student exhibits no major errors or omissions regarding the simpler details and processes, such as . . .** • recognizing and recalling specific terminology (*e.g., biography, autobiography*); and • recognizing and recalling isolated details, such as . . . ○ the characteristics of various forms of nonfiction. **However, the student exhibits major errors or omissions with score 3.0 elements.**
Grade 5	
Score 3.0	**While engaged in grade-appropriate tasks, the student demonstrates an ability to identify and analyze literary genre by . . .** • comparing and contrasting different types of fiction (*e.g., understanding that some fiction takes the form of a novel, some takes the form of a short story, and some is meant for specific audiences, such as children*). **The student exhibits no major errors or omissions.**
Score 2.0	**The student exhibits no major errors or omissions regarding the simpler details and processes, such as . . .** • recognizing and recalling specific terminology (*e.g., novel, short story*); and • recognizing and recalling isolated details such as . . . ○ the characteristics of various forms of fiction. **However, the student exhibits major errors or omissions with score 3.0 elements.**
Grade 4	
Score 3.0	**While engaged in grade-appropriate tasks, the student demonstrates an ability to identify and analyze literary genre by . . .** • comparing and contrasting basic features of fiction, nonfiction, drama, and poetry (*e.g., understanding that if a story has been made up, it is fiction, and if that story consists mainly of dialogue and stage directions, then it is a play*). **The student exhibits no major errors or omissions.**
Score 2.0	**The student exhibits no major errors or omissions regarding the simpler details and processes, such as . . .** • recognizing and recalling specific terminology (*e.g., poetry, drama*); and • recognizing and recalling isolated details, such as . . . ○ the basic characteristics of poetry, drama, fiction, and nonfiction. **However, the student exhibits major errors or omissions with score 3.0 elements.**
Grade 3	
Score 3.0	**While engaged in grade-appropriate tasks, the student demonstrates an ability to identify and analyze literary genre by . . .** • comparing and contrasting various imaginative forms of literature (*e.g., understanding that a comic book is a fantasy told mainly through illustrations, whereas folk and fairy tales are stories made up to teach some kind of lesson*). **The student exhibits no major errors or omissions.**
Score 2.0	**The student exhibits no major errors or omissions regarding the simpler details and processes, such as . . .** • recognizing and recalling specific terminology (*e.g., fairy tale, folk tale*); and • recognizing and recalling isolated details, such as . . . ○ the basic characteristics of various imaginative forms of literature. **However, the student exhibits major errors or omissions with score 3.0 elements.**

Grade 2	
Score 3.0	**While engaged in grade-appropriate tasks, the student demonstrates an ability to identify and analyze literary genre by . . .** • explaining the basic features of fiction and nonfiction texts (*e.g., chapters and chapter headings, glossary, index*). **The student exhibits no major errors or omissions.**
Score 2.0	**The student exhibits no major errors or omissions regarding the simpler details and processes, such as . . .** • recognizing and recalling specific terminology (*e.g., chapter, table of contents*); and • recognizing and recalling isolated details, such as . . . ○ fiction and nonfiction have similarities and differences. **However, the student exhibits major errors or omissions with score 3.0 elements.**
Grade 1	
Score 3.0	**While engaged in grade-appropriate tasks, the student demonstrates an ability to identify and analyze literary genre by . . .** • distinguishing between stories that are true and stories that are made up (*e.g., understanding that comic books cannot be considered true because people do not really have superhuman powers*). **The student exhibits no major errors or omissions.**
Score 2.0	**The student exhibits no major errors or omissions regarding the simpler details and processes, such as . . .** • recognizing and recalling specific terminology (*e.g., reality, make-believe*); and • recognizing and recalling isolated details, such as . . . ○ identifying basic characteristics of true stories and stories that are made up. **However, the student exhibits major errors or omissions with score 3.0 elements.**
Grade K	
Score 3.0	**While engaged in grade-appropriate tasks, the student demonstrates an ability to identify and analyze literary genre by . . .** • identifying basic features of picture books and nursery rhymes (*e.g., picture books and nursery rhymes tell stories that teach us things*). **The student exhibits no major errors or omissions.**
Score 2.0	**The student exhibits no major errors or omissions regarding the simpler details and processes, such as . . .** • recognizing and recalling specific terminology (*e.g., picture book, nursery rhyme*); and • recognizing and recalling isolated details, such as . . . ○ picture books and nursery rhymes are both forms of literature. **However, the student exhibits major errors or omissions with score 3.0 elements.**

Listening and Speaking

Oral Comprehension

Grade 8		
Score 4.0	**In addition to score 3.0 performance, the student demonstrates in-depth inferences and applications that go beyond what was taught.**	
	Score 3.5	In addition to score 3.0 performance, the student demonstrates in-depth inferences and applications with partial success.
Score 3.0	**While participating in grade-appropriate oral communication, the student demonstrates the ability to listen critically and respond appropriately by . . .** • analyzing the logic of an extended oral presentation (*e.g., analyzing how effectively the speaker supports claims made during a presentation*); • asking questions that require the speaker to reconcile apparent inconsistencies in the content and information presented by the speaker that contradicts other information on the topic (*e.g., generating questions designed to clarify inconsistencies and/or contradictions apparent in an oral presentation*); and • using the speaker's nonverbal messages to infer the speaker's point of view toward the content (*e.g., analyzing gestures, facial expressions, posture, and other body language to determine a speaker's point of view toward the content in an oral presentation*). **The student exhibits no major errors or omissions.**	
	Score 2.5	The student exhibits no major errors or omissions regarding the score 2.0 elements and partial knowledge of the score 3.0 elements.

Score 2.0	**The student exhibits no major errors or omissions regarding the simpler details and processes, such as . . .**
	• recognizing and recalling specific terminology (*e.g., contradiction, body language*); and
	• performing basic processes, such as . . .
	  ○ identifying the overall logic of an oral presentation;
	  ○ recognizing inconsistencies in an oral presentation; and
	  ○ recognizing basic nonverbal behaviors that indicate point of view.
	However, the student exhibits major errors or omissions with score 3.0 elements.	

	Score 1.5	The student demonstrates partial knowledge of the score 2.0 elements but major errors or omissions regarding the score 3.0 elements.
Score 1.0	**With help, the student demonstrates partial understanding of some of the score 2.0 elements and some of the score 3.0 elements.**	
	Score 0.5	With help, the student demonstrates partial understanding of some of the score 2.0 elements but not the score 3.0 elements.
Score 0.0	**Even with help, the student demonstrates no understanding or skill.**	
Grade 7		
Score 3.0	**While participating in grade-appropriate oral communication, the student demonstrates the ability to listen critically and respond appropriately by . . .**	

Score 3.0 (continued)	• summarizing the logic of an extended oral presentation (*e.g., providing a summary of the key points of an extended oral presentation and determining whether those points logically support claims made by the speaker*); • asking questions that require the speaker to reconcile apparent inconsistencies (*e.g., generating questions designed to clarify inconsistencies apparent in an oral presentation*); and • using the speaker's nonverbal messages to infer the speaker's general attitude toward the content (*e.g., analyzing gestures, facial expressions, posture, and other body language to determine the speaker's general attitude about the content in an oral presentation*). **The student exhibits no major errors or omissions.**

Score 2.0	**The student exhibits no major errors or omissions regarding the simpler details and processes, such as . . .**
	 • recognizing and recalling specific terminology (*e.g., analysis, logic, inconsistency, facial expression*); and
	 • performing basic processes, such as . . .
	     ○ identifying the basic logic of an oral presentation;
	     ○ recognizing inconsistencies in an oral presentation; and
	     ○ recognizing basic nonverbal messages.
	 However, the student exhibits major errors or omissions with score 3.0 elements.

Grade 6	
Score 3.0	**While participating in grade-appropriate oral communication, the student demonstrates the ability to listen critically and respond appropriately by . . .** • summarizing main idea and supporting details from extended oral presentations (*e.g., providing a summary of the main idea and the most critical points that support the main idea in an extended oral presentation*); • asking questions of the speaker that help clarify confusing aspects of the presentation (*e.g., generating questions designed to clarify confusing aspects of an oral presentation that significantly impact meaning*); and • recognizing basic nonverbal messages (*e.g., explaining and exemplifying facial expressions that are a basic form of nonverbal communication*). **The student exhibits no major errors or omissions.**

Score 2.0	**The student exhibits no major errors or omissions regarding the simpler details and processes, such as . . .**
	 • recognizing and recalling specific terminology (*e.g., nonverbal messages, point of view, inference*); and
	 • performing basic processes, such as . . .
	     ○ identifying the main idea but not the supporting details of an oral presentation;
	     ○ asking basic questions of the speaker; and
	     ○ identifying basic forms of nonverbal communication.
	 However, the student exhibits major errors or omissions with score 3.0 elements.

Grade 5	
Score 3.0	**While participating in grade-appropriate oral communication, the student demonstrates the ability to listen critically and respond appropriately by . . .** • summarizing the main idea and supporting details from extended oral presentations (*e.g., providing a summary of the main idea and the general points offered by the presenter to support the main idea in an extended oral presentation*); and • asking questions of the speaker that help clarify confusing aspects of the presentation (*e.g., generating questions designed to clarify any confusing aspects of an oral presentation*). **The student exhibits no major errors or omissions.**

Score 2.0	The student exhibits no major errors or omissions regarding the simpler details and processes, such as . . .
	• recognizing and recalling specific terminology (*e.g., supporting detail, clarification*); and
	• performing basic processes, such as . . .
	   ○ identifying supporting details but not the main idea of an oral presentation; and
	   ○ asking basic questions of the speaker.
	However, the student exhibits major errors or omissions with score 3.0 elements.

Grade 4	
Score 3.0	While participating in grade-appropriate oral communication, the student demonstrates the ability to listen critically and respond appropriately by . . . • summarizing the main idea from extended oral presentations (*e.g., providing a summary of the main idea of an extended oral presentation*); and • asking questions of the speaker that help add detail to the content of the presentation (*e.g., generating questions to gain further information about a key point of a presentation*). **The student exhibits no major errors or omissions.**

Score 2.0	The student exhibits no major errors or omissions regarding the simpler details and processes, such as . . .
	• recognizing and recalling specific terminology (*e.g., main idea, detail, content*); and
	• performing basic processes, such as . . .
	   ○ identifying important information from an oral presentation; and
	   ○ asking basic questions of the speaker.
	However, the student exhibits major errors or omissions with score 3.0 elements.

Grade 3	
Score 3.0	While participating in grade-appropriate oral communication, the student demonstrates the ability to listen critically and respond appropriately by . . . • summarizing short oral presentations (*e.g., providing a summary of the main idea and supporting details of a short oral presentation*); and • asking basic questions of the speaker (*e.g., asking a speaker to repeat information that was not heard correctly*). **The student exhibits no major errors or omissions.**

Score 2.0	The student exhibits no major errors or omissions regarding the simpler details and processes, such as . . .
	• recognizing and recalling specific terminology (*e.g., oral presentation, speaker*); and
	• performing basic processes, such as . . .
	   ○ identifying the main idea of a short oral presentation but not the supporting points; and
	   ○ identifying when a question should be asked of the speaker.
	However, the student exhibits major errors or omissions with score 3.0 elements.

Grade 2	
Score 3.0	While participating in grade-appropriate oral communication, the student demonstrates the ability to listen critically and respond appropriately by . . . • restating and carrying out multiple-step directions (*e.g., describing and executing a set of multiple-step directions provided by the teacher*). **The student exhibits no major errors or omissions.**
Score 2.0	The student exhibits no major errors or omissions regarding the simpler details and processes, such as . . . • recognizing and recalling specific terminology (*e.g., performance, restate/restating*); and • performing basic processes, such as . . . ○ identifying directions that involve multiple steps. **However, the student exhibits major errors or omissions with score 3.0 elements.**

	Grade 1
Score 3.0	**While participating in grade-appropriate oral communication, the student demonstrates the ability to listen critically and respond appropriately by . . .** • restating and carrying out basic directions with more than one step (*e.g., describing and executing basic directions with three steps*). **The student exhibits no major errors or omissions.**
Score 2.0	**The student exhibits no major errors or omissions regarding the simpler details and processes, such as . . .** • recognizing and recalling specific terminology (*e.g., summary, process*); and • performing basic processes, such as . . . ○ identifying basic directions that involve more than one step. **However, the student exhibits major errors or omissions with score 3.0 elements.**
	Grade K
Score 3.0	**While participating in grade-appropriate oral communication, the student demonstrates the ability to listen critically and respond appropriately by . . .** • restating and carrying out simple one-step directions (*e.g., describing and executing simple directions with one step*). **The student exhibits no major errors or omissions.**
Score 2.0	**The student exhibits no major errors or omissions regarding the simpler details and processes, such as . . .** • recognizing and recalling specific terminology (*e.g., directions, step*); and • performing basic processes, such as . . . ○ identifying simple directions that involve a single step. **However, the student exhibits major errors or omissions with score 3.0 elements.**

Analysis and Evaluation of Oral Media

	Grade 8	
Score 4.0	**In addition to score 3.0 performance, the student demonstrates in-depth inferences and applications that go beyond what was taught.**	
	Score 3.5	In addition to score 3.0 performance, the student demonstrates in-depth inferences and applications with partial success.
Score 3.0	**While participating in grade-appropriate oral communication, the student formulates thoughtful conclusions about the content and delivery by . . .** • analyzing the speaker's presentation for less common informal fallacies, such as use of faulty reasoning and presence of obstacles to clarity and accuracy (*e.g., determining when a speaker makes an incorrect assumption and explaining why the assumption is inaccurate*); • analyzing the speaker's use of invalid and less common persuasive techniques, such as appeals to personality, tradition, and rhetoric (*e.g., determining when a speaker appeals to tradition and explaining why this type of argument is invalid*); • analyzing the credibility of the speaker (*e.g., determining credibility on an issue by checking a speaker's bio for degrees, publications, and other information that might indicate adequate knowledge to present opinions about the topic*); and • checking the accuracy of information presented by the speaker (*e.g., confirming the accuracy of a speaker's use of statistics to support a claim that appears unlikely to be true*). **The student exhibits no major errors or omissions.**	
	Score 2.5	The student exhibits no major errors or omissions regarding the score 2.0 elements and partial knowledge of the score 3.0 elements.

Score 2.0	**The student exhibits no major errors or omissions regarding the simpler details and processes, such as . . .**
	• recognizing and recalling specific terminology (*e.g., regression toward the mean, appeal to personality, appeal to tradition, appeal to rhetoric*);
	• recognizing and recalling isolated details, such as . . .
	  ○ characteristics of faulty reasoning and characteristics of obstacles to clarity and accuracy;
	  ○ characteristics of persuasive techniques;
	  ○ characteristics of a credible speaker; and
	  ○ characteristics of accurate information.
	However, the student exhibits major errors or omissions with score 3.0 elements.	

	Score 1.5	The student demonstrates partial knowledge of the score 2.0 elements but major errors or omissions regarding the score 3.0 elements.
Score 1.0	**With help, the student demonstrates partial understanding of some of the score 2.0 elements and some of the score 3.0 elements.**	
	Score 0.5	With help, the student demonstrates partial understanding of some of the score 2.0 elements but not the score 3.0 elements.
Score 0.0	**Even with help, the student demonstrates no understanding or skill.**	
	Grade 7	
Score 3.0	**While participating in grade-appropriate oral communication, the student formulates thoughtful conclusions about the content and delivery by . . .** • analyzing the speaker's presentation for common informal fallacies, such as using attack strategies or faulty logic (*e.g., determining when a speaker attacks a position without support, explaining why this is invalid, and describing how the position should have been supported*);	

Score 3.0 (continued)	• analyzing the speaker's use of valid and common persuasive techniques, such as use of facts, evidence, examples, and appeal to reason (*e.g., determining when a speaker uses evidence to support a claim and explaining why the evidence is a valid support for the claim*); and • analyzing the credibility of the speaker (*e.g., determining if a speaker is credible and explaining reasons for that determination*). **The student exhibits no major errors or omissions.**

Score 2.0	**The student exhibits no major errors or omissions regarding the simpler details and processes, such as . . .**
	• recognizing and recalling specific terminology (*e.g., evading the issue, arguing from ignorance, composition/division, appeal to reason*); and
	• recognizing and recalling isolated details, such as . . .
	  ◦ characteristics of attack strategies and characteristics of faulty logic;
	  ◦ characteristics of persuasive techniques; and
	  ◦ characteristics of a credible speaker.
	However, the student exhibits major errors or omissions with score 3.0 elements.

Grade 6

Score 3.0	**While participating in grade-appropriate oral communication, the student formulates thoughtful conclusions about the content and delivery by . . .** • analyzing the speaker's presentation for basic informal fallacies, such as misinforming the audience or using weak, biased, or emotionally based support (*e.g., determining if a speaker's support for a claim is biased and explaining reasons for that determination*). **The student exhibits no major errors or omissions.**
Score 2.0	**The student exhibits no major errors or omissions regarding the simpler details and processes, such as . . .** • recognizing and recalling specific terminology (*e.g., fallacy, misinformation, bias, credibility*); and • recognizing and recalling isolated details, such as . . . ◦ characteristics of basic informal fallacies. **However, the student exhibits major errors or omissions with score 3.0 elements.**

Grade 5

Score 3.0	Not applicable.
Score 2.0	Not applicable.

Grade 4

Score 3.0	Not applicable.
Score 2.0	Not applicable.

Grade 3

Score 3.0	Not applicable.
Score 2.0	Not applicable.

Grade 2

Score 3.0	Not applicable.

Score 2.0	Not applicable.
Grade 1	
Score 3.0	Not applicable.
Score 2.0	Not applicable.
Grade K	
Score 3.0	Not applicable.
Score 2.0	Not applicable.

Speaking Applications

	Grade 8	
Score 4.0	**In addition to score 3.0 performance, the student demonstrates in-depth inferences and applications that go beyond what was taught.**	
	Score 3.5	In addition to score 3.0 performance, the student demonstrates in-depth inferences and applications with partial success.
Score 3.0	**While participating in grade-appropriate tasks, the student makes both formal and informal presentations, such as . . .** • making extended persuasive presentations (*e.g., delivering a presentation on effects of global warming, possible solutions, and steps for implementing one of the solutions with reasons why the solution would be the most effective*); • adjusting presentations based on audience reactions (*e.g., using appropriate humor to re-engage the audience during a presentation*); and • using Microsoft PowerPoint while making formal presentations (*e.g., using PowerPoint slides throughout a presentation to highlight key ideas and display charts, diagrams, and other information to support points made in the presentation*). **The student exhibits no major errors or omissions.**	
	Score 2.5	The student exhibits no major errors or omissions regarding the score 2.0 elements and partial knowledge of the score 3.0 elements.

Score 2.0	**The student exhibits no major errors or omissions regarding the simpler details and processes, such as . . .**
	• recognizing and recalling specific terminology (*e.g., adjustment, appropriate humor*); and
	• performing basic processes, such as . . .
	   ○ identifying whether a presentation was persuasive or not and why;
	   ○ recognizing when a presentation should be adjusted; and
	   ○ developing Microsoft PowerPoint slides to accompany a presentation.
	However, the student exhibits major errors or omissions with score 3.0 elements.	

	Score 1.5	The student demonstrates partial knowledge of the score 2.0 elements but major errors or omissions regarding the score 3.0 elements.
Score 1.0	**With help, the student demonstrates partial understanding of some of the score 2.0 elements and some of the score 3.0 elements.**	
	Score 0.5	With help, the student demonstrates partial understanding of some of the score 2.0 elements but not the score 3.0 elements.
Score 0.0	**Even with help, the student demonstrates no understanding or skill.**	
	Grade 7	
Score 3.0	**While participating in grade-appropriate tasks, the student makes both formal and informal presentations, such as . . .** • making extended persuasive presentations (*e.g., delivering a presentation on the benefits of seat belts and reasons for making and enforcing mandatory seat belt laws*); • demonstrating awareness of audience reaction to presentations (*e.g., repeating key points during a presentation when the audience appears confused*); and • using basic features of Microsoft PowerPoint while making formal presentations (*e.g., using PowerPoint slides to provide the audience with a simple outline of the presentation and definitions of terms that may be misunderstood*). **The student exhibits no major errors or omissions.**	

Score 2.0	**The student exhibits no major errors or omissions regarding the simpler details and processes, such as . . .**
	• recognizing and recalling specific terminology (*e.g., audience reaction, PowerPoint*); and
	• performing basic processes, such as . . .
	   ○ identifying whether a presentation was persuasive or not and why;
	   ○ recognizing when a presenter is aware of audience reactions; and
	   ○ developing basic PowerPoint slides to accompany a presentation.
	However, the student exhibits major errors or omissions with score 3.0 elements.

	**Grade 6**
Score 3.0	**While participating in grade-appropriate tasks, the student makes both formal and informal presentations, such as . . .** • making extended presentations involving taking and defending a position (*e.g., delivering a presentation that defends a position on a topic provided by the teacher*); • using appropriate volume, pitch, and tone when making formal presentations (*e.g., modifying the voice throughout a presentation to help keep the audience interested in the topic*); and • using visual aids such as pictures, charts, or graphs (*e.g., using a graph depicting the results of a survey to support claims made using those results*). **The student exhibits no major errors or omissions.**

Score 2.0	**The student exhibits no major errors or omissions regarding the simpler details and processes, such as . . .**
	• recognizing and recalling specific terminology (*e.g., persuasion, vocal modulation*); and
	• performing basic processes, such as . . .
	   ○ identifying whether a presentation was persuasive or not and why;
	   ○ identifying appropriate and inappropriate verbal expression in formal presentations; and
	   ○ preparing visual aids for a formal presentation.
	However, the student exhibits major errors or omissions with score 3.0 elements.

	**Grade 5**
Score 3.0	**While participating in grade-appropriate tasks, the student makes both formal and informal presentations, such as . . .** • making formal but basic presentations involving taking and defending a position (*e.g., delivering a basic presentation that defends a position on a topic provided by the teacher*); • using appropriate volume, pitch, and tone when making formal presentations (*e.g., avoiding speaking in a monotone during a presentation*); and • using basic visual aids such as pictures, charts, or graphs (*e.g., using pictures during a presentation to help the audience create a mental picture of the topic*). **The student exhibits no major errors or omissions.**

Score 2.0	**The student exhibits no major errors or omissions regarding the simpler details and processes, such as . . .**
	• recognizing and recalling specific terminology (*e.g., taking a position, defending a position, appropriate pitch, appropriate tone*); and
	• performing basic processes, such as . . .
	   ○ identifying whether a basic presentation defends a position;
	   ○ identifying appropriate use of volume, pitch, and tone in a formal presentation; and
	   ○ preparing basic visual aids to accompany a presentation.
	However, the student exhibits major errors or omissions with score 3.0 elements.

	**Grade 4**
Score 3.0	**While participating in grade-appropriate tasks, the student makes both formal and informal presentations, such as . . .**

Score 3.0 (continued)	• making formal narrative and descriptive presentations (*e.g., delivering a presentation on the life of an important historical figure*); and • attending to appropriate volume when making formal presentations (*e.g., avoiding talking too loudly or too quietly during a presentation*). **The student exhibits no major errors or omissions.**

Score 2.0	**The student exhibits no major errors or omissions regarding the simpler details and processes, such as . . .**
	• recognizing and recalling specific terminology (*e.g., appropriate volume, formal versus informal presentation*); and
	• recognizing and recalling isolated details, such as . . .
	   ○ characteristics of formal narrative and descriptive presentations; and
	   ○ characteristics of appropriate use of volume.
	However, the student exhibits major errors or omissions with score 3.0 elements.

Grade 3	
Score 3.0	**While participating in grade-appropriate tasks, the student makes both formal and informal presentations, such as . . .** • making formal narrative presentations (*e.g., delivering a presentation that tells a story about a family vacation*); and • making formal descriptive presentations (*e.g., delivering a presentation that describes the solar system*). **The student exhibits no major errors or omissions.**

Score 2.0	**The student exhibits no major errors or omissions regarding the simpler details and processes, such as . . .**
	• recognizing and recalling specific terminology (*e.g., narrative presentation, descriptive presentation*); and
	• recognizing and recalling isolated details, such as . . .
	   ○ characteristics of narrative presentations; and
	   ○ characteristics of descriptive presentations.
	However, the student exhibits major errors or omissions with score 3.0 elements.

Grade 2	
Score 3.0	**While participating in grade-appropriate tasks, the student makes both formal and informal presentations, such as . . .** • making informal presentations about narrative events with a clear but simple plot (*e.g., telling a short story to the class about a made-up character's journey to outer space*); and • making informal presentations describing a person, place, or thing with attention to details (*e.g., telling the class about the early childhood of Abraham Lincoln*). **The student exhibits no major errors or omissions.**

Score 2.0	**The student exhibits no major errors or omissions regarding the simpler details and processes, such as . . .**
	• recognizing and describing basic terminology (*e.g., plot, narration*); and
	• recognizing and recalling isolated details, such as . . .
	   ○ characteristics of narrative events; and
	   ○ characteristics of details that enhance a description.
	However, the student exhibits major errors or omissions with score 3.0 elements.

Grade 1	
Score 3.0	**While participating in grade-appropriate tasks, the student makes both formal and informal presentations, such as . . .**

Score 3.0 (*continued*)	• making informal class presentations about an important life event using a simple sequence (*e.g., telling the class about the wedding of a relative*); and • making informal presentations describing a person, place, or thing with some attention to details (*e.g., telling the class about a favorite restaurant*). **The student exhibits no major errors or omissions.**

Score 2.0	**The student exhibits no major errors or omissions regarding the simpler details and processes, such as . . .**
	• recognizing and recalling specific terminology (*e.g., description, detail*); and
	• performing basic processes, such as . . .
	  ◦ telling a teacher or peers about an important life event; and
	  ◦ describing a person, place, or thing to teachers or peers.
	However, the student exhibits major errors or omissions with score 3.0 elements.

Grade K	
Score 3.0	**While participating in grade-appropriate tasks, the student makes both formal and informal presentations, such as . . .** • making informal class presentations about an important life event using a simple sequence (*e.g., telling the class about a birthday celebration*). **The student exhibits no major errors or omissions.**
Score 2.0	**The student exhibits no major errors or omissions regarding the simpler details and processes, such as . . .** • recognizing and recalling specific terminology (*e.g., event, sequence*); and • performing basic processes, such as . . . ◦ telling a teacher or peers about an important life event. **However, the student exhibits major errors or omissions with score 3.0 elements.**

Scoring Scales for
Mathematics

Mathematics

―――

Note: For each measurement topic, the scale for the first grade level (the highest grade level to which the topic extends) shows all scores, including half-point scores. For all other grade levels, the scale shows scores 3.0 and 2.0 only, because the descriptors for the other scores on the scale do not change from grade level to grade level.

Note: In Scoring Scales for Mathematics, some rules of punctuation and consistency have been waived for clarity. For example, we've elected to omit a semicolon following some mathematical equations and geometric shapes because the punctuation may be distracting and cause confusion.

Numbers and Operations

Number Sense and Number Systems

	Grade 8	
Score 4.0	**In addition to score 3.0 performance, the student demonstrates in-depth inferences and applications that go beyond what was taught.**	
	Score 3.5	In addition to score 3.0 performance, the student demonstrates in-depth inferences and applications with partial success.
Score 3.0	**While engaged in grade-appropriate tasks, the student demonstrates an understanding of numbers and number systems by . . .** • determining the union and intersection of various sets (*e.g., explaining and exemplifying the union of two sets as the set of elements that are in either set*); • using scientific notation to express large numbers and small numbers between 0 and 1 (*e.g., 0.256 written in scientific notation is 2.56 × 10⁻¹*); and • distinguishing between subsets of the real number system (*e.g., explaining and exemplifying.that a rational number is one that can be written as a simple fraction and providing examples of rational versus irrational numbers*). **The student exhibits no major errors or omissions.**	
	Score 2.5	The student exhibits no major errors or omissions regarding the score 2.0 elements and partial knowledge of the score 3.0 elements.

Score 2.0	**The student exhibits no major errors or omissions regarding the simpler details and processes, such as . . .**
	• recognizing and recalling specific terminology (*e.g., union, intersection, real number system*); and
	• recognizing and recalling the accuracy of basic solutions and information, such as . . .
	  ○ if set A = {1, 3, 5} and set B = {1, 5, 6}, the union of A and B, written A ∪ B = {1, 3, 5, 6};
	  ○ in scientific notation, numbers are written using powers of 10 (*e.g., 2,000 in scientific notation is 2 × 10³*); and
	  ○ pi is a famous irrational number.
	However, the student exhibits major errors or omissions with score 3.0 elements.	

	Score 1.5	The student demonstrates partial knowledge of the score 2.0 elements but major errors or omissions regarding the score 3.0 elements.
Score 1.0	**With help, the student demonstrates partial understanding of some of the score 2.0 elements and some of the score 3.0 elements.**	
	Score 0.5	With help, the student demonstrates partial understanding of some of the score 2.0 elements but not the score 3.0 elements.
Score 0.0	**Even with help, the student demonstrates no understanding or skill.**	
	Grade 7	
Score 3.0	**While engaged in grade-appropriate tasks, the student demonstrates an understanding of numbers and number systems by . . .**	

Score 3.0 (*continued*)	• expressing various large numbers in multiple ways (*e.g., explaining and exemplifying how the same number can be expressed in scientific and standard notations*); • expressing various numbers in exponential form (*e.g., explaining and exemplifying the meaning of exponents that are negative or 0*); and • comparing and ordering a variety of integers, fractions, decimals, and percents (*e.g., converting between different types of rational numbers for accurate comparison*). **The student exhibits no major errors or omissions.**

Score 2.0	**The student exhibits no major errors or omissions regarding the simpler details and processes, such as . . .**
	• recognizing and recalling specific terminology (*e.g., scientific notation, rational number, irrational number*);
	• recognizing and recalling the accuracy of basic solutions and information, such as . . .
	   ○ 275,000 written in scientific notation is 2.75×10^5;
	   ○ exponents can be positive or negative; and
	   ○ 5^{-2} can be expressed as $(1/5)^2$ or 0.04 or 4%.
	However, the student exhibits major errors or omissions with score 3.0 elements.

Grade 6

Score 3.0	**While engaged in grade-appropriate tasks, the student demonstrates an understanding of numbers and number systems by . . .** • expressing various small numbers in multiple ways (*e.g., explaining and exemplifying how factors and exponents can be used to decompose and recompose whole numbers*); • using prime factorization (*e.g., explaining and exemplifying how prime factorization was used to solve a given problem*); and • expressing decimal numbers in multiple ways (*e.g., explaining and exemplifying how a decimal number can be used to express the concepts of ratio, proportion, and percent*). **The student exhibits no major errors or omissions.**

Score 2.0	**The student exhibits no major errors or omissions regarding the simpler details and processes, such as . . .**
	• recognizing and recalling specific terminology (*e.g., decompose, recompose, exponent*); and
	• recognizing and recalling the accuracy of basic solutions and information, such as . . .
	   ○ $27 = 3 \times 3 \times 3 = 3^3$;
	   ○ $2 \times 3 \times 5$ is the prime factorization of 30; and
	   ○ 3.762 written in expanded notation is $3 + 0.7 + 0.06 + 0.002$.
	However, the student exhibits major errors or omissions with score 3.0 elements.

Grade 5

Score 3.0	**While engaged in grade-appropriate tasks, the student demonstrates an understanding of numbers and number systems by . . .** • expressing equivalent forms of various simple fractions (*e.g., explaining and exemplifying how to convert between simple fractions, decimals, and percents*); • rounding decimals to a given place value and fractions (including mixed numbers) to the nearest half (*e.g., explaining and exemplifying the rules for rounding a variety of numbers*); and • finding the greatest common factor (GCF) and least common multiple (LCM) of a variety of numbers (*e.g., explaining and exemplifying the concepts of common multiples and factors*). **The student exhibits no major errors or omissions.**
Score 2.0	**The student exhibits no major errors or omissions regarding the simpler details and processes, such as . . .** • recognizing and recalling specific terminology (*e.g., prime factorization, greatest common factor [GCF], least common multiple [LCM]*); and

Score 2.0 (*continued*)	• recognizing and recalling the accuracy of basic solutions and information, such as . . . ◦ 75% = 0.75 = 3/4; ◦ 5.375 rounded to the nearest tenth is 5.4; and ◦ the least common multiple of 3 and 5 is 15. **However, the student exhibits major errors or omissions with score 3.0 elements.**

Grade 4	
Score 3.0	**While engaged in grade-appropriate tasks, the student demonstrates an understanding of numbers and number systems by . . .** • ordering and comparing whole numbers (millions), decimals (thousandths), and fractions with like denominators (*e.g., converting between whole numbers, decimals, and fractions for accurate comparison*); • expressing complex money amounts in a variety of ways (*e.g., explaining and exemplifying how the same amount of money can be expressed differently*); and • finding factors and multiples of whole numbers through 100 (*e.g., explaining and exemplifying the difference between a factor and a multiple*). **The student exhibits no major errors or omissions.**
Score 2.0	**The student exhibits no major errors or omissions regarding the simpler details and processes, such as . . .** • recognizing and recalling specific terminology (*e.g., factor, multiple, prime*); and • recognizing and recalling the accuracy of basic solutions and information, such as . . . ◦ 0.5 = 1/2; ◦ $25.00 is written as twenty-five dollars; and ◦ 4 is a factor of 12. **However, the student exhibits major errors or omissions with score 3.0 elements.**

Grade 3	
Score 3.0	**While engaged in grade-appropriate tasks, the student demonstrates an understanding of numbers and number systems by . . .** • using mathematical language and symbols to compare and order whole numbers (up to 9999), decimals (hundredths), and commonly used fractions and mixed numbers (*e.g., explaining and exemplifying the difference between < and ≤*); and • generating equivalent forms of whole numbers (*e.g., explaining and exemplifying how different forms of a whole number are the same*). **The student exhibits no major errors or omissions.**
Score 2.0	**The student exhibits no major errors or omissions regarding the simpler details and processes, such as . . .** • recognizing and recalling specific terminology (*e.g., less than, greater than, mixed number*); and • recognizing and recalling the accuracy of basic solutions and information, such as . . . ◦ < is a symbol that means "less than"; > is a symbol that means "greater than"; and ◦ 15 + 10 is the same as 25. **However, the student exhibits major errors or omissions with score 3.0 elements.**

Grade 2	
Score 3.0	**While engaged in grade-appropriate tasks, the student demonstrates an understanding of numbers and number systems by . . .** • using place-value concepts to represent, compare, and order whole numbers (up to 999) (*e.g., explaining and exemplifying how each place represents a power of 10*); and • representing different forms of money (*e.g., explaining and exemplifying how common decimal numbers, 0.10, 0.25, 0.50, and 0.75, are related to money*). **The student exhibits no major errors or omissions.**

Score 2.0	The student exhibits no major errors or omissions regarding the simpler details and processes, such as . . . • recognizing and recalling specific terminology (*e.g., sixths, eighths, decimal form*); and • recognizing and recalling the accuracy of basic solutions and information, such as . . . ○ in the number 765, 6 is in the 10s place; and ○ 0.25 is twenty-five cents. **However, the student exhibits major errors or omissions with score 3.0 elements.**
Grade 1	
Score 3.0	**While engaged in grade-appropriate tasks, the student demonstrates an understanding of numbers and number systems by . . .** • generating equivalent forms for the same number (*e.g., explaining the difference between two equivalent forms of the same number*); • describing the value of a small collection of coins (total value up to one dollar) (*e.g., explaining the difference in value between different coins*); and • describing and using ordinal numbers (1st to 10th) (*e.g., explaining the position of different ordinal numbers*). **The student exhibits no major errors or omissions.**
Score 2.0	The student exhibits no major errors or omissions regarding the simpler details and processes, such as . . . • recognizing and recalling specific terminology (*e.g., place value, expanded notation, fraction*); and • recognizing and recalling the accuracy of basic solutions and information, such as . . . ○ 5 + 5 is the same as 10; ○ a dime is 10 cents; and ○ in (a, b, c, d, e, f, g), b is second, f is sixth. **However, the student exhibits major errors or omissions with score 3.0 elements.**
Grade K	
Score 3.0	**While engaged in grade-appropriate tasks, the student demonstrates an understanding of numbers and number systems by . . .** • comparing and ordering whole numbers up to 10 (*e.g., explaining the quantity represented by different whole numbers*); • placing simple sets of objects into ordinal position (*e.g., explaining why one set of objects belongs in a specific ordinal position*); and • constructing multiple sets of objects, each containing the same number of objects (*e.g., making and describing equal sets out of a group of different objects*). **The student exhibits no major errors or omissions.**
Score 2.0	The student exhibits no major errors or omissions regarding the simpler details and processes, such as . . . • recognizing and recalling specific terminology (*e.g., whole number, ordinal position [1st to 10th], numeral*); and • recognizing and recalling the accuracy of basic solutions and information, such as . . . ○ 5, 3, 7 should be ordered as 3, 5, 7; ○ in the set {ball, cookie, tree, leaf} the third element is "tree"; and ○ set A has five rubber bands, set B has four marbles, set C has five erasers; both A and C have the same number of objects. **However, the student exhibits major errors or omissions with score 3.0 elements.**

Basic Addition and Subtraction

	Grade 8
Score 3.0	Not applicable.
Score 2.0	Not applicable.

	Grade 7
Score 3.0	Not applicable.
Score 2.0	Not applicable.

	Grade 6	
Score 4.0	**In addition to score 3.0 performance, the student demonstrates in-depth inferences and applications that go beyond what was taught.**	
	Score 3.5	In addition to score 3.0 performance, the student demonstrates in-depth inferences and applications with partial success.
Score 3.0	**While engaged in grade-appropriate tasks, the student demonstrates an understanding of basic addition and subtraction by . . .** • performing addition and subtraction of decimals and fractions greater than zero (*e.g., explaining and modeling the steps required to solve an equation containing both decimals and fractions*). **The student exhibits no major errors or omissions.**	
	Score 2.5	The student exhibits no major errors or omissions regarding the score 2.0 elements and partial knowledge of the score 3.0 elements.
Score 2.0	**The student exhibits no major errors or omissions regarding the simpler details and processes, such as . . .** • recognizing and recalling specific terminology (*e.g., computation, ratio, percent*); and • recognizing and recalling the accuracy of basic solutions and information, such as . . . 　○ 5/8 – 2/7 = 35/56 – 16/56 = 19/56. **However, the student exhibits major errors or omissions with score 3.0 elements.**	
	Score 1.5	The student demonstrates partial knowledge of the score 2.0 elements but major errors or omissions regarding the score 3.0 elements.
Score 1.0	**With help, the student demonstrates partial understanding of some of the score 2.0 elements and some of the score 3.0 elements.**	
	Score 0.5	With help, the student demonstrates partial understanding of some of the score 2.0 elements but not the score 3.0 elements.
Score 0.0	**Even with help, the student demonstrates no understanding or skill.**	

	Grade 5
Score 3.0	**While engaged in grade-appropriate tasks, the student demonstrates an understanding of basic addition and subtraction by . . .** • performing addition and subtraction of whole numbers (up to seven digits) (*e.g., explaining and modeling the steps required to solve an addition or subtraction problem containing seven-digit whole numbers*); • performing addition and subtraction of fractions with common and uncommon denominators (*e.g., explaining and modeling the steps required to solve an addition or subtraction problem containing fractions with uncommon denominators*); and

Score 3.0 (continued)	• performing addition and subtraction of decimals (hundredths) (*e.g., explaining and modeling the steps required to solve an addition or subtraction problem containing decimals to the hundredths place*). **The student exhibits no major errors or omissions.**

Score 2.0	**The student exhibits no major errors or omissions regarding the simpler details and processes, such as . . .**
	• recognizing and recalling specific terminology (*e.g., hundredths place, uncommon denominator, mixed number*); and
	• recognizing and recalling the accuracy of basic solutions and information, such as . . .
	    ○ 12,000 + 235,750 = 247,750;
	    ○ 1/2 + 5/8 = 4/8 + 5/8 = 9/8 = 1 1/8; and
	    ○ 5.27 – 3.15 = 2.12.
	However, the student exhibits major errors or omissions with score 3.0 elements.

Grade 4

Score 3.0	**While engaged in grade-appropriate tasks, the student demonstrates an understanding of basic addition and subtraction by . . .** • performing addition and subtraction of whole numbers (up to four digits) with and without regrouping (*e.g., explaining and modeling the steps required to solve an addition or subtraction problem containing four-digit whole numbers by regrouping*); • performing addition and subtraction of fractions with common denominators (*e.g., explaining and modeling the steps required to solve an addition or subtraction problem containing fractions with common denominators*); and • performing addition and subtraction of decimals (tenths) (*e.g., explaining and modeling the steps required to solve an addition or subtraction problem containing decimals to the tenths place*). **The student exhibits no major errors or omissions.**

Score 2.0	**The student exhibits no major errors or omissions regarding the simpler details and processes, such as . . .**
	• recognizing and recalling specific terminology (*e.g., tenths place, fraction, common denominator*); and
	• recognizing and recalling the accuracy of basic solutions and information, such as . . .
	    ○ 5250 – 725 = 4525;
	    ○ 3/7 + 2/7 = 5/7; and
	    ○ 5.7 – 5.3 = 0.4.
	However, the student exhibits major errors or omissions with score 3.0 elements.

Grade 3

Score 3.0	**While engaged in grade-appropriate tasks, the student demonstrates an understanding of basic addition and subtraction by . . .** • modeling the associative and commutative properties for addition (*e.g., explaining and modeling the difference between the associative and commutative properties for addition*); and • performing addition and subtraction of two- and three-digit whole numbers with and without regrouping (*e.g., explaining and modeling the steps required to solve an addition or subtraction problem with three-digit whole numbers by regrouping*). **The student exhibits no major errors or omissions.**
Score 2.0	**The student exhibits no major errors or omissions regarding the simpler details and processes, such as . . .** • recognizing and recalling specific terminology (*e.g., associative property, commutative property*); and • recognizing and recalling the accuracy of basic solutions and information, such as . . .

Score 2.0 *(continued)*	○ the following example shows the associative property for addition

$$5 + (2 + 8) = (5 + 2) + 8$$
$$5 + (10) = (7) + 8$$
$$15 = 15$$

○ $355 + 143 = 498$.

However, the student exhibits major errors or omissions with score 3.0 elements.

Grade 2

Score 3.0	**While engaged in grade-appropriate tasks, the student demonstrates an understanding of basic addition and subtraction by . . .**

- representing subtraction as comparison, take-away, and part-to-whole (*e.g., explaining and modeling the basic processes of comparison, take-away, and part-to-whole*);
- exemplifying the commutative property for addition (*e.g., explaining basic reasons why the order of addition is not important*); and
- performing addition and subtraction of whole numbers (two digits) with and without regrouping (*e.g., explaining and modeling the steps required to solve an addition or subtraction problem with two-digit whole numbers by regrouping*).

The student exhibits no major errors or omissions.

Score 2.0	**The student exhibits no major errors or omissions regarding the simpler details and processes, such as . . .**

- recognizing and recalling specific terminology (*e.g., part-to-whole, regrouping*); and
- recognizing and recalling the accuracy of basic solutions and information, such as . . .
  - ○ taking away three pieces of a pie that was cut into seven pieces leaves four pieces;
  - ○ the example $1 + 3 = 3 + 1$ shows the commutative property for addition; and
  - ○ the following example shows how to subtract $35 - 18$ by regrouping

$$\overset{\overset{2\ 15}{}}{\cancel{35}}$$
$$-18$$
$$\overline{17}$$

However, the student exhibits major errors or omissions with score 3.0 elements.

Grade 1

Score 3.0	**While engaged in grade-appropriate tasks, the student demonstrates an understanding of basic addition and subtraction by . . .**

- representing addition as combining sets and counting on (*e.g., explaining and modeling the basic processes of combining sets and counting on*);
- representing subtraction as take-away and comparison (*e.g., explaining and modeling the basic processes of take-away and comparison*); and
- performing addition and subtraction of one- and two-digit whole numbers without regrouping (*e.g., explaining and modeling the steps required to solve an addition or subtraction problem with one- and two-digit whole numbers without regrouping*).

The student exhibits no major errors or omissions.

Score 2.0	**The student exhibits no major errors or omissions regarding the simpler details and processes, such as . . .**

- recognizing and recalling specific terminology (*e.g., combining sets, equal*); and
- recognizing and recalling the accuracy of basic solutions and information, such as . . .
  - ○ addition can be explained as combining one set of three marbles with another set of two marbles to make one set of five marbles;
  - ○ subtraction can be explained as comparing one set of five cookies to a set of two cookies and determining that the second set is missing three cookies; and
  - ○ $27 - 12 = 15$.

However, the student exhibits major errors or omissions with score 3.0 elements.

Grade K	
Score 3.0	**While engaged in grade-appropriate tasks, the student demonstrates an understanding of basic addition and subtraction by . . .** • representing addition as counting on using numbers totaling 10 or less (*e.g., explaining and modeling the basic process of counting on to model addition*); and • representing subtraction as counting back using numbers less than or equal to 10 (*e.g., explaining and modeling the basic process of counting back to model subtraction*). **The student exhibits no major errors or omissions.**

Score 2.0	**The student exhibits no major errors or omissions regarding the simpler details and processes, such as . . .**
	
	• recognizing and recalling specific terminology (*e.g., counting on, counting back*); and
	
	• recognizing and recalling the accuracy of basic solutions and information, such as . . .
	  ◦ 1, 2, 3 is an example of counting forward; and
	  ◦ 3, 2, 1 is an example of counting backward.
	
	However, the student exhibits major errors or omissions with score 3.0 elements.

Basic Multiplication and Division

Grade 8		
Score 3.0	Not applicable.	
Score 2.0	Not applicable.	
Grade 7		
Score 3.0	Not applicable.	
Score 2.0	Not applicable.	
Grade 6		
Score 4.0	**In addition to score 3.0 performance, the student demonstrates in-depth inferences and applications that go beyond what was taught.**	
	Score 3.5	In addition to score 3.0 performance, the student demonstrates in-depth inferences and applications with partial success.
Score 3.0	**While engaged in grade-appropriate tasks, the student demonstrates an understanding of basic multiplication and division by . . .** • explaining and exemplifying the relationship between a quotient and a dividend (*e.g., explaining that a quotient may be larger than the dividend when the divisor is a fraction*); and • performing multiplication and division of decimals and fractions greater than zero (*e.g., explaining and modeling the steps required to solve a multiplication or division problem containing both decimals and fractions*). **The student exhibits no major errors or omissions.**	
	Score 2.5	The student exhibits no major errors or omissions regarding the score 2.0 elements and partial knowledge of the score 3.0 elements.

Score 2.0	**The student exhibits no major errors or omissions regarding the simpler details and processes, such as . . .**
	• recognizing and recalling specific terminology (*e.g., ratio, percent, computation*); and
	• recognizing and recalling the accuracy of basic solutions and information, such as . . .
	  ◦ a quotient can be larger than the dividend;
	  ◦ $0.235 \times 0.45 = 0.10575$; and
	  ◦ $25/80 \div 10/25 = 25/80 \times 25/10 = 625/800 = 25/32$.
	However, the student exhibits major errors or omissions with score 3.0 elements.	

	Score 1.5	The student demonstrates partial knowledge of the score 2.0 elements but major errors or omissions regarding the score 3.0 elements.
Score 1.0	**With help, the student demonstrates partial understanding of some of the score 2.0 elements and some of the score 3.0 elements.**	
	Score 0.5	With help, the student demonstrates partial understanding of some of the score 2.0 elements but not the score 3.0 elements.
Score 0.0	**Even with help, the student demonstrates no understanding or skill.**	
Grade 5		
Score 3.0	**While engaged in grade-appropriate tasks, the student demonstrates an understanding of basic multiplication and division by . . .** • performing multiplication of whole numbers (two-digit multipliers) (*e.g., explaining and modeling the steps required to solve a multiplication problem containing two-digit whole-number multipliers*); and	

Score 3.0 (continued)	• performing division of whole numbers (two-digit divisors) (*e.g., explaining and modeling the steps required to solve a division problem containing two-digit whole-number divisors*). **The student exhibits no major errors or omissions.**

Score 2.0	**The student exhibits no major errors or omissions regarding the simpler details and processes, such as . . .**
	• recognizing and recalling specific terminology (*e.g., quotient, dividend, divisor*); and
	• recognizing and recalling the accuracy of basic solutions and information, such as . . .
	    ○ 25 × 30 = 750; and
	    ○ 3125 ÷ 25 = 125.
	However, the student exhibits major errors or omissions with score 3.0 elements.

Grade 4	
Score 3.0	**While engaged in grade-appropriate tasks, the student demonstrates an understanding of basic multiplication and division by . . .** • representing the associative, commutative, and distributive properties for multiplication (*e.g., explaining basic reasons why multiplication distributes over addition*); • performing multiplication of three-digit whole numbers (two-digit multipliers) (*e.g., explaining and modeling the steps required to solve a multiplication problem containing three-digit whole numbers with two-digit multipliers*); and • performing division of three-digit whole numbers (one-digit divisors) (*e.g., explaining and modeling the steps required to solve a division problem containing three-digit whole numbers with one-digit divisors*). **The student exhibits no major errors or omissions.**

Score 2.0	**The student exhibits no major errors or omissions regarding the simpler details and processes, such as . . .**
	• recognizing and recalling specific terminology (*e.g., multiplier, multiplicand, distributive property*); and
	• recognizing and recalling the accuracy of basic solutions and information, such as . . .
	    ○ the example 5 × (2 + 8) = (5 × 2) + (5 × 8) shows the distributive property;
	    ○ 220 × 10 = 2200; and
	    ○ 102 ÷ 4 = 25 with a remainder of 2.
	However, the student exhibits major errors or omissions with score 3.0 elements.

Grade 3	
Score 3.0	**While engaged in grade-appropriate tasks, the student demonstrates an understanding of basic multiplication and division by . . .** • describing how a remainder may affect an answer in a real-world situation (*e.g., explaining and demonstrating the result of 10 cupcakes being shared by 3 children*); • performing multiplication of two-digit whole numbers (one-digit multiplier) with and without regrouping (*e.g., explaining and modeling the steps required to solve a multiplication problem containing two-digit whole numbers with one-digit multipliers*); and • performing division of two-digit whole numbers (one-digit divisor) without remainders (*e.g., explaining and modeling the steps required to solve a division problem containing two-digit whole numbers with one-digit divisors*). **The student exhibits no major errors or omissions.**
Score 2.0	**The student exhibits no major errors or omissions regarding the simpler details and processes, such as . . .** • recognizing and recalling specific terminology (*e.g., inverse, associative property, remainder*); and • recognizing and recalling the accuracy of basic solutions and information, such as . . . ○ if 10 cupcakes are shared by 3 children, each child would get 3 cupcakes with 1 cupcake left over;

Score 2.0 *(continued)*	○ $15 \times 2 = 30$; and ○ $25 \div 5 = 5$. **However, the student exhibits major errors or omissions with score 3.0 elements.**

Grade 2	
Score 3.0	**While engaged in grade-appropriate tasks, the student demonstrates an understanding of basic multiplication and division by . . .** • representing multiplication as repeated addition, rectangular arrays, and skip counting (*e.g., explaining and modeling the basic processes of repeated addition, rectangular arrays, and skip counting*); • representing division as sharing equally and repeated subtraction (*e.g., explaining and modeling the basic processes of sharing equally and repeated subtraction*); and • explaining the commutative and associative properties for multiplication (*e.g., explaining and modeling basic reasons why the order of multiplication is not important*). **The student exhibits no major errors or omissions.**
Score 2.0	**The student exhibits no major errors or omissions regarding the simpler details and processes, such as . . .** • recognizing and recalling specific terminology (*e.g., repeated subtraction, commutative property, regrouping*); and • recognizing and recalling the accuracy of basic solutions and information, such as . . . ○ 3×3 by skip counting is 3, 6, 9; ○ $8 \div 2$ by repeated subtraction means counting the number of times 2 can be subtracted from 8 until the answer is 0 (*e.g., $8 - 2 = 6$ [1], $6 - 2 = 4$ [2], $4 - 2 = 2$ [3], $2 - 2 = 0$ [4], so $8 \div 2$ is 4*); and ○ the example $2 \times (4 \times 3) = (2 \times 4) \times 3$ shows the associative property. **However, the student exhibits major errors or omissions with score 3.0 elements.**

Grade 1	
Score 3.0	**While engaged in grade-appropriate tasks, the student demonstrates an understanding of basic multiplication and division by . . .** • representing multiplication as repeated addition and rectangular arrays (*e.g., explaining and modeling basic processes of repeated addition and rectangular arrays*); and • representing division as sharing equally in contextual situations (*e.g., explaining and modeling the basic process of sharing equally*). **The student exhibits no major errors or omissions.**
Score 2.0	**The student exhibits no major errors or omissions regarding the simpler details and processes, such as . . .** • recognizing and recalling specific terminology (*e.g., repeated addition, sharing*); and • recognizing and recalling the accuracy of basic solutions and information, such as . . . ○ multiplication as repeated addition would be $2 \times 4 = 2 + 2 + 2 + 2 = 8$; and ○ four cupcakes shared equally by two classmates is two cupcakes each. **However, the student exhibits major errors or omissions with score 3.0 elements.**

Grade K	
Score 3.0	**While engaged in grade-appropriate tasks, the student demonstrates an understanding of basic multiplication and division by . . .** • joining multiple groups of objects, each containing the same number of objects (*e.g., putting together more than one group containing four objects of different type*); and • partitioning (sharing) a small set of objects into groups of equal size (*e.g., splitting a set of eight objects into groups of two objects and groups of four objects*). **The student exhibits no major errors or omissions.**

Score 2.0	**The student exhibits no major errors or omissions regarding the simpler details and processes, such as . . .**
	• recognizing and recalling specific terminology (*e.g., sets, groups*); and
	• recognizing and recalling the accuracy of basic solutions and information, such as . . .
	  ◦ joining groups of three pears, three apples, and three oranges would make a new group with a total of nine objects; and
	  ◦ partitioning six marbles into groups of equal size could be three groups of two marbles each or two groups of three marbles each.
	However, the student exhibits major errors or omissions with score 3.0 elements.

Operations, Computation, and Estimation

Grade 8		
Score 4.0	**In addition to score 3.0 performance, the student demonstrates in-depth inferences and applications that go beyond what was taught.**	
	Score 3.5	In addition to score 3.0 performance, the student demonstrates in-depth inferences and applications with partial success.
Score 3.0	**While engaged in grade-appropriate tasks, the student demonstrates an understanding of operations, computation, and estimation by . . .** • using order of operations to simplify expressions and perform computations involving integer exponents and radicals (*e.g., explaining and modeling the steps required to solve and/or simplify an equation containing integer exponents and radicals*); • using the inverse and identity properties and inverse relationships (*e.g., explaining and exemplifying the relationships between addition/subtraction, multiplication/division, and squaring/square roots*); and • evaluating whole number powers and square roots of perfect squares and estimating the square root of nonperfect squares (*e.g., approximating the square root of nonperfect squares as consecutive integers between which the root lies*). **The student exhibits no major errors or omissions.**	
	Score 2.5	The student exhibits no major errors or omissions regarding the score 2.0 elements and partial knowledge of the score 3.0 elements.
Score 2.0	**The student exhibits no major errors or omissions regarding the simpler details and processes, such as . . .** • recognizing and recalling specific terminology (*e.g., powers, radical expression*); and • recognizing and recalling the accuracy of basic solutions and information, such as . . . $\circ$ $\sqrt{25x \times 3x + 25x^2} = \sqrt{75x^2 + 25x^2} = \sqrt{100x^2} = 10x$; $\circ$ the identity is any number that when multiplied to a given number, produces the given number as the result; and $\circ$ $\sqrt{130}$ is between 11 and 12. **However, the student exhibits major errors or omissions with score 3.0 elements.**	
	Score 1.5	The student demonstrates partial knowledge of the score 2.0 elements but major errors or omissions regarding the score 3.0 elements.
Score 1.0	**With help, the student demonstrates partial understanding of some of the score 2.0 elements and some of the score 3.0 elements.**	
	Score 0.5	With help, the student demonstrates partial understanding of some of the score 2.0 elements but not the score 3.0 elements.
Score 0.0	**Even with help, the student demonstrates no understanding or skill.**	
Grade 7		
Score 3.0	**While engaged in grade-appropriate tasks, the student demonstrates an understanding of operations, computation, and estimation by . . .** • using order of operations and properties to simplify expressions involving integers, fractions, and decimals (*e.g., explaining and modeling the steps required to simplify expressions containing integers, fractions, and decimals*); • evaluating square roots of perfect squares through 225 (*e.g., explaining and exemplifying the concepts of square roots and perfect squares*); • computing absolute values (*e.g., explaining and exemplifying the concept of absolute value*); and	

Score 3.0 (continued)	• using a variety of estimation strategies (e.g., *explaining and exemplifying how estimation can be used to assist in verifying solutions to problems*). **The student exhibits no major errors or omissions.**
Score 2.0	**The student exhibits no major errors or omissions regarding the simpler details and processes, such as . . .** • recognizing and recalling specific terminology (e.g., *square root, absolute value*); and • recognizing and recalling the accuracy of basic solutions and information, such as . . . ○ $5x - \dfrac{1}{2}(4+x) - 2.2x = \dfrac{2}{2} \times 5x - \dfrac{4}{2} - \dfrac{x}{2} - \dfrac{2}{2} \times 2.2x = \dfrac{10x - 4 - x - 4.4x}{2} =$ $\dfrac{9x - 4.4x - 4}{2} = \dfrac{4.6x - 4}{2} = \dfrac{2(2.3x - 2)}{2} = 2.3x - 2;$ ○ $\sqrt{144} = 12;$ ○ $|-25| = 25;$ and ○ a reasonable estimate of 550 + 45 + 3000 + 212 would be to add 3000 + 500 + 200 = 3700 as a starting point; 50 + 45 is close to 100, so 100 should be added to the estimate, making 3800 more reasonable (actual answer 3807). **However, the student exhibits major errors or omissions with score 3.0 elements.**
Grade 6	
Score 3.0	**While engaged in grade-appropriate tasks, the student demonstrates an understanding of operations, computation, and estimation by . . .** • using properties (commutative, associative, distributive, identity, inverse) to simplify and evaluate algebraic expressions (e.g., *explaining and modeling the steps required to simplify and evaluate an algebraic expression using the inverse property*); • using order of operations (including the use of exponents) to simplify and evaluate numerical expressions (e.g., *explaining and modeling the steps required to simplify and evaluate numerical expressions containing exponents*); • using ratios to represent comparisons (e.g., *explaining and exemplifying the concept of a ratio*); and • using a variety of estimation strategies (e.g., *explaining and modeling the steps required to estimate a solution using a specific strategy*). **The student exhibits no major errors or omissions.**
Score 2.0	**The student exhibits no major errors or omissions regarding the simpler details and processes, such as . . .** • recognizing and recalling specific terminology (e.g., *ratio, order of operations— PEMDAS [parentheses, exponents, multiplication, division, addition, subtraction]*); and • recognizing and recalling the accuracy of basic solutions and information, such as . . . ○ in the example $6x \times (1/6) = 7 \times (1/6)$, the quantities in parentheses show how the multiplicative inverse would be applied; ○ using PEMDAS, the example $8 \div 2^3 \times 3 + (10 - 5)$ would be evaluated in the following sequence: (step 1) $8 \div 2^3 \times 3 + \mathbf{(10 - 5)}$, (step 2) $8 \div 2^3 \times 3 + 5$, (step 3) $8 \div \mathbf{8} \times 3 + 5$, (step 4) $\mathbf{8 \div 24} + 5$, (step 5) $\mathbf{3} + 5$; ○ ratios can be written as a fraction; and ○ a reasonable estimate of 0.235×0.45 would be rounding to the nearest tenth: $0.2 \times 0.5 = 0.1$ (actual answer 0.10575). **However, the student exhibits major errors or omissions with score 3.0 elements.**
Grade 5	
Score 3.0	**While engaged in grade-appropriate tasks, the student demonstrates an understanding of operations, computation, and estimation by . . .** • using properties (commutative, associative, distributive, identity, inverse) to simplify and evaluate algebraic expressions (e.g., *explaining and modeling the steps required to simplify and evaluate an algebraic expression using the distributive property*);

Score 3.0 (continued)	• using order of operations (including use of parentheses) to simplify and evaluate numerical expressions (*e.g., explaining and modeling the steps required to simplify and evaluate a numerical expression containing parentheses*); • using a variety of estimation strategies (*e.g., estimating and exemplifying the results of the same computation using different strategies*); and • describing strategies for performing computations mentally (*e.g., explaining and modeling the mental steps used to perform a computation*). **The student exhibits no major errors or omissions.**

Score 2.0	**The student exhibits no major errors or omissions regarding the simpler details and processes, such as . . .**
	• recognizing and recalling specific terminology (*e.g., identity property, order of operations—PMDAS [parentheses, multiplication, division, addition, subtraction]*); and
	• recognizing and recalling the accuracy of basic solutions and information, such as . . .
	  ○ in the example x + 7 + (−7) = 12 + (−7), the quantities in parentheses show how the additive inverse would be applied;
	  ○ using PMDAS, the example 8 × 2 ÷ 2 + (10 − 5) would be evaluated in the following sequence: (step 1) 8 × 2 ÷ 2 + (**10 − 5**), (step 2) **8 × 2 ÷ 2** + 5, (step 3) **16 ÷ 2** + 5, (step 4) **8 + 5**;
	  ○ 3125 ÷ 25 = 125 using front-end estimation without rounding would be 3000 ÷ 20 = 150; and
	  ○ while developing a mental strategy for performing computations, it can be helpful to verify the mental results on paper.
	However, the student exhibits major errors or omissions with score 3.0 elements.

Grade 4	
Score 3.0	**While engaged in grade-appropriate tasks, the student demonstrates an understanding of operations, computation, and estimation by . . .** • describing the proper order of operations in an expression (*e.g., explaining and exemplifying how the result changes based on the order in which operations are performed*); and • using a variety of estimation strategies (*e.g., estimating and explaining the results of the same computation using different strategies*). **The student exhibits no major errors or omissions.**

Score 2.0	**The student exhibits no major errors or omissions regarding the simpler details and processes, such as . . .**
	• recognizing and recalling specific terminology (*e.g., distributive property, order of operations—MDAS [multiplication, division, addition, subtraction]*); and
	• recognizing and recalling the accuracy of basic solutions and information, such as . . .
	  ○ given the expression 4 × 3 + 5 − 4, operations are done left to right, multiplication first, addition next, and subtraction last; and
	  ○ 234 × 27 = 6318 using front-end estimation with rounding would be 200 × 30 = 6000; without rounding would be 200 × 20 = 4000.
	However, the student exhibits major errors or omissions with score 3.0 elements.

Grade 3	
Score 3.0	**While engaged in grade-appropriate tasks, the student demonstrates an understanding of operations, computation, and estimation by . . .** • evaluating the reasonableness of estimations (*e.g., explaining why one estimation is more reasonable than another*). **The student exhibits no major errors or omissions.**
Score 2.0	**The student exhibits no major errors or omissions regarding the simpler details and processes, such as . . .** • recognizing and recalling specific terminology (*e.g., associative property, front-end estimation*); and

Score 2.0 *(continued)*	• recognizing and recalling the accuracy of basic solutions and information, such as . . . ○ 355 + 143 by front-end estimation produces 400 as an estimate, which is not reasonable as it is almost 100 less than the correct answer of 498. **However, the student exhibits major errors or omissions with score 3.0 elements.**
Grade 2	
Score 3.0	**While engaged in grade-appropriate tasks, the student demonstrates an understanding of operations, computation, and estimation by . . .** • using front-end estimation to estimate the results of addition and subtraction of whole numbers (two digits) (*e.g., explaining and modeling the basic process of front-end estimation using whole numbers*). **The student exhibits no major errors or omissions.**
Score 2.0	**The student exhibits no major errors or omissions regarding the simpler details and processes, such as . . .** • recognizing and recalling specific terminology (*e.g., repeated subtraction, commutative property*); and • recognizing and recalling the accuracy of basic solutions and information, such as . . . ○ 35 – 18 using front-end estimation would be 20. **However, the student exhibits major errors or omissions with score 3.0 elements.**
Grade 1	
Score 3.0	Not applicable.
Score 2.0	Not applicable.
Grade K	
Score 3.0	Not applicable.
Score 2.0	Not applicable.

Algebra

Basic Patterns

Grade 8		
Score 3.0	Not applicable.	
Score 2.0	Not applicable.	
Grade 7		
Score 3.0	Not applicable.	
Score 2.0	Not applicable.	
Grade 6		
Score 3.0	Not applicable.	
Score 2.0	Not applicable.	
Grade 5		
Score 3.0	Not applicable.	
Score 2.0	Not applicable.	
Grade 4		
Score 4.0	**In addition to score 3.0 performance, the student demonstrates in-depth inferences and applications that go beyond what was taught.**	
	Score 3.5	In addition to score 3.0 performance, the student demonstrates in-depth inferences and applications with partial success.
Score 3.0	**While engaged in grade-appropriate tasks, the student demonstrates an understanding of basic patterns by . . .** • analyzing a variety of patterns (*e.g., explaining and exemplifying the rule for a given pattern; finding missing values in a whole-number pattern*); and • extending patterns and relationships (*e.g., explaining and exemplifying the rule to extend a given pattern*). **The student exhibits no major errors or omissions.**	
	Score 2.5	The student exhibits no major errors or omissions regarding the score 2.0 elements and partial knowledge of the score 3.0 elements.

Score 2.0	**The student exhibits no major errors or omissions regarding the simpler details and processes, such as . . .**
	• recognizing and recalling specific terminology (*e.g., table, graph, function*); and
	• recognizing and recalling the accuracy of basic solutions and information, such as . . .
	   ◦ in the pattern 3, 7, 15, ?, 43, the missing element is 27; and
	   ◦ to extend the pattern 4, 8, 12, 16, the next number would be 20.
	However, the student exhibits major errors or omissions with score 3.0 elements.	

	Score 1.5	The student demonstrates partial knowledge of the score 2.0 elements but major errors or omissions regarding the score 3.0 elements.
Score 1.0		**With help, the student demonstrates partial understanding of some of the score 2.0 elements and some of the score 3.0 elements.**
	Score 0.5	With help, the student demonstrates partial understanding of some of the score 2.0 elements but not the score 3.0 elements.
Score 0.0		**Even with help, the student demonstrates no understanding or skill.**

Grade 3		
Score 3.0		**While engaged in grade-appropriate tasks, the student demonstrates an understanding of basic patterns by . . .** • creating simple decreasing patterns (*e.g., making and describing simple decreasing patterns with manipulatives, numbers, and graphic representations*); and • using patterns to make predictions (*e.g., supporting a prediction by a simple rule*). **The student exhibits no major errors or omissions.**
Score 2.0		**The student exhibits no major errors or omissions regarding the simpler details and processes, such as . . .** • recognizing and recalling specific terminology (*e.g., decreasing pattern, relationship*); and • recognizing and recalling the accuracy of basic solutions and information, such as . . . ◦ 25, 19, 13, 7, 1 is a decreasing pattern; and ◦ in the pattern 20, 18, 15, 11, the next element would be 6. **However, the student exhibits major errors or omissions with score 3.0 elements.**

Grade 2		
Score 3.0		**While engaged in grade-appropriate tasks, the student demonstrates an understanding of basic patterns by . . .** • creating simple increasing patterns (*e.g., making and describing simple increasing patterns with manipulatives, numbers, and graphic representations*); and • using patterns to make generalizations and predictions (*e.g., explaining why a basic prediction is supported by a given simple pattern*). **The student exhibits no major errors or omissions.**
Score 2.0		**The student exhibits no major errors or omissions regarding the simpler details and processes, such as . . .** • recognizing and recalling specific terminology (*e.g., generalization, prediction, increasing pattern*); and • recognizing and recalling the accuracy of basic solutions and information, such as . . . ◦ a picture showing triangle, circle, square, triangle, triangle, circle, circle, square, square is an increasing pattern; and ◦ in the pattern 3, 6, 9, 12, the next element would be 15. **However, the student exhibits major errors or omissions with score 3.0 elements.**

Grade 1		
Score 3.0		**While engaged in grade-appropriate tasks, the student demonstrates an understanding of basic patterns by . . .** • creating four-element patterns (*e.g., making and describing four-element patterns with manipulatives and graphic representations*); and • sorting, classifying, and ordering objects by two or more attributes (*e.g., explaining attributes used to classify objects*). **The student exhibits no major errors or omissions.**

Score 2.0	The student exhibits no major errors or omissions regarding the simpler details and processes, such as . . .
	• recognizing and recalling specific terminology (*e.g., drawing/picture, attribute*); and
	• recognizing and recalling the accuracy of basic solutions and information, such as . . .
	   ○ a picture showing square, circle, rectangle, triangle, square, circle, rectangle, triangle is a four-element pattern; and
	   ○ a group of triangles of different sizes and colors can be sorted by size and color.
	However, the student exhibits major errors or omissions with score 3.0 elements.

Grade K	
Score 3.0	While engaged in grade-appropriate tasks, the student demonstrates an understanding of basic patterns by . . . • replicating three-element patterns using manipulatives (*e.g., replicating and describing three-element patterns with concrete objects*); and • classifying objects by size/number/other attributes (*e.g., explaining basic attributes that can be used to sort objects*). **The student exhibits no major errors or omissions.**

Score 2.0	The student exhibits no major errors or omissions regarding the simpler details and processes, such as . . .
	• recognizing and recalling specific terminology (*e.g., model, pattern*); and
	• recognizing and recalling the accuracy of basic solutions and information, such as . . .
	   ○ the pattern 2, 5, 8 can be replicated with one group of two marbles, one group of five marbles, and one group of eight marbles; and
	   ○ a group of large and small marbles can be sorted into groups of large marbles and small marbles.
	However, the student exhibits major errors or omissions with score 3.0 elements.

Functions and Equations

Grade 8	
Score 4.0	**In addition to score 3.0 performance, the student demonstrates in-depth inferences and applications that go beyond what was taught.**
	Score 3.5 In addition to score 3.0 performance, the student demonstrates in-depth inferences and applications with partial success.
Score 3.0	**While engaged in grade-appropriate tasks, the student demonstrates an understanding of functions and equations by . . .** • evaluating various linear equations (with integer coefficients and solutions) and algebraic expressions (given integer values for variables) (*e.g., explaining and modeling the steps required to solve a multistep linear equation with integer coefficients and solutions; explaining the steps required to evaluate an algebraic expression given integer values for variables*); • classifying a variety of variables and relations (*e.g., explaining why a variable in a given function is independent; explaining why a given relation is nonlinear*); and • determining functions from information in tables, sets of ordered pairs, equations, graphs, and mappings (*e.g., explaining and modeling how a function was determined from a set of ordered pairs*). **The student exhibits no major errors or omissions.**
	Score 2.5 The student exhibits no major errors or omissions regarding the score 2.0 elements and partial knowledge of the score 3.0 elements.

Score 2.0	**The student exhibits no major errors or omissions regarding the simpler details and processes, such as . . .**
	• recognizing and recalling specific terminology (*e.g., linear relation, nonlinear relation, dependent variable, independent variable*); and
	• recognizing and recalling the accuracy of basic solutions and information, such as . . .
	   ○ linear equation: $3(5x - 2) = 9$; solution: $15x - 6 = 9$, $15x = 15$, $x = 1$;
	   ○ the relation $\{(-4, 12), (3, 2), (3, 7)\}$ is nonlinear; and
	   ○ ordered pairs: $(-2, -4)$, $(0, 2)$, $(2, 8)$; function: $f(x) = 3x + 2$.
	However, the student exhibits major errors or omissions with score 3.0 elements.

	Score 1.5 The student demonstrates partial knowledge of the score 2.0 elements but major errors or omissions regarding the score 3.0 elements.
Score 1.0	**With help, the student demonstrates partial understanding of some of the score 2.0 elements and some of the score 3.0 elements.**
	Score 0.5 With help, the student demonstrates partial understanding of some of the score 2.0 elements but not the score 3.0 elements.
Score 0.0	**Even with help, the student demonstrates no understanding or skill.**
Grade 7	
Score 3.0	**While engaged in grade-appropriate tasks, the student demonstrates an understanding of functions and equations by . . .** • evaluating various one- and two-step linear equations (with whole-number coefficients and solutions), algebraic expressions (given whole-number values for variables), and inequalities (with one variable) (*e.g., explaining and modeling the steps required to solve a two-step linear equation with whole-number coefficients; explaining and modeling the steps required to evaluate an algebraic expression given whole-number values for variables; explaining and modeling the steps required to solve an inequality with one variable*); and • determining if a constant rate of change exists in a pattern (*e.g., explaining and exemplifying whether a constant rate of change in a pattern is increasing or decreasing*). **The student exhibits no major errors or omissions.**

Score 2.0	The student exhibits no major errors or omissions regarding the simpler details and processes, such as . . .
	• recognizing and recalling specific terminology (*e.g., linear equation, algebraic expression, inequality, coefficient*); and
	• recognizing and recalling the accuracy of basic solutions and information, such as . . .
	  ○ inequality: $x + 7 > 3$; solution: $x > $ -4; and
	  ○ if the graph of a pattern is a straight line, the rate of change is constant.
	However, the student exhibits major errors or omissions with score 3.0 elements.

Grade 6

Score 3.0	While engaged in grade-appropriate tasks, the student demonstrates an understanding of functions and equations by . . . • evaluating various numerical and geometric rules and functions (*e.g., explaining and exemplifying why a description of a rule for a given function is valid or invalid*); and • analyzing a rule for a function given the input and output (*e.g., explaining and exemplifying all possible rules for a given input and output, i.e., input: 8, output: 4, rule: 1/2 of the input or subtract 4 from the input*). **The student exhibits no major errors or omissions.**

Score 2.0	The student exhibits no major errors or omissions regarding the simpler details and processes, such as . . .
	• recognizing and recalling specific terminology (*e.g., input, output*); and
	• recognizing and recalling the accuracy of basic solutions and information, such as . . .
	  ○ adding 5 to any number given can be written as the function $f(x) = x + 5$; and
	  ○ input: 6, output: 2, input: 10, output: 4, rule: take half of the input number and subtract 1.
	However, the student exhibits major errors or omissions with score 3.0 elements.

Grade 5

Score 3.0	While engaged in grade-appropriate tasks, the student demonstrates an understanding of functions and equations by . . . • evaluating general rules for basic functions (*e.g., explaining and exemplifying why a general rule for a basic function is valid*); • describing the basic concept of a variable (*e.g., explaining and exemplifying how a variable can be used to represent a fixed quantity, i.e., x + 2 = 5, the only possible value for the variable is 3; explaining and exemplifying how a variable can be used to represent any value in a formula, i.e., P = 2l + 2w, the formula for determining the perimeter for rectangles, any length and width can be substituted in place of the variables to calculate the perimeter*); and • solving simple open sentences involving operations on whole numbers (*e.g., explaining and modeling the steps required to solve a simple open sentence involving an operation on whole numbers*). **The student exhibits no major errors or omissions.**

Score 2.0	The student exhibits no major errors or omissions regarding the simpler details and processes, such as . . .
	• recognizing and recalling specific terminology (*e.g., variable, open sentence*); and
	• recognizing and recalling the accuracy of basic solutions and information, such as . . .
	  ○ a function works like a machine—put something in, get something out;
	  ○ a variable is often used to represent an unknown quantity; and
	  ○ open sentence: ? + 17 = 23; solution: 6.
	However, the student exhibits major errors or omissions with score 3.0 elements.

Grade 4

Score 3.0	Not applicable.

Score 2.0	Not applicable.
Grade 3	
Score 3.0	Not applicable.
Score 2.0	Not applicable.
Grade 2	
Score 3.0	Not applicable.
Score 2.0	Not applicable.
Grade 1	
Score 3.0	Not applicable.
Score 2.0	Not applicable.
Grade K	
Score 3.0	Not applicable.
Score 2.0	Not applicable.

Algebraic Representations and Mathematical Models

	Grade 8
Score 4.0	**In addition to score 3.0 performance, the student demonstrates in-depth inferences and applications that go beyond what was taught.**

	Score 3.5	In addition to score 3.0 performance, the student demonstrates in-depth inferences and applications with partial success.

Score 3.0	**While engaged in grade-appropriate tasks, the student demonstrates an understanding of algebraic representations and mathematical models by . . .** • graphing linear relations (*e.g., explaining and modeling the steps required to graph a linear relation by plotting points; explaining the steps required to graph a linear relation using the slope and y-intercept*); • computing and interpreting slope, midpoint, and distance, given a set of ordered pairs (*e.g., explaining and modeling the steps required to compute the slope, midpoint, and distance of a set of ordered pairs*); • calculating the slope of a linear relation given as a table or graph (*e.g., explaining and modeling the steps required to calculate the slope of a linear relation from a table; explaining and modeling the steps required to calculate the slope of a linear relation from a graph*); and • solving simple quadratic equations graphically (*e.g., explaining and modeling the steps required to solve a simple quadratic equation and graph the solution*). **The student exhibits no major errors or omissions.**

	Score 2.5	The student exhibits no major errors or omissions regarding the score 2.0 elements and partial knowledge of the score 3.0 elements.

Score 2.0	**The student exhibits no major errors or omissions regarding the simpler details and processes, such as . . .**
	• recognizing and recalling specific terminology (*e.g., slope, y-intercept, x-intercept, quadratic equation*); and
	• recognizing and recalling the accuracy of basic solutions and information, such as . . .
	  ○ the points $(-2, -1)$ and $(2, 7)$ form a line that will cross the x-axis at -1.5 and the y-axis at 3;
	  ○ the midpoint between $(-1, 2)$ and $(3, -6)$ is $(1, -2)$;
	  ○ the slope of the following table is 2

x	-4	-2	0	2
y	-5	-1	3	7

○ the graph of the equation $y = x^2 - 16$ is a parabola with a vertex at $(0, -16)$ pointing up and crossing the x-axis at points $(-4, 0)$ and $(4, 0)$. **However, the student exhibits major errors or omissions with score 3.0 elements.**

	Score 1.5	The student demonstrates partial knowledge of the score 2.0 elements but major errors or omissions regarding the score 3.0 elements.

Score 1.0	**With help, the student demonstrates partial understanding of some of the score 2.0 elements and some of the score 3.0 elements.**

	Score 0.5	With help, the student demonstrates partial understanding of some of the score 2.0 elements but not the score 3.0 elements.

Score 0.0	**Even with help, the student demonstrates no understanding or skill.**

	Grade 7
Score 3.0	While engaged in grade-appropriate tasks, the student demonstrates an understanding of algebraic representations and mathematical models by . . . • translating word phrases into algebraic expressions and algebraic expressions into word phrases (*e.g., explaining how an algebraic expression accurately represents information described in a word problem*); • graphing solution sets of inequalities on a number line (*e.g., explaining and modeling the steps required to solve an inequality and graph the solution set on a number line*); and • solving problems with linear functions and graphing the resulting ordered pairs (*e.g., explaining and modeling the steps required to solve a problem with a linear function and graph the resulting ordered pairs*). **The student exhibits no major errors or omissions.**

Score 2.0	The student exhibits no major errors or omissions regarding the simpler details and processes, such as . . .
	• recognizing and recalling specific terminology (*e.g., inequality, linear function, linear relation*); and
	• recognizing and recalling the accuracy of basic solutions and information, such as . . .
	   ◦ word problem: a new room is being built that needs to be three times the width of the adjacent room and twice the length; find the area of the new room; algebraic expression: $A = 3w \times 2l$;
	   ◦ the graph of $x \geq -2$ is the following
	
	$$\xleftarrow{\quad} \underset{\substack{-5 \;\; -4 \;\; -3 \;\; -2 \;\; -1 \;\;\; 0 \;\;\; 1 \;\;\; 2 \;\;\; 3 \;\;\; 4 \;\;\; 5}}{\rule{0pt}{0pt}} \xrightarrow{\quad}$$
	
	   ◦ linear function: $y = 2x + 3$; ordered pairs: $\{(-4, -5), (-2, -1), (0, 3), (2, 7)\}$.
	However, the student exhibits major errors or omissions with score 3.0 elements.

	Grade 6
Score 3.0	While engaged in grade-appropriate tasks, the student demonstrates an understanding of algebraic representations and mathematical models by . . . • finding the value of a variable within an algebraic expression involving any whole-number operation (*e.g., explaining and modeling the steps required to find the value of a variable within an algebraic expression involving division of whole numbers*); and • using the Cartesian plane (*e.g., explaining basic concepts of the coordinate system and modeling the steps required to plot points in all four quadrants of the Cartesian plane*). **The student exhibits no major errors or omissions.**

Score 2.0	The student exhibits no major errors or omissions regarding the simpler details and processes, such as . . .
	• recognizing and recalling specific terminology (*e.g., coordinate, evaluate*); and
	• recognizing and recalling the accuracy of basic solutions and information, such as . . .
	   ◦ $25 \div z = 5$; and
	   ◦ the point $(-2, -3)$ is in quadrant III.
	However, the student exhibits major errors or omissions with score 3.0 elements.

	Grade 5
Score 3.0	While engaged in grade-appropriate tasks, the student demonstrates an understanding of algebraic representations and mathematical models by . . . • finding the value of a variable within an algebraic expression involving addition and subtraction using whole numbers (*e.g., explaining and modeling the steps required to find the value of a variable within an algebraic expression involving addition of whole numbers*);

Score 3.0 (continued)	• finding a horizontal or vertical length between two points on a graph (*e.g., explaining and modeling the steps required to determine the horizontal length between two points on a graph*); and • finding and graphing positive ordered pairs that fit a linear equation and drawing the line they determine (*e.g., explaining and modeling the steps required to determine the positive ordered pairs that fit a linear equation and drawing the line they determine on the Cartesian plane*). **The student exhibits no major errors or omissions.**

Score 2.0	**The student exhibits no major errors or omissions regarding the simpler details and processes, such as . . .**
	• recognizing and recalling specific terminology (*e.g., Cartesian plane, vertex*); and
	• recognizing and recalling the accuracy of basic solutions and information, such as . . .
	  ◦ in the expression $a + 7 = 10$, a is a variable representing an unknown quantity;
	  ◦ the vertical length between $(0, 3)$ and $(0, 6)$ is 3; and
	  ◦ the points $(3, 0)$ and $(0, -6)$ fit the equation $y = 2x - 6$.
	However, the student exhibits major errors or omissions with score 3.0 elements.

Grade 4

Score 3.0	**While engaged in grade-appropriate tasks, the student demonstrates an understanding of algebraic representations and mathematical models by . . .** • writing and solving number sentences for word problems involving multiplication and division (*e.g., explaining and modeling the steps required to write a number sentence for a word problem involving multiplication and the steps required to find the solution*); • plotting and labeling whole numbers on a number line to 100 (*e.g., explaining and exemplifying how to construct a number line and modeling the steps required to plot and label various whole numbers up to 100*); and • finding locations on a map or grid using ordered pairs (*e.g., explaining and modeling the steps required to find the location of an ordered pair on a grid*). **The student exhibits no major errors or omissions.**

Score 2.0	**The student exhibits no major errors or omissions regarding the simpler details and processes, such as . . .**
	• recognizing and recalling specific terminology (*e.g., ordered pair, grid*); and
	• recognizing and recalling the accuracy of basic solutions and information, such as . . .
	  ◦ word problem: if there are six cookies for Jill and Jane to share, how many will they both get? number sentence: $6 \div 2 = ?$;
	  ◦ the number 76 is between 75 and 80 on the number line; and
	  ◦ on a 3×3 grid, the pair $(1, 1)$ is directly in the center of the grid.
	However, the student exhibits major errors or omissions with score 3.0 elements.

Grade 3

Score 3.0	**While engaged in grade-appropriate tasks, the student demonstrates an understanding of algebraic representations and mathematical models by . . .** • writing and solving number sentences for word problems involving addition and subtraction (*e.g., explaining and modeling the steps required to write a number sentence for a word problem involving addition and the steps required to find the solution*); • plotting and labeling whole numbers on a number line to 10 (*e.g., explaining and exemplifying how to construct a number line and modeling the steps required to plot and label various whole numbers up to 10*); and • specifying locations on a simple grid using horizontal and vertical movements (*e.g., describing and exemplifying how many squares to move up, down, left, or right from a given reference point on a simple grid—for example, on a 6×6 coordinate grid [5, 2] would be five squares to the right and two squares up when starting at [0, 0]*). **The student exhibits no major errors or omissions.**

Score 2.0	**The student exhibits no major errors or omissions regarding the simpler details and processes, such as . . .**
	
	• recognizing and recalling specific terminology (*e.g., number sentence, number line*); and
	• recognizing and recalling the accuracy of basic solutions and information, such as . . .
	    ○ "Ted has five apples and buys four more apples at the store; how many does he have?" is written as 5 + 4 = ? ;
	    ○ the missing numbers on the following number line are 1, 4, 7, and 10
	
	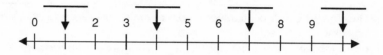
	
	    ○ the location (3, 2) on a coordinate grid is three units to the right (horizontal) and two units up (vertical).
	However, the student exhibits major errors or omissions with score 3.0 elements.

Grade 2	
Score 3.0	Not applicable.
Score 2.0	Not applicable.

Grade 1	
Score 3.0	Not applicable.
Score 2.0	Not applicable.

Grade K	
Score 3.0	Not applicable.
Score 2.0	Not applicable.

Geometry

Lines, Angles, and Geometric Objects

Grade 8		
Score 4.0	**In addition to score 3.0 performance, the student demonstrates in-depth inferences and applications that go beyond what was taught.**	
	Score 3.5	In addition to score 3.0 performance, the student demonstrates in-depth inferences and applications with partial success.
Score 3.0	**While engaged in grade-appropriate tasks, the student demonstrates an understanding of lines, angles, and geometric objects by . . .** • classifying lines, rays, segments, angles, and two- and three-dimensional objects (*e.g., explaining and exemplifying the distinctions between various geometric objects*); • constructing polygons, angles, angle bisectors, perpendicular bisectors, segments, and lines (parallel and perpendicular) (*e.g., explaining and modeling the steps required to construct an angle bisector*); • applying the Pythagorean theorem and its converse (*e.g., explaining and modeling the steps required to apply the Pythagorean theorem and its converse*); and • applying the triangle inequality theorem (*e.g., explaining and modeling the steps required to apply the triangle inequality theorem*). **The student exhibits no major errors or omissions.**	
	Score 2.5	The student exhibits no major errors or omissions regarding the score 2.0 elements and partial knowledge of the score 3.0 elements.

Score 2.0	**The student exhibits no major errors or omissions regarding the simpler details and processes, such as . . .**
	 • recognizing and recalling specific terminology (*e.g., triangle inequality theorem, converse, bisector*);
	 • recognizing and recalling the accuracy of basic solutions and information, such as . . .
	    ○ three-dimensional objects have depth, whereas two-dimensional objects do not;
	    ○ an angle bisector divides an angle in half;
	    ○ the Pythagorean theorem can be expressed as $a^2 + b^2 = c^2$; and
	    ○ for a triangle with sides of 4, 7, and 10, 7 is less than the sum of the other two sides $(4 + 10 = 14)$ and is greater than the difference between the other two sides $(10 - 4 = 6)$.
	 However, the student exhibits major errors or omissions with score 3.0 elements.	

	Score 1.5	The student demonstrates partial knowledge of the score 2.0 elements but major errors or omissions regarding the score 3.0 elements.
Score 1.0	**With help, the student demonstrates partial understanding of some of the score 2.0 elements and some of the score 3.0 elements.**	
	Score 0.5	With help, the student demonstrates partial understanding of some of the score 2.0 elements but not the score 3.0 elements.
Score 0.0	**Even with help, the student demonstrates no understanding or skill.**	

Grade 7	
Score 3.0	**While engaged in grade-appropriate tasks, the student demonstrates an understanding of lines, angles, and geometric objects by . . .** • classifying lines, rays, segments, and angles (*e.g., explaining and exemplifying distinctions between various geometric figures*); • analyzing geometric relationships among two- and three-dimensional objects (*e.g., explaining and exemplifying how a two-dimensional figure is a representation of a three-dimensional object*); and • drawing geometric figures when given specified components (such as base/height) (*e.g., explaining and modeling the steps required to draw a geometric figure when given partial dimensions—such as length of the base and height of a triangle*). **The student exhibits no major errors or omissions.**

Score 2.0	**The student exhibits no major errors or omissions regarding the simpler details and processes, such as . . .**
	• recognizing and recalling specific terminology (*e.g., base, Pythagorean theorem, hypotenuse*); and
	• recognizing and recalling the accuracy of basic solutions and information, such as . . .
	   ◦ angles of more than 180° are called reflex angles;
	   ◦ two-dimensional figures are often representations of three-dimensional objects; and
	   ◦ the Pythagorean theorem can be used to determine the length of an unknown side.
	However, the student exhibits major errors or omissions with score 3.0 elements.

Grade 6	
Score 3.0	**While engaged in grade-appropriate tasks, the student demonstrates an understanding of lines, angles, and geometric objects by . . .** • classifying two- and three-dimensional figures based on attributes, properties, and component parts (*e.g., explaining and exemplifying distinctions between component parts of various geometric figures*); • classifying various triangles (*e.g., explaining and exemplifying distinctions between types of triangles, such as equilateral, isosceles, scalene, right, acute, obtuse, equiangular*); and • drawing quadrilaterals and triangles based on given information (*e.g., explaining and modeling the steps required to draw a quadrilateral based on given information*). **The student exhibits no major errors or omissions.**

Score 2.0	**The student exhibits no major errors or omissions regarding the simpler details and processes, such as . . .**
	• recognizing and recalling specific terminology (*e.g., right triangle, obtuse triangle, acute triangle*); and
	• recognizing and recalling the accuracy of basic solutions and information, such as . . .
	   ◦ a hexagon is a two-dimensional figure with six sides;
	   ◦ an obtuse triangle has one angle greater than 90°; and
	   ◦ a rhomboid is a parallelogram with adjacent sides of unequal lengths.
	However, the student exhibits major errors or omissions with score 3.0 elements.

Grade 5	
Score 3.0	**While engaged in grade-appropriate tasks, the student demonstrates an understanding of lines, angles, and geometric objects by . . .** • classifying polygons (regular and congruent) and angles (right, obtuse, acute, and straight) (*e.g., explaining and exemplifying distinctions between regular and congruent polygons*); • drawing triangles (equilateral, isosceles, scalene, right, acute, obtuse, equiangular) and polygons (pentagons, hexagons) (*e.g., explaining and modeling the steps required to draw a scalene triangle*); and

Score 3.0 (continued)	• measuring and drawing angles, perpendicular/parallel lines, rectangles, triangles, and circles (including radius and diameter) with appropriate tools (*e.g., explaining and modeling the steps required to draw a 155° angle with a protractor*). **The student exhibits no major errors or omissions.**

Score 2.0	**The student exhibits no major errors or omissions regarding the simpler details and processes, such as . . .**
	• recognizing and recalling specific terminology (*e.g., isosceles, scalene, equiangular*); and
	• recognizing and recalling the accuracy of basic solutions and information, such as . . .
	   ◦ an obtuse angle is greater than 90° and less than 180°;
	   ◦ an equiangular triangle has three angles that are equal; and
	   ◦ the following lines are parallel
	
	However, the student exhibits major errors or omissions with score 3.0 elements.

Grade 4

Score 3.0	**While engaged in grade-appropriate tasks, the student demonstrates an understanding of lines, angles, and geometric objects by . . .** • drawing and comparing parallelograms, rhombuses, and trapezoids (*e.g., explaining and modeling the steps required to draw a parallelogram; explaining basic distinctions between parallelograms, rhombuses, and trapezoids*); • drawing and comparing parallel, perpendicular, and oblique lines (*e.g., explaining and modeling the steps required to draw oblique lines; explaining basic distinctions between parallel, perpendicular, and oblique lines*); • drawing and comparing rays, right angles, acute angles, obtuse angles, and straight angles (*e.g., explaining and modeling the steps required to draw a ray; explaining basic distinctions between rays and various angles*); and • constructing and comparing cubes and prisms (*e.g., explaining and modeling the steps required to construct a prism; explaining basic distinctions between cubes and prisms*). **The student exhibits no major errors or omissions.**

Score 2.0	**The student exhibits no major errors or omissions regarding the simpler details and processes, such as . . .**
	• recognizing and recalling specific terminology (*e.g., oblique, ray, acute angle*); and
	• recognizing and recalling the accuracy of basic solutions and information, such as . . .
	   ◦ a parallelogram is a shape in which both pairs of opposite sides are parallel;
	   ◦ two lines are considered to be perpendicular if one falls on the other in a way that creates four 90° angles;
	   ◦ a ray is a half-line; and
	   ◦ a prism is a solid figure whose bases have the same size and shape and are parallel to one another, and each of whose sides is a parallelogram.
	However, the student exhibits major errors or omissions with score 3.0 elements.

Grade 3

Score 3.0	**While engaged in grade-appropriate tasks, the student demonstrates an understanding of lines, angles, and geometric objects by . . .** • analyzing cubes, spheres, prisms, pyramids, cones, and cylinders (*e.g., explaining the basic characteristics of a pyramid*); and • describing, drawing, and comparing line segments and lines (*e.g., explaining basic distinctions between a line and a line segment*). **The student exhibits no major errors or omissions.**

Score 2.0	The student exhibits no major errors or omissions regarding the simpler details and processes, such as . . .
	• recognizing and recalling specific terminology (*e.g., sphere, pyramid, cylinder*); and
	• recognizing and recalling the accuracy of basic solutions and information, such as . . .
	  ○ a sphere has no sharp points or flat surfaces; and
	  ○ a line segment is a part of a line bounded by two end points.
	However, the student exhibits major errors or omissions with score 3.0 elements.

Grade 2

Score 3.0	While engaged in grade-appropriate tasks, the student demonstrates an understanding of lines, angles, and geometric objects by . . . • describing basic attributes of two-dimensional (plane) and three-dimensional (solid) figures (*e.g., explaining basic distinctions between two- and three-dimensional figures*); • drawing circles, squares, rectangles, and triangles (*e.g., explaining and modeling the steps required to draw a triangle*); • describing quadrilaterals, pentagons, hexagons, and octagons (*e.g., explaining basic characteristics of a hexagon, such as number of sides, lengths of sides, angles*); and • constructing cubes and rectangular prisms (*e.g., explaining and modeling the steps required to construct a rectangular prism*). **The student exhibits no major errors or omissions.**

Score 2.0	The student exhibits no major errors or omissions regarding the simpler details and processes, such as . . .
	• recognizing and recalling specific terminology (*e.g., quadrilateral, pentagon, hexagon*); and
	• recognizing and recalling the accuracy of basic solutions and information, such as . . .
	  ○ a cube has six sides;
	  ○ a square has four equal sides and each angle is a right angle;
	  ○ pentagons have five sides; and
	  ○ a cube looks like the following picture
	
	However, the student exhibits major errors or omissions with score 3.0 elements.

Grade 1

Score 3.0	While engaged in grade-appropriate tasks, the student demonstrates an understanding of lines, angles, and geometric objects by . . . • describing why objects are two- or three-dimensional (*e.g., three-dimensional objects have depth like solid figures that can be found in the environment*); • using rules to classify and sort plane and solid objects by position, shape, size, roundness, and other attributes (*e.g., classifying all plane figures with four sides of equal length as squares*); and • describing triangles, rectangles, squares, and circles (*e.g., explaining basic characteristics of a rectangle, such as number of sides, differences between lengths of sides*). **The student exhibits no major errors or omissions.**

Score 2.0	The student exhibits no major errors or omissions regarding the simpler details and processes, such as . . .
	• recognizing and recalling specific terminology (*e.g., cube, depth, side*); and
	• recognizing and recalling the accuracy of basic solutions and information, such as . . .
	  ○ pictures of things are different from the real thing because they are flat;
	  ○ all triangles have three sides; and
	  ○ circles have no angles.
	However, the student exhibits major errors or omissions with score 3.0 elements.

	Grade K
Score 3.0	**While engaged in grade-appropriate tasks, the student demonstrates an understanding of lines, angles, and geometric objects by . . .** • creating rectangles, squares, circles, and triangles using shapes or drawings (*e.g., demonstrating how to combine shapes to create a new one, such as combining a circle and triangle to make a cone*); and • sorting objects by size, position, shape, roundness, number of vertices, and other attributes (*e.g., grouping all triangles together because they have three sides*). **The student exhibits no major errors or omissions.**
Score 2.0	**The student exhibits no major errors or omissions regarding the simpler details and processes, such as . . .** • recognizing and recalling specific terminology (*e.g., triangle, size, shape*); and • recognizing and recalling the accuracy of basic solutions and information, such as . . . ◦ squares can be combined to form other types of shapes; and ◦ when grouped by number of sides, rectangles and squares can be grouped together. **However, the student exhibits major errors or omissions with score 3.0 elements.**

Transformations, Congruency, and Similarity

		Grade 8
Score 4.0		**In addition to score 3.0 performance, the student demonstrates in-depth inferences and applications that go beyond what was taught.**
	Score 3.5	In addition to score 3.0 performance, the student demonstrates in-depth inferences and applications with partial success.
Score 3.0		**While engaged in grade-appropriate tasks, the student demonstrates an understanding of transformations, congruency, and similarity by . . .** • drawing a variety of transformations of figures (dilation, translation, reflection, rotation) (*e.g., explaining and modeling the steps required to draw a dilation of a given figure*); • analyzing relationships between basic properties of geometric shapes (*e.g., explaining and exemplifying how two different types of geometric shapes can have the same perimeter*); and • drawing congruent angles, congruent segments, and congruent figures (*e.g., explaining and modeling the steps required to draw a figure that is congruent to another one*). **The student exhibits no major errors or omissions.**
	Score 2.5	The student exhibits no major errors or omissions regarding the score 2.0 elements and partial knowledge of the score 3.0 elements.
Score 2.0		**The student exhibits no major errors or omissions regarding the simpler details and processes, such as . . .** • recognizing and recalling specific terminology (*e.g., congruent angle, congruent segment*); and • recognizing and recalling the accuracy of basic solutions and information, such as . . . 　○ the following picture shows a dilation and rotation 　○ the perimeter of one figure might be twice that of another figure; and 　○ a line segment with endpoints (–3, 2) and (1, 4) is congruent to one with endpoints (–5, –5) and (–1, –3). **However, the student exhibits major errors or omissions with score 3.0 elements.**
	Score 1.5	The student demonstrates partial knowledge of the score 2.0 elements but major errors or omissions regarding the score 3.0 elements.
Score 1.0		**With help, the student demonstrates partial understanding of some of the score 2.0 elements and some of the score 3.0 elements.**
	Score 0.5	With help, the student demonstrates partial understanding of some of the score 2.0 elements but not the score 3.0 elements.
Score 0.0		**Even with help, the student demonstrates no understanding or skill.**
		Grade 7
Score 3.0		**While engaged in grade-appropriate tasks, the student demonstrates an understanding of transformations, congruency, and similarity by . . .** • drawing transformations of figures (translation, reflection, rotation) (*e.g., explaining and modeling the steps required to draw a reflection of a given figure*);

Score 3.0 (continued)	• graphing transformations of quadrilaterals on the Cartesian plane by plotting the vertices (*e.g., explaining and modeling the steps required to graph a transformation of a given quadrilateral on the Cartesian plane*); and • graphing figures that are similar to other figures using dilations (*e.g., explaining and modeling the steps required to graph a dilation of a given figure*). **The student exhibits no major errors or omissions.**

Score 2.0	**The student exhibits no major errors or omissions regarding the simpler details and processes, such as . . .**
	• recognizing and recalling specific terminology (*e.g., dilation, vertices*); and
	• recognizing and recalling the accuracy of basic solutions and information, such as . . .
	  ◦ the following picture shows a translation
	
	  ◦ a quadrilateral with vertices in quadrant I at the following points (1, 1), (1, 5), (2, 4), and (4, 5) can be reflected in quadrant IV at the following points (1, –1), (1, –5), (2, –4), and (4, –5); and
	  ◦ the following picture shows a dilation
	
	However, the student exhibits major errors or omissions with score 3.0 elements.

Grade 6	
Score 3.0	**While engaged in grade-appropriate tasks, the student demonstrates an understanding of transformations, congruency, and similarity by . . .** • describing line and rotational symmetries of various polygons (*e.g., explaining and exemplifying distinctions between line and rotational symmetry; explaining how to determine the order of rotational symmetry of a given polygon*); • classifying congruent objects by their properties (*e.g., explaining and exemplifying the characteristics that make two objects congruent*); • drawing two-dimensional shapes that are similar (*e.g., explaining and exemplifying how two different two-dimensional shapes are similar*); and • drawing translations and reflections of shapes (*e.g., explaining and modeling the steps required to draw a translation of a given shape*). **The student exhibits no major errors or omissions.**

Score 2.0	**The student exhibits no major errors or omissions regarding the simpler details and processes, such as . . .**
	• recognizing and recalling specific terminology (*e.g., reflection, translation*); and
	• recognizing and recalling the accuracy of basic solutions and information, such as . . .
	  ◦ some polygons can be rotated 90° and still be an exact match of the original position;
	  ◦ triangles can be classified as congruent if they have a corresponding side, angle, side that are the same;

Score 2.0 (*continued*)	○ the following two dimensional shapes are similar ○ the following shapes are reflections of each other **However, the student exhibits major errors or omissions with score 3.0 elements.**
Grade 5	
Score 3.0	**While engaged in grade-appropriate tasks, the student demonstrates an understanding of transformations, congruency, and similarity by . . .** • determining whether reflectional or rotational symmetry exists between various geometric figures (*e.g., explaining and exemplifying how to determine if two figures exhibit rotational symmetry*); and • predicting the results of a flip (reflection), turn (rotation), or slide (translation) of various geometric figures (*e.g., describing the new position and location of a given figure after a slide in a given direction, such as to the right, and a rotation of a given degree, such as 90°*). **The student exhibits no major errors or omissions.**

Score 2.0	**The student exhibits no major errors or omissions regarding the simpler details and processes, such as . . .**
	• recognizing and recalling specific terminology (*e.g., midpoint, shape symmetry*); and
	• recognizing and recalling the accuracy of basic solutions and information, such as . . .
	  ○ one figure is a reflection of another if it is the mirror opposite of the first; and
	  ○ the first figure (below) rotated 90° to the right would look like the second figure
	
	However, the student exhibits major errors or omissions with score 3.0 elements.

Grade 4	
Score 3.0	**While engaged in grade-appropriate tasks, the student demonstrates an understanding of transformations, congruency, and similarity by . . .** • demonstrating slides (translations), flips (reflections), and turns (rotations) using quadrilaterals, pentagons, hexagons, and octagons (*e.g., explaining and exemplifying basic distinctions between sliding, flipping, and turning a pentagon*);

Score 3.0 (*continued*)	• drawing lines of symmetry in quadrilaterals, pentagons, hexagons, and octagons (*e.g., explaining and exemplifying how to determine where to draw each line of symmetry in a quadrilateral*); and • describing how to determine whether two quadrilaterals are congruent (*e.g., explaining and exemplifying the characteristics that two quadrilaterals need to have in common to be considered congruent*). **The student exhibits no major errors or omissions.**

Score 2.0	**The student exhibits no major errors or omissions regarding the simpler details and processes, such as . . .**
	
	 • recognizing and recalling specific terminology (*e.g., rotation, flip transformation*); and
	
	 • recognizing and recalling the accuracy of basic solutions and information, such as . . .
	     ○ the following picture shows a hexagon that has been turned
	
	     ○ the following picture shows a line of symmetry in a pentagon
	
	     ○ two quadrilaterals are congruent if they have corresponding sides that are the same.
	
	 However, the student exhibits major errors or omissions with score 3.0 elements.

Grade 3	
Score 3.0	**While engaged in grade-appropriate tasks, the student demonstrates an understanding of transformations, congruency, and similarity by . . .** • demonstrating slides (translations), flips (reflections), and turns (rotations) using triangles, squares, and rectangles (*e.g., explaining and exemplifying what happens to a triangle when it is flipped in a given direction*); • drawing lines of symmetry in triangles, squares, and rectangles (*e.g., explaining and exemplifying basic distinctions between lines of symmetry in triangles, squares, and rectangles, such as number of lines, location of lines*); and • drawing a shape that is congruent to another (*e.g., explaining and modeling how to draw a shape that is congruent to another*). **The student exhibits no major errors or omissions.**
Score 2.0	**The student exhibits no major errors or omissions regarding the simpler details and processes, such as . . .** • recognizing and recalling specific terminology (*e.g., shape similarity, shape transformation*); and • recognizing and recalling the accuracy of basic solutions and information, such as . . . ○ the following picture shows a slide

Score 2.0 (continued)	○ the following picture shows the lines of symmetry in a square 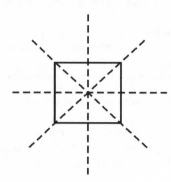 ○ the following picture shows congruent shapes 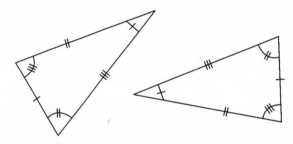 **However, the student exhibits major errors or omissions with score 3.0 elements.**
	Grade 2
Score 3.0	**While engaged in grade-appropriate tasks, the student demonstrates an understanding of transformations, congruency, and similarity by . . .** • creating designs that exhibit line symmetry (*e.g., explaining and exemplifying how a design exhibits line symmetry*); • describing the results of changing the position (transformation) of objects or shapes by sliding (translation), turning (rotation), or flipping (reflection) (*e.g., explaining and exemplifying what happens to the position of a given shape when it is turned—for example, the top of the shape moves to the side*); and • explaining why two shapes in any position are congruent (*e.g., describing how a second shape can be manipulated so it matches exactly when placed over the first shape*). **The student exhibits no major errors or omissions.**

Score 2.0	**The student exhibits no major errors or omissions regarding the simpler details and processes, such as . . .**
	• recognizing and recalling specific terminology (*e.g., position, congruent*); and
	• recognizing and recalling the accuracy of basic solutions and information, such as . . .
	  ○ the following picture has line symmetry
	
	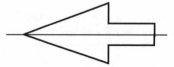
	
	  ○ flipping a shape creates a mirror image; and
	  ○ shapes can be congruent no matter what their position might be.
	However, the student exhibits major errors or omissions with score 3.0 elements.

	Grade 1
Score 3.0	**While engaged in grade-appropriate tasks, the student demonstrates an understanding of transformations, congruency, and similarity by . . .** • transferring shape combinations from one dimension to another (*e.g., explaining and modeling how to represent a given three-dimensional object with a two-dimensional figure*); • finding real-life examples of line symmetry (*e.g., explaining how a real-life example exhibits line symmetry*); and • changing the position of objects or shapes by sliding (translation) and turning (rotation) (*e.g., explaining and exemplifying what has happened to the position of an object that has been turned*). **The student exhibits no major errors or omissions.**

Score 2.0	**The student exhibits no major errors or omissions regarding the simpler details and processes, such as . . .**
	• recognizing and recalling specific terminology (*e.g., sliding, turning*); and
	• recognizing and recalling the accuracy of basic solutions and information, such as . . .
	  ◦ a cone can be represented by a triangle
	
	  ◦ the reflection of a mountain in a lake where the base of the mountain meets the top of the reflection is an example of line symmetry;
	  ◦ the following example shows a rectangle that has been turned on its side
	
	However, the student exhibits major errors or omissions with score 3.0 elements.

	Grade K
Score 3.0	**While engaged in grade-appropriate tasks, the student demonstrates an understanding of transformations, congruency, and similarity by . . .** • finding like shapes in the environment (*e.g., identifying several like shapes that can be found in the environment, such as in the classroom, school, home*); • finding shapes that are symmetrical (*e.g., identifying several shapes that are symmetrical among groups of shapes that are both symmetrical and nonsymmetrical*); and • finding two equal sets of objects in different spatial arrangements (*e.g., identifying equal sets of objects in a variety of spatial arrangements among groups of objects that are both identical and nonidentical*). **The student exhibits no major errors or omissions.**

Score 2.0	**The student exhibits no major errors or omissions regarding the simpler details and processes, such as . . .**
	• recognizing and recalling specific terminology (*e.g., above, below*); and
	• recognizing and recalling the accuracy of basic solutions and information, such as . . .
	○ an ice cream cone and a traffic cone have the same shape;
	○ the following triangles are symmetrical

	○ the following sets of objects are equal

	However, the student exhibits major errors or omissions with score 3.0 elements.

Measurement

Measurement Systems

	Grade 8	
Score 4.0	**In addition to score 3.0 performance, the student demonstrates in-depth inferences and applications that go beyond what was taught.**	
	Score 3.5	In addition to score 3.0 performance, the student demonstrates in-depth inferences and applications with partial success.
Score 3.0	**While engaged in grade-appropriate tasks, the student demonstrates an understanding of measurement systems by . . .** • selecting and applying appropriate units (U.S. customary and metric) and tools to estimate and measure length, weight, and capacity (*e.g., explaining and modeling how to use a variety of tools to measure the weight of a given object*); • converting weight/mass between U.S. customary and metric systems (*e.g., explaining and modeling the steps required to convert the weight of a given object between U.S. customary and metric systems—for example, pound to kilogram*); and • converting capacity/volume between U.S. customary and metric systems (*e.g., explaining and modeling the steps required to convert the capacity of a given object between U.S. customary and metric systems—for example, milliliter to teaspoon*). **The student exhibits no major errors or omissions.**	
	Score 2.5	The student exhibits no major errors or omissions regarding the score 2.0 elements and partial knowledge of the score 3.0 elements.

Score 2.0	**The student exhibits no major errors or omissions regarding the simpler details and processes, such as . . .**
	• recognizing and recalling specific terminology (*e.g., precision, measures of capacity [U.S./metric]*); and
	• recognizing and recalling the accuracy of basic solutions and information, such as . . .
	  ◦ if object A weighs 5 kilograms and object B weighs almost two-and-a-half times as much, how much does B weigh? answer: approximately 12.5 kilograms;
	  ◦ 1 ton = 907.18 kilograms; and
	  ◦ 1 cup = 236.59 milliliters.
	However, the student exhibits major errors or omissions with score 3.0 elements.	

	Score 1.5	The student demonstrates partial knowledge of the score 2.0 elements but major errors or omissions regarding the score 3.0 elements.
Score 1.0	**With help, the student demonstrates partial understanding of some of the score 2.0 elements and some of the score 3.0 elements.**	
	Score 0.5	With help, the student demonstrates partial understanding of some of the score 2.0 elements but not the score 3.0 elements.
Score 0.0	**Even with help, the student demonstrates no understanding or skill.**	

Grade 7	
Score 3.0	**While engaged in grade-appropriate tasks, the student demonstrates an understanding of measurement systems by . . .** • selecting and applying appropriate units (U.S. customary and metric) and tools to estimate and measure length, weight, and capacity (*e.g., explaining and modeling how to apply the appropriate unit of measurement, both U.S. customary and metric, to measure capacity—for example, gram for smaller units of weight*); • converting length between U.S. customary and metric systems (*e.g., explaining and modeling the steps required to convert the length of a given object between U.S. customary and metric systems—for example, foot to meter, kilometer to mile*); and • converting common measurements to equivalent measurements within the same system (*e.g., explaining and modeling the steps required to convert a given measurement to an equivalent one within the same system—for example, quart to gallon in the U.S. customary system and millimeter to centimeter in the metric system*). **The student exhibits no major errors or omissions.**

Score 2.0	**The student exhibits no major errors or omissions regarding the simpler details and processes, such as . . .**
	• recognizing and recalling specific terminology (*e.g., kilogram, metric ton*); and
	• recognizing and recalling the accuracy of basic solutions and information, such as . . .
	  ◦ measuring cups are often used to measure ingredients in cooking;
	  ◦ 5 miles = 8.05 kilometers; and
	  ◦ 1 tablespoon = 3 teaspoons.
	However, the student exhibits major errors or omissions with score 3.0 elements.

Grade 6	
Score 3.0	**While engaged in grade-appropriate tasks, the student demonstrates an understanding of measurement systems by . . .** • selecting and applying appropriate units and tools to measure time and temperature (*e.g., explaining and modeling how various tools are used to measure temperature; explaining basic distinctions between various tools used to measure temperature and which tool would be the best one to use to safely measure the temperature of a given object*); • selecting and applying appropriate units and tools to measure length, weight, and capacity using U.S. customary and metric units (*e.g., explaining and exemplifying basic distinctions between various tools that can be used to measure the capacity of a given object*); and • converting temperature between °F and °C (*e.g., explaining and modeling the steps required to convert a given temperature from Fahrenheit to Celsius*). **The student exhibits no major errors or omissions.**

Score 2.0	**The student exhibits no major errors or omissions regarding the simpler details and processes, such as . . .**
	• recognizing and recalling specific terminology (*e.g., square units, mile, kilometer*); and
	• recognizing and recalling the accuracy of basic solutions and information, such as . . .
	  ◦ an infrared thermometer could be used to safely determine the surface temperature of a frying pan on a stove;
	  ◦ distances between cities are measured in miles or kilometers; and
	  ◦ 75° Celsius = 167° Fahrenheit.
	However, the student exhibits major errors or omissions with score 3.0 elements.

Grade 5	
Score 3.0	**While engaged in grade-appropriate tasks, the student demonstrates an understanding of measurement systems by . . .** • selecting and applying appropriate units and tools to measure time and temperature (*e.g., explaining and modeling how to use various tools to measure time; explaining and exemplifying basic distinctions between various tools used to measure time and which tool would be the best one to use to measure time in a given situation*);

Score 3.0 (continued)	• selecting and applying appropriate units and tools to measure length using U.S. customary and metric units (*e.g., explaining basic distinctions between various tools that can be used to measure the length of a given object*); • converting units of measure within the same system (larger unit to smaller) (*e.g., explaining and modeling the steps required to convert a unit of measure from larger to smaller within the same system—for example, tablespoon to teaspoon in the U.S. customary system or meter to centimeter in the metric system*); and • comparing various temperatures (°F and °C) (*e.g., comparing the boiling point of water in both Fahrenheit and Celsius; comparing the freezing point of water in both Fahrenheit and Celsius; comparing classroom temperature in both Fahrenheit and Celsius*). **The student exhibits no major errors or omissions.**
Score 2.0	**The student exhibits no major errors or omissions regarding the simpler details and processes, such as . . .** • recognizing and recalling specific terminology (*e.g., Fahrenheit, Celsius*); and • recognizing and recalling the accuracy of basic solutions and information, such as . . . ○ a thermometer calibrated for temperatures between 50 and 500 degrees Fahrenheit would not be capable of measuring the temperature of ice water; ○ a room in a building is usually measured in feet and inches; ○ 10 centimeters is 100 millimeters; and ○ the boiling point of water is 212°F/100°C. **However, the student exhibits major errors or omissions with score 3.0 elements.**
Grade 4	
Score 3.0	**While engaged in grade-appropriate tasks, the student demonstrates an understanding of measurement systems by . . .** • selecting and applying appropriate units and tools to measure time and temperature (°F and °C) (*e.g., determining the appropriate unit—for example, days—to measure the length of time for a given event*); • selecting and applying appropriate units (U.S. customary and metric) and tools to measure length (*e.g., determining the appropriate unit—for example, feet—to measure the length of a given distance*); • estimating and measuring length to the nearest 1/4 inch, 1/8 inch, and millimeter (*e.g., explaining and exemplifying the rules governing measuring to the nearest 1/4 inch—for example, explaining when to round up, when to round down*); and • calculating elapsed time (hour and minute) (*e.g., explaining and modeling the steps required to calculate elapsed time to the hour and minute*). **The student exhibits no major errors or omissions.**
Score 2.0	**The student exhibits no major errors or omissions regarding the simpler details and processes, such as . . .** • recognizing and recalling specific terminology (*e.g., equivalent representation, unit conversion, time zone*); and • recognizing and recalling the accuracy of basic solutions and information, such as . . . ○ a 100-yard dash should be measured by a stopwatch in seconds; ○ a person should be measured by a tape measure in feet and inches; ○ a pencil that is between five-and-one-quarter inches and five-and-one-half inches long that is less than halfway to five-and-one-half inches measured to the nearest quarter inch would be five-and-one-quarter inches; and ○ the elapsed time between 10:15 a.m. and 6:35 p.m. is 8 hours 20 minutes. **However, the student exhibits major errors or omissions with score 3.0 elements.**
Grade 3	
Score 3.0	**While engaged in grade-appropriate tasks, the student demonstrates an understanding of measurement systems by . . .**

Score 3.0 (continued)	• estimating/measuring length, weight, and capacity in metric and standard units (*e.g., measuring multiple objects and distances with both a metric and a standard ruler to determine the length of each object/distance in both inches and centimeters; weighing multiple objects on a scale to determine the weight of each object in both pounds and kilograms; measuring the volume of various containers using both metric and standard measuring cups to determine the capacity of each container in both cups and milliliters*); • determining elapsed time to the day with calendars and to the hour with a clock (*e.g., using a clock to find out how many hours the class was on a school field trip*); and • comparing and telling time using both analog and digital clocks to the nearest minute using a.m. and p.m. (*e.g., comparing various given times on both analog and digital clocks and specifying whether each time is a.m. or p.m.*). **The student exhibits no major errors or omissions.**

Score 2.0	**The student exhibits no major errors or omissions regarding the simpler details and processes, such as . . .**
	 • recognizing and recalling specific terminology (*e.g., English system of measurement, metric system, elapsed time*); and
	 • recognizing and recalling the accuracy of basic solutions and information, such as . . .
	   ◦ a large rock weighs two pounds, so a rock that is half the size should weigh about one pound;
	   ◦ a three-day vacation that starts on Monday would end on Wednesday; and
	   ◦ 3:59 in the afternoon is 3:59 p.m.
	 However, the student exhibits major errors or omissions with score 3.0 elements.

Grade 2

Score 3.0	**While engaged in grade-appropriate tasks, the student demonstrates an understanding of measurement systems by . . .** • describing the use of basic measurement tools (ruler, yardstick, meterstick, tape measure) (*e.g., explaining when a yardstick should be used to measure a distance or length of an object*); • measuring/estimating length to the nearest inch/foot/yard/centimeter/meter (*e.g., measuring multiple objects and distances to the nearest inch to determine the length of each object/distance*); • measuring/estimating capacity using cups and pints (*e.g., measuring the volume of various containers in cups and pints to determine the capacity of each container*); and • comparing and telling time using both analog and digital clocks to the nearest minute (*e.g., comparing various given times on both analog and digital clocks*). **The student exhibits no major errors or omissions.**

Score 2.0	**The student exhibits no major errors or omissions regarding the simpler details and processes, such as . . .**
	 • recognizing and recalling specific terminology (*e.g., time interval, standard measures of time, standard measures of weight*); and
	 • recognizing and recalling the accuracy of basic solutions and information, such as . . .
	   ◦ an object greater than three feet in length cannot be measured on a single yardstick;
	   ◦ a plant that measures three feet and four inches to the nearest foot is three feet;
	   ◦ a container with two cups of liquid would also measure one pint of liquid; and
	   ◦ 4:35:34 to the nearest minute would be 4:36.
	 However, the student exhibits major errors or omissions with score 3.0 elements.

Grade 1

Score 3.0	**While engaged in grade-appropriate tasks, the student demonstrates an understanding of measurement systems by . . .** • measuring/estimating length to nearest inch/centimeter (*e.g., measuring multiple objects and distances to the nearest centimeter to determine the length of each object/distance*);

Score 3.0 (continued)	• comparing and ordering objects according to length/capacity/weight using nonstandard units (*e.g., using paper clips to compare the lengths of several objects*); • telling time using both analog and digital clocks to the nearest half hour (*e.g., verbalizing the correct time to the nearest half hour on both analog and digital clocks; writing down the correct time to the nearest half hour as displayed on both analog and digital clocks*); and • locating days, dates, and months on a calendar (*e.g., finding a given date, such as February 23, on a calendar*). **The student exhibits no major errors or omissions.**
Score 2.0	**The student exhibits no major errors or omissions regarding the simpler details and processes, such as . . .** • recognizing and recalling specific terminology (*e.g., measuring cup, standard measures of length*); and • recognizing and recalling the accuracy of basic solutions and information, such as . . . ◦ an object that is five-and-three-quarter inches long measured to the nearest inch would be six inches long; ◦ object A is three pencils long, object B is one pencil long, and object C is five pencils long; ordered from shortest to longest: B, A, C; ◦ the small hand is on the 2, and the large hand is on the 5; the time at the nearest half-hour is 2:30; and ◦ October is before November and after September on the calendar used in the United States. **However, the student exhibits major errors or omissions with score 3.0 elements.**
Grade K	
Score 3.0	**While engaged in grade-appropriate tasks, the student demonstrates an understanding of measurement systems by . . .** • using a thermometer to measure temperature (*e.g., reading the temperature of the classroom on a wall-mounted thermometer*); • applying basic concepts of time (*e.g., counting the number of days until a class party*); and • comparing a variety of objects (length, height, capacity, weight) (*e.g., determining which of two objects weights more or less than the other object*). **The student exhibits no major errors or omissions.**
Score 2.0	**The student exhibits no major errors or omissions regarding the simpler details and processes, such as . . .** • recognizing and recalling specific terminology (*e.g., longer than/as long as, shorter than/as short as*); and • recognizing and recalling the accuracy of basic solutions and information, such as . . . ◦ one thermometer placed inside the classroom and one outside the classroom will show if it is hotter inside or outside; ◦ Friday comes after Thursday and before Saturday; and ◦ the larger cup holds more water than the smaller cup. **However, the student exhibits major errors or omissions with score 3.0 elements.**

Perimeter, Area, and Volume

	Grade 8	
Score 4.0	**In addition to score 3.0 performance, the student demonstrates in-depth inferences and applications that go beyond what was taught.**	
	Score 3.5	In addition to score 3.0 performance, the student demonstrates in-depth inferences and applications with partial success.
Score 3.0	**While engaged in grade-appropriate tasks, the student demonstrates an understanding of perimeter, area, and volume by . . .** • using formulas to find the perimeter and area of regular and irregular plane figures (*e.g., explaining and modeling the steps required to find the area of an irregular polygon*); • describing surface area and volume using appropriate units of measure (*e.g., explaining and exemplifying why surface area is measured in square units and volume is measured in cubic units*); • using formulas to find surface area and volume of rectangular prisms, cylinders, and pyramids (*e.g., explaining and modeling the steps required to find the volume of a cylinder*); and • finding the ratios of the perimeters and areas of similar triangles, trapezoids, and parallelograms (*e.g., explaining and modeling the steps required to find the ratios of the areas of similar parallelograms*). **The student exhibits no major errors or omissions.**	
	Score 2.5	The student exhibits no major errors or omissions regarding the score 2.0 elements and partial knowledge of the score 3.0 elements.

Score 2.0	**The student exhibits no major errors or omissions regarding the simpler details and processes, such as . . .**
	• recognizing and recalling specific terminology (*e.g., volume formula for cylinder, volume formula for pyramid, volume formula for prism*); and
	• recognizing and recalling the accuracy of basic solutions and information, such as . . .
	  ◦ the formula for finding the perimeter of a regular polygon is *Perimeter = the sum of the lengths of all the sides*;
	  ◦ the volume of a cube measured in centimeters would be described in cubic centimeters or cm^3;
	  ◦ the formula for finding the volume of a pyramid is *Volume = one-third times the base times the height*; and
	  ◦ the ratio of triangle 1 with a perimeter of 9 to triangle 2 with a perimeter of 15 is 3 to 5.
	However, the student exhibits major errors or omissions with score 3.0 elements.	

	Score 1.5	The student demonstrates partial knowledge of the score 2.0 elements but major errors or omissions regarding the score 3.0 elements.
Score 1.0	**With help, the student demonstrates partial understanding of some of the score 2.0 elements and some of the score 3.0 elements.**	
	Score 0.5	With help, the student demonstrates partial understanding of some of the score 2.0 elements but not the score 3.0 elements.
Score 0.0	**Even with help, the student demonstrates no understanding or skill.**	
	Grade 7	
Score 3.0	**While engaged in grade-appropriate tasks, the student demonstrates an understanding of perimeter, area, and volume by . . .** • using circumference and diameter to approximate the value of π (*e.g., explaining and exemplifying basic reasons why computing the ratio of the circumference and diameter of various circles can provide an approximation of the constant value of π*);	

Score 3.0 (continued)	• using formulas to find circumference and area of circles (*e.g., explaining and modeling the steps required to find the area of a circle*); and • using formulas to find the perimeter and area of triangles and trapezoids (*e.g., explaining and modeling the steps required to find the area of a trapezoid*). **The student exhibits no major errors or omissions.**

Score 2.0	**The student exhibits no major errors or omissions regarding the simpler details and processes, such as . . .**
	• recognizing and recalling specific terminology (*e.g., area formula for circle, circumference*); and
	• recognizing and recalling the accuracy of basic solutions and information, such as . . .
	   ○ π is a constant;
	   ○ the formula for finding the area of a circle is $A = \pi r^2$; and
	   ○ the formula for finding the area of a trapezoid is $A = ((b1 + b2) / 2) \times h$.
	However, the student exhibits major errors or omissions with score 3.0 elements.

Grade 6

Score 3.0	**While engaged in grade-appropriate tasks, the student demonstrates an understanding of perimeter, area, and volume by . . .** • determining appropriate units of measure to describe perimeter and area (*e.g., explaining and exemplifying why a given unit of measure would not be appropriate to describe perimeter—for example, using feet to describe a rectangle with sides measured in inches*); • using formulas to find perimeter and area of parallelograms and rectangles (*e.g., explaining and modeling the steps required to find the area of a parallelogram*); and • explaining the concept of π and knowing common estimates (*e.g., explaining the basic characteristics of π*). **The student exhibits no major errors or omissions.**

Score 2.0	**The student exhibits no major errors or omissions regarding the simpler details and processes, such as . . .**
	• recognizing and recalling specific terminology (*e.g., area formula for parallelogram, dimension, π*); and
	• recognizing and recalling the accuracy of basic solutions and information, such as . . .
	   ○ the area of a shape is described in square units, such as square inches, square centimeters;
	   ○ the formula for finding the area of a parallelogram is $A = b \times h$; and
	   ○ a common estimate for π is 3.14159.
	However, the student exhibits major errors or omissions with score 3.0 elements.

Grade 5

Score 3.0	**While engaged in grade-appropriate tasks, the student demonstrates an understanding of perimeter, area, and volume by . . .** • calculating perimeter of rectangles from measured dimensions (*e.g., explaining and modeling the steps required to calculate the perimeter of a rectangle with given or measured dimensions*); • using formulas to find areas of a triangle, a parallelogram, and a trapezoid from diagrams or word problems (*e.g., explaining and modeling the steps required to find the area of a trapezoid from dimensions described in a word problem*); • finding the surface area and volume of rectangular solids (*e.g., explaining and modeling the steps required to find the volume of a rectangular solid*); and • finding the area of complex shapes (*e.g., explaining and modeling how to use basic shapes to help find the area of a complex shape—for example, explaining that a hexagon can be broken into a rectangle and two triangles, the measurements of which can be used to calculate the area of each basic shape and added together to determine the area of the hexagon*). **The student exhibits no major errors or omissions.**

Score 2.0	The student exhibits no major errors or omissions regarding the simpler details and processes, such as . . .
	• recognizing and recalling specific terminology (*e.g., volume formula for rectangular solid, area formula for trapezoid, surface area*); and
	• recognizing and recalling the accuracy of basic solutions and information, such as . . .
	  ○ a rectangle with top and bottom lengths of 8 and left and right widths of 3 would have a perimeter of 22 ($P = 2l + 2w = 2(8) + 2(3) = 16 + 6 = 22$);
	  ○ a triangle with a base length of 10 and height of 7 would have an area of 35 ($A = (1/2)bh = (1/2)(10)(7) = (5)(7) = 35$);
	  ○ the formula for the volume of a rectangular solid is $V = l \times w \times h$; and
	  ○ simple shapes can be used to find the area of complex shapes.
	However, the student exhibits major errors or omissions with score 3.0 elements.

Grade 4	
Score 3.0	**While engaged in grade-appropriate tasks, the student demonstrates an understanding of perimeter, area, and volume by . . .** • using formulas to find perimeter/area of triangles, rectangles, and squares (*e.g., explaining and modeling the steps required to find the area of a triangle*); • demonstrating that shapes with the same perimeters can have different areas and shapes with same areas can have different perimeters (*e.g., explaining and exemplifying how two shapes with the same perimeter can have different areas—for example, a square with side lengths of 4 has a perimeter of 16 [Perimeter = 4 × side = 4 × 4 = 16] and an area of 16 [Area = side × side = 4 × 4 = 16]; a rectangle with top and bottom lengths of 6 and left and right widths of 2 has a perimeter of 16 [Perimeter = 2 × length + 2 × width = 2 × 6 + 2 × 2 = 12 + 4 = 16] and an area of 12 [Area = length × width = 6 × 2 = 12]*); and • using formulas to find the volume of a cube (*e.g., explaining and modeling the steps required to find the volume of a cube*). **The student exhibits no major errors or omissions.**

Score 2.0	The student exhibits no major errors or omissions regarding the simpler details and processes, such as . . .
	• recognizing and recalling specific terminology (*e.g., perimeter formula for triangle, perimeter formula for square, perimeter formula for rectangle*);
	• recognizing and recalling the accuracy of basic solutions and information, such as . . .
	  ○ the formula for finding the area of a rectangle is *Area = length × width*;
	  ○ two different shapes can have the same perimeter and different areas; and
	  ○ the formula for finding the volume of a cube is *Volume = length × width × height*).
	However, the student exhibits major errors or omissions with score 3.0 elements.

Grade 3	
Score 3.0	**While engaged in grade-appropriate tasks, the student demonstrates an understanding of perimeter, area, and volume by . . .** • finding the perimeter of a polygon (*e.g., explaining and exemplifying the basic concept of perimeter and modeling the steps required to find the perimeter of a polygon*); • estimating/calculating area using squares (*e.g., explaining and modeling how small squares with a known area can be used to help estimate the area of larger squares and rectangles*); and • estimating/calculating volume of objects using cubes (*e.g., explaining and modeling how small cubes with a known volume can be used to help estimate the volume of larger objects*). **The student exhibits no major errors or omissions.**
Score 2.0	The student exhibits no major errors or omissions regarding the simpler details and processes, such as . . . • recognizing and recalling specific terminology (*e.g., perimeter, area, volume*); and • recognizing and recalling the accuracy of basic solutions and information, such as . . .

Score 2.0 (*continued*)	○ a polygon with sides of 4, 4, 3, and 3 has a perimeter of 14; ○ using a square with a known area of 9, a larger rectangle that can fit two squares inside would have an area of 18 (*9 + 9*); and ○ using a cube with a known volume of 27, a larger object that can fit three cubes inside would have a volume of 81 (*27 + 27 + 27*). **However, the student exhibits major errors or omissions with score 3.0 elements.**
Grade 2	
Score 3.0	Not applicable.
Score 2.0	Not applicable.
Grade 1	
Score 3.0	Not applicable.
Score 2.0	Not applicable.
Grade K	
Score 3.0	Not applicable.
Score 2.0	Not applicable.

Data Analysis and Probability

Data Organization and Interpretation

	Grade 8	
Score 4.0	**In addition to score 3.0 performance, the student demonstrates in-depth inferences and applications that go beyond what was taught.**	
	Score 3.5	In addition to score 3.0 performance, the student demonstrates in-depth inferences and applications with partial success.
Score 3.0	**While engaged in grade-appropriate tasks, the student demonstrates an understanding of data organization and interpretation by . . .** • computing various measures of central tendency (mean, median, mode, range, quartiles, extremes, and outliers) (*e.g., explaining and modeling the steps required to compute extremes for a given set of data*); and • analyzing and representing data with the most appropriate graph, including box-and-whisker plot, circle graph, and scatterplot (*e.g., explaining and modeling how to represent data with a box-and-whisker plot; explaining how to interpret data depicted by a box-and-whisker plot*). **The student exhibits no major errors or omissions.**	
	Score 2.5	The student exhibits no major errors or omissions regarding the score 2.0 elements and partial knowledge of the score 3.0 elements.

Score 2.0	**The student exhibits no major errors or omissions regarding the simpler details and processes, such as . . .**
	• recognizing and recalling specific terminology (*e.g., quartile, extreme, outlier, box-and-whisker plot*); and
	• recognizing and recalling the accuracy of basic solutions and information, such as . . .
	  ○ given the ordered data set (65, 65, 70, 75, 80, 80, 85, 90, 95, 100), the lower quartile would be 70 and the upper quartile would be 90; and
	  ○ the box-and-whisker plot for the data set above would look like the following picture
	
	However, the student exhibits major errors or omissions with score 3.0 elements.	

	Score 1.5	The student demonstrates partial knowledge of the score 2.0 elements but major errors or omissions regarding the score 3.0 elements.
Score 1.0	**With help, the student demonstrates partial understanding of some of the score 2.0 elements and some of the score 3.0 elements.**	
	Score 0.5	With help, the student demonstrates partial understanding of some of the score 2.0 elements but not the score 3.0 elements.

Score 0.0	Even with help, the student demonstrates no understanding or skill.
Grade 7	
Score 3.0	**While engaged in grade-appropriate tasks, the student demonstrates an understanding of data organization and interpretation by . . .** • computing measures of central tendency (mean, median, and mode) and the range using a given set of data or graphs, including histograms, frequency tables, and stem-and-leaf plots (*e.g., explaining and modeling the steps required to compute the median of a given set of data—for example, explaining frequency tables*); • describing the effect of outliers on the mean, median, and mode (*e.g., explaining the impact outliers have on the mean of a given set of data*); and • analyzing and representing data using histograms (*e.g., explaining and modeling how to represent data with a histogram; explaining how to interpret data depicted by a histogram*). **The student exhibits no major errors or omissions.**

Score 2.0	**The student exhibits no major errors or omissions regarding the simpler details and processes, such as . . .**
	• recognizing and recalling specific terminology (*e.g., histogram, stem-and-leaf plot, range, central tendency*); and
	• recognizing and recalling the accuracy of basic solutions and information, such as . . .
	  ○ given a set of numbers {13, 18, 13, 14, 13, 16, 14, 21, 13}, the range would be 8;
	  ○ outliers can cause the mean of the data set to be inflated, that is, higher than would otherwise be expected; and
	  ○ the following histogram shows that a majority of households have two pets
	
	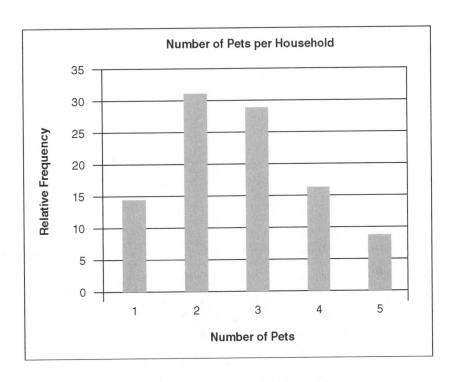
	
	However, the student exhibits major errors or omissions with score 3.0 elements.

Grade 6	
Score 3.0	**While engaged in grade-appropriate tasks, the student demonstrates an understanding of data organization and interpretation by . . .** • selecting the most appropriate measure (mean, median, mode) for a given set of data (*e.g., explaining the function and purpose for each measure of central tendency and the reason for choosing one of the measures as the most appropriate for the given set of data*); and • collecting and representing information (categorical, numerical) using bar graphs, line graphs, and circle graphs (*e.g., explaining and modeling how to systematically collect and represent information with a bar graph; explaining how to interpret information depicted by a bar graph; explaining the function and purpose for each graph and the reason for choosing one of the graphs as the most appropriate for the type of information being represented*). **The student exhibits no major errors or omissions.**

Score 2.0	**The student exhibits no major errors or omissions regarding the simpler details and processes, such as . . .**
	
	• recognizing and recalling specific terminology (*e.g., bar graph, line graph, circle graph*); and
	
	• recognizing and recalling the accuracy of basic solutions and information, such as . . .
	
	   ○ mode would be most appropriate to determine the greatest frequency of responses for categorical data; and
	
	   ○ a student's test scores for the previous week of 3.5, 2.5, 3.5, 4.0, and 3.5 can be displayed as in the following line graph
	
	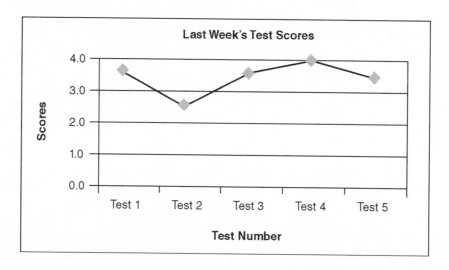
	
	However, the student exhibits major errors or omissions with score 3.0 elements.

Grade 5	
Score 3.0	**While engaged in grade-appropriate tasks, the student demonstrates an understanding of data organization and interpretation by . . .** • evaluating different representations of the same data (*e.g., explaining and exemplifying how to determine how well various representations show important aspects of the data*); • systematically collecting, representing, and analyzing categorical data using bar graphs (*e.g., explaining and modeling how to systematically collect and represent categorical data with a bar graph; explaining how to interpret information depicted by a bar graph*); and • computing mean, median, and mode for data sets (*e.g., explaining and modeling the steps required to compute the median of a given set of data*). **The student exhibits no major errors or omissions.**

Score 2.0	**The student exhibits no major errors or omissions regarding the simpler details and processes, such as . . .**
	• recognizing and recalling specific terminology (*e.g., mean, median, mode*); and
	• recognizing and recalling the accuracy of basic solutions and information, such as . . .
	    ○ a line graph shows growth over time in a manner that is easy to visualize;
	    ○ data collected about the sleeping habits of the classroom could be displayed in a bar graph like the following
	
	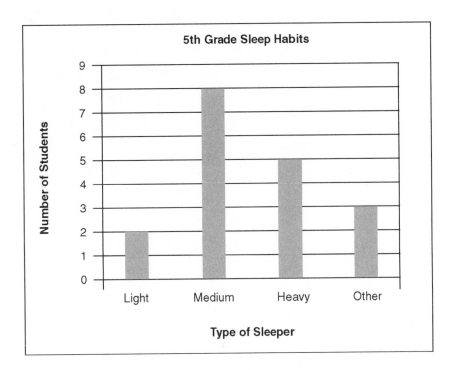
	
	    ○ given the set of numbers {1, 3, 7, 9}, the median is 5.
	However, the student exhibits major errors or omissions with score 3.0 elements.

Grade 4

Score 3.0	**While engaged in grade-appropriate tasks, the student demonstrates an understanding of data organization and interpretation by . . .** • collecting data using observations, surveys, or experiments and creating tally charts to represent the data (*e.g., explaining and modeling how to record the results of an informal class survey on a tally chart*); • representing categorical data using tables and graphs (bar graphs, line graphs, line plots) (*e.g., explaining and modeling how to represent a given set of categorical data on a line graph*); and • representing numerical data in tables and graphs (bar graphs, line graphs) (*e.g., explaining and modeling how to represent a given set of numerical data in a table*). **The student exhibits no major errors or omissions.**
Score 2.0	**The student exhibits no major errors or omissions regarding the simpler details and processes, such as . . .** • recognizing and recalling specific terminology (*e.g., survey, tally chart, line plot*); and • recognizing and recalling the accuracy of basic solutions and information, such as . . . ○ a survey and tally chart can be used to determine if classmates enjoyed a recent movie, as shown (*on the next page*)

Score 2.0
(continued)

Liked movie	x x x x x x
Did not like movie	x x x x x
Did not see movie	x x x x x x

- the tally chart above can be displayed as the following bar graph

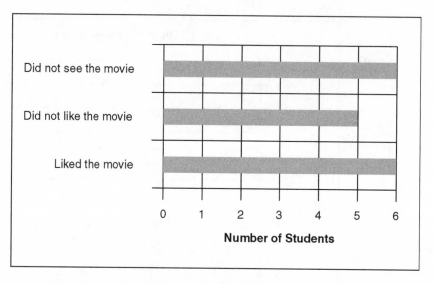

- the amount of growth of a plant in the classroom can be shown in a line graph as pictured here

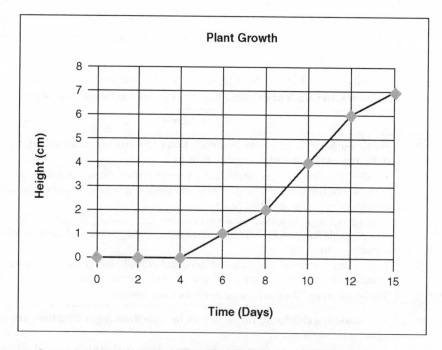

However, the student exhibits major errors or omissions with score 3.0 elements.

	Grade 3
Score 3.0	**While engaged in grade-appropriate tasks, the student demonstrates an understanding of data organization and interpretation by . . .** • describing data as either categorical or numerical (*e.g., explaining and exemplifying the difference between categorical and numerical data; determining whether a given set of data is categorical or numerical*); and • representing simple data using graphs and Venn diagrams (*e.g., explaining and modeling how to represent a given set of data with a Venn diagram*). **The student exhibits no major errors or omissions.**

Score 2.0	**The student exhibits no major errors or omissions regarding the simpler details and processes, such as . . .**
	• recognizing and recalling specific terminology (*e.g., Venn diagram, data*); and
	• recognizing and recalling the accuracy of basic solutions and information, such as . . .
	   ○ the following picture shows a categorical display of students' hair color
	
	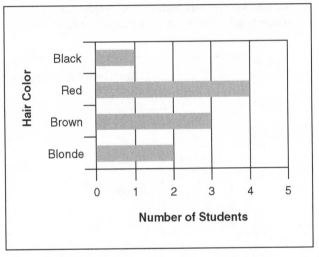
	
	   ○ information about two sisters and things they have in common and things they don't can be shown in a Venn diagram like the following picture
	
	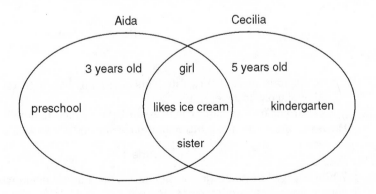
	
	However, the student exhibits major errors or omissions with score 3.0 elements.

Grade 2	
Score 3.0	**While engaged in grade-appropriate tasks, the student demonstrates an understanding of data organization and interpretation by . . .** • creating and labeling displays for a given set of data using pictographs, tally charts, bar graphs, or single- or double-loop Venn diagrams (*e.g., demonstrating how to create a double-loop Venn diagram for a given set of data and where to place appropriate labels*); • interpreting basic graphic displays (*e.g., describing the information depicted in a basic graphic display*); and • collecting and recording numerical data in systematic ways (*e.g., demonstrating different types of data that can be collected and displayed*). **The student exhibits no major errors or omissions.**

Score 2.0	**The student exhibits no major errors or omissions regarding the simpler details and processes, such as . . .**
	• recognizing and recalling specific terminology (*e.g., tally, table*); and
	• recognizing and recalling the accuracy of basic solutions and information, such as . . .
	   ○ the following picture shows a bar graph that can be created to count the number of students with birthdays from January to June
	
	Birthdays from January to June
	
	Months (vertical axis): Jan, Feb, Mar, Apr, May, June
	Number of Students (horizontal axis): 0 1 2 3 4 5 6
	Mar: 2, Apr: 3, May: 4, June: 1
	
	   ○ the picture shows that two students have a birthday in March, three in April, four in May, and one in June; and
	   ○ classroom temperatures can be recorded for a month and displayed in a table.
	However, the student exhibits major errors or omissions with score 3.0 elements.

Grade 1	
Score 3.0	**While engaged in grade-appropriate tasks, the student demonstrates an understanding of data organization and interpretation by . . .** • organizing objects or information into predetermined and labeled data displays (pictographs, tally charts, bar graphs, double-loop Venn diagrams) (*e.g., completing a given tally chart—for example, providing missing labels, supplying some missing tallies based on information provided with the tally chart*);

Score 3.0 (continued)	• generating simple questions for data collection (*e.g., demonstrating how organizing student responses into categories would answer the question about who went to the movie over the weekend*); and • creating simple graphic displays with appropriate labels (*e.g., making a simple tally chart with appropriate labels in the correct places*). **The student exhibits no major errors or omissions.**

Score 2.0	**The student exhibits no major errors or omissions regarding the simpler details and processes, such as . . .**
	• recognizing and recalling specific terminology (*e.g., list, graph*); and
	• recognizing and recalling the accuracy of basic solutions and information, such as . . .
	    ○ a bar graph listing students in the class can be colored in with information about how many pockets each one has on his or her clothes;
	    ○ "What is your favorite color?" is an example of a simple question that can be used to collect data; and
	    ○ a tally chart counting the different hair colors in the class would have labels for the number of students and each hair color.
	However, the student exhibits major errors or omissions with score 3.0 elements.

<div align="center">**Grade K**</div>	
Score 3.0	**While engaged in grade-appropriate tasks, the student demonstrates an understanding of data organization and interpretation by . . .** • sorting real objects into a set (or sets) of data and communicating conclusions about the resulting set or sets (*e.g., grouping different colored pencils by color and describing the groups that result—for example, by stating how many pencils are in each group, which group has the most number of pencils, and which group has the least number of pencils*). **The student exhibits no major errors or omissions.**
Score 2.0	**The student exhibits no major errors or omissions regarding the simpler details and processes, such as . . .** • recognizing and recalling specific terminology (*e.g., grouping, set*); and • recognizing and recalling the accuracy of basic solutions and information, such as . . . ○ grouping different colored erasers into sets by color—set A: 5 blue erasers, set B: 7 pink erasers, set C: 4 green erasers; set A is greater than set C but less than set B. **However, the student exhibits major errors or omissions with score 3.0 elements.**

Probability

Grade 8		
Score 4.0	**In addition to score 3.0 performance, the student demonstrates in-depth inferences and applications that go beyond what was taught.**	
	Score 3.5	In addition to score 3.0 performance, the student demonstrates in-depth inferences and applications with partial success.
Score 3.0	**While engaged in grade-appropriate tasks, the student demonstrates an understanding of probability by . . .** • determining the probability of complementary events (*e.g., explaining the concept of complementary events and modeling how to determine the probability of an event and its complement*); • determining whether two events are mutually exclusive (*e.g., explaining the concept of mutually exclusive events and modeling how to determine whether two events are mutually exclusive*); • determining the probability of independent events (*e.g., explaining the concept of independent events and modeling how to determine the probability of an independent event*); and • determining the probability of dependent events (*e.g., explaining the concept of dependent events and modeling how to determine the probability of a dependent event*). **The student exhibits no major errors or omissions.**	
	Score 2.5	The student exhibits no major errors or omissions regarding the score 2.0 elements and partial knowledge of the score 3.0 elements.

Score 2.0	**The student exhibits no major errors or omissions regarding the simpler details and processes, such as . . .**
	• recognizing and recalling specific terminology (*e.g., complementary event, independent event, dependent event, mutually exclusive event*); and
	• recognizing and recalling the accuracy of basic solutions and information, such as . . .
	   ○ the probability of rolling a 2 or less on a die is 1/3 and the probability of its complement (rolling a 3 or greater) is 2/3;
	   ○ rolling a 4 or doubles on a pair of dice is not mutually exclusive because the outcome (2, 2) is common for both events;
	   ○ one coin is taken out of a jar containing 3 quarters, 7 dimes, 4 nickels, and 10 pennies and then replaced; another coin is taken from the jar; the probability of the first coin being a quarter and the second a nickel is P(quarter and nickel) = P(quarter) × P(nickel) = 3/24 × 4/24 = 12/576 = 1/48; and
	   ○ if the events in the previous example were dependent, the probability would be 3/24 × 4/23 = 12/552 = 1/46.
	However, the student exhibits major errors or omissions with score 3.0 elements.	

	Score 1.5	The student demonstrates partial knowledge of the score 2.0 elements but major errors or omissions regarding the score 3.0 elements.
Score 1.0	**With help, the student demonstrates partial understanding of some of the score 2.0 elements and some of the score 3.0 elements.**	
	Score 0.5	With help, the student demonstrates partial understanding of some of the score 2.0 elements but not the score 3.0 elements.
Score 0.0	**Even with help, the student demonstrates no understanding or skill.**	
Grade 7		
Score 3.0	**While engaged in grade-appropriate tasks, the student demonstrates an understanding of probability by . . .**	

Score 3.0 *(continued)*	• determining the experimental and theoretical probability of the same event (*e.g.,* *explaining the concepts of experimental and theoretical probability and modeling how to* *determine both the experimental and theoretical probability of the same event*); and • determining the number of possible arrangements of several objects using a tree diagram or the fundamental counting principle (*e.g., explaining the concept of the fundamental* *counting principle and modeling how to determine the number of possible arrangements of* *several objects using the principle*). **The student exhibits no major errors or omissions.**
Score 2.0	**The student exhibits no major errors or omissions regarding the simpler details and** **processes, such as . . .** • recognizing and recalling specific terminology (*e.g., fundamental counting principle,* *theoretical probability, experimental probability*); and • recognizing and recalling the accuracy of basic solutions and information, such as . . . ○ a spinner landing on one of four colors (equally divided) has a theoretical probability of 25 percent, whereas landing on one color eight times results in an experimental probability of 40 percent; and ○ 3 red balls, 5 green balls, 7 paper clips, and 4 pencils can be arranged $3 \times 5 \times 7 \times 4 = 420$ ways. **However, the student exhibits major errors or omissions with score 3.0 elements.**
Grade 6	
Score 3.0	**While engaged in grade-appropriate tasks, the student demonstrates an understanding of** **probability by . . .** • making a sample space for selected experiments and representing it as a list, chart, picture, or tree diagram (*e.g., explaining the concept of sample space and modeling how to* *represent the sample space for a given experiment as a chart*); and • determining the probability of an event occurring from a given sample space and representing the probability as a ratio, decimal, or percent, as appropriate (*e.g., explaining* *and modeling how to determine the probability of an event occurring from a given sample* *space; explaining and modeling how to represent probability—i.e., ratio, decimal, and* *percent—and the reason for choosing one as the most appropriate for representing the* *probability of an event occurring from a given sample space*). **The student exhibits no major errors or omissions.**
Score 2.0	**The student exhibits no major errors or omissions regarding the simpler details and** **processes, such as . . .** • recognizing and recalling specific terminology (*e.g., sample space, ratio, percent*); and • recognizing and recalling the accuracy of basic solutions and information, such as . . . ○ a jar containing 20 dimes, 15 nickels, and 5 pennies would have a sample space of {all 40 coins in the jar}; and ○ the probability of picking one of the 15 nickels at random from the sample space would be 3/8 or 0.4 (rounded to the nearest tenth) or 40 percent. **However, the student exhibits major errors or omissions with score 3.0 elements.**
Grade 5	
Score 3.0	**While engaged in grade-appropriate tasks, the student demonstrates an understanding of** **probability by . . .** • using common fractions to represent probabilities (*e.g., explaining and exemplifying why* *common fractions can represent probability*); • expressing the probability of an event taking place as a value between 0 and 1 (*e.g.,* *explaining and exemplifying why probability is expressed as a value between 0 and 1*); and • expressing probability of situations verbally (in words) and numerically (*e.g., explaining* *and modeling how to express probability in both words and numbers*). **The student exhibits no major errors or omissions.**

Score 2.0	**The student exhibits no major errors or omissions regarding the simpler details and processes, such as . . .**
	
	• recognizing and recalling specific terminology (*e.g., odds, common fraction, event probability*); and
	• recognizing and recalling the accuracy of basic solutions and information, such as . . .
	  ○ the probability of a child being born male is 1/2;
	  ○ the probability of rolling two dice with a sum of 6 or 8 is 5/36; and
	  ○ expressing the previous example in words would be as follows: the probability of rolling two dice with a sum of six or eight is five out of thirty-six.
	
	However, the student exhibits major errors or omissions with score 3.0 elements.

	Grade 4
Score 3.0	**While engaged in grade-appropriate tasks, the student demonstrates an understanding of probability by . . .** • determining if outcomes of simple events are likely, unlikely, certain, equally likely, or impossible (*e.g., explaining the concept of "equally likely" and analyzing whether describing the outcome of a given simple event as equally likely makes sense*); • summarizing results of probability experiments in a clear and organized way (*e.g., explaining and modeling how to use a tally chart to describe the results of an experiment—for example, recording the sum of two dice rolled at the same time for a specified number of rolls to determine the number of times 6 appears as the sum*); and • predicting possible outcomes of a given situation or event (*e.g., explaining and exemplifying how possible outcomes can be determined for a given event*). **The student exhibits no major errors or omissions.**

Score 2.0	**The student exhibits no major errors or omissions regarding the simpler details and processes, such as . . .**
	
	• recognizing and recalling specific terminology (*e.g., certainty, possible outcome, probability experiment*); and
	• recognizing and recalling the accuracy of basic solutions and information, such as . . .
	  ○ when rolling a single die, it is equally likely for any of the six numbers to appear;
	  ○ the following tally chart shows that the difference between two dice rolled at the same time is likely to be 1, 2, or 3

0	x
1	x x x x x x
2	x x x x x
3	x x x x
4	x x
5	x x

○ the following chart shows all possible outcomes for the sum of two dice

+	1	2	3	4	5	6
1	2	3	4	5	6	7
2	3	4	5	6	7	8
3	4	5	6	7	8	9
4	5	6	7	8	9	10
5	6	7	8	9	10	11
6	7	8	9	10	11	12

However, the student exhibits major errors or omissions with score 3.0 elements.

	Grade 3
Score 3.0	**While engaged in grade-appropriate tasks, the student demonstrates an understanding of probability by . . .** • determining the likelihood of different outcomes in a simple experiment (*e.g., explaining and modeling basic ways to determine how likely an outcome, such as the number of times a spinner might land on one color, might appear in future experiments*); and • identifying events as certain, likely, unlikely, or impossible (*e.g., explaining the differences between the concepts certain, likely, unlikely, and impossible, and basic reasons for choosing one to describe an event*). **The student exhibits no major errors or omissions.**

Score 2.0	**The student exhibits no major errors or omissions regarding the simpler details and processes, such as . . .**
	• recognizing and recalling specific terminology (*e.g., event likelihood, simple experiment*); and
	• recognizing and recalling the accuracy of basic solutions and information, such as . . .
	   ○ tallying the sum of two dice for 20 rolls would provide information to help determine the likelihood of a value appearing on future rolls of the dice; and
	   ○ rolling a 7 on two dice would be likely, while rolling a 2 would be unlikely.
	However, the student exhibits major errors or omissions with score 3.0 elements.

	Grade 2
Score 3.0	**While engaged in grade-appropriate tasks, the student demonstrates an understanding of probability by . . .** • comparing likelihoods of two events (*e.g., explaining basic reasons why one event is more likely/less likely than another*); and • performing and recording results of simple probability experiments (*e.g., tallying the number of times a spinner lands on a color using an unequally divided spinner*). **The student exhibits no major errors or omissions.**

Score 2.0	**The student exhibits no major errors or omissions regarding the simpler details and processes, such as . . .**
	• recognizing and recalling specific terminology (*e.g., more likely/less likely, unequally divided spinner*); and
	• recognizing and recalling the accuracy of basic solutions and information, such as . . .
	   ○ on an unequally divided spinner, the spinner is more likely to land on the color with the largest section; and
	   ○ the following tally chart shows the number of times an unequally divided spinner landed on two colors when spun 20 times
	
		Color 1 (larger)	x x x x x x x x x x x x x |
			
				Color 2 (smaller)	x x x x x x x |
					
					However, the student exhibits major errors or omissions with score 3.0 elements.

	Grade 1
Score 3.0	**While engaged in grade-appropriate tasks, the student demonstrates an understanding of probability by . . .** • performing and recording (with tally marks) simple probability experiments (*e.g., tallying the number of times a coin lands on heads*). **The student exhibits no major errors or omissions.**

| Score 2.0 | **The student exhibits no major errors or omissions regarding the simpler details and processes, such as . . .**
• recognizing and recalling specific terminology (*e.g., grouping, equally divided spinner*); and
• recognizing and recalling the accuracy of basic solutions and information, such as . . .
 ○ the following tally chart shows the number of times the numbers 1 to 6 appeared when tossing a number cube 20 times

| | |
\|---\|---\|
\| 1 \| x x x x x \|
\| 2 \| x x \|
\| 3 \| x \|
\| 4 \| x x x \|
\| 5 \| x x x \|
\| 6 \| x x x x x x \|

However, the student exhibits major errors or omissions with score 3.0 elements. |

The tally chart in Score 2.0:

1	x x x x x
2	x x
3	x
4	x x x
5	x x x
6	x x x x x x

However, the student exhibits major errors or omissions with score 3.0 elements.

Grade K	
Score 3.0	**While engaged in grade-appropriate tasks, the student demonstrates an understanding of probability by . . .** • describing what the data show from simple data representations (*e.g., tallying the results of a simple class survey—for example, tallying the results of a survey showing how many pets each student has; explaining the results of a simple class survey—for example, stating which student has the most pets, which student has the fewest pets*). **The student exhibits no major errors or omissions.**
Score 2.0	**The student exhibits no major errors or omissions regarding the simpler details and processes, such as . . .** • recognizing and recalling specific terminology (*e.g., greater than/less than, class survey*); and • recognizing and recalling the accuracy of basic solutions and information, such as . . . ○ the following tally chart shows the size of each family in the class; using the tally chart we can see who has the largest family and who has the smallest.

Beth	x x x x x
Steve	x x
Mark	x x
Susan	x x x
Mike	x x x

However, the student exhibits major errors or omissions with score 3.0 elements.

Scoring Scales
for Science

Science

Note: For each measurement topic, the scale for the first grade level (the highest grade level to which the topic extends) shows all scores, including half-point scores. For all other grade levels, the scale shows scores 3.0 and 2.0 only, because the descriptors for the other scores on the scale do not change from grade level to grade level.

Earth and Space Sciences

Atmospheric Processes and the Water Cycle

		Grade 8
Score 4.0		**In addition to score 3.0 performance, the student demonstrates in-depth inferences and applications that go beyond what was taught.**
	Score 3.5	In addition to score 3.0 performance, the student demonstrates in-depth inferences and applications with partial success.
Score 3.0		**While engaged in tasks that address atmospheric processes and the water cycle, the student demonstrates an understanding of important information, such as . . .** • how water-cycle processes affect climatic patterns (temperature, wind, clouds) (*e.g., explaining how temperature is affected by water-cycle processes, such as precipitation—for example, explaining why rainfall on a hot day can lower the temperature*); and • the effects of temperature and pressure in different layers of the earth's atmosphere (troposphere, stratosphere, mesosphere, thermosphere) (*e.g., explaining why temperature and pressure are not the same in different layers of the earth's atmosphere—for example, explaining how small amounts of residual oxygen cause temperatures in the atmosphere to increase with altitude*). **The student exhibits no major errors or omissions.**
	Score 2.5	The student exhibits no major errors or omissions regarding the score 2.0 elements and partial knowledge of the score 3.0 elements.

Score 2.0		**The student exhibits no major errors or omissions regarding the simpler details and processes, such as . . .**
		• recognizing and recalling specific terminology (*e.g., climatic pattern, troposphere, stratosphere*); and
		• recognizing and recalling isolated details, such as . . .
		   ○ precipitation can cause temperature change; and
		   ○ the troposphere is the lowest portion of the earth's atmosphere.
		However, the student exhibits major errors or omissions with score 3.0 elements.

	Score 1.5	The student demonstrates partial knowledge of the score 2.0 elements but major errors or omissions regarding the score 3.0 elements.
Score 1.0		**With help, the student demonstrates partial understanding of some of the score 2.0 elements and some of the score 3.0 elements.**
	Score 0.5	With help, the student demonstrates partial understanding of some of the score 2.0 elements but not the score 3.0 elements.
Score 0.0		**Even with help, the student demonstrates no understanding or skill.**
		Grade 7
Score 3.0		**While engaged in tasks that address atmospheric processes and the water cycle, the student demonstrates an understanding of important information, such as . . .**

Score 3.0 *(continued)*	• interactions of the processes in the water cycle (condensation, precipitation, surface run-off, percolation, evaporation) (*e.g., explaining how each process of the water cycle affects the other processes—for example, explaining why precipitation would not occur without the evaporation and condensation of surface water on the earth*); • why water is an essential component of the earth system (impact on life forms, human uses) (*e.g., explaining how a specific use for water affects humanity—for example, how using water to generate electricity affects people living today*); • how changes in atmospheric composition can affect the earth's climate (temperature, humidity) (*e.g., explaining how increases in "greenhouse" gases affect temperature on the earth—for example, how temperature on the earth is affected by increases in the amount of gases in the atmosphere that absorb infrared radiation emitted by the earth*); and • how clouds affect climate (temperature, humidity) (*e.g., explaining how clouds affect temperature on the earth—for example, how temperature on the earth is affected by the clouds' reflection of some of the incoming radiation from the sun*). **The student exhibits no major errors or omissions.**

Score 2.0	**The student exhibits no major errors or omissions regarding the simpler details and processes, such as . . .**
	• recognizing and recalling specific terminology (*e.g., water cycle, surface run-off, heat retention*); and
	• recognizing and recalling isolated details, such as . . .
	  ◦ surface run-off is one of the processes of the water cycle;
	  ◦ water is considered a universal solvent;
	  ◦ the earth's atmosphere contains nitrogen; and
	  ◦ the type and amount of clouds can vary throughout a day.
	However, the student exhibits major errors or omissions with score 3.0 elements.

	**Grade 6**
Score 3.0	**While engaged in tasks that address atmospheric processes and the water cycle, the student demonstrates an understanding of important information, such as . . .** • the impact of the sun on the earth (*e.g., explaining how a specific type of energy from the sun affects the earth—for example, how life on earth, in the form of plants, is affected by sunlight*); • how various factors (changes in ocean temperature, geological shifts, meteors, the advance and retreat of glaciers) affect the earth's climate (temperature, humidity) (*e.g., explaining how changes in ocean temperature affect the earth's climate—for example, how regional precipitation is affected by an El Niño/La Niña episode*); and • interactions between the moon and the earth (*e.g., explaining how ocean tides on the earth are affected by the moon—for example, how the height of the tide is affected by both the position of the moon as the earth completes a revolution and the position of the moon as it orbits the earth*). **The student exhibits no major errors or omissions.**

Score 2.0	**The student exhibits no major errors or omissions regarding the simpler details and processes, such as . . .**
	• recognizing and recalling specific terminology (*e.g., atmosphere, climate change, geological shift*); and
	• recognizing and recalling isolated details, such as . . .
	  ◦ the sun, like other stars, produces energy;
	  ◦ a glacier is a large, long-lasting river of ice; and
	  ◦ the moon makes one complete orbit about the earth every 27.3 days.
	However, the student exhibits major errors or omissions with score 3.0 elements.

	**Grade 5**
Score 3.0	**While engaged in tasks that address atmospheric processes and the water cycle, the student demonstrates an understanding of important information, such as . . .**

Score 3.0 (continued)	• basic impact of the sun on the earth (*e.g., explaining basic ways the earth is affected by the sun—for example, explaining basic forms of energy [ultraviolet light] transmitted by the sun to the earth*); and • basic effects of the tilt of the earth's axis as the earth orbits the sun (impact on seasons, impact on weather patterns) (*e.g., explaining how the tilt of the earth's axis affects seasons—for example, explaining basic reasons why seasons are the opposite in each hemisphere*). **The student exhibits no major errors or omissions.**

Score 2.0	**The student exhibits no major errors or omissions regarding the simpler details and processes, such as . . .**
	• recognizing and recalling specific terminology (*e.g., climate, hemisphere, ocean current*); and
	• recognizing and recalling isolated details, such as . . .
	  ◦ the average amount of visible sunlight is 10 to 12 hours a day in North America during the summer; and
	  ◦ one of the earth's hemispheres is tilted away from the sun.
	However, the student exhibits major errors or omissions with score 3.0 elements.

Grade 4

Score 3.0	**While engaged in tasks that address atmospheric processes and the water cycle, the student demonstrates an understanding of important information, such as . . .** • general characteristics of water (color, ability to change states, ability to dissolve many types of substances) (*e.g., explaining general information known about water—for example, that water has the ability to dissolve many substances into smaller particles that cannot be seen by the naked eye*); and • how water changes states (liquid to solid, liquid to gas, solid to liquid, gas to liquid) (*e.g., explaining the basic process of how water changes from one state to another—for example, what happens to ice placed in a glass of water*). **The student exhibits no major errors or omissions.**

Score 2.0	**The student exhibits no major errors or omissions regarding the simpler details and processes, such as . . .**
	• recognizing and recalling specific terminology (*e.g., forms of water, condensation, evaporation*); and
	• recognizing and recalling isolated details, such as . . .
	  ◦ many substances dissolve when placed in water; and
	  ◦ water on earth goes through a cycle.
	However, the student exhibits major errors or omissions with score 3.0 elements.

Grade 3

Score 3.0	**While engaged in tasks that address atmospheric processes and the water cycle, the student demonstrates an understanding of important information, such as . . .** • general characteristics of various types of precipitation (liquid, freezing, frozen) (*e.g., explaining general information known about a specific type of precipitation—for example, that hail is a form of precipitation that consists of balls of ice*); and • general characteristics of air (cannot be seen, can be felt as wind, basic impact of wind on different objects) (*e.g., explaining general information known about air—for example, even though air cannot be seen, it can be felt as wind*). **The student exhibits no major errors or omissions.**
Score 2.0	**The student exhibits no major errors or omissions regarding the simpler details and processes, such as . . .** • recognizing and recalling specific terminology (*e.g., air movement, wind patterns, precipitation*); and

Score 2.0 (*continued*)	• recognizing and recalling isolated details, such as . . . ○ rain and drizzle are types of liquid precipitation; and ○ air is a substance that surrounds us and takes up space. **However, the student exhibits major errors or omissions with score 3.0 elements.**

Grade 2	
Score 3.0	**While engaged in tasks that address atmospheric processes and the water cycle, the student demonstrates an understanding of important information, such as . . .** • basic forms of water (*e.g., explaining that water can be found in different forms—for example, ice is water in a solid form*); and • general characteristics of weather (ability to change, types of weather) (*e.g., explaining general information known about weather—for example, weather can change several times a day, as when the sun shines in the morning, is covered by a thunderstorm in the early afternoon, and reappears after the storm*). **The student exhibits no major errors or omissions.**
Score 2.0	**The student exhibits no major errors or omissions regarding the simpler details and processes, such as . . .** • recognizing and recalling specific terminology (*e.g., temperature, weather pattern, monsoon*); and • recognizing and recalling isolated details, such as . . . ○ water on the earth is always changing; and ○ there are different types of weather. **However, the student exhibits major errors or omissions with score 3.0 elements.**

Grade 1	
Score 3.0	**While engaged in tasks that address atmospheric processes and the water cycle, the student demonstrates an understanding of important information, such as . . .** • sources of freshwater on the earth (rivers, lakes, glaciers, underground) (*e.g., explaining that there are several sources of freshwater on the earth—for example, a well draws freshwater from underground*); • general characteristics of water on the earth (saltwater, freshwater) (*e.g., explaining general information known about water on the earth—for example, the earth's oceans are saltwater*); and • general characteristics of seasons (types of weather) (*e.g., explaining general information known about seasons—for example, leaves change colors during autumn*). **The student exhibits no major errors or omissions.**
Score 2.0	**The student exhibits no major errors or omissions regarding the simpler details and processes, such as . . .** • recognizing and recalling specific terminology (*e.g., wind, rain, snow*); and • recognizing and recalling isolated details, such as . . . ○ only a small portion of the earth's water is freshwater; ○ more than half of the earth is covered with water; and ○ each season is different. **However, the student exhibits major errors or omissions with score 3.0 elements.**

Grade K	
Score 3.0	**While engaged in tasks that address atmospheric processes and the water cycle, the student demonstrates an understanding of important information, such as . . .** • basic differences between forms of water found on the earth (liquid, solid) (*e.g., explaining that water on the earth can be found in different forms—for example, icebergs are solid water*); and

Score 3.0 (continued)	• basic differences between the seasons of the year (changes to plants, changes to trees, temperature) (*e.g., explaining that each season is different—for example, some trees will lose their leaves in the autumn to prepare for the freezing temperatures of winter*). **The student exhibits no major errors or omissions.**

Score 2.0	**The student exhibits no major errors or omissions regarding the simpler details and processes, such as . . .**
	 • recognizing and recalling specific terminology (*e.g., water, season, rainy*); and
	 • recognizing and recalling isolated details, such as . . .
	    ◦ water is very important to the earth; and
	    ◦ there are four seasons on earth.
	 However, the student exhibits major errors or omissions with score 3.0 elements.

Composition and Structure of the Earth

Grade 8		
Score 4.0	**In addition to score 3.0 performance, the student demonstrates in-depth inferences and applications that go beyond what was taught.**	
	Score 3.5	In addition to score 3.0 performance, the student demonstrates in-depth inferences and applications with partial success.
Score 3.0	**While engaged in tasks that address the composition and structure of the earth, the student demonstrates an understanding of important information, such as . . .** • how the earth's layers interact and their impact on the earth (plates move away from each other, plates move toward each other, plates grind past each other) (*e.g., explaining how the earth is affected when tectonic plates grind past each other—for example, how earthquakes can result when two tectonic plates grind past each other*); • how landforms are created (constructive forces, destructive forces) (*e.g., explaining how a destructive force created a specific landform—for example, how erosion created the Grand Canyon*); and • components and interactions of the rock cycle (transition to igneous rock, transition to metamorphic rock, transition to sedimentary rock) (*e.g., explaining how a specific type of rock is formed—for example, describing the processes involved in the formation of igneous rock*). **The student exhibits no major errors or omissions.**	
	Score 2.5	The student exhibits no major errors or omissions regarding the score 2.0 elements and partial knowledge of the score 3.0 elements.

Score 2.0	**The student exhibits no major errors or omissions regarding the simpler details and processes, such as . . .**
	• recognizing and recalling specific terminology (*e.g., tectonic plate, sedimentary rock, igneous rock*); and
	• recognizing and recalling isolated details, such as . . .
	   ◦ the earth's tectonic plates are around 100 kilometers (60 miles) thick;
	   ◦ some landforms were created by destructive forces; and
	   ◦ sedimentary rocks make up about three-fourths of the rocks at the earth's surface.
	However, the student exhibits major errors or omissions with score 3.0 elements.	

	Score 1.5	The student demonstrates partial knowledge of the score 2.0 elements but major errors or omissions regarding the score 3.0 elements.
Score 1.0	**With help, the student demonstrates partial understanding of some of the score 2.0 elements and some of the score 3.0 elements.**	
	Score 0.5	With help, the student demonstrates partial understanding of some of the score 2.0 elements but not the score 3.0 elements.
Score 0.0	**Even with help, the student demonstrates no understanding or skill.**	
Grade 7		
Score 3.0	**While engaged in tasks that address the composition and structure of the earth, the student demonstrates an understanding of important information, such as . . .** • characteristics of various layers of the earth (depth, types of rock, types of minerals) (*e.g., explaining information known about a specific layer of the earth—for example, describing the types of rock and minerals that can be found in the earth's crust*); and	

Score 3.0 (*continued*)	• how constructive forces create or change landforms (crustal deformation, volcanic eruptions, deposition of sediment) (*e.g., explaining how landforms are affected by constructive forces—for example, how the depth of a river is affected by the deposition of sediment*). **The student exhibits no major errors or omissions.**

Score 2.0	**The student exhibits no major errors or omissions regarding the simpler details and processes, such as . . .**
	• recognizing and recalling specific terminology (*e.g., lithosphere, hydrosphere, and rock cycle*); and
	• recognizing and recalling isolated details, such as . . .
	  ○ the lithosphere is the crust and the upper part of the mantle; and
	  ○ deposition of sediment is a constructive force.
	However, the student exhibits major errors or omissions with score 3.0 elements.

Grade 6	
Score 3.0	**While engaged in tasks that address the composition and structure of the earth, the student demonstrates an understanding of important information, such as . . .** • materials that make up the earth's layers (rocks, minerals) (*e.g., explaining that specific materials can be found in the earth's layers—for example, describing general types of rock that can be found in each of the earth's layers*); and • how destructive forces create or change landforms (weathering, erosion) (*e.g., explaining how landforms are affected by destructive forces—for example, how the shoreline of a river is affected by erosion*). **The student exhibits no major errors or omissions.**

Score 2.0	**The student exhibits no major errors or omissions regarding the simpler details and processes, such as . . .**
	• recognizing and recalling specific terminology (*e.g., mineral vein, mantle, landform*); and
	• recognizing and recalling isolated details, such as . . .
	  ○ the earth has four layers; and
	  ○ weathering is a destructive force.
	However, the student exhibits major errors or omissions with score 3.0 elements.

Grade 5	
Score 3.0	**While engaged in tasks that address the composition and structure of the earth, the student demonstrates an understanding of important information, such as . . .** • names and locations of the earth's layers (*e.g., explaining the location of a specific layer of the earth—for example, describing the outer core as the layer between the mantle and the inner core*); and • how features on the earth's surface constantly change (river width, river depth) (*e.g., explaining that some features on the earth's surface continuously change—for example, explaining why a river gets wider each year*). **The student exhibits no major errors or omissions.**

Score 2.0	**The student exhibits no major errors or omissions regarding the simpler details and processes, such as . . .**
	• recognizing and recalling specific terminology (*e.g., core, crust, sediment*); and
	• recognizing and recalling isolated details, such as . . .
	  ○ the earth is composed of layers; and
	  ○ features on the earth's surface can be changed.
	However, the student exhibits major errors or omissions with score 3.0 elements.

	Grade 4
Score 3.0	**While engaged in tasks that address the composition and structure of the earth, the student demonstrates an understanding of important information, such as . . .** • basic composition and properties of soil (organic materials, inorganic materials) (*e.g., explaining general information known about the composition and properties of soil—for example, every soil type is a mixture of sand, silt, clay, and organic matter*); and • examples of common minerals and their basic properties and uses (color, shape, texture, weight) (*e.g., explaining general information known about a common mineral—for example, quartz is one of the most common minerals in the earth's crust and is clear and colorless in its pure form*). **The student exhibits no major errors or omissions.**
Score 2.0	**The student exhibits no major errors or omissions regarding the simpler details and processes, such as . . .** • recognizing and recalling specific terminology (*e.g., mineral, silt, clay*); and • recognizing and recalling isolated details, such as . . . ○ soils can be classified by physical appearance; and ○ minerals can be classified by physical properties. **However, the student exhibits major errors or omissions with score 3.0 elements.**
	Grade 3
Score 3.0	**While engaged in tasks that address the composition and structure of the earth, the student demonstrates an understanding of important information, such as . . .** • examples of natural materials found on earth (solid rock, soil, water, gases) (*e.g., explaining that some materials found on the earth are natural materials—for example, saltwater is a natural material found in the earth's oceans*); and • basic composition and characteristics of rocks (color, shape, texture, weight, how they were formed) (*e.g., explaining general information known about the basic composition and characteristics of a specific type of rock—for example, some rocks are formed from molten magma*). **The student exhibits no major errors or omissions.**
Score 2.0	**The student exhibits no major errors or omissions regarding the simpler details and processes, such as . . .** • recognizing and recalling specific terminology (*e.g., weathered rock, bedrock, magma*); and • recognizing and recalling isolated details, such as . . . ○ the earth is made of a variety of types of natural materials; and ○ rocks can be classified by their composition. **However, the student exhibits major errors or omissions with score 3.0 elements.**
	Grade 2
Score 3.0	**While engaged in tasks that address the composition and structure of the earth, the student demonstrates an understanding of important information, such as . . .** • basic distinctions between different types of rock (shape, size, color, texture) (*e.g., explaining general differences between two types of rock—for example, explaining that one rock is smooth whereas another rock is rough*); and • constant change of surface features on the earth (basic impact of wind, basic impact of water, basic impact of ice) (*e.g., explaining that some features on the earth's surface change constantly—for example, heavy rains can cause the side of a mountain to erode*). **The student exhibits no major errors or omissions.**
Score 2.0	**The student exhibits no major errors or omissions regarding the simpler details and processes, such as . . .** • recognizing and recalling specific terminology (*e.g., soil, erosion, glacier*); and

Score 2.0 (continued)	• recognizing and recalling isolated details, such as . . .
	     ○ there are three types of rocks; and
	     ○ mountains are one of many physical features of the earth.
	 However, the student exhibits major errors or omissions with score 3.0 elements.

Grade 1	
Score 3.0	**While engaged in tasks that address the composition and structure of the earth, the student demonstrates an understanding of important information, such as . . .** • features on the earth's surface can be suddenly changed (mountains, beaches, rivers) (*e.g., explaining that some features on the earth's surface can be changed suddenly—for example, the top of a volcano can be blown away when it erupts*). **The student exhibits no major errors or omissions.**
Score 2.0	**The student exhibits no major errors or omissions regarding the simpler details and processes, such as . . .** • recognizing and recalling specific terminology (*e.g., landslide, volcanic eruption, earthquake*); and • recognizing and recalling isolated details, such as . . . ○ an active volcano can erupt with little or no warning. **However, the student exhibits major errors or omissions with score 3.0 elements.**
Grade K	
Score 3.0	Not applicable.
Score 2.0	Not applicable.

Composition and Structure of the Universe and the Earth's Place in It

Grade 8		
Score 4.0	**In addition to score 3.0 performance, the student demonstrates in-depth inferences and applications that go beyond what was taught.**	
	Score 3.5	In addition to score 3.0 performance, the student demonstrates in-depth inferences and applications with partial success.
Score 3.0	**While engaged in tasks that address the composition and structure of the universe and the earth's place in it, the student demonstrates an understanding of important information, such as . . .** • how the regular and predictable motions of the earth and the moon explain phenomena on the earth (the day, the year, phases of the moon, eclipses, tides, shadows) (*e.g., explaining why motions of the earth and the moon are responsible for phenomena on the earth—for example, describing how the orbit of the moon makes it appear to go through several phases when seen from the earth*); • distinctions between the planets in the solar system (shape, size, characteristics of rings, characteristics of moons, distance from the sun) (*e.g., explaining differences between two planets in the solar system—for example, describing how Neptune and Mars differ in size, shape, and distance from the sun*); • basic interactions between the sun and the planets in the solar system (gravitational forces, orbits, source of energy, source of light) (*e.g., explaining the basic ways the sun and the planets interact within the solar system—for example, explaining why the planets stay in orbit around the sun*); and • general characteristics of various celestial objects in the universe (stars, star clusters, planets, asteroids, comets) (*e.g., explaining general information known about a specific celestial object that can be found in the universe—for example, explaining that a star cluster is a group of stars bound together by gravity*). **The student exhibits no major errors or omissions.**	
	Score 2.5	The student exhibits no major errors or omissions regarding the score 2.0 elements and partial knowledge of the score 3.0 elements.

Score 2.0	**The student exhibits no major errors or omissions regarding the simpler details and processes, such as . . .**
	• recognizing and recalling specific terminology (*e.g., planetary rings, light year, astronomical unit*); and
	• recognizing and recalling isolated details, such as . . .
	   ○ the moon is about one-third the size of the earth;
	   ○ astronomers most often measure distances within the solar system in astronomical units (AU);
	   ○ the path of objects around the sun travel according to a law of planetary motion discovered by German astronomer Johannes Kepler in the early 1600s; and
	   ○ the term "celestial object" does not include the earth.
	However, the student exhibits major errors or omissions with score 3.0 elements.	

	Score 1.5	The student demonstrates partial knowledge of the score 2.0 elements but major errors or omissions regarding the score 3.0 elements.
Score 1.0	**With help, the student demonstrates partial understanding of some of the score 2.0 elements and some of the score 3.0 elements.**	
	Score 0.5	With help, the student demonstrates partial understanding of some of the score 2.0 elements but not the score 3.0 elements.
Score 0.0	**Even with help, the student demonstrates no understanding or skill.**	

	Grade 7
Score 3.0	**While engaged in tasks that address the composition and structure of the universe and the earth's place in it, the student demonstrates an understanding of important information, such as . . .** • distinctions between various celestial objects in the solar system (asteroid, comet, meteor, moon, planet) (*e.g., explaining the differences between two celestial objects in the solar system—for example, describing how an asteroid and a planet differ*); and • composition and characteristics of the sun (size, surface temperature, physical structure, sunspots, solar flares, forms of energy produced) (*e.g., explaining information known about the composition and characteristics of the sun—for example, describing the four layers that make up the physical structure of the sun*). **The student exhibits no major errors or omissions.**
Score 2.0	**The student exhibits no major errors or omissions regarding the simpler details and processes, such as . . .** • recognizing and recalling specific terminology (*e.g., eclipse, celestial object, dwarf planet*); and • recognizing and recalling isolated details, such as . . . ◦ Ceres, the first asteroid to be discovered, is now classified as a dwarf planet; and ◦ the ancient Greeks grouped the sun together with the other celestial bodies that moved across the sky, calling them all planets. **However, the student exhibits major errors or omissions with score 3.0 elements.**
	Grade 6
Score 3.0	**While engaged in tasks that address the composition and structure of the universe and the earth's place in it, the student demonstrates an understanding of important information, such as . . .** • basic distinctions between the planets in the solar system (time to orbit the sun, type of atmosphere, number of moons, rings/no rings) (*e.g., explaining general differences between two planets in the solar system—for example, describing how the time it takes to orbit the sun differs between Uranus and Venus*). **The student exhibits no major errors or omissions.**
Score 2.0	**The student exhibits no major errors or omissions regarding the simpler details and processes, such as . . .** • recognizing and describing basic terminology (*e.g., meteor, asteroid, gravitational force*); and • recognizing and recalling isolated details, such as . . . ◦ the solar system comprises the sun and all celestial objects bound to it by gravity. **However, the student exhibits major errors or omissions with score 3.0 elements.**
	Grade 5
Score 3.0	**While engaged in tasks that address the composition and structure of the universe and the earth's place in it, the student demonstrates an understanding of important information, such as . . .** • general characteristics of major features of the universe (galaxies, black holes, the solar system, extrasolar planetary systems) (*e.g., explaining general information known about a specific major feature of the universe—for example, explaining that planets discovered beyond our solar system are members of planetary systems that orbit a star and are called extrasolar planets or exoplanets*). **The student exhibits no major errors or omissions.**
Score 2.0	**The student exhibits no major errors or omissions regarding the simpler details and processes, such as . . .** • recognizing and recalling specific terminology (*e.g., exoplanet, black hole, star cluster*); and

Score 2.0 (continued)	• recognizing and recalling isolated details, such as . . . ◦ the Milky Way galaxy is one of billions of galaxies known to exist. **However, the student exhibits major errors or omissions with score 3.0 elements.**
Grade 4	
Score 3.0	**While engaged in tasks that address the composition and structure of the universe and the earth's place in it, the student demonstrates an understanding of important information, such as . . .** • general characteristics of basic patterns of the earth, the sun, and the moon (shape of the earth's orbit around the sun, shape of the moon's orbit around the earth, position of the earth as it rotates) (*e.g., explaining general information known about a basic pattern of the earth, the sun, and the moon—for example, describing the basic shape of the earth's orbit around the sun*); and • general characteristics of basic patterns of the stars (appearance in the sky from different hemispheres, position of constellations in the sky, apparent movement of the stars) (*e.g., explaining general information known about a basic pattern of the stars—for example, describing basic reasons why stars appear to move in the night sky*). **The student exhibits no major errors or omissions.**

Score 2.0	**The student exhibits no major errors or omissions regarding the simpler details and processes, such as . . .**
	• recognizing and recalling specific terminology (*e.g., galaxy, lunar phase, constellation*); and
	• recognizing and recalling isolated details, such as . . .
	   ◦ the moon orbits the earth much more quickly than the earth orbits the sun; and
	   ◦ stars have been used for celestial navigation.
	However, the student exhibits major errors or omissions with score 3.0 elements.

Grade 3	
Score 3.0	**While engaged in tasks that address the composition and structure of the universe and the earth's place in it, the student demonstrates an understanding of important information, such as . . .** • general characteristics of major features of the solar system (order of the planets from the sun, types of objects in the asteroid belt, amount of time planets take to orbit the sun) (*e.g., explaining general information known about a major feature of the solar system—for example, describing basic types of objects that can be found in the asteroid belt*). **The student exhibits no major errors or omissions.**
Score 2.0	**The student exhibits no major errors or omissions regarding the simpler details and processes, such as . . .** • recognizing and recalling specific terminology (*e.g., solar system, comet, orbit*); and • recognizing and recalling isolated details, such as . . . ◦ the inner and outer planets of the solar system are separated by the asteroid belt. **However, the student exhibits major errors or omissions with score 3.0 elements.**
Grade 2	
Score 3.0	**While engaged in tasks that address the composition and structure of the universe and the earth's place in it, the student demonstrates an understanding of important information, such as . . .** • general characteristics of the sun (source of heat, source of light, apparent movement of the sun) (*e.g., explaining general information known about the sun—for example, basic reasons why heat from the sun can be felt on earth*). **The student exhibits no major errors or omissions.**
Score 2.0	**The student exhibits no major errors or omissions regarding the simpler details and processes, such as . . .**

Score 2.0 (*continued*)	• recognizing and recalling specific terminology (*e.g., solar energy, star, star age*); and • recognizing and recalling isolated details, such as . . . ◦ the sun is the closest star to the earth. **However, the student exhibits major errors or omissions with score 3.0 elements.**
Grade 1	
Score 3.0	**While engaged in tasks that address the composition and structure of the universe and the earth's place in it, the student demonstrates an understanding of important information, such as . . .** • general characteristics of the moon (apparent movement of the moon, phases of the moon) (*e.g., explaining general information known about the moon—for example, describing basic reasons why the moon looks different throughout the month*); and • general characteristics of the earth (earth's rotation, seasons, day and night) (*e.g., explaining general information known about the earth—for example, basic reasons for day and night*). **The student exhibits no major errors or omissions.**

Score 2.0	**The student exhibits no major errors or omissions regarding the simpler details and processes, such as . . .**
	• recognizing and recalling specific terminology (*e.g., earth rotation, earth axis, season*); and
	• recognizing and recalling isolated details, such as . . .
	   ◦ the moon is the only celestial body on which human beings have landed; and
	   ◦ the earth is the third planet from the sun.
	However, the student exhibits major errors or omissions with score 3.0 elements.

Grade K	
Score 3.0	**While engaged in tasks that address the composition and structure of the universe and the earth's place in it, the student demonstrates an understanding of important information, such as . . .** • general characteristics of major features of the sky (the sun, the moon, clouds, stars) (*e.g., explaining general information known about a major feature of the sky—for example, explaining that stars cannot be seen during the day because the sun is so bright*). **The student makes no major errors or omissions.**
Score 2.0	**The student exhibits no major errors or omissions regarding the simpler details and processes, such as . . .** • recognizing and recalling specific terminology (*e.g., earth, sun, moon*); and • recognizing and recalling isolated details, such as . . . ◦ the sun is very important to life on earth. **However, the student exhibits major errors or omissions with score 3.0 elements.**

Life Sciences

Principles of Heredity and Related Concepts

Grade 8		
Score 4.0	**In addition to score 3.0 performance, the student demonstrates in-depth inferences and applications that go beyond what was taught.**	
	Score 3.5	In addition to score 3.0 performance, the student demonstrates in-depth inferences and applications with partial success.
Score 3.0	**While engaged in tasks that address principles of heredity and related concepts, the student demonstrates an understanding of important information, such as . . .** • distinctions between asexual and sexual reproduction (risk of mutation, energy requirements, similarity of offspring to parent, processes involved) (*e.g., explaining how asexual and sexual reproduction differ in their impact on potential mutation of offspring—for example, describing which type of reproduction has a greater risk of mutation and why the risk is greater*); and • the impact of heredity on organisms (traits, diseases, genetic disorders) (*e.g., explaining how organisms are affected by heredity—for example, describing how a genetic disorder, such as cystic fibrosis, can be passed from parents to offspring when the parents are healthy*). **The student exhibits no major errors or omissions.**	
	Score 2.5	The student exhibits no major errors or omissions regarding the score 2.0 elements and partial knowledge of the score 3.0 elements.
Score 2.0	**The student exhibits no major errors or omissions regarding the simpler details and processes, such as . . .** • recognizing and recalling specific terminology (*e.g., egg, sperm, genetic mutation*); and • recognizing and recalling isolated details, such as . . . 　○ half the genes come from each parent in sexual reproduction; and 　○ heritable characteristics determine an organism's likelihood to survive and reproduce. **However, the student exhibits major errors or omissions with score 3.0 elements.**	
	Score 1.5	The student demonstrates partial knowledge of the score 2.0 elements but major errors or omissions regarding the score 3.0 elements.
Score 1.0	**With help, the student demonstrates partial understanding of some of the score 2.0 elements and some of the score 3.0 elements.**	
	Score 0.5	With help, the student demonstrates partial understanding of some of the score 2.0 elements but not the score 3.0 elements.
Score 0.0	**Even with help, the student demonstrates no understanding or skill.**	
Grade 7		
Score 3.0	**While engaged in tasks that address principles of heredity and related concepts, the student demonstrates an understanding of important information, such as . . .**	

Score 3.0 (*continued*)	• general implications of altering or combining genes (risk of mutation, treatment of disease) (*e.g., explaining the basic impact of altering/combining genes on humanity—for example, describing how gene therapy can treat certain diseases*); and • general characteristics of asexual and sexual reproduction (types of asexual reproduction and their basic processes, distinctions between sexual reproduction in plants and mammals) (*e.g., explaining general information known about a specific type of asexual reproduction—for example, describing how binary fission differs from other types of asexual reproduction*). **The student exhibits no major errors or omissions.**

Score 2.0	**The student exhibits no major errors or omissions regarding the simpler details and processes, such as . . .**
	• recognizing and recalling specific terminology (*e.g., asexual reproduction, sexual reproduction, disease*); and
	• recognizing and recalling isolated details, such as . . .
	  ○ genes can be combined or altered; and
	  ○ most animals reproduce sexually.
	However, the student exhibits major errors or omissions with score 3.0 elements.

Grade 6

Score 3.0	**While engaged in tasks that address principles of heredity and related concepts, the student demonstrates an understanding of important information, such as . . .** • general characteristics of genes (basic role of DNA, basic role of RNA, basic impact on inherited traits) (*e.g., explaining general information known about genes—for example, describing the basic roles of DNA and RNA*); and • how species are classified (taxonomic levels, ability to reproduce, similarity of physical characteristics) (*e.g., explaining how to classify a variety of species—for example, describing why modern humans have been classified as* Homo sapiens). **The student exhibits no major errors or omissions.**

Score 2.0	**The student exhibits no major errors or omissions regarding the simpler details and processes, such as . . .**
	• recognizing and recalling specific terminology (*e.g., gene, chromosome, DNA/RNA*); and
	• recognizing and recalling isolated details, such as . . .
	  ○ current estimates place the human genome at about 25,000 genes; and
	  ○ the science of classifying living organisms is known as alpha taxonomy.
	However, the student exhibits major errors or omissions with score 3.0 elements.

Grade 5

Score 3.0	**While engaged in tasks that address principles of heredity and related concepts, the student demonstrates an understanding of important information, such as . . .** • distinctions between instinct and learned behavior in animals (*e.g., explaining how instinct and learned behavior are different—for example, explaining that some behaviors, such as an instinct for swimming, are traits/instincts that the animal is born with, and some behaviors, such as being able to cross a crocodile-infested river safely, have to be taught, often by the animal's parents*); and • general distinctions between how plants and animals reproduce (pollination, external fertilization, internal fertilization) (*e.g., explaining basic differences between how plants and animals reproduce—for example, describing the basic processes involved in pollination in plants and how it differs from external fertilization in animals*). **The student exhibits no major errors or omissions.**

Score 2.0	**The student exhibits no major errors or omissions regarding the simpler details and processes, such as . . .**
	• recognizing and recalling specific terminology (*e.g., pollination, species, organism*); and
	• recognizing and recalling isolated details, such as . . .
	  ◦ some traits are learned from parents; and
	  ◦ reproduction is a fundamental feature of all known life.
	However, the student exhibits major errors or omissions with score 3.0 elements.

Grade 4

Score 3.0	**While engaged in tasks that address principles of heredity and related concepts, the student demonstrates an understanding of important information, such as . . .** • general distinctions between types of traits (learned trait, inherited trait) (*e.g., explaining the basic difference between learned and inherited traits—for example, some traits have to be learned over time whereas others are present at birth*). **The student exhibits no major errors or omissions.**
Score 2.0	**The student exhibits no major errors or omissions regarding the simpler details and processes, such as . . .** • recognizing and recalling specific terminology (*e.g., learned trait, inherited trait*); and • recognizing and recalling isolated details, such as . . . ◦ identical twins will have the same traits. **However, the student exhibits major errors or omissions with score 3.0 elements.**

Grade 3

Score 3.0	**While engaged in tasks that address principles of heredity and related concepts, the student demonstrates an understanding of important information, such as . . .** • examples of inherited traits (hair color, eye color, height, skin color) (*e.g., explaining that some traits are inherited—for example, physical attributes, such as hair color, are inherited from the parents*). **The student exhibits no major errors or omissions.**
Score 2.0	**The student exhibits no major errors or omissions regarding the simpler details and processes, such as . . .** • recognizing and recalling specific terminology (*e.g., physical attribute, trait*); and • recognizing and recalling isolated details, such as . . . ◦ inherited traits come from parents. **However, the student exhibits major errors or omissions with score 3.0 elements.**

Grade 2

Score 3.0	**While engaged in tasks that address principles of heredity and related concepts, the student demonstrates an understanding of important information, such as . . .** • basic ways in which siblings resemble each other (hair color, eye color, skin color, facial shape) (*e.g., explaining that siblings often resemble each other in specific ways—for example, siblings sometimes have the same eye color*). **The student exhibits no major errors or omissions.**
Score 2.0	**The student exhibits no major errors or omissions regarding the simpler details and processes, such as . . .** • recognizing and recalling specific terminology (*e.g., sibling, similarity*); and • recognizing and recalling isolated details, such as . . . ◦ siblings have the same parents. **However, the student exhibits major errors or omissions with score 3.0 elements.**

Grade 1	
Score 3.0	**While engaged in tasks that address principles of heredity and related concepts, the student demonstrates an understanding of important information, such as . . .** • basic ways in which animals resemble their parents (hair color, eye color, skin color, facial shape) (*e.g., explaining that animals often resemble their parents in specific ways—for example, a parent and offspring sometimes have the same hair color*). **The student exhibits no major errors or omissions.**
Score 2.0	**The student exhibits no major errors or omissions regarding the simpler details and processes, such as . . .** • recognizing and recalling specific terminology (*e.g., parent, offspring*); and • recognizing and recalling isolated details, such as . . . ○ animal offspring resemble their parents. **However, the student exhibits major errors or omissions with score 3.0 elements.**
Grade K	
Score 3.0	Not applicable.
Score 2.0	Not applicable.

Structure and Function of Cells and Organisms

Grade 8		
Score 4.0	**In addition to score 3.0 performance, the student demonstrates in-depth inferences and applications that go beyond what was taught.**	
	Score 3.5	In addition to score 3.0 performance, the student demonstrates in-depth inferences and applications with partial success.
Score 3.0	**While engaged in tasks that address the structure and function of cells and organisms, the student demonstrates an understanding of important information, such as . . .** • basic processes of cell division and differentiation (prokaryotic organisms, eukaryotic organisms) (*e.g., explaining basic processes of cell division—for example, describing how the process of cell division differs between prokaryotic and eukaryotic organisms*); • the purpose of various specialized cells within multicellular organisms (red blood cells, white blood cells) (*e.g., explaining the purpose of a specific specialized cell that can be found within a multicellular organism—for example, describing the primary function of a red blood cell*); and • basic interactions between the levels of organization in living systems (specialized cells within tissues, specialized tissues within organs, specialized organs within organ systems) (*e.g., explaining basic ways the levels of organization in living systems interact—for example, describing how specialized cells group together to perform specific functions as a tissue*). **The student exhibits no major errors or omissions.**	
	Score 2.5	The student exhibits no major errors or omissions regarding the score 2.0 elements and partial knowledge of the score 3.0 elements.

Score 2.0	**The student exhibits no major errors or omissions regarding the simpler details and processes, such as . . .**
	• recognizing and recalling specific terminology (*e.g., cell division, cell differentiation, specialized cells*); and
	• recognizing and recalling isolated details, such as . . .
	  ○ cell division is the biological basis of life;
	  ○ groups of specialized cells cooperate to form a tissue; and
	  ○ all components of an organism must interact to maintain a balanced internal environment.
	However, the student exhibits major errors or omissions with score 3.0 elements.	

	Score 1.5	The student demonstrates partial knowledge of the score 2.0 elements but major errors or omissions regarding the score 3.0 elements.
Score 1.0	**With help, the student demonstrates partial understanding of some of the score 2.0 elements and some of the score 3.0 elements.**	
	Score 0.5	With help, the student demonstrates partial understanding of some of the score 2.0 elements but not the score 3.0 elements.
Score 0.0	**Even with help, the student demonstrates no understanding or skill.**	
Grade 7		
Score 3.0	**While engaged in tasks that address the structure and function of cells and organisms, the student demonstrates an understanding of important information, such as . . .** • basic distinctions between prokaryotes and eukaryotes (cellular structure, cellular reproduction, function of cell components) (*e.g., explaining basic differences between prokaryotes and eukaryotes—for example, describing how the cellular structure of a prokaryote differs from that of a eukaryote*);	

Score 3.0 (continued)	• basic purpose and functions of various specialized tissues within multicellular organisms (connective tissue, muscle tissue, nervous tissue) (*e.g., explaining the basic purpose and function of a specific specialized tissue that can be found within a multicellular organism—for example, describing the basic function of connective tissue*); • basic implications of an organism's ability to regulate its internal environment (basic impact on disease prevention) (*e.g., explaining how the ability to regulate its internal environment affects an organism—for example, describing the basic effect of internal regulation on disease prevention within an organism*); and • basic distinctions between the levels of organization in living systems (purpose, functions) (*e.g., explaining the basic differences between two levels of organization in a living system—for example, describing basic ways that tissues and organs differ*). **The student exhibits no major errors or omissions.**

Score 2.0	**The student exhibits no major errors or omissions regarding the simpler details and processes, such as . . .**
	• recognizing and recalling specific terminology (*e.g., specialized tissue, prokaryote, eukaryote*); and
	• recognizing and recalling isolated details, such as . . .
	  ◦ prokaryotes are unicellular organisms;
	  ◦ different tissues group together to form an organ;
	  ◦ many multicellular organisms have structures and systems that help regulate their internal environment; and
	  ◦ living systems have levels of organization.
	However, the student exhibits major errors or omissions with score 3.0 elements.

Grade 6

Score 3.0	**While engaged in tasks that address the structure and function of cells and organisms, the student demonstrates an understanding of important information, such as . . .** • basic functions of various cell parts (membrane, cytoplasm, organelle, nucleus) (*e.g., explaining the basic function of a specific cell part—for example, describing the basic function of cytoplasm within a cell*); and • basic purpose and functions of various specialized organs and organ systems within multicellular organisms (muscular system, nervous system, digestive system, cardiovascular system) (*e.g., explaining the basic purpose and function of a specific specialized organ/organ system that can be found within a multicellular organism—for example, describing the basic function of the cardiovascular system*). **The student exhibits no major errors or omissions.**

Score 2.0	**The student exhibits no major errors or omissions regarding the simpler details and processes, such as . . .**
	• recognizing and recalling specific terminology (*e.g., tissue, organ, organelle*); and
	• recognizing and recalling isolated details, such as . . .
	  ◦ cells are the fundamental units of life; and
	  ◦ multicellular organisms have a variety of specialized organs and organ systems that perform specialized functions.
	However, the student exhibits major errors or omissions with score 3.0 elements.

Grade 5

Score 3.0	**While engaged in tasks that address the structure and function of cells and organisms, the student demonstrates an understanding of important information, such as . . .** • basic distinctions between the composition of various organisms (unicellular, multicellular) (*e.g., explaining the basic differences between unicellular and multicellular organisms—for example, describing basic ways that the digestive functions of unicellular and multicellular organisms differ*);

Score 3.0 (continued)	• basic influences on organism behavior (internal cues, external cues) (*e.g., explaining how internal cues can influence organism behavior—for example, describing the basic effect of hunger on an organism*); and • how green plants obtain energy (basic stages of photosynthesis, basic function of chloroplasts) (*e.g., explaining how green plants get energy from sunlight—for example, describing the basic stages of photosynthesis*). **The student exhibits no major errors or omissions.**

Score 2.0	**The student exhibits no major errors or omissions regarding the simpler details and processes, such as . . .**
	• recognizing and recalling specific terminology (*e.g., multicellular organism, unicellular organism, cell*); and
	• recognizing and recalling isolated details, such as . . .
	  ◦ all organisms are composed of cells;
	  ◦ the behavior of individual organisms can be influenced; and
	  ◦ photosynthesis is a two-stage process.
	However, the student exhibits major errors or omissions with score 3.0 elements.

Grade 4	
Score 3.0	**While engaged in tasks that address the structure and function of cells and organisms, the student demonstrates an understanding of important information, such as . . .** • how plants can live in different environments (external features, internal features) (*e.g., explaining why plants can live in a specific environment—for example, describing the external features that allow plants to live in water, such as leaves that float atop the water*); • how animals can live in different environments (external features, internal features) (*e.g., explaining why animals can live in a specific environment—for example, describing the internal features, such as ability to hibernate, that allow bears to survive through winter*); • basic distinctions between the life cycles of different organisms (duration, stages) (*e.g., explaining the basic differences between the life cycles of two organisms—for example, describing how the duration of the life cycle of humans differs from the duration of the life cycle of dogs*); and • basic distinctions between the life needs of plants and animals (sources of food, sources of water) (*e.g., explaining the basic differences between the life needs of plants and animals—for example, describing how the source of food for a plant differs from the source of food for an animal*). **The student exhibits no major errors or omissions.**

Score 2.0	**The student exhibits no major errors or omissions regarding the simpler details and processes, such as . . .**
	• recognizing and recalling specific terminology (*e.g., photosynthetic plant, plant organ, external cues*); and
	• recognizing and recalling isolated details, such as . . .
	  ◦ plants have features to help them live in different environments;
	  ◦ animals have features to help them live in different environments;
	  ◦ the details of life cycles are different for different organisms; and
	  ◦ all organisms have basic life needs.
	However, the student exhibits major errors or omissions with score 3.0 elements.

Grade 3	
Score 3.0	**While engaged in tasks that address the structure and function of cells and organisms, the student demonstrates an understanding of important information, such as . . .** • the stages of the life cycle of various organisms (humans, animals, plants) (*e.g., explaining each stage of the life cycle of a specific organism—for example, describing the stages a butterfly goes through from birth to death*); and

Score 3.0 (continued)	• basic impact of light on plants (*e.g., explaining the basic impact light has on plants—for example, explaining that most plants use sunlight to make their own food*). **The student exhibits no major errors or omissions.**

Score 2.0	**The student exhibits no major errors or omissions regarding the simpler details and processes, such as . . .**
	• recognizing and recalling specific terminology (*e.g., senses, organism, life cycle*); and
	• recognizing and recalling isolated details, such as . . .
	  ◦ growth and development are part of the life cycle; and
	  ◦ most plants make their own food.
	However, the student exhibits major errors or omissions with score 3.0 elements.

Grade 2	
Score 3.0	**While engaged in tasks that address the structure and function of cells and organisms, the student demonstrates an understanding of important information, such as . . .** • basic needs of animals (why food is necessary, why water is necessary, why shelter is necessary) (*e.g., explaining the basic needs of animals—for example, describing basic reasons why animals need shelter*); and • basic needs of plants (why food is necessary, why water is necessary) (*e.g., explaining the basic needs of plants—for example, describing basic reasons why plants need water*). **The student exhibits no major errors or omissions.**

Score 2.0	**The student exhibits no major errors or omissions regarding the simpler details and processes, such as . . .**
	• recognizing and recalling specific terminology (*e.g., growth, development, reproduction*); and
	• recognizing and recalling isolated details, such as . . .
	  ◦ animals need shelter; and
	  ◦ plants need water.
	However, the student exhibits major errors or omissions with score 3.0 elements.

Grade 1	
Score 3.0	**While engaged in tasks that address the structure and function of cells and organisms, the student demonstrates an understanding of important information, such as . . .** • general characteristics of specific types of animals (body structures, locomotion, food consumption) (*e.g., explaining general information known about a specific type of animal—for example, describing the basic body structure of a lion*); and • general characteristics of plant and animal changes (physical growth, social development, aging) (*e.g., explaining that plants and animals experience different types of change throughout their lives—for example, explaining that both plants and animals grow physically*). **The student exhibits no major errors or omissions.**

Score 2.0	**The student exhibits no major errors or omissions regarding the simpler details and processes, such as . . .**
	• recognizing and recalling specific terminology (*e.g., body structure, movement, old age*); and
	• recognizing and recalling isolated details, such as . . .
	  ◦ animals have distinct body structures for walking, flying, and swimming; and
	  ◦ animals change throughout life.
	However, the student exhibits major errors or omissions with score 3.0 elements.

Grade K	
Score 3.0	**While engaged in tasks that address the structure and function of cells and organisms, the student demonstrates an understanding of important information, such as . . .** • examples of different types of animals that walk, fly, and swim (mammals, birds, reptiles, insects, fish) (*e.g., explaining that different types of animals can swim—for example, explaining that both salmon and tigers can swim*); and

Score 3.0 (continued)	• examples of resources that both plants and animals need to survive (*e.g., explaining that both plants and animals will die without certain resources—for example, explaining that without food and water, plants and animals will die*). **The student exhibits no major errors or omissions.**

Score 2.0	**The student exhibits no major errors or omissions regarding the simpler details and processes, such as . . .**
	 • recognizing and recalling specific terminology (*e.g., birth, death, reptile*); and
	 • recognizing and recalling isolated details, such as . . .
	    ◦ a bird is an animal with feathers; and
	    ◦ animals eat different kinds of food.
	 However, the student exhibits major errors or omissions with score 3.0 elements.

Relationships Between Organisms and Their Physical Environment

Grade 8		
Score 4.0	**In addition to score 3.0 performance, the student demonstrates in-depth inferences and applications that go beyond what was taught.**	
	Score 3.5	In addition to score 3.0 performance, the student demonstrates in-depth inferences and applications with partial success.
Score 3.0	**While engaged in tasks that address the relationships between organisms and their physical environment, the student demonstrates an understanding of important information, such as . . .** • implications of interactions between humans and ecosystems (impact on equilibrium, extinction of species) (*e.g., explaining how interactions between humans and an ecosystem affect the ecosystem—for example, describing the effect humans can have on the extinction of a species within an ecosystem*); • implications of how organisms interact with one another through food chains and webs in an ecosystem (mutualism, commensalism) (*e.g., explaining how interactions between organisms within a food chain affect one another—for example, describing how a mutualistic relationship between two organisms affects each organism*); and • how matter is recycled within ecosystems (scavengers, decomposers) (*e.g., explaining the processes involved in the recycling of matter within an ecosystem—for example, describing how a decomposer recycles matter in an ecosystem*). **The student exhibits no major errors or omissions.**	
	Score 2.5	The student exhibits no major errors or omissions regarding the score 2.0 elements and partial knowledge of the score 3.0 elements.

Score 2.0	**The student exhibits no major errors or omissions regarding the simpler details and processes, such as . . .**
	• recognizing and recalling specific terminology (*e.g., equilibrium, nervous system, symbiosis*); and
	• recognizing and recalling isolated details, such as . . .
	  ○ humans often interact with multiple ecosystems;
	  ○ symbiosis is a close association between two different types of organisms in a community; and
	  ○ fungi are one of three types of decomposers.
	However, the student exhibits major errors or omissions with score 3.0 elements.	

	Score 1.5	The student demonstrates partial knowledge of the score 2.0 elements but major errors or omissions regarding the score 3.0 elements.
Score 1.0	**With help, the student demonstrates partial understanding of some of the score 2.0 elements and some of the score 3.0 elements.**	
	Score 0.5	With help, the student demonstrates partial understanding of some of the score 2.0 elements but not the score 3.0 elements.
Score 0.0	**Even with help, the student demonstrates no understanding or skill.**	
Grade 7		
Score 3.0	**While engaged in tasks that address the relationships between organisms and their physical environment, the student demonstrates an understanding of important information, such as . . .** • impact of various factors on ecosystems (abiotic, biotic) (*e.g., explaining how a specific abiotic factor affects an ecosystem—for example, describing the effect weather can have on an ecosystem*); and	

Score 3.0 (continued)	• implications of how organisms interact with one another through food chains and webs in an ecosystem (producer/consumer, parasite/host) (*e.g., explaining how interactions between organisms within a food chain affect one another—for example, describing how a parasite/host relationship between two organisms affects each organism*). **The student exhibits no major errors or omissions.**
Score 2.0	**The student exhibits no major errors or omissions regarding the simpler details and processes, such as . . .** • recognizing and recalling specific terminology (*e.g., ecosystem, decomposer, parasite*); and • recognizing and recalling isolated details, such as . . . 　◦ quantity of water can affect an ecosystem; and 　◦ herbivore is one of the three groups of consumers. **However, the student exhibits major errors or omissions with score 3.0 elements.**
Grade 6	
Score 3.0	**While engaged in tasks that address the relationships between organisms and their physical environment, the student demonstrates an understanding of important information, such as . . .** • the impact of various factors on organisms within an ecosystem (impact on the number of organisms an ecosystem can support, impact on the types of organisms an ecosystem can support) (*e.g., explaining how a specific factor affects organisms within an ecosystem—for example, describing why the number of organisms an ecosystem can support is affected by the number of organisms present in the ecosystem*); and • implications of how organisms interact with one another through food chains and webs in an ecosystem (predator/prey) (*e.g., explaining how interactions between organisms within a food chain affect one another—for example, describing how a predator/prey relationship between two organisms affects each organism*). **The student exhibits no major errors or omissions.**
Score 2.0	**The student exhibits no major errors or omissions regarding the simpler details and processes, such as . . .** • recognizing and recalling specific terminology (*e.g., population, predation, predator*); and • recognizing and recalling isolated details, such as . . . 　◦ a lack of resources can affect every organism in an ecosystem; and 　◦ a predator at the top of its food chain is called an apex predator. **However, the student exhibits major errors or omissions with score 3.0 elements.**
Grade 5	
Score 3.0	**While engaged in tasks that address the relationships between organisms and their physical environment, the student demonstrates an understanding of important information, such as . . .** • the impact of various abiotic factors on the number and types of organisms an ecosystem can support (amount of water, amount of light, range of temperatures, soil composition) (*e.g., explaining the impact of a specific abiotic factor on the number and types of organisms an ecosystem can support—for example, describing how the amount of water affects the number and types of organisms an ecosystem can support*); • examples of simple food chains and food webs (desert, temperate rainforest, arctic, coniferous forest) (*e.g., explaining that a specific food chain can be found in a specific region—for example, describing a simple food chain that can be found in Africa: trees/shrubs—giraffes—lions*); and • basic implications of changes in the environment on the survival of different organisms (loss of habitat, severe weather, change in temperature) (*e.g., explaining how a specific change in the environment affects the survival of a specific organism—for example, describing how a loss of habitat affects the survival of a pride of lions*). **The student exhibits no major errors or omissions.**

Score 2.0	**The student exhibits no major errors or omissions regarding the simpler details and processes, such as . . .**
	
	• recognizing and recalling specific terminology (*e.g., abiotic, biotic, food web*); and
	• recognizing and recalling isolated details, such as . . .
	   ∘ range of temperatures can affect an ecosystem;
	   ∘ a food chain describes the feeding relationships between species in a biotic community; and
	   ∘ changes in the environment can affect different organisms in different ways.
	However, the student exhibits major errors or omissions with score 3.0 elements.

Grade 4	

Score 3.0	**While engaged in tasks that address the relationships between organisms and their physical environment, the student demonstrates an understanding of important information, such as . . .** • general effects that changes in the environment can have on different organisms (flood, fire, changes in weather) (*e.g., explaining the basic impact a specific change in the environment can have on a specific organism—for example, describing the basic effects a fire would have on deer living in a forest*); and • general changes an organism can cause in its environment (beneficial changes, harmful changes) (*e.g., explaining that an organism can have a beneficial impact on its environment—for example, beaver dams are the primary natural method of establishing wetlands*). **The student exhibits no major errors or omissions.**

Score 2.0	**The student exhibits no major errors or omissions regarding the simpler details and processes, such as . . .**
	
	• recognizing and recalling specific terminology (*e.g., survival, stored energy, photosynthesis*); and
	• recognizing and recalling isolated details, such as . . .
	   ∘ changes in the environment can affect an organism; and
	   ∘ all organisms cause changes to their environment.
	However, the student exhibits major errors or omissions with score 3.0 elements.

Grade 3	

Score 3.0	**While engaged in tasks that address the relationships between organisms and their physical environment, the student demonstrates an understanding of important information, such as . . .** • general characteristics and examples of herbivores (examples from North America and their sources of food, examples from South America and their sources of food, examples from Africa and their sources of food) (*e.g., explaining general information known about a specific herbivore that can be found in South America—for example, describing the green iguana as a large lizard from Central and South America that feeds on leaves, flowers, and fruit*); • general characteristics and examples of carnivores (examples from North America and their sources of food, examples from South America and their sources of food, examples from Africa and their sources of food) (*e.g., explaining general information known about a specific carnivore that can be found in Africa—for example, explaining that the African wild dog can be found only in Africa and often preys on medium-sized hoofed mammals such as the impala*); • general characteristics and examples of changes organisms make to their environment (changes to habitat, changes to levels of available food) (*e.g., explaining that all organisms cause changes in their environment—for example, explaining that the construction of new homes in an undeveloped area may reduce the size of an organism's habitat*); and

Score 3.0 (continued)	• general characteristics and examples of how an organism's pattern of behavior is related to the availability of resources in its environment (limited availability) (*e.g., explaining that the availability of resources influences the behavior of an organism—for example, explaining that when a natural shelter has been destroyed or altered, most organisms will attempt to change the available environment to meet their needs, as exemplified by birds nesting on building ledges in cities*). **The student exhibits no major errors or omissions.**

Score 2.0	**The student exhibits no major errors or omissions regarding the simpler details and processes, such as . . .**
	• recognizing and recalling specific terminology (*e.g., herbivore, carnivore, omnivore*); and
	• recognizing and recalling isolated details, such as . . .
	  ◦ some animals eat plants only;
	  ◦ some animals eat meat only;
	  ◦ environments can be changed; and
	  ◦ the availability of resources in a habitat can change.
	However, the student exhibits major errors or omissions with score 3.0 elements.

Grade 2	
Score 3.0	**While engaged in tasks that address the relationships between organisms and their physical environment, the student demonstrates an understanding of important information, such as . . .** • an organism's pattern of behavior is related to the physical characteristics of its environment (access to food sources, protection from predators) (*e.g., explaining that the physical characteristics of the environment influence the behavior of an organism—for example, small mammals often look for food close to rocks and shrubs that can be used to hide from birds and other predators*); and • distinct environments support the life of different plants (desert, rain forest, mountains) (*e.g., explaining that there are different environments that support the life of different types of plants—for example, describing basic differences between the desert and rain forest and the types of plants that can be found in them*). **The student exhibits no major errors or omissions.**

Score 2.0	**The student exhibits no major errors or omissions regarding the simpler details and processes, such as . . .**
	• recognizing and describing basic terminology (*e.g., habitat, balance, rain forest*); and
	• recognizing and recalling isolated details, such as . . .
	  ◦ some environments are rocky; and
	  ◦ cactus can be found in desert regions.
	However, the student exhibits major errors or omissions with score 3.0 elements.

Grade 1	
Score 3.0	**While engaged in tasks that address the relationships between organisms and their physical environment, the student demonstrates an understanding of important information, such as . . .** • an organism's pattern of behavior is related to the availability of food in its environment (limited availability) (*e.g., explaining that the availability of food in the environment can influence the behavior of an organism—for example, explaining that when food is limited, a lion has to search a greater distance to find food*); and • distinct environments support the life of different animals (desert, rain forest, mountains) (*e.g., explaining that there are different environments that support the life of different types of animals—for example, describing basic differences between the desert and mountains and the types of animals that are found in them*). **The student exhibits no major errors or omissions.**

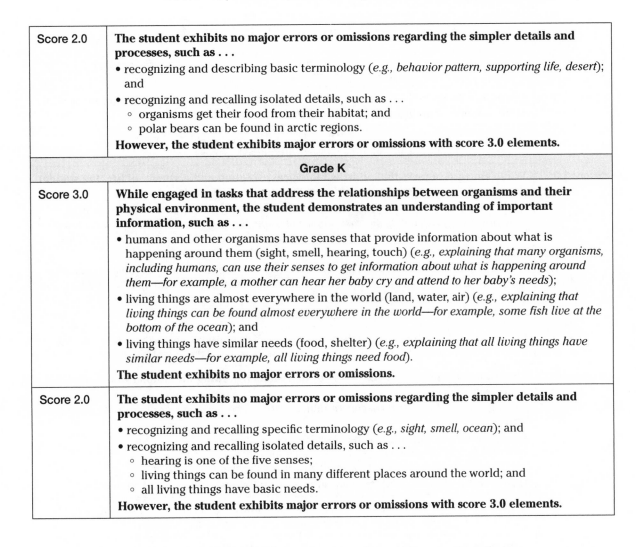

Score 2.0	The student exhibits no major errors or omissions regarding the simpler details and processes, such as . . .
	• recognizing and describing basic terminology (*e.g., behavior pattern, supporting life, desert*); and
	• recognizing and recalling isolated details, such as . . .
	  ○ organisms get their food from their habitat; and
	  ○ polar bears can be found in arctic regions.
	However, the student exhibits major errors or omissions with score 3.0 elements.

Grade K	
Score 3.0	While engaged in tasks that address the relationships between organisms and their physical environment, the student demonstrates an understanding of important information, such as . . . • humans and other organisms have senses that provide information about what is happening around them (sight, smell, hearing, touch) (*e.g., explaining that many organisms, including humans, can use their senses to get information about what is happening around them—for example, a mother can hear her baby cry and attend to her baby's needs*); • living things are almost everywhere in the world (land, water, air) (*e.g., explaining that living things can be found almost everywhere in the world—for example, some fish live at the bottom of the ocean*); and • living things have similar needs (food, shelter) (*e.g., explaining that all living things have similar needs—for example, all living things need food*). **The student exhibits no major errors or omissions.**

Score 2.0	The student exhibits no major errors or omissions regarding the simpler details and processes, such as . . .
	• recognizing and recalling specific terminology (*e.g., sight, smell, ocean*); and
	• recognizing and recalling isolated details, such as . . .
	  ○ hearing is one of the five senses;
	  ○ living things can be found in many different places around the world; and
	  ○ all living things have basic needs.
	However, the student exhibits major errors or omissions with score 3.0 elements.

Biological Evolution and Diversity of Life

Grade 8		
Score 4.0	**In addition to score 3.0 performance, the student demonstrates in-depth inferences and applications that go beyond what was taught.**	
	Score 3.5	In addition to score 3.0 performance, the student demonstrates in-depth inferences and applications with partial success.
Score 3.0	**While engaged in tasks that address biological evolution and diversity of life, the student demonstrates an understanding of important information, such as . . .** • basic implications of how life is thought to have begun (scientific theories, religious theories) (*e.g., explaining the basic impact of a specific theory on how life is thought to have begun—for example, determining whether the big bang theory answers the question of how life began and describing basic reasons for making that determination*); and • basic implications of natural selection (diversity of present life, unity of present life) (*e.g., explaining the basic impact of natural selection on present life—for example, describing basic effects of natural selection on the diversity that can be found in present life*). **The student exhibits no major errors or omissions.**	
	Score 2.5	The student exhibits no major errors or omissions regarding the score 2.0 elements and partial knowledge of the score 3.0 elements.

Score 2.0	**The student exhibits no major errors or omissions regarding the simpler details and processes, such as . . .**
	• recognizing and recalling specific terminology (*e.g., species diversity, unity of life, taxon*); and
	• recognizing and recalling isolated details, such as . . .
	  ○ Aristotle held that life is generated from nonliving matter; and
	  ○ Charles Darwin did not introduce the phrase "survival of the fittest."
	However, the student exhibits major errors or omissions with score 3.0 elements.	

	Score 1.5	The student demonstrates partial knowledge of the score 2.0 elements but major errors or omissions regarding the score 3.0 elements.
Score 1.0	**With help, the student demonstrates partial understanding of some of the score 2.0 elements and some of the score 3.0 elements.**	
	Score 0.5	With help, the student demonstrates partial understanding of some of the score 2.0 elements but not the score 3.0 elements.
Score 0.0	**Even with help, the student demonstrates no understanding or skill.**	
Grade 7		
Score 3.0	**While engaged in tasks that address biological evolution and diversity of life, the student demonstrates an understanding of important information, such as . . .** • distinctions between how life is thought to have begun (scientific theories, religious theories) (*e.g., explaining the key points of different explanations for how life is thought to have begun—for example, describing basic differences between common scientific and religious theories that attempt to explain how life is thought to have begun*); and • basic implications of natural selection (diversity of past life, unity of past life) (*e.g., explaining the basic impact of natural selection on past life—for example, describing basic effects of natural selection on the unity that can be found in past life*). **The student exhibits no major errors or omissions.**	
Score 2.0	• recognizing and recalling specific terminology (*e.g., natural selection, decomposer, diversity of life*); and	

Score 2.0 (continued)	• recognizing and recalling isolated details, such as . . . ○ a few facts give insight into the conditions in which life may have emerged, but the mechanisms are still elusive; and ○ the concept of natural selection was introduced by Charles Darwin.
Grade 6	
Score 3.0	**While engaged in tasks that address biological evolution and diversity of life, the student demonstrates an understanding of important information, such as . . .** • basic implications of key concepts of biological evolution (common ancestry, adaptation) (*e.g., explaining the basic impact of a specific key concept of biological evolution—for example, describing basic effects of adaptation on the survivability of organisms*); and • general characteristics of various taxonomic groups (fungi, plants, animals) (*e.g., explaining general information known about a specific taxonomic group—for example, describing the defining qualities of an animal*). **The student exhibits no major errors or omissions.**
Score 2.0	**The student exhibits no major errors or omissions regarding the simpler details and processes, such as . . .** • recognizing and recalling specific terminology (*e.g., adaptive characteristics, fossil record, adaptation*); and • recognizing and recalling isolated details, such as . . . ○ universal common descent is the theory that all life on earth originated from the same common ancestor billions of years ago; and ○ the science of classifying living organisms is known as alpha taxonomy. **However, the student exhibits major errors or omissions with score 3.0 elements.**
Grade 5	
Score 3.0	**While engaged in tasks that address biological evolution and diversity of life, the student demonstrates an understanding of important information, such as . . .** • basic implications of fossils (diversity of past life, similarity to present life) (*e.g., explaining the basic impact of fossils on present life—for example, describing basic reasons why studying a past ecosystem found in the fossil record can help predict the response of modern ecosystems to environmental change*); • general characteristics of key concepts of biological evolution (adaptation, common ancestry) (*e.g., explaining general information known about a specific key concept of biological evolution—for example, explaining that the theory of universal common descent proposes that all organisms on earth are descended from a common ancestor*); and • general characteristics of ways living things can be classified (producer, consumer, decomposer) (*e.g., explaining general information known about a specific way to classify living things—for example, describing the defining qualities of a decomposer*). **The student exhibits no major errors or omissions.**
Score 2.0	**The student exhibits no major errors or omissions regarding the simpler details and processes, such as . . .** • recognizing and recalling specific terminology (*e.g., extinction, evolution, common ancestry*); and • recognizing and recalling isolated details, such as . . . ○ the totality of fossils and their placement in fossil-containing rock formations and sedimentary layers is known as the fossil record; ○ the theory of adaptation was introduced by Jean-Baptiste Lamarck; and ○ a living thing can be classified as a producer, a consumer, or a decomposer. **However, the student exhibits major errors or omissions with score 3.0 elements.**
Grade 4	
Score 3.0	**While engaged in tasks that address biological evolution and diversity of life, the student demonstrates an understanding of important information, such as . . .**

Score 3.0 (continued)	• basic distinctions between fossils and living organisms of today (size, structure) (*e.g., explaining basic differences between fossils and organisms alive today—for example, explaining that some dinosaur fossils are much larger than organisms alive today*); and • various ways to group living things (grouping by genus, grouping by species) (*e.g., explaining how to group living things in a specific way—for example, grouping several given animals by genus and species and describing basic reasons why they were grouped that way*). **The student exhibits no major errors or omissions.**

Score 2.0	**The student exhibits no major errors or omissions regarding the simpler details and processes, such as . . .**
	• recognizing and recalling specific terminology (*e.g., fossil evidence, prehistoric organisms, genus*); and
	• recognizing and recalling isolated details, such as . . .
	  ○ some fossils that have been found are only part of a larger creature; and
	  ○ the Bengal tiger is the most common tiger.
	However, the student exhibits major errors or omissions with score 3.0 elements.

Grade 3	
Score 3.0	**While engaged in tasks that address biological evolution and diversity of life, the student demonstrates an understanding of important information, such as . . .** • basic distinctions between various fossils (size, structure) (*e.g., explaining basic differences between two fossils—for example, describing basic differences in size and structure between two leaf fossils*); • basic distinctions in the behavior of various plants (food gathering, water gathering) (*e.g., explaining the basic differences between the behavior of two different types of plants—for example, describing the basic ways that green plants and carnivorous plants get their food and how those ways are different*); and • various ways to group living things (grouping by external features, grouping by internal features) (*e.g., explaining how to group living things in a specific way—for example, grouping several given animals by an internal feature and describing basic reasons why they were grouped that way, such as bones versus no bones*). **The student exhibits no major errors or omissions.**

Score 2.0	**The student exhibits no major errors or omissions regarding the simpler details and processes, such as . . .**
	• recognizing and recalling specific terminology (*e.g., plant behavior, green plant, carnivorous plant*); and
	• recognizing and recalling isolated details, such as . . .
	  ○ fossils are not exactly alike;
	  ○ sunflowers will rotate to remain pointed toward the sun throughout the day; and
	  ○ spiders do not have internal bones.
	However, the student exhibits major errors or omissions with score 3.0 elements.

Grade 2	
Score 3.0	**While engaged in tasks that address biological evolution and diversity of life, the student demonstrates an understanding of important information, such as . . .** • basic distinctions in the behavior of various animals (food gathering, social grouping, parenting) (*e.g., explaining basic differences between the behavior of two animals—for example, describing the basic ways lions and wolves hunt for food and how those ways differ*); • kinds of organisms that have completely disappeared (plants, animals) (*e.g., explaining that a specific kind of organism can no longer be found on earth—for example, explaining that some fossils are plants that cannot be found on earth today*); and

Score 3.0 (continued)	• various ways to group living things (grouping by type of animal, grouping by type of plant) (*e.g., explaining how to group living things in a specific way—for example, grouping several given animals by type and describing basic reasons why they were grouped that way [e.g., mammals/amphibians/birds/insects/fish]*). **The student exhibits no major errors or omissions.**

Score 2.0	**The student exhibits no major errors or omissions regarding the simpler details and processes, such as . . .**
	• recognizing and recalling specific terminology (*e.g., animal behavior, fossil, organism*); and
	• recognizing and recalling isolated details, such as . . .
	   ○ as kittens' mobility increases, many mother cats will invent a "call sign" to signal the bolder kittens that have strayed too far;
	   ○ dinosaurs no longer live on the earth; and
	   ○ insects have six legs when fully grown.
	However, the student exhibits major errors or omissions with score 3.0 elements.

Grade 1

Score 3.0	**While engaged in tasks that address biological evolution and diversity of life, the student demonstrates an understanding of important information, such as . . .** • basic distinctions in the appearance of various plants (leaves, flowers) (*e.g., explaining basic differences in the appearance of two plants—for example, describing how the shape of leaves from an oak tree differs from the shape of leaves from a maple tree*); and • various ways to group living things (grouping by appearance, grouping by behavior) (*e.g., explaining how to group living things in a specific way—for example, grouping several given animals by behavior, such as awake during the day versus awake during the night, and describing basic reasons why they were grouped that way*). **The student exhibits no major errors or omissions.**

Score 2.0	**The student exhibits no major errors or omissions regarding the simpler details and processes, such as . . .**
	• recognizing and recalling specific terminology (*e.g., animal features, plant features, prehistoric animal*); and
	• recognizing and recalling isolated details, such as . . .
	   ○ one plant does not look exactly like another; and
	   ○ some plants have red flowers; some plants have yellow flowers.
	However, the student exhibits major errors or omissions with score 3.0 elements.

Grade K

Score 3.0	**While engaged in tasks that address biological evolution and diversity of life, the student demonstrates an understanding of important information, such as . . .** • basic distinctions in the appearance of various animals (hair, body) (*e.g., explaining basic differences in the appearance of two animals—for example, describing how the color of the fur of a polar bear differs from the color of the fur of a black bear*); and • groups of living things (plants, animals) (*e.g., explaining basic ways living things can be grouped—for example, explaining that cats and dogs can be grouped together because they are both animals; birds and oak trees cannot be grouped together because a bird is an animal and an oak tree is a plant*). **The student exhibits no major errors or omissions.**

Score 2.0	**The student exhibits no major errors or omissions regarding the simpler details and processes, such as . . .**
	• recognizing and recalling specific terminology (*e.g., plant, animal, body*); and
	• recognizing and recalling isolated details, such as . . .
	   ○ some cats have short fur; and
	   ○ a cat is a type of animal.
	However, the student exhibits major errors or omissions with score 3.0 elements.

Physical Sciences

Structure and Properties of Matter

Grade 8		
Score 4.0	**In addition to score 3.0 performance, the student demonstrates in-depth inferences and applications that go beyond what was taught.**	
	Score 3.5	In addition to score 3.0 performance, the student demonstrates in-depth inferences and applications with partial success.
Score 3.0	**While engaged in tasks that address the structure and properties of matter, the student demonstrates an understanding of important information, such as . . .** • distinctions between various thermodynamic systems (isolated, closed, open) (*e.g., explaining the differences between two thermodynamic systems—for example, describing how energy and matter are exchanged with the environment in an open system and how this differs from the exchange of energy and matter with the environment in a closed system*); • distinctions between various states of matter (solid, liquid, gas, plasma) (*e.g., explaining the differences between two states of matter—for example, describing unique properties of plasma and how these properties differ from unique properties of gas*); and • general characteristics of various elements (composition, atomic number, melting point, boiling point) (*e.g., explaining general information known about a specific element—for example, explaining that the boiling point of nitrogen is 77.36 K [–195.79°C, –320.42°F]*). **The student exhibits no major errors or omissions.**	
	Score 2.5	The student exhibits no major errors or omissions regarding the score 2.0 elements and partial knowledge of the score 3.0 elements.

Score 2.0	**The student exhibits no major errors or omissions regarding the simpler details and processes, such as . . .**
	• recognizing and recalling specific terminology (*e.g., conservation of mass, atomic arrangement, thermodynamic system*); and
	• recognizing and recalling isolated details, such as . . .
	  ◦ total weight in a closed system does not change;
	  ◦ plasma is a state of matter; and
	  ◦ the atomic number of an element is equal to the number of protons that defines the element.
	However, the student exhibits major errors or omissions with score 3.0 elements.	

	Score 1.5	The student demonstrates partial knowledge of the score 2.0 elements but major errors or omissions regarding the score 3.0 elements.
Score 1.0	**With help, the student demonstrates partial understanding of some of the score 2.0 elements and some of the score 3.0 elements.**	
	Score 0.5	With help, the student demonstrates partial understanding of some of the score 2.0 elements but not the score 3.0 elements.
Score 0.0	**Even with help, the student demonstrates no understanding or skill.**	

Grade 7	
Score 3.0	**While engaged in tasks that address the structure and properties of matter, the student demonstrates an understanding of important information, such as . . .** • distinctions between various ways elements can be grouped (highly reactive metals, less reactive metals, highly reactive nonmetals, almost completely nonreactive gases) (*e.g., explaining the differences between two ways that elements can be grouped—for example, describing how highly reactive metals differ from less reactive metals*); and • general characteristics of various common chemical compounds (component elements, ratio of elements, chemical formula) (*e.g., explaining general information known about a specific common chemical compound—for example, explaining that salt is composed of the elements sodium and chloride*). **The student exhibits no major errors or omissions.**

Score 2.0	**The student exhibits no major errors or omissions regarding the simpler details and processes, such as . . .**
	• recognizing and recalling specific terminology (*e.g., properties of elements, chemical compound, chemical formula*); and
	• recognizing and recalling isolated details, such as . . .
	   ○ oxygen is a nonmetal; and
	   ○ a chemical formula is a concise way of expressing information about the atoms that constitute a particular chemical compound.
	However, the student exhibits major errors or omissions with score 3.0 elements.

Grade 6	
Score 3.0	**While engaged in tasks that address the structure and properties of matter, the student demonstrates an understanding of important information, such as . . .** • general characteristics of matter in different states (solid, liquid, gas) (*e.g., explaining general information known about a specific state of matter—for example, explaining that liquids generally expand when heated and contract when cooled*); and • general characteristics of chemical reactions (oxidation-reduction, acid-base reaction) (*e.g., explaining general information known about a specific chemical reaction—for example, explaining that when an acid and a base are placed together they react to neutralize the acid and base properties*). **The student exhibits no major errors or omissions.**

Score 2.0	**The student exhibits no major errors or omissions regarding the simpler details and processes, such as . . .**
	• recognizing and recalling specific terminology (*e.g., chemical element, chemical substance, chemical reaction*); and
	• recognizing and recalling isolated details, such as . . .
	   ○ solids resist deformation; and
	   ○ a base will neutralize an acid.
	However, the student exhibits major errors or omissions with score 3.0 elements.

Grade 5	
Score 3.0	**While engaged in tasks that address the structure and properties of matter, the student demonstrates an understanding of important information, such as . . .** • general characteristics of matter (*e.g., explaining general information known about matter, such as the fact that matter has the same molecular structure regardless of state—for example, water has two hydrogen atoms and one oxygen atom whether its physical state is water, vapor, or ice*); and

Score 3.0 (*continued*)	• general characteristics of various ways substances can be classified (magnetism, conductivity, density, solubility, boiling point, melting point) (*e.g., explaining general information known about ways substances can be classified—for example, explaining that the boiling point of a substance is the temperature at which the substance boils at a fixed pressure, usually measured at sea level*). **The student exhibits no major errors or omissions.**
Score 2.0	**The student exhibits no major errors or omissions regarding the simpler details and processes, such as . . .** • recognizing and recalling specific terminology (*e.g., mass, atom, boiling point*); and • recognizing and recalling isolated details, such as . . . ◦ all matter can move from one state to another; and ◦ water has a boiling point of 212 degrees Fahrenheit. **However, the student exhibits major errors or omissions with score 3.0 elements.**

Grade 4

Score 3.0	**While engaged in tasks that address the structure and properties of matter, the student demonstrates an understanding of important information, such as . . .** • examples of common substances that can change state and the types of state change they make (solid to liquid, liquid to solid, liquid to gas) (*e.g., explaining that some substances can change from one state to another by heating or cooling—for example, explaining that water can change from solid to liquid or liquid to gas by heating; water can change from liquid to solid or gas to liquid by cooling*); and • how breaking an object into parts affects the weight of the object (*e.g., explaining the basic effect breaking an object into parts has on its weight—for example, describing that the broken parts of an object will have the same total weight as the original object*). **The student exhibits no major errors or omissions.**
Score 2.0	**The student exhibits no major errors or omissions regarding the simpler details and processes, such as . . .** • recognizing and recalling specific terminology (*e.g., state change, matter, cooling*); and • recognizing and recalling isolated details, such as . . . ◦ some substances, such as water, change states when heated; and ◦ the parts of an object can be weighed to find out the weight of the entire object. **However, the student exhibits major errors or omissions with score 3.0 elements.**

Grade 3

Score 3.0	**While engaged in tasks that address the structure and properties of matter, the student demonstrates an understanding of important information, such as . . .** • basic distinctions between general characteristics of common materials (visible properties, physical properties) (*e.g., explaining basic differences between the general characteristics of two common materials—for example, describing how wood and rubber feel different, in that wood feels hard and rubber feels elastic*); and • basic impact of heating and cooling on the properties of common materials (shape, texture, size) (*e.g., explaining the basic effect heat has on the shape of a common material—for example, explaining that plastic will shrink when heated*). **The student exhibits no major errors or omissions.**
Score 2.0	**The student exhibits no major errors or omissions regarding the simpler details and processes, such as . . .** • recognizing and recalling specific terminology (*e.g., magnifier, magnification, elastic*); and • recognizing and recalling isolated details, such as . . . ◦ wood is a common material for building things; and ◦ the shape of some materials can be changed. **However, the student exhibits major errors or omissions with score 3.0 elements.**

Grade 2	
Score 3.0	**While engaged in tasks that address the structure and properties of matter, the student demonstrates an understanding of important information, such as . . .** • various ways to describe objects and their physical properties (*e.g., explaining how objects can be described in different ways, such as by color, by texture, or by the materials they are made of*); and • basic distinctions between how materials respond to what is done to them (heating, freezing, mixing, cutting, dissolving, bending, wetting, exposing to light) (*e.g., explaining basic differences between how two materials respond to cutting—for example, explaining that cutting a piece of paper with scissors will separate the paper where it has been cut, whereas cutting a wood pencil with scissors will leave an indentation mark where it has been cut*). **The student exhibits no major errors or omissions.**

Score 2.0	**The student exhibits no major errors or omissions regarding the simpler details and processes, such as . . .**
	• recognizing and recalling specific terminology (*e.g., heating, freezing, texture*); and
	• recognizing and recalling isolated details, such as . . .
	  ○ two balls can be the same size but different colors; and
	  ○ some things can bend without breaking.
	However, the student exhibits major errors or omissions with score 3.0 elements.

Grade 1	
Score 3.0	**While engaged in tasks that address the structure and properties of matter, the student demonstrates an understanding of important information, such as . . .** • some objects are made of different materials (paper, metal, cloth, wood) (*e.g., explaining that a given object is made of a specific material—for example, explaining that the chairs in the classroom are made of plastic and metal*); and • some objects have different observable properties (color, shape, size, weight) (*e.g., explaining that a given object has a specific property or properties—for example, explaining that the ball on the left is red and is smaller than the ball on the right*). **The student exhibits no major errors or omissions.**

Score 2.0	**The student exhibits no major errors or omissions regarding the simpler details and processes, such as . . .**
	• recognizing and recalling specific terminology (*e.g., observation, weight, material*); and
	• recognizing and recalling isolated details, such as . . .
	  ○ some objects are made of only one kind of material; and
	  ○ some objects are similar in some ways and different in others.
	However, the student exhibits major errors or omissions with score 3.0 elements.

Grade K	
Score 3.0	**While engaged in tasks that address the structure and properties of matter, the student demonstrates an understanding of important information, such as . . .** • various ways to classify objects (color, shape, size) (*e.g., explaining how a given set of objects can be classified—for example, explaining that three red pencils, four red erasers, and two red marbles can be classified as red objects because they all have the same color*). **The student exhibits no major errors or omissions.**
Score 2.0	**The student exhibits no major errors or omissions regarding the simpler details and processes, such as . . .** • recognizing and recalling specific terminology (*e.g., color, classify, shape*); and • recognizing and recalling isolated details, such as . . . ○ classifying objects helps us see their similarities. **However, the student exhibits major errors or omissions with score 3.0 elements.**

Sources and Properties of Energy

Grade 8		
Score 4.0	**In addition to score 3.0 performance, the student demonstrates in-depth inferences and applications that go beyond what was taught.**	
	Score 3.5	In addition to score 3.0 performance, the student demonstrates in-depth inferences and applications with partial success.
Score 3.0	**While engaged in tasks that address the sources and properties of energy, the student demonstrates an understanding of important information, such as . . .** • characteristics of various forms of potential energy (gravitational energy, nuclear energy, stored mechanical energy, chemical energy) (*e.g., explaining the concept of potential energy and information known about a specific form of potential energy—for example, explaining that chemical potential energy is related to the structural arrangement of atoms or molecules*); • characteristics of various forms of kinetic energy (electrical energy, radiant energy, thermal energy, motion energy, sound) (*e.g., explaining the concept of kinetic energy and information known about a specific form of kinetic energy—for example, explaining that radiant energy is the energy of electromagnetic waves*); and • characteristics of various types of renewable energy (geothermal, hydrogen, hydropower, ocean, solar, wind) (*e.g., explaining information known about a specific type of renewable energy—for example, explaining that geothermal power is the use of geothermal heat to generate electricity*). **The student exhibits no major errors or omissions.**	
	Score 2.5	The student exhibits no major errors or omissions regarding the score 2.0 elements and partial knowledge of the score 3.0 elements.

Score 2.0	**The student exhibits no major errors or omissions regarding the simpler details and processes, such as . . .**
	• recognizing and recalling specific terminology (*e.g., chemical energy, heat retention, kinetic energy*); and
	• recognizing and recalling isolated details, such as . . .
	  ○ a compressed spring is an example of stored mechanical energy;
	  ○ wind is an example of motion energy; and
	  ○ the earth's oceans produce mechanical energy from the tides and waves.
	However, the student exhibits major errors or omissions with score 3.0 elements.	

	Score 1.5	The student demonstrates partial knowledge of the score 2.0 elements but major errors or omissions regarding the score 3.0 elements.
Score 1.0	**With help, the student demonstrates partial understanding of some of the score 2.0 elements and some of the score 3.0 elements.**	
	Score 0.5	With help, the student demonstrates partial understanding of some of the score 2.0 elements but not the score 3.0 elements.
Score 0.0	**Even with help, the student demonstrates no understanding or skill.**	
Grade 7		
Score 3.0	**While engaged in tasks that address the sources and properties of energy, the student demonstrates an understanding of important information, such as . . .** • characteristics of various forms of energy (thermal, chemical, electrical, radiant, nuclear) (*e.g., explaining information known about a specific form of energy—for example, explaining that nuclear energy is released from the atomic nucleus*); and	

Score 3.0 (*continued*)	• characteristics of various sources of energy (renewable, nonrenewable) (*e.g., explaining information known about a specific source of energy—for example, explaining that wind power is a common renewable energy source that produces electricity by using airflow to rotate the blades on wind turbines*). **The student exhibits no major errors or omissions.**

Score 2.0	**The student exhibits no major errors or omissions regarding the simpler details and processes, such as . . .**
	• recognizing and recalling specific terminology (*e.g., mechanical energy, electrical energy, renewable energy*); and
	• recognizing and recalling isolated details, such as . . .
	    ○ nuclear energy was discovered accidentally by French physicist Henri Becquerel in 1896; and
	    ○ natural gas is a common nonrenewable source of heat energy in the United States.
	However, the student exhibits major errors or omissions with score 3.0 elements.

Grade 6	
Score 3.0	**While engaged in tasks that address the sources and properties of energy, the student demonstrates an understanding of important information, such as . . .** • basic properties of energy (*e.g., explaining general information known about the basic properties of energy, such as the fact that energy can be converted from one form to another but can never be created or destroyed*); • characteristics of various ways to transfer heat energy (conduction, convection, radiation) (*e.g., describing a specific way to transfer heat energy—for example, describing convection as a way that heat energy is transferred by the movement of currents in a gas or a liquid*); and • characteristics of electrical circuits (purpose, function of circuit components, forms of energy produced) (*e.g., explaining information known about electrical circuits, such as the fact that a resistor will reduce the flow of electricity through a circuit*). **The student exhibits no major errors or omissions.**

Score 2.0	**The student exhibits no major errors or omissions regarding the simpler details and processes, such as . . .**
	• recognizing and recalling specific terminology (*e.g., energy source, heat convection, heat radiation*); and
	• recognizing and recalling isolated details, such as . . .
	    ○ energy is defined as the ability to do work;
	    ○ conduction is one of the three most common ways to transfer heat energy; and
	    ○ a power source is a necessary component of an electrical circuit.
	However, the student exhibits major errors or omissions with score 3.0 elements.

Grade 5	
Score 3.0	**While engaged in tasks that address the sources and properties of energy, the student demonstrates an understanding of important information, such as . . .** • general characteristics of heat energy (direction of heat flow, basic impact on temperature) (*e.g., explaining general information known about heat energy, such as the fact that heat transfer always goes in the direction of hot to cold*); • general characteristics of electrical circuits (impact of an open loop on circuit function, basic purpose of circuit components) (*e.g., explaining general information known about electrical circuits, such as the fact that a broken wire or an open switch in an electrical circuit will prevent electricity from flowing through the circuit*); and • general characteristics of light energy (light absorption, light refraction, light reflection) (*e.g., explaining general information known about light energy, such as the fact that light can be absorbed by atoms and molecules*). **The student exhibits no major errors or omissions.**

Score 2.0	The student exhibits no major errors or omissions regarding the simpler details and processes, such as . . .
	• recognizing and recalling specific terminology (*e.g., heat conduction, heat transfer, heat energy*); and
	• recognizing and recalling isolated details, such as . . .
	  ◦ the transfer rate of heat energy is measured in watts;
	  ◦ a switch is a common component of electrical circuits; and
	  ◦ the speed of light is a fixed definition, not a measurement.
	However, the student exhibits major errors or omissions with score 3.0 elements.

	Grade 4
Score 3.0	**While engaged in tasks that address the sources and properties of energy, the student demonstrates an understanding of important information, such as . . .** • general characteristics of various common heat sources (human body, radiator, the sun, furnace) (*e.g., explaining general information known about a specific source of heat, such as the fact that the human body constantly releases energy in the form of heat through the skin*); • general characteristics of various components of a simple electrical circuit (power source, motor, light bulb, small appliance, large appliance) (*e.g., explaining general information known about a specific component of a simple electrical circuit—for example, turning a light switch to the "on" position provides electrical power to the light bulb, and turning a light switch to the "off" position removes electrical power from the light bulb*); • general characteristics of various common objects and substances that can refract light (prism, water, glass) (*e.g., explaining general information known about a common object or substance that can refract light—for example, water can make objects under its surface appear to be in a different location than they actually are*); and • general characteristics of various sounds (*e.g., explaining general information known about a specific sound—for example, a high-pitched sound is produced when an object vibrates at a high frequency*). **The student exhibits no major errors or omissions.**

Score 2.0	**The student exhibits no major errors or omissions regarding the simpler details and processes, such as . . .**
	• recognizing and recalling specific terminology (*e.g., electrical circuit, high frequency, low frequency*); and
	• recognizing and recalling isolated details, such as . . .
	  ◦ a thermometer would be used to measure the temperature of a heat source;
	  ◦ an electrical circuit will not work without a power source;
	  ◦ light can be refracted; and
	  ◦ some sounds have different frequencies.
	However, the student exhibits major errors or omissions with score 3.0 elements.

	Grade 3
Score 3.0	**While engaged in tasks that address the sources and properties of energy, the student demonstrates an understanding of important information, such as . . .** • examples of various common materials that conduct heat (*e.g., explaining that different materials conduct heat, and some of those materials conduct heat better than others—for example, metals conduct heat efficiently, whereas wood conducts heat poorly*); • examples of various common objects and substances that reflect light (*e.g., explaining that different objects and substances reflect light—for example, reflection of the sun can be seen on the surface of a lake*); and • general characteristics of pitch (*e.g., explaining general information known about pitch, such as the fact that pitch is the highness or lowness of a sound*). **The student exhibits no major errors or omissions.**

Score 2.0	The student exhibits no major errors or omissions regarding the simpler details and processes, such as . . .
	• recognizing and recalling specific terminology (*e.g., pitch, light reflection, light refraction*); and
	• recognizing and recalling isolated details, such as . . .
	    ◦ some materials conduct heat;
	    ◦ light can be reflected; and
	    ◦ sounds can be high or low.
	However, the student exhibits major errors or omissions with score 3.0 elements.

Grade 2	
Score 3.0	While engaged in tasks that address the sources and properties of energy, the student demonstrates an understanding of important information, such as . . . • basic ways heat can be produced (friction, motion, burning) (*e.g., explaining that heat can be produced in different ways—for example, rubbing two objects together produces heat by a process called friction*); • basic products of electricity in circuits (heat, sound, magnetic effects) (*e.g., explaining that different products result from electricity in circuits—for example, electricity in an electrical circuit can create a magnet*); and • basic interactions between vibration and sound (*e.g., explaining that changes in vibration affect the sound that is heard—for example, the more an object vibrates, the louder the sound that is produced*). **The student exhibits no major errors or omissions.**

Score 2.0	The student exhibits no major errors or omissions regarding the simpler details and processes, such as . . .
	• recognizing and recalling specific terminology (*e.g., magnet, friction, properties of light*); and
	• recognizing and recalling isolated details, such as . . .
	    ◦ some actions can produce heat;
	    ◦ Benjamin Franklin flew a kite during a thunderstorm to study electricity; and
	    ◦ when a guitar string vibrates, it produces a sound.
	However, the student exhibits major errors or omissions with score 3.0 elements.

Grade 1	
Score 3.0	While engaged in tasks that address the sources and properties of energy, the student demonstrates an understanding of important information, such as . . . • general characteristics of sound (*e.g., explaining general information known about sound, such as the fact that vibrating objects produce sound*); and • examples of various common uses for electricity (light, heat, sound) (*e.g., explaining that electricity is used for different purposes—for example, to power the lights in a home*). **The student exhibits no major errors or omissions.**

Score 2.0	The student exhibits no major errors or omissions regarding the simpler details and processes, such as . . .
	• recognizing and recalling specific terminology (*e.g., vibration, sound, electricity*); and
	• recognizing and recalling isolated details, such as . . .
	    ◦ some sounds are louder than others; and
	    ◦ a desk lamp will not work if it is not plugged in.
	However, the student exhibits major errors or omissions with score 3.0 elements.

Grade K	
Score 3.0	While engaged in tasks that address the sources and properties of energy, the student demonstrates an understanding of important information, such as . . .

Score 3.0 (continued)	• general characteristics of vibrating objects (*e.g., explaining general information known about vibrating objects, such as the fact that an object can vibrate quickly or slowly*); and • basic impact of light on how we see objects (*e.g., explaining that we see an object because light strikes it—for example, explaining that pointing a flashlight in a dark room allows us to see an object the light is pointing at*). **The student exhibits no major errors or omissions.**

Score 2.0	**The student exhibits no major errors or omissions regarding the simpler details and processes, such as . . .**
	• recognizing and recalling specific terminology (*e.g., loud, soft, light*); and
	• recognizing and recalling isolated details, such as . . .
	  ◦ vibrations can be felt; and
	  ◦ objects are hard to see in the dark.
	However, the student exhibits major errors or omissions with score 3.0 elements.

Forces and Motion

	Grade 8	
Score 4.0	**In addition to score 3.0 performance, the student demonstrates in-depth inferences and applications that go beyond what was taught.**	
	Score 3.5	In addition to score 3.0 performance, the student demonstrates in-depth inferences and applications with partial success.
Score 3.0	**While engaged in tasks that address forces and motion, the student demonstrates an understanding of important information, such as . . .** • implications of various factors on the motion of an object (more than one force acting on an object along a straight line, friction) (*e.g., explaining how a specific factor affects the motion of an object—for example, describing the effect of more than one force acting on an object that is moving along a straight line*); • characteristics and implications of the relationship between electricity and magnetism (*e.g., explaining information known about the relationship between electricity and magnetism—for example, describing how magnets can be used to generate electricity and examples of basic applications; describing how electricity can be used to generate a magnetic field and examples of basic applications*); and • basic implications of mass and distance on gravitational force (*e.g., explaining the basic impact that both mass and distance have on the strength of gravitational pull—for example, describing basic differences between how both a long and a short distance affect the gravitational pull between two objects*). **The student exhibits no major errors or omissions.**	
	Score 2.5	The student exhibits no major errors or omissions regarding the score 2.0 elements and partial knowledge of the score 3.0 elements.
Score 2.0	**The student exhibits no major errors or omissions regarding the simpler details and processes, such as . . .** • recognizing and recalling specific terminology (*e.g., inertia, electromagnetic force, gravitational pull*); and • recognizing and recalling isolated details, such as . . . 　○ friction can affect an object's motion; 　○ magnets can be used to generate electricity; and 　○ Sir Isaac Newton first thought of his system of gravitation when he saw an apple fall from a tree. **However, the student exhibits major errors or omissions with score 3.0 elements.**	
	Score 1.5	The student demonstrates partial knowledge of the score 2.0 elements but major errors or omissions regarding the score 3.0 elements.
Score 1.0	**With help, the student demonstrates partial understanding of some of the score 2.0 elements and some of the score 3.0 elements.**	
	Score 0.5	With help, the student demonstrates partial understanding of some of the score 2.0 elements but not the score 3.0 elements.
Score 0.0	**Even with help, the student demonstrates no understanding or skill.**	
	Grade 7	
Score 3.0	**While engaged in tasks that address forces and motion, the student demonstrates an understanding of important information, such as . . .**	

Score 3.0 (*continued*)	• implications of various forces on various objects (impact on position, impact on speed, impact on direction, effect of the same force on objects of varying size, effect of different forces on objects of the same size) (*e.g., explaining the impact of a specific force on a specific object—for example, predicting which of two different-sized objects will travel farther when kicked on the ground with the same force, and reasons for making the prediction*); • various ways to represent an object's change in position, direction, and speed (graphically, textually, mathematically) (*e.g., explaining how to represent an object's change in position, direction, and speed in a specific way—for example, explaining and exemplifying how to graph an object's change in speed*); and • implications of the effect of gravitational force on objects (impact on position, impact on speed, impact on direction, impact on objects of varying size, impact on objects of the same size) (*e.g., explaining the impact of gravity on a specific object—for example, predicting which of two different-sized objects will reach a given point first when pushed with equal force, and reasons for making the prediction*). **The student exhibits no major errors or omissions.**

Score 2.0	**The student exhibits no major errors or omissions regarding the simpler details and processes, such as . . .**
	• recognizing and recalling specific terminology (*e.g., gravitational force, kinetic, point of impact*); and
	• recognizing and recalling isolated details, such as . . .
	   ◦ force can affect an object's position, speed, and direction;
	   ◦ an object's change in position over time can be represented graphically; and
	   ◦ every object exerts a gravitational force.
	However, the student exhibits major errors or omissions with score 3.0 elements.

Grade 6	
Score 3.0	**While engaged in tasks that address forces and motion, the student demonstrates an understanding of important information, such as . . .** • characteristics of various ways to describe an object's motion (direction, speed, position over time) (*e.g., explaining information known about a specific way to describe the motion of an object—for example, explaining and exemplifying how to describe the position of an object over time by recording the object's position at different intervals*); • implications of the size of an object on the effect of a given force (impact on position, impact on direction, impact on speed) (*e.g., explaining the impact that the size of an object has on the effect of a given force—for example, describing how a large ball would be affected by a slight push*); • general characteristics of gravity (*e.g., explaining general information known about gravity, such as the fact that gravity decreases with altitude*); and • basic interactions between electrically charged material and other materials (charged versus noncharged) (*e.g., explaining the interaction between an electrically charged material and another given material—for example, predicting how an electrically charged material will interact with another material that is not electrically charged, and general reasons for making the prediction*). **The student exhibits no major errors or omissions.**

Score 2.0	**The student exhibits no major errors or omissions regarding the simpler details and processes, such as . . .**
	• recognizing and recalling specific terminology (*e.g., direction of a force, direction of motion, electrically charged material*); and
	• recognizing and recalling isolated details, such as . . .
	   ◦ a moving object's direction can be described and graphed;
	   ◦ a force's effect can vary;
	   ◦ gravity affects physical objects in a variety of ways; and
	   ◦ some materials can be electrically charged.
	However, the student exhibits major errors or omissions with score 3.0 elements.

Grade 5		
Score 3.0	**While engaged in tasks that address forces and motion, the student demonstrates an understanding of important information, such as . . .** • impact of force on motion (increase in force, decrease in force) (*e.g., explaining the impact that force has on motion—for example, predicting how a decrease in force would affect the motion of an object, and reasons for making the prediction*); • basic interactions between magnets and other materials (magnets versus nonmagnets) (*e.g., explaining the interaction between a magnet and another given material—for example, predicting how a magnet will interact with another magnet and general reasons for making the prediction*); and • basic implications of gravity (gravity versus no gravity) (*e.g., explaining the basic impact of gravity—for example, describing what would happen to the speed of a moving object if gravity did not exist*). **The student exhibits no major errors or omissions.**	

Score 2.0	**The student exhibits no major errors or omissions regarding the simpler details and processes, such as . . .**
	• recognizing and recalling specific terminology (*e.g., magnetic repulsion, magnetic attraction, gravity*); and
	• recognizing and recalling isolated details, such as . . .
	  ○ a force can affect the motion of an object;
	  ○ magnets do not attract all types of metal; and
	  ○ gravity is a necessary property of the earth.
	However, the student exhibits major errors or omissions with score 3.0 elements.	

Grade 4		
Score 3.0	**While engaged in tasks that address forces and motion, the student demonstrates an understanding of important information, such as . . .** • impact of force on speed and direction (increase in force, decrease in force, direction of force) (*e.g., explaining the impact that force has on direction—for example, predicting how changing the direction of a force affects the direction of an object in motion, and reasons for making the prediction*); and • general characteristics of magnetism (*e.g., explaining general information known about magnetism, such as the fact that magnets can attract other magnets and certain metals*). **The student exhibits no major errors or omissions.**	

Score 2.0	**The student exhibits no major errors or omissions regarding the simpler details and processes, such as . . .**
	• recognizing and recalling specific terminology (*e.g., force strength, friction, magnetism*); and
	• recognizing and recalling isolated details, such as . . .
	  ○ objects respond to forces applied to them; and
	  ○ a magnet is an object that has a magnetic field.
	However, the student exhibits major errors or omissions with score 3.0 elements.	

Grade 3		
Score 3.0	**While engaged in tasks that address forces and motion, the student demonstrates an understanding of important information, such as . . .** • impact of pushing or pulling on an object (impact on motion, impact on position) (*e.g., explaining how pushing or pulling would affect a given object—for example, predicting how pulling on an object would affect its position, and reasons for making the prediction*); and • general characteristics of magnets (*e.g., explaining general information known about magnets, such as the fact that magnets can attract or repel other magnets*). **The student exhibits no major errors or omissions.**	

Score 2.0	**The student exhibits no major errors or omissions regarding the simpler details and processes, such as . . .**
	• recognizing and recalling specific terminology (*e.g., change of speed, change of direction, magnet*); and
	• recognizing and recalling isolated details, such as . . .
	  ○ some objects may be harder to push than others; and
	  ○ magnets are used as tools to move things.
	However, the student exhibits major errors or omissions with score 3.0 elements.

Grade 2	
Score 3.0	**While engaged in tasks that address forces and motion, the student demonstrates an understanding of important information, such as . . .** • basic ways to describe the position of an object (relative to another object, relative to the background) (*e.g., explaining that the position of an object can be described in different ways—for example, an object can be described by its relationship to the position of another object or the background*); and • general characteristics of basic types of motion (circular, straight line, zigzag) (*e.g., explaining general information known about a specific type of motion, such as the fact that an object moving in a circular motion is forming a circle with its movement*). **The student exhibits no major errors or omissions.**

Score 2.0	**The student exhibits no major errors or omissions regarding the simpler details and processes, such as . . .**
	• recognizing and recalling specific terminology (*e.g., circular motion, straight-line motion, zigzag motion*); and
	• recognizing and recalling isolated details, such as . . .
	  ○ the position of an object can be described in different ways; and
	  ○ there are many different types of motion.
	However, the student exhibits major errors or omissions with score 3.0 elements.

Grade 1	
Score 3.0	**While engaged in tasks that address forces and motion, the student demonstrates an understanding of important information, such as . . .** • basic ways objects can be moved (sinking, pushing, pulling) (*e.g., explaining that an object can be moved in a specific way—for example, sinking an object in a bucket of water will move it from the surface to the bottom*); and • basic ways that the motion of objects can be stopped (*e.g., explaining that an object can be kept from falling to the ground—for example, a ball can be caught before it hits the ground*). **The student exhibits no major errors or omissions.**

Score 2.0	**The student exhibits no major errors or omissions regarding the simpler details and processes, such as . . .**
	• recognizing and recalling specific terminology (*e.g., vibration, position, sinking*); and
	• recognizing and recalling isolated details, such as . . .
	  ○ objects can be moved in different ways; and
	  ○ objects can be stopped before they fall to the ground.
	However, the student exhibits major errors or omissions with score 3.0 elements.

Grade K	
Score 3.0	**While engaged in tasks that address forces and motion, the student demonstrates an understanding of important information, such as . . .** • basic ways objects can be moved (*e.g., explaining that an object can be moved by pushing or pulling—for example, a wagon can be pulled across the classroom*); and

Score 3.0 (continued)	• basic ways things can fall to the ground (*e.g., explaining that an object can fall to the ground—for example, an apple can fall off a tree to the ground*). **The student exhibits no major errors or omissions.**

Score 2.0	**The student exhibits no major errors or omissions regarding the simpler details and processes, such as . . .**
	• recognizing and recalling specific terminology (*e.g., pushing, pulling, falling*); and
	• recognizing and recalling isolated details, such as . . .
	    ○ objects are frequently moved by people or other forces; and
	    ○ objects that are above the ground commonly fall to the ground.
	However, the student exhibits major errors or omissions with score 3.0 elements.

Nature of Science

Nature of Scientific Inquiry

Grade 8		
Score 4.0	**In addition to score 3.0 performance, the student demonstrates in-depth inferences and applications that go beyond what was taught.**	
	Score 3.5	In addition to score 3.0 performance, the student demonstrates in-depth inferences and applications with partial success.
Score 3.0	**While engaged in tasks that address the nature of scientific inquiry, the student demonstrates important skills, such as . . .** • designing and conducting two or more experiments with an emphasis on replication (*e.g., designing and implementing an experiment to test a hypothesis that has been constructed, replicating the experiment with appropriate controls, and then examining and explaining the combined results of the original experiment and the replication*). **The student exhibits no major errors or omissions.**	
	Score 2.5	The student exhibits no major errors or omissions regarding the score 2.0 elements and partial knowledge of the score 3.0 elements.
Score 2.0	**The student exhibits no major errors or omissions regarding the simpler details and processes, such as . . .** • recognizing and recalling specific terminology (*e.g., alternative explanation of data, experimental confirmation, replication*); and • performing basic processes, such as . . . ○ carrying out a predesigned replication and comparing the results with the original experiment. **However, the student exhibits major errors or omissions with score 3.0 elements.**	
	Score 1.5	The student demonstrates partial knowledge of the score 2.0 elements but major errors or omissions regarding the score 3.0 elements.
Score 1.0	**With help, the student demonstrates partial understanding of some of the score 2.0 elements and some of the score 3.0 elements.**	
	Score 0.5	With help, the student demonstrates partial understanding of some of the score 2.0 elements but not the score 3.0 elements.
Score 0.0	**Even with help, the student demonstrates no understanding or skill.**	
Grade 7		
Score 3.0	**While engaged in tasks that address the nature of scientific inquiry, the student demonstrates important skills, such as . . .** • designing and conducting an experiment with a focus on alternative hypotheses (*e.g., generating a primary hypothesis along with an alternative hypothesis, designing a way to test the primary hypothesis and the alternative hypothesis, and evaluating the accuracy of the primary and alternative hypotheses based on the results*). **The student exhibits no major errors or omissions.**	

Score 2.0	The student exhibits no major errors or omissions regarding the simpler details and processes, such as . . . • recognizing and recalling specific terminology (*e.g., faulty reasoning, experimental control, scientific skepticism*); and • performing basic processes, such as . . . ◦ conducting a predesigned experiment to test two different hypotheses. **However, the student exhibits major errors or omissions with score 3.0 elements.**

Grade 6	
Score 3.0	While engaged in tasks that address the nature of scientific inquiry, the student demonstrates important skills, such as . . . • designing and conducting an experiment with a focus on controls (*e.g., generating a basic hypothesis, designing a way to test that hypothesis while controlling for specific factors, and evaluating the accuracy of the original hypothesis based on the results*). **The student exhibits no major errors or omissions.**
Score 2.0	The student exhibits no major errors or omissions regarding the simpler details and processes, such as . . . • recognizing and recalling specific terminology (*e.g., hypothesis, logic, scientific method*); and • performing basic processes, such as . . . ◦ designing a way to control for a specific variable. **However, the student exhibits major errors or omissions with score 3.0 elements.**

Grade 5	
Score 3.0	While engaged in tasks that address the nature of scientific inquiry, the student demonstrates important skills, such as . . . • designing and conducting a simple experiment and evaluating the results in light of the original hypothesis (*e.g., generating a basic hypothesis regarding something that has been observed, setting up a way to test the hypothesis, and then evaluating the accuracy of the hypothesis based on the results*). **The student exhibits no major errors or omissions.**
Score 2.0	The student exhibits no major errors or omissions regarding the simpler details and processes, such as . . . • recognizing and recalling specific terminology (*e.g., data analysis, data presentation, replicable experiment*); and • performing basic processes, such as . . . ◦ evaluating the accuracy of a hypothesis based on the findings of an experiment that has already been conducted. **However, the student exhibits major errors or omissions with score 3.0 elements.**

Grade 4	
Score 3.0	While engaged in tasks that address the nature of scientific inquiry, the student demonstrates important skills, such as . . . • designing and conducting a simple experiment (*e.g., generating basic hypotheses about something observed at home and then setting up a simple way to test the hypotheses*). **The student exhibits no major errors or omissions.**
Score 2.0	The student exhibits no major errors or omissions regarding the simpler details and processes, such as . . . • recognizing and recalling specific terminology (*e.g., controlled experiment, scientific evidence, reproducible result*); and

Score 2.0 (continued)	• performing basic processes, such as . . . ○ conducting a predesigned experiment to test a given hypothesis. **However, the student exhibits major errors or omissions with score 3.0 elements.**
Grade 3	
Score 3.0	**While engaged in tasks that address the nature of scientific inquiry, the student demonstrates important skills, such as . . .** • generating a feasible hypothesis about something that has been observed (*e.g., after observing that a pet rabbit kept in class sleeps most of the day, the student generates a viable hypothesis as to why*). **The student exhibits no major errors or omissions.**
Score 2.0	**The student exhibits no major errors or omissions regarding the simpler details and processes, such as . . .** • recognizing and recalling specific terminology (*e.g., scientific equipment, question formulation, scientific knowledge*); and • performing basic processes, such as . . . ○ determining whether a given hypothesis is a viable way to explain something that has been observed in class. **However, the student exhibits major errors or omissions with score 3.0 elements.**
Grade 2	
Score 3.0	**While engaged in tasks that address the nature of scientific inquiry, the student demonstrates important skills, such as . . .** • using simple tools (thermometers, magnifiers, rulers) (*e.g., using a ruler to measure the size of students' hands and then making a generalization about the data*). **The student exhibits no major errors or omissions.**
Score 2.0	**The student exhibits no major errors or omissions regarding the simpler details and processes, such as . . .** • recognizing and recalling specific terminology (*e.g., scientific investigation, duplication, scientific tools*); and • performing basic processes, such as . . . ○ determining the appropriate tool to be used in a given situation. **However, the student exhibits major errors or omissions with score 3.0 elements.**
Grade 1	
Score 3.0	**While engaged in tasks that address the nature of scientific inquiry, the student demonstrates important skills, such as . . .** • using simple tools to gather information and extend the senses (thermometers, magnifiers, rulers) (*e.g., demonstrating how to place and read a thermometer to determine the temperature of a liquid*). **The student exhibits no major errors or omissions.**
Score 2.0	**The student exhibits no major errors or omissions regarding the simpler details and processes, such as . . .** • recognizing and recalling specific terminology (*e.g., magnify, simple experiment, thermometer*); and • recognizing and recalling isolated details, such as . . . ○ thermometers come in many different forms. **However, the student exhibits major errors or omissions with score 3.0 elements.**
Grade K	
Score 3.0	**While engaged in tasks that address the nature of scientific inquiry, the student demonstrates important skills and understanding such as . . .**

Score 3.0 (continued)	• generating basic questions about the physical world (*e.g., asking why the weather changes frequently*). **The student exhibits no major errors or omissions.**
Score 2.0	**The student exhibits no major errors or omissions regarding the simpler details and processes, such as . . .** • recognizing and recalling specific terminology (*e.g., the senses, observation, magnifier*); and • recognizing and recalling isolated details, such as . . . ○ a magnifier can be used to see small objects more clearly. **However, the student exhibits major errors or omissions with score 3.0 elements.**

Scientific Enterprise

		Grade 8
Score 4.0		**In addition to score 3.0 performance, the student demonstrates in-depth inferences and applications that go beyond what was taught.**
	Score 3.5	In addition to score 3.0 performance, the student demonstrates in-depth inferences and applications with partial success.
Score 3.0		**While engaged in tasks that address scientific enterprise, the student demonstrates an understanding of important information, such as . . .** • how various scientists (including Antoine Lavoisier, Marie Curie, and Pierre Curie) have added to our scientific knowledge (*e.g., explaining how Antoine Lavoisier, Marie Curie, Pierre Curie, and other scientists contributed to our scientific knowledge—for example, explaining that Antoine Lavoisier invented the first periodic table with 33 elements; Marie Curie discovered the chemical elements polonium and radium with her husband Pierre; Pierre Curie discovered piezoelectric effects with his brother Jacques*); and • implications of ethical issues on the scientific enterprise (research on animals, human drug trials) (*e.g., explaining how scientists and their research are affected by an ethical issue—for example, describing how research to find a cure for a disease would be affected if the scientists involved considered research on animals to be a violation of their personal code of ethics*). **The student exhibits no major errors or omissions.**
	Score 2.5	The student exhibits no major errors or omissions regarding the score 2.0 elements and partial knowledge of the score 3.0 elements.

Score 2.0		**The student exhibits no major errors or omissions regarding the simpler details and processes, such as . . .**
		• recognizing and recalling specific terminology (*e.g., ethics in science, clinical trial*); and
		• recognizing and recalling isolated details, such as
		  ○ Antoine Lavoisier is considered "the father of modern chemistry"; Marie Curie was the first two-time Nobel laureate and the only female laureate in two different sciences, physics and chemistry; Pierre Curie shared the 1903 Nobel Prize with his wife Marie and Henri Becquerel; and
		  ○ scientists must consider ethical issues regarding their studies.
		However, the student exhibits major errors or omissions with score 3.0 elements.

	Score 1.5	The student demonstrates partial knowledge of the score 2.0 elements but major errors or omissions regarding the score 3.0 elements.
Score 1.0		**With help, the student demonstrates partial understanding of some of the score 2.0 elements and some of the score 3.0 elements.**
	Score 0.5	With help, the student demonstrates partial understanding of some of the score 2.0 elements but not the score 3.0 elements.
Score 0.0		**Even with help, the student demonstrates no understanding or skill.**
		Grade 7
Score 3.0		**While engaged in tasks that address scientific enterprise, the student demonstrates an understanding of important information, such as . . .** • how various scientists (including Louis Pasteur, Edward Jenner, and Sir Isaac Newton) have added to our scientific knowledge (*e.g., explaining how Louis Pasteur, Edward Jenner, Sir Isaac Newton, and other scientists contributed to our scientific knowledge—for example, explaining that Louis Pasteur created the first vaccine for rabies; Edward Jenner was the first doctor to introduce and study the smallpox vaccine; and Sir Isaac Newton shares credit with Gottfried Leibniz for the development of calculus*); and

Score 3.0 (continued)	• implications of various issues on the scientific enterprise (whether the study might harm people or the environment, whether the cost of the study is justified for what might be discovered, whether the study might damage scientific equipment) (*e.g., explaining how scientists and their research are affected by a specific issue—for example, describing how a research project would be affected if it is determined that portions of the study might damage scientific equipment used in the project*). **The student exhibits no major errors or omissions.**

Score 2.0	**The student exhibits no major errors or omissions regarding the simpler details and processes, such as . . .**
	• recognizing and recalling specific terminology (*e.g., intellectual honesty, environmental impact*); and
	• recognizing and recalling isolated details, such as . . .
	  ◦ Louis Pasteur is best known for inventing a process called pasteurization; Edward Jenner coined the term "vaccination"; Sir Isaac Newton is regarded by many as the greatest figure in the history of science; and
	  ◦ scientists must consider how their studies might affect others and the environment.
	However, the student exhibits major errors or omissions with score 3.0 elements.

Grade 6	
Score 3.0	**While engaged in tasks that address scientific enterprise, the student demonstrates an understanding of important information, such as . . .** • how various scientists (including Galileo Galilei, Nicolaus Copernicus, and Johannes Kepler) have added to our scientific knowledge (*e.g., explaining how Galileo Galilei, Nicolaus Copernicus, Johannes Kepler, and other scientists contributed to our scientific knowledge—for example, explaining that Galileo Galilei pioneered the use of quantitative experiments whose results could be analyzed with mathematical precision; Nicolaus Copernicus was the first European astronomer to formulate a modern heliocentric theory of the solar system; Johannes Kepler's first major astronomical work,* Mysterium Cosmographicum (The Sacred Mystery of the Cosmos), *was the first published defense of the Copernican system*); and • general characteristics of effective scientists (including being willing to work in teams, being willing to work alone, seeing things in different ways, being willing to live with ambiguity, being willing to question assumptions and ideas) (*e.g., explaining general information known about being an effective scientist—for example, describing an effective scientist as one who is willing to question assumptions and ideas*). **The student exhibits no major errors or omissions.**

Score 2.0	**The student exhibits no major errors or omissions regarding the simpler details and processes, such as . . .**
	• recognizing and recalling specific terminology (*e.g., ambiguity, informed subject*); and
	• recognizing and recalling isolated details, such as . . .
	  ◦ Galileo Galilei is often referred to as the "father of modern astronomy"; Nicolaus Copernicus's conception of the sun is considered among the most important landmarks in the history of science; Johannes Kepler is best known for his laws of planetary motion; and
	  ◦ being a good scientist involves a specific set of skills and abilities.
	However, the student exhibits major errors or omissions with score 3.0 elements.

Grade 5	
Score 3.0	**While engaged in tasks that address scientific enterprise, the student demonstrates an understanding of important information, such as . . .** • how various scientists (including Alexander Graham Bell, Thomas Edison, and Benjamin Franklin) have added to our scientific knowledge (*e.g., explaining how Alexander Graham Bell, Thomas Edison, Benjamin Franklin, and other scientists contributed to our scientific knowledge—for example, explaining that Alexander Graham Bell is credited with the invention of the metal detector; Thomas Edison patented an electric distribution system in 1880; Benjamin Franklin invented bifocal glasses*);

Score 3.0 (continued)	• how societal challenges (disease, disability, convenience) inspire scientific research (*e.g., explaining that challenges faced by society often inspire scientific research—for example, prosthetic devices were developed to help disabled people gain more mobility in society*); and • how scientific investigation can take years to complete (*e.g., explaining why scientific investigations can sometimes take years to complete—for example, describing basic reasons why the polio vaccine developed by Jonas Salk in 1952 was not licensed until three years later*). **The student exhibits no major errors or omissions.**

Score 2.0	**The student exhibits no major errors or omissions regarding the simpler details and processes, such as . . .**
	• recognizing and recalling specific terminology (*e.g., ongoing process of science, innovation*); and
	• recognizing and recalling isolated details, such as . . .
	    ◦ Alexander Graham Bell is widely acclaimed for inventing and developing the telephone in 1876; Thomas Edison invented the phonograph in 1877; Benjamin Franklin invented the lightning rod; and
	    ◦ the Artificial Limb Program was started in 1945 by National Academy of Sciences; and
	    ◦ some scientific studies can take years before reaching a definitive conclusion.
	However, the student exhibits major errors or omissions with score 3.0 elements.

Grade 4

Score 3.0	**While engaged in tasks that address scientific enterprise, the student demonstrates an understanding of important information, such as . . .** • general characteristics of various scientific and technological contributions (development of the polio vaccine, invention of the light bulb, invention of the telephone) (*e.g., explaining general information about a specific scientific or technological contribution—for example, the first effective polio vaccine, developed by Jonas Salk in 1952, was not announced safe and effective until almost three years after it was first developed*). **The student exhibits no major errors or omissions.**
Score 2.0	**The student exhibits no major errors or omissions regarding the simpler details and processes, such as . . .** • recognizing and recalling specific terminology (*e.g., scientific contribution, technological contribution*); and • recognizing and recalling isolated details, such as . . . ◦ some scientific and technological innovations involve many cycles of trial and error before results are accepted. **However, the student exhibits major errors or omissions with score 3.0 elements.**

Grade 3

Score 3.0	**While engaged in tasks that address scientific enterprise, the student demonstrates an understanding of important information, such as . . .** • general benefits of scientists sharing their findings with others (adds to our knowledge of the world, gets the reactions of other scientists) (*e.g., explaining general benefits associated with scientists sharing their findings from a scientific study—for example, findings from a scientific study can be validated by other scientists*). **The student exhibits no major errors or omissions.**
Score 2.0	**The student exhibits no major errors or omissions regarding the simpler details and processes, such as . . .** • recognizing and recalling specific terminology (*e.g., history of science, findings*); and • recognizing and recalling isolated details, such as . . . ◦ the process of science often involves sharing results with other scientists. **However, the student exhibits major errors or omissions with Score 3.0 elements.**

Grade 2	
Score 3.0	**While engaged in tasks that address scientific enterprise, the student demonstrates an understanding of important information, such as . . .** • general benefits of scientists working in teams (helps them identify errors, helps them look at different explanations for things) (*e.g., explaining general benefits associated with scientists working on research in teams, such as the fact that a team of scientists working on a project might notice errors in the research that a scientist working alone might otherwise miss*). **The student exhibits no major errors or omissions.**
Score 2.0	**The student exhibits no major errors or omissions regarding the simpler details and processes, such as . . .** • recognizing and recalling specific terminology (*e.g., scientist, technology*); and • recognizing and recalling isolated details, such as . . . 　○ in science it is useful to work with a team. **However, the student exhibits major errors or omissions with score 3.0 elements.**

Grade 1	
Score 3.0	**While engaged in tasks that address scientific enterprise, the student demonstrates an understanding of important information, such as . . .** • general characteristics of the basic process of science (making predictions, testing predictions) (*e.g., explaining general information known about the basic process of science—for example, science involves making a prediction and testing that prediction to see if it is correct*). **The student exhibits no major errors or omissions.**
Score 2.0	**The student exhibits no major errors or omissions regarding the simpler details and processes, such as . . .** • recognizing and recalling specific terminology (*e.g., prediction, testing*); and • recognizing and recalling isolated details, such as . . . 　○ science involves testing predictions. **However, the student exhibits major errors or omissions with score 3.0 elements.**

Grade K	
Score 3.0	**While engaged in tasks that address scientific enterprise, the student demonstrates an understanding of important information, such as . . .** • general characteristics of science (*e.g., explaining general information known about science—for example, science involves trying to determine how things work or why things happen*). **The student exhibits no major errors or omissions.**
Score 2.0	**The student exhibits no major errors or omissions regarding the simpler details and processes, such as . . .** • recognizing and recalling specific terminology (*e.g., science, question*); and • recognizing and recalling isolated details, such as . . . 　○ students engage in science when they ask questions about how things work. **However, the student exhibits major errors or omissions with score 3.0 elements.**

Scoring Scales for
Social Studies

Social Studies

―――

Note: For each measurement topic, the scale for the first grade level (the highest grade level to which the topic extends) includes all scores, including half-point scores. For all other grade levels, the scale shows scores 3.0 and 2.0 only, because the descriptors for the other scores on the scale do not change from grade level to grade level.

Citizenship, Government, and Democracy

Rights, Responsibilities, and Participation in the Political Process

Grade 8		
Score 4.0	**In addition to score 3.0 performance, the student demonstrates in-depth inferences and applications that go beyond what was taught.**	
	Score 3.5	In addition to score 3.0 performance, the student demonstrates in-depth inferences and applications with partial success.
Score 3.0	**While engaged in tasks that address the topic of rights, responsibilities, and participation in the political process, the student demonstrates an understanding of important information, such as . . .** • the influence of various political rights on society in the United States (*e.g., explaining and exemplifying how Americans' right to petition affects elected officials at all levels of government—for example, petitioning a state representative to urge a policy change in the governor's office*); • the influence of commonly held civic responsibilities on society in the United States (*e.g., explaining and exemplifying how performing public service affects a local community—for example, donating time as a mentor at a youth center*); and • the impact of various contemporary issues involving civic responsibility on society in the United States (*e.g., explaining and exemplifying how a contemporary issue affects U.S. citizens—for example, explaining how low voter turnout influences election results*). **The student exhibits no major errors or omissions.**	
	Score 2.5	The student exhibits no major errors or omissions regarding the score 2.0 elements and partial knowledge of the score 3.0 elements.
Score 2.0	**The student exhibits no major errors or omissions regarding the simpler details and processes, such as . . .** • recognizing and recalling specific terminology, events, people, and locations (*e.g., freedom of elections, equality of justice, public service, voter participation*); and • recognizing and recalling isolated details, such as . . . ○ signatures on a petition often have to be authenticated before the petition is accepted; ○ performing public service is considered a civic responsibility; and ○ voter turnout is usually higher during a presidential election. **However, the student exhibits major errors or omissions regarding score 3.0 elements.**	
	Score 1.5	The student demonstrates partial knowledge of the score 2.0 elements but major errors or omissions regarding the score 3.0 elements.
Score 1.0	**With help, the student demonstrates partial understanding of some of the score 2.0 elements and some of the score 3.0 elements.**	
	Score 0.5	With help, the student demonstrates partial understanding of some of the score 2.0 elements but not the score 3.0 elements.

Score 0.0	Even with help, the student demonstrates no understanding or skill.

Grade 7

Score 3.0	While engaged in tasks that address the topic of rights, responsibilities, and participation in the political process, the student demonstrates an understanding of important information, such as . . . • the impact of major civil rights legislation on society in the United States (*e.g., explaining and exemplifying how U.S. citizens have been affected by the Civil Rights Act of 1964—for example, how outlawing discrimination based on race, color, religion, sex, or national origin has changed hiring policies from then until now*); and • the influence of commonly held civic responsibilities on society in the United States (*e.g., explaining and exemplifying how considering the rights and interests of others affects a local community—for example, how a charity might be affected if citizens stopped volunteering their time*). **The student exhibits no major errors or omissions.**

Score 2.0	The student exhibits no major errors or omissions regarding the simpler details and processes, such as . . .
	
	• recognizing and recalling specific terminology, events, people, and locations (*e.g., political rights, civil rights legislation, civic responsibility*); and
	
	• recognizing and recalling isolated details, such as . . .
	  ○ Title I of the Civil Rights Act of 1964 deals with voter rights; and
	  ○ the rights and interests of others is considered a civic responsibility.
	
	However, the student exhibits major errors or omissions regarding score 3.0 elements.

Grade 6

Score 3.0	While engaged in tasks that address the topic of rights, responsibilities, and participation in the political process, the student demonstrates an understanding of important information, such as . . . • the influence of political rights on individuals (*e.g., explaining and exemplifying how freedom of speech affects individuals—for example, how an individual can influence change in local policy through a public speech*); and • the impact of the U.S. Constitution and the Bill of Rights on society in the United States (*e.g., explaining and exemplifying how the news media is affected by the First Amendment—for example, explaining why information published in newspapers might be limited without a free press*). **The student exhibits no major errors or omissions.**

Score 2.0	The student exhibits no major errors or omissions regarding the simpler details and processes, such as . . .
	
	• recognizing and recalling specific terminology, events, people, and locations (*e.g., right to petition, freedom of the press, U.S. Constitution, Bill of Rights*); and
	
	• recognizing and recalling isolated details, such as . . .
	  ○ freedom of speech is considered a political right; and
	  ○ the First Amendment to the U.S. Constitution deals with religion, speech, the press, petition, and assembly.
	
	However, the student exhibits major errors or omissions regarding score 3.0 elements.

Grade 5

Score 3.0	While engaged in tasks that address the topic of rights, responsibilities, and participation in the political process, the student demonstrates an understanding of important information, such as . . . • the impact of the Declaration of Independence on society in the United States (*e.g., explaining and exemplifying how deriving its powers from the consent of the governed affects the U.S. government—for example, explaining why each state is represented in the U.S. House of Representatives proportionally according to its population*); and

Score 3.0 (continued)	• the influence of commonly held personal responsibilities on society in the United States (*e.g., explaining and exemplifying how accepting, or failing to accept, responsibility for the consequences of one's actions affects a local community—for example, explaining why a hero graciously accepting a medal of honor helps give citizens a greater sense of pride in their community*). **The student exhibits no major errors or omissions.**

Score 2.0	**The student exhibits no major errors or omissions regarding the simpler details and processes, such as . . .**
	• recognizing and recalling specific terminology, events, people, and locations (*e.g., right to vote, right to assemble, unalienable rights, personal responsibility*); and
	• recognizing and recalling isolated details, such as . . .
	   ◦ the preamble to the Declaration of Independence deals with rights of all men; and
	   ◦ accepting responsibility for the consequences of one's actions is considered a personal responsibility.
	However, the student exhibits major errors or omissions regarding score 3.0 elements.

Grade 4

Score 3.0	**While engaged in tasks that address the topic of rights, responsibilities, and participation in the political process, the student demonstrates an understanding of important information, such as . . .** • basic implications of being a citizen of the United States (*e.g., explaining and exemplifying basic reasons why citizens owe allegiance or loyalty to the United States—for example, for protection from foreign enemies; explaining basic reasons why citizens need to respect the law—for example, to maintain a peaceful society; explaining basic reasons why citizens need to vote—for example, to give citizens a way to let politicians know what issues are important to them*); and • basic influence of fundamental values of democracy in the United States (equality of opportunity, diversity, truth, patriotism) on U.S. society (*e.g., explaining and exemplifying the basic effect of equality of opportunity on employees—for example, explaining that each potential employee should have an equal chance to get hired if the person meets the requirements for the job*). **The student exhibits no major errors or omissions.**

Score 2.0	**The student exhibits no major errors or omissions regarding the simpler details and processes, such as . . .**
	• recognizing and recalling specific terminology, events, people, and locations (*e.g., diversity, truth, patriotism*); and
	• recognizing and recalling isolated details, such as . . .
	   ◦ a citizen of the United States owes allegiance or loyalty to the United States; and
	   ◦ equality of opportunity is considered a fundamental value of democracy in the United States.
	However, the student exhibits major errors or omissions regarding score 3.0 elements.

Grade 3

Score 3.0	**While engaged in tasks that address the topic of rights, responsibilities, and participation in the political process, the student demonstrates an understanding of important information, such as . . .** • why a citizen of the United States receives protection (military protection) and other services (financial assistance, food stamps) from the U.S. government (*e.g., explaining and exemplifying basic services U.S. citizens can and cannot receive from the federal government—for example, explaining that many Americans incorrectly believe that the government is required to help citizens pay their bills in time of financial crisis*); and

Score 3.0 (continued)	• basic influence of fundamental values of democracy in the United States (individual rights, the public or common good, justice) on U.S. society (e.g., *explaining and exemplifying how citizens' working together affects a local community—for example, explaining why a group of citizens volunteering to repair an old library helps people in the community*). **The student exhibits no major errors or omissions.**

Score 2.0	**The student exhibits no major errors or omissions regarding the simpler details and processes, such as . . .**
	• recognizing and recalling specific terminology, events, people, and locations (e.g., *protection, common good, justice*); and
	• recognizing and recalling isolated details, such as . . .
	  ○ the U.S. government provides a military to help protect its citizens from harm; and
	  ○ individual rights are considered a fundamental value of democracy in the United States.
	However, the student exhibits major errors or omissions regarding score 3.0 elements.

Grade 2	

Score 3.0	**While engaged in tasks that address the topic of rights, responsibilities, and participation in the political process, the student demonstrates an understanding of important information, such as . . .** • a citizen of the United States is a legally recognized member who has privileges and responsibilities (e.g., *explaining that the right to vote is a privilege of being a U.S. citizen that can be lost—for example, convicted criminals are prohibited from voting*). **The student exhibits no major errors or omissions.**
Score 2.0	**The student exhibits no major errors or omissions regarding the simpler details and processes, such as . . .** • recognizing and recalling specific terminology, events, people, and locations (e.g., *privilege, responsibility, rights*); and • recognizing and recalling isolated details, such as . . . ○ only a citizen of the United States can vote in government elections within the United States. **However, the student exhibits major errors or omissions regarding score 3.0 elements.**

Grade 2

Grade 1

Score 3.0	**While engaged in tasks that address the topic of rights, responsibilities, and participation in the political process, the student demonstrates an understanding of important information, such as . . .** • basic values of democracy in the United States, including life, liberty, and the common good (e.g., *explaining that democracy in the United States is based on fundamental values—for example, "common good" means that laws should benefit all members of society*); and • basic protections government should provide its citizens, including individual rights (e.g., *explaining that the free exercise of religion is a basic protection that should be given to the citizens of a government—for example, citizens should not be persecuted for their religious beliefs*). **The student exhibits no major errors or omissions.**

Score 2.0	**The student exhibits no major errors or omissions regarding the simpler details and processes, such as . . .**
	• recognizing and recalling specific terminology, events, people, and locations (e.g., *democracy, citizen, government*); and
	• recognizing and recalling isolated details, such as . . .
	  ○ democracy in the United States has fundamental values; and
	  ○ government should protect its citizens.
	However, the student exhibits major errors or omissions regarding score 3.0 elements.

Grade K	
Score 3.0	Not applicable.
Score 2.0	Not applicable.

The U.S. and State Constitutions

Grade 8		
Score 4.0	In addition to score 3.0 performance, the student demonstrates in-depth inferences and applications that go beyond what was taught.	
	Score 3.5	In addition to score 3.0 performance, the student demonstrates in-depth inferences and applications with partial success.
Score 3.0	While engaged in tasks that address the U.S. and state constitutions, the student demonstrates an understanding of important information, such as . . . • implications of alternative plans and major compromises considered by the delegates during the Constitutional Convention (*e.g., explaining and exemplifying how the Virginia Plan, if approved, would have affected the states and the new federal government—for example, explaining how having both houses of the legislature based on proportional representation might affect the states with smaller populations*); • implications of amendments to the U.S. Constitution (*e.g., explaining and exemplifying how passage of the Fifteenth Amendment affected women in the United States—for example, explaining how excluding women influenced women's suffrage groups of the time*); and • implications of various challenges to the Bill of Rights (*e.g., explaining and exemplifying the arguments by the Federalists and the Anti-Federalists over the need for a Bill of Rights—for example, explaining why Alexander Hamilton feared the Bill of Rights would limit the rights of the people*). **The student exhibits no major errors or omissions.**	
	Score 2.5	The student exhibits no major errors or omissions regarding the score 2.0 elements and partial knowledge of the score 3.0 elements.

Score 2.0	The student exhibits no major errors or omissions regarding the simpler details and processes, such as . . .
	• recognizing and recalling specific terminology, events, people, and locations (*e.g., equal protection of the laws, separation of church and state, Virginia Plan, New Jersey Plan*); and
	• recognizing and recalling isolated details, such as . . .
	  ○ the Virginia Plan was created by James Madison;
	  ○ the Fifteenth Amendment deals with voting qualifications; and
	  ○ Alexander Hamilton was one of the Federalists.
	However, the student exhibits major errors or omissions with score 3.0 elements.	

	Score 1.5	The student demonstrates partial knowledge of the score 2.0 elements but major errors or omissions regarding the score 3.0 elements.
Score 1.0	With help, the student demonstrates partial understanding of some of the score 2.0 elements and some of the score 3.0 elements.	
	Score 0.5	With help, the student demonstrates partial understanding of some of the score 2.0 elements but not the score 3.0 elements.
Score 0.0	Even with help, the student demonstrates no understanding or skill.	
Grade 7		
Score 3.0	While engaged in tasks that address the U.S. and state constitutions, the student demonstrates an understanding of important information, such as . . . • events that led to and shaped the Constitutional Convention (*e.g., explaining and exemplifying how Shays's Rebellion influenced those participating in the convention—for example, explaining how nationalists used the rebellion to scare the country into supporting a more vigorous federal government*);	

Score 3.0 (*continued*)	• implications of the Bill of Rights (*e.g., explaining and exemplifying how the Fourth Amendment affects law enforcement—for example, explaining how the exclusionary rule affects a criminal trial if the defendant's Fourth Amendment rights are found to have been violated*); and • implications of challenges to the Bill of Rights (*e.g., explaining and exemplifying how the Sedition Act violated the Bill of Rights—for example, explaining why Thomas Jefferson believed the Sedition Act violated the Tenth Amendment*). **The student exhibits no major errors or omissions.**

Score 2.0	**The student exhibits no major errors or omissions regarding the simpler details and processes, such as . . .**
	• recognizing and recalling specific terminology, events, people, and locations (*e.g., Shays's Rebellion, Articles of Confederation, search and seizure, privacy*); and
	• recognizing and recalling isolated details, such as . . .
	  ○ Shays's Rebellion was led by Daniel Shays;
	  ○ the Bill of Rights deals with rights of U.S. citizens; and
	  ○ the Sedition Act of 1798 had an expiration date of March 3, 1801.
	However, the student exhibits major errors or omissions with score 3.0 elements.

Grade 6	
Score 3.0	**While engaged in tasks that address the U.S. and state constitutions, the student demonstrates an understanding of important information, such as . . .** • the impact of various concepts within the U.S. Constitution on society in the United States (habeas corpus, trial by jury, ex post facto, due process of law, right to counsel) (*e.g., explaining and exemplifying how the right to counsel affects a defendant in a criminal trial—for example, explaining how a poor defendant might be affected if an attorney were not provided*). **The student exhibits no major errors or omissions.**
Score 2.0	**The student exhibits no major errors or omissions regarding the simpler details and processes, such as . . .** • recognizing and recalling specific terminology, events, people, and locations (*e.g., habeas corpus, ex post facto, due process of law, right to counsel*); and • recognizing and recalling isolated details, such as . . . ○ the writ of habeas corpus is mentioned in Article I of the United States Constitution. **However, the student exhibits major errors or omissions with score 3.0 elements.**
Grade 5	
Score 3.0	Not applicable.
Score 2.0	Not applicable.
Grade 4	
Score 3.0	Not applicable.
Score 2.0	Not applicable.
Grade 3	
Score 3.0	Not applicable.
Score 2.0	Not applicable.
Grade 2	
Score 3.0	Not applicable.

Score 2.0	Not applicable.
Grade 1	
Score 3.0	Not applicable.
Score 2.0	Not applicable.
Grade K	
Score 3.0	Not applicable.
Score 2.0	Not applicable.

The Civil and Criminal Legal Systems

	Grade 8	
Score 4.0	**In addition to score 3.0 performance, the student demonstrates in-depth inferences and applications that go beyond what was taught.**	
	Score 3.5	In addition to score 3.0 performance, the student demonstrates in-depth inferences and applications with partial success.
Score 3.0	**While engaged in tasks that address the civil and criminal legal systems, the student demonstrates an understanding of important information, such as . . .** • implications of various concepts of criminal law in the United States (criminal law serving to deter crime, juvenile offenders tried as adults, the appeals process, jury trials) (*e.g., explaining and exemplifying how all jurors being required to reach a unanimous verdict affects a criminal trial—for example, explaining what happens to a person actually guilty of an accused crime if the jury cannot agree on circumstantial evidence*); and • implications of various concepts of civil law in the United States (civil law serving to compensate, standards of proof in a civil trial) (*e.g., explaining and exemplifying how being able to bring a civil suit against someone acquitted of a crime affects society in the United States—for example, explaining how the perceived validity of a criminal verdict might be influenced if a person acquitted of murder is found liable for the victim's death in civil court*). **The student exhibits no major errors or omissions.**	
	Score 2.5	The student exhibits no major errors or omissions regarding the score 2.0 elements and partial knowledge of the score 3.0 elements.

Score 2.0	**The student exhibits no major errors or omissions regarding the simpler details and processes, such as . . .**
	• recognizing and recalling specific terminology, events, people, and locations (*e.g., compensate, deter, punish*); and
	• recognizing and recalling isolated details, such as . . .
	  ○ a jury of "peers" determines whether the defendant in a criminal trial is guilty beyond a reasonable doubt; and
	  ○ there is a lower standard of proof in civil trials than criminal trials.
	However, the student exhibits major errors or omissions with score 3.0 elements.	

	Score 1.5	The student demonstrates partial knowledge of the score 2.0 elements but major errors or omissions regarding the score 3.0 elements.
Score 1.0	**With help, the student demonstrates partial understanding of some of the score 2.0 elements and some of the score 3.0 elements.**	
	Score 0.5	With help, the student demonstrates partial understanding of some of the score 2.0 elements but not the score 3.0 elements.
Score 0.0	**Even with help, the student demonstrates no understanding or skill.**	
	Grade 7	
Score 3.0	**While engaged in tasks that address the civil and criminal legal systems, the student demonstrates an understanding of important information, such as . . .** • the impact of distinctions between misdemeanor and felony crimes on society in the United States (*e.g., explaining and exemplifying how sentences affect the deterrence of crime—for example, determining whether a lenient sentence would be effective as a deterrent for a repeat offense and explaining reasons for that determination*); • the impact of sealing a juvenile's criminal record on society in the United States (*e.g., explaining and exemplifying how a sealed record affects the juvenile—for example, explaining whether a sealed record might influence rehabilitation of a juvenile offender and explaining reasons for that determination*);	

Score 3.0 *(continued)*	• distinctions between the different roles in a criminal trial (judge, jury, prosecutor, defense attorney, defendant) (*e.g., explaining and exemplifying the functions and purpose of the different roles in a criminal trial—for example, explaining that the judge rules on the validity of objections by either the prosecution or the defense*); and • implications of frivolous civil suits on society in the United States (*e.g., explaining and exemplifying how frivolous civil suits affect health care costs in the United States—for example, explaining why increases in malpractice insurance often lead to increases in consumer costs*). **The student exhibits no major errors or omissions.**
Score 2.0	**The student exhibits no major errors or omissions regarding the simpler details and processes, such as . . .** • recognizing and recalling specific terminology, events, people, and locations (*e.g., misdemeanor, felony, prosecutor, defense attorney, appeal*); and • recognizing and recalling isolated details, such as . . . ○ a misdemeanor is considered a "lesser" crime than a felony; ○ juvenile criminal records are often sealed so they cannot be seen; ○ the job of the prosecutor in a criminal trial is to prove that the defendant is guilty of all charges; and ○ a civil trial involves settling a disagreement between two parties. **However, the student exhibits major errors or omissions with score 3.0 elements.**

Grade 6

Score 3.0	**While engaged in tasks that address the civil and criminal legal systems, the student demonstrates an understanding of important information, such as . . .** • distinctions between criminal and civil law (purpose, types of trials, types of verdicts) (*e.g., explaining and exemplifying the difference between the purpose of a criminal trial and the purpose of a civil trial—for example, explaining that the purpose of civil law is to compensate or withhold compensation from the person bringing the civil suit, whereas one purpose of criminal law is to deter other individuals from committing a crime*); and • basic rights of defendants and their impact on society in the United States (to have counsel, to "confront their accuser," to avoid self-incrimination, to have a fair and speedy trial) (*e.g., explaining and exemplifying how the defendant's right to confront the accuser affects the accuser—for example, explaining how a child could be affected if forced to testify in open court during a trial of someone accused of killing his parents*). **The student exhibits no major errors or omissions.**
Score 2.0	**The student exhibits no major errors or omissions regarding the simpler details and processes, such as . . .** • recognizing and recalling specific terminology, events, people, and locations (*e.g., criminal law, civil law, defendant, plaintiff*); and • recognizing and recalling isolated details, such as . . . ○ a criminal trial involves finding a person "guilty" or "not guilty" of one or more crimes; and ○ defendants in a criminal trial have the right to avoid self-incrimination. **However, the student exhibits major errors or omissions with score 3.0 elements.**

Grade 5

Score 3.0	**While engaged in tasks that address the civil and criminal legal systems, the student demonstrates an understanding of important information, such as . . .** • the impact of laws on the power of people in government (term-limit laws) (*e.g., explaining and exemplifying how term-limit laws affect elected officials—for example, explaining how a politician's last year in office is affected when she cannot run for reelection*); and

Score 3.0 (continued)	• basic distinctions between state and national laws and the impact of these distinctions on society in the United States (*e.g., explaining and exemplifying how jurisdiction affects the criminal legal system in the United States—for example, describing the basic effect on society of a person committing the same crime in more than one state*). **The student exhibits no major errors or omissions.**
Score 2.0	**The student exhibits no major errors or omissions regarding the simpler details and processes, such as . . .** • recognizing and recalling specific terminology, events, people, and locations (*e.g., federal court, state court, municipal court*); and • recognizing and recalling isolated details, such as . . . 　○ the president of the United States can serve only two terms in office; and 　○ the Congress makes the laws for the United States. **However, the student exhibits major errors or omissions with score 3.0 elements.**

Grade 4

Score 3.0	**While engaged in tasks that address the civil and criminal legal systems, the student demonstrates an understanding of important information, such as . . .** • how laws can be used (provide predictability, provide security, protect rights, provide benefits, assign burdens) and their basic impact on society in the United States (*e.g., explaining and exemplifying how laws that protect against discrimination affect people in the local community—for example, explaining that laws that require wheelchair access to public facilities help give people with disabilities the ability to conduct business with minimal assistance from other people*); • general reasons why there should be consequences for disobeying laws (punishment) (*e.g., explaining and exemplifying basic reasons why disobedience is usually punished—for example, explaining that most people dislike being punished and will keep from disobeying a law to avoid the unpleasant consequence of a punishment*); and • general reasons why laws can be more or less effective (enforceable, clearly written) (*e.g., explaining and exemplifying basic reasons why some laws can be more effective than they currently are—for example, explaining that some laws have been written in a way that is difficult to enforce and need to be changed so that they can be enforced*). **The student exhibits no major errors or omissions.**
Score 2.0	**The student exhibits no major errors or omissions regarding the simpler details and processes, such as . . .** • recognizing and recalling specific terminology, events, people, and locations (*e.g., personal responsibility, courts, enforceable*); and • recognizing and recalling isolated details, such as . . . 　○ some laws protect the rights of citizens; 　○ consequences of violating laws often involve some form of punishment; and 　○ some laws are difficult to enforce. **However, the student exhibits major errors or omissions with score 3.0 elements.**

Grade 3

Score 3.0	**While engaged in tasks that address the civil and criminal legal systems, the student demonstrates an understanding of important information, such as . . .** • how laws can be used (describe how people should behave, provide order, assign responsibilities, limit the power of people in authority) and their basic impact on society in the United States (*e.g., explaining that some laws tell people how to behave in public—for example, in most communities it is against the law to disturb the peace with a loud party in the middle of the night*); • general reasons why there should be consequences for responsible actions (reward/acknowledgment) (*e.g., explaining basic reasons why responsible actions should be acknowledged—for example, rewards help to reinforce good behaviors*);

Score 3.0 (continued)	• general reasons why there should be consequences for irresponsible actions (punishment) (*e.g., explaining basic reasons why irresponsible actions should be punished—for example, punishment helps to discourage bad behaviors*); and • general reasons why some laws might not work (easily misunderstood) (*e.g., explaining basic reasons why some laws don't work—for example, a law is difficult to follow if it is easily misunderstood*). **The student exhibits no major errors or omissions.**

Score 2.0	**The student exhibits no major errors or omissions regarding the simpler details and processes, such as . . .**
	• recognizing and recalling specific terminology, events, people, and locations (*e.g., law enforcement, lawmaker, privilege*); and
	• recognizing and recalling isolated details, such as . . .
	   ○ some laws describe how people should behave;
	   ○ a consequence for a responsible action is sometimes a reward;
	   ○ a consequence for an irresponsible action is sometimes a punishment; and
	   ○ laws can be misunderstood.
	However, the student exhibits major errors or omissions with score 3.0 elements.

Grade 2	
Score 3.0	**While engaged in tasks that address the civil and criminal legal systems, the student demonstrates an understanding of important information, such as . . .** • general reasons for the differences between rules at home and at school (types of rules, types of consequences) (*e.g., explaining basic reasons why there might be a difference between the rules at home and at school—for example, chewing gum is generally not allowed in class because it can be a distraction, but some parents allow their children to chew gum as a special treat*); • how rules can be used (encourage acceptable behavior, discourage unacceptable behavior) and their basic impact on families (*e.g., explaining that rules can be used to encourage acceptable behavior—for example, the rule "only one person may speak at a time" encourages students to respect each other and the person speaking*); and • general reasons why sometimes rules need to be changed (outdated rule, enforceability) (*e.g., explaining basic reasons why a rule should be changed—for example, a rule that is hard to understand is usually hard to enforce and would need to be changed to be more clear*). **The student exhibits no major errors or omissions.**

Score 2.0	**The student exhibits no major errors or omissions regarding the simpler details and processes, such as . . .**
	• recognizing and recalling specific terminology, events, people, and locations (*e.g., duty, good law*); and
	• recognizing and recalling isolated details, such as . . .
	   ○ sometimes there are differences between rules at home and rules at school;
	   ○ rules can be used to discourage certain actions; and
	   ○ some rules may need to be changed.
	However, the student exhibits major errors or omissions with score 3.0 elements.

Grade 1	
Score 3.0	**While engaged in tasks that address the civil and criminal legal systems, the student demonstrates an understanding of important information, such as . . .** • general reasons why school and family rules exist (protection, direction, correction) (*e.g., explaining that some family rules exist to protect students—for example, a rule that prohibits touching the stove without adult supervision can help prevent severe burns*); • behaviors that are not accepted in most schools (cheating, stealing, fighting) (*e.g., explaining that some behaviors are not allowed at school—for example, cheating is not acceptable in class*); and

Score 3.0 (*continued*)	• behaviors that are not accepted in most families (lying, fighting, stealing) (*e.g., explaining that some behaviors are not allowed at home—for example, lying is not acceptable in most homes*). **The student exhibits no major errors or omissions.**

Score 2.0	**The student exhibits no major errors or omissions regarding the simpler details and processes, such as . . .**
	
	• recognizing and recalling specific terminology, events, people, and locations (*e.g., rule, law*); and
	• recognizing and recalling isolated details, such as . . .
	  ○ schools have rules that students are required to follow;
	  ○ some behaviors are not acceptable in most schools; and
	  ○ some behaviors are not acceptable in most families.
	
	However, the student exhibits major errors or omissions with score 3.0 elements.

Grade K	
Score 3.0	**While engaged in tasks that address the civil and criminal legal systems, the student demonstrates an understanding of important information, such as . . .** • general consequences for breaking rules ("time out," loss of a privilege) (*e.g., explaining that there are consequences for breaking rules—for example, lying to parents might result in loss of TV time for a day*); • general characteristics of basic rules in the classroom, school, and home (discourage bad behavior, encourage good behavior) (*e.g., explaining that rules often discourage bad behavior—for example, the rule "keep your hands to yourself" discourages pushing others*); and • general reasons why some behaviors are not acceptable in most families or schools (pushing, fighting, biting) (*e.g., explaining basic reasons why biting is not acceptable at home or school—for example, biting can cut the skin and is usually very painful*). **The student exhibits no major errors or omissions.**

Score 2.0	**The student exhibits no major errors or omissions regarding the simpler details and processes, such as . . .**
	
	• recognizing and recalling specific terminology, events, people, and locations (*e.g., honesty, responsibility*); and
	• recognizing and recalling isolated details, such as . . .
	  ○ rules have consequences for breaking them;
	  ○ classroom rules should be followed by all students; and
	  ○ some behaviors are not acceptable.
	
	However, the student exhibits major errors or omissions with score 3.0 elements.

Culture and Cultural Diversity

The Nature and Influence of Culture

Grade 8		
Score 4.0	**In addition to score 3.0 performance, the student demonstrates in-depth inferences and applications that go beyond what was taught.**	
	Score 3.5	In addition to score 3.0 performance, the student demonstrates in-depth inferences and applications with partial success.
Score 3.0	**While engaged in tasks that address the nature and influence of culture, the student demonstrates an understanding of important information, such as . . .** • the influence of cultural characteristics of different places throughout the United States (architecture, cuisine, education, customs) (*e.g., explaining and exemplifying how architectural styles from various cultures influenced building in the United States—for example, analyzing Spanish-style homes in Miami Springs, Florida*); • how migrant populations contributed to the United States (belief systems, languages, art, technology, foods) (*e.g., explaining and exemplifying how various immigrants affected society in the United States—for example, analyzing the influence of Irish settlers in Massachusetts*); and • how migrant populations stimulate diversity (beliefs, customs) (*e.g., explaining and exemplifying ways that immigrants stimulate diversity through the celebration of major holidays—for example, comparing African Americans' celebration of Kwanzaa and Jewish Americans' celebration of Hanukkah*). **The student exhibits no major errors or omissions.**	
	Score 2.5	The student exhibits no major errors or omissions regarding the score 2.0 elements and partial knowledge of the score 3.0 elements.

Score 2.0	**The student exhibits no major errors or omissions regarding the simpler details and processes, such as . . .**
	• recognizing and recalling specific terminology, events, people, and locations (*e.g., transmission of culture, transmission of beliefs, tribal identity*); and
	• recognizing and recalling isolated details, such as . . .
	   ○ Chinatowns in the United States exhibit Chinese architectural influences;
	   ○ early European immigrants helped contribute to the image of the United States as a "melting pot" of immigrant cultures; and
	   ○ migrant populations bring their own perspectives on a variety of issues.
	However, the student exhibits major errors or omissions with score 3.0 elements.	

	Score 1.5	The student demonstrates partial knowledge of the score 2.0 elements but major errors or omissions regarding the score 3.0 elements.
Score 1.0	**With help, the student demonstrates partial understanding of some of the score 2.0 elements and some of the score 3.0 elements.**	
	Score 0.5	With help, the student demonstrates partial understanding of some of the score 2.0 elements but not the score 3.0 elements.
Score 0.0	**Even with help, the student demonstrates no understanding or skill.**	

Grade 7	
Score 3.0	**While engaged in tasks that address the nature and influence of culture, the student demonstrates an understanding of important information, such as . . .** • the influence of cultural characteristics of different places throughout the student's state (e.g., California—music, art, customs) (*e.g., explaining and exemplifying how music in different parts of California might reflect a different cultural influence—for example, explaining why some radio stations play music with Asian influence near Chinatown in San Francisco and Spanish influence near the border with Mexico*). • how individuals or groups contributed to the student's state (e.g., Colorado—railroad engineers, miners, migrant workers, musicians) (*e.g., explaining and exemplifying the contributions to Colorado society made by railroad engineers—for example, explaining the danger associated with building railroads to connect old mining towns with the rest of Colorado*); and • how diversity benefits society in the United States (beliefs, customs) (*e.g., explaining and exemplifying ways that diversity benefits society in the United States—for example, explaining why acceptance of different customs can help build a tolerance of new beliefs and ideas and help increase a sense of national identity*). **The student exhibits no major errors or omissions.**

Score 2.0	**The student exhibits no major errors or omissions regarding the simpler details and processes, such as . . .**
	• recognizing and recalling specific terminology, events, people, and locations (*e.g., ethnic group, ethnic identity, ethnic minority*); and
	• recognizing and recalling isolated details, such as . . .
	  ◦ Chinatown is a major tourist attraction in San Francisco;
	  ◦ the Georgetown Loop Railroad, completed in 1884, was considered an engineering marvel for its time; and
	  ◦ diversity fosters a variety of viewpoints.
	However, the student exhibits major errors or omissions with score 3.0 elements.

Grade 6	
Score 3.0	**While engaged in tasks that address the nature and influence of culture, the student demonstrates an understanding of important information, such as . . .** • how ancient civilizations influence the modern world (technology, music, art, religion) (*e.g., explaining and exemplifying how ancient civilizations affect society today—for example, discussing the influence of ancient Egyptian architecture on buildings constructed today*); and • how classical civilizations influence later civilizations and modern society (technology, beliefs, customs, language) (*e.g., explaining and exemplifying how classical civilizations affected later civilizations—for example, describing the influence of Greek beliefs and customs on the Roman civilization*). **The student exhibits no major errors or omissions.**

Score 2.0	**The student exhibits no major errors or omissions regarding the simpler details and processes, such as . . .**
	• recognizing and recalling specific terminology, events, people, and locations (*e.g., philosophy, ethnic art, cultural heritage*); and
	• recognizing and recalling isolated details, such as . . .
	  ◦ the Parthenon was a model used to design some of the buildings in Washington, D.C.; and
	  ◦ Plato's writings had a major influence on modern philosophers.
	However, the student exhibits major errors or omissions with score 3.0 elements.

Grade 5	
Score 3.0	**While engaged in tasks that address the nature and influence of culture, the student demonstrates an understanding of important information, such as . . .**

Score 3.0 (*continued*)	• the influence of basic components of culture (social organizations, religious organizations) on society in the United States (*e.g., explaining and exemplifying how religious organizations have helped to shape society in the United States—for example, explaining how religious groups have helped provide a moral compass for many Americans to follow*); • how specific individuals contributed to cultural development within the United States (poets, authors, musicians, actors, politicians, educators) (*e.g., explaining and exemplifying ways that specific individuals have helped to influence cultural development in the United States—for example, discussing how the poetry of Maya Angelou often confronts racism*); and • how specific cultural groups (the National Rifle Association, the Moral Majority) contributed to cultural development within the United States (*e.g., explaining and exemplifying ways that specific cultural groups have helped to influence cultural development in the United States—for example, explaining that the purpose of the Anti-Defamation League is to fight anti-Semitism, bigotry, and racism*). **The student exhibits no major errors or omissions.**

Score 2.0	**The student exhibits no major errors or omissions regarding the simpler details and processes, such as . . .**
	 • recognizing and recalling specific terminology, events, people, and locations (*e.g., cultural influence, belief*); and
	 • recognizing and recalling isolated details, such as . . .
	   ◦ social organizations are a basic component of culture;
	   ◦ Samuel L. Clemens (known by the pen name Mark Twain) is an author from the United States; and
	   ◦ the National Association of the Deaf (NAD) represents members of the deaf and hard of hearing community in the United States.
	 However, the student exhibits major errors or omissions with score 3.0 elements.

Grade 4

Score 3.0	**While engaged in tasks that address the nature and influence of culture, the student demonstrates an understanding of important information, such as . . .** • how music and drama are transmitters of culture (beliefs, customs) (*e.g., explaining and exemplifying ways that drama can transmit culture—for example, explaining that a play can show how a specific culture celebrates the journey from childhood to adulthood*); and • how traditions are expressed in a variety of literature (holiday celebrations, wedding celebrations, birthday celebrations) (*e.g., explaining and exemplifying ways that different traditions are depicted in literature—for example, citing a chapter in a story that describes how weddings are celebrated in a small Russian village*). **The student exhibits no major errors or omissions.**

Score 2.0	**The student exhibits no major errors or omissions regarding the simpler details and processes, such as . . .**
	 • recognizing and recalling specific terminology, events, people, and locations (*e.g., culture, celebration*); and
	 • recognizing and recalling isolated details, such as . . .
	   ◦ artistic creations are an expression of culture; and
	   ◦ wedding celebrations are performed in many different cultures.
	 However, the student exhibits major errors or omissions with score 3.0 elements.

Grade 3

Score 3.0	**While engaged in tasks that address the nature and influence of culture, the student demonstrates an understanding of important information, such as . . .** • specific examples of how culture is expressed in language, stories, and folktales (beliefs, customs, history) (*e.g., explaining and exemplifying how a specific story describes the beliefs/customs/history of a specific culture—for example, explaining that "Sagwa, the Chinese Siamese Cat" describes life in ancient China from the perspective of a cat*); and

Score 3.0 (continued)	• specific examples of different versions of the same story from different cultures (creation stories, flood stories) (*e.g., explaining and exemplifying how the same story may have different versions in different cultures—for example, explaining that many cultures have folktales about a trickster and identifying examples from two or more cultures*). **The student exhibits no major errors or omissions.**

Score 2.0	**The student exhibits no major errors or omissions regarding the simpler details and processes, such as . . .**
	• recognizing and recalling specific terminology, events, people, and locations (*e.g., epic, myth*); and
	• recognizing and recalling isolated details, such as . . .
	  ○ folktales exist in many different cultures; and
	  ○ stories about a great flood exist in many different cultures.
	However, the student exhibits major errors or omissions with score 3.0 elements.

Grade 2

Score 3.0	**While engaged in tasks that address the nature and influence of culture, the student demonstrates an understanding of important information, such as . . .** • specific examples of works of art that reflect the cultural heritage of the community (*e.g., explaining and exemplifying how a specific work of art reflects a specific culture important to the history of the local community—for example, explaining that the statue of Chief Seattle in Seattle, Washington, pays tribute to the leader of the Suquamish and Duwamish Native American tribes who lived in Washington*); • specific examples of major works by individuals of various cultures who have contributed significantly to the arts and humanities (poets, authors, musicians, actors) (*e.g., explaining and exemplifying how a specific author wrote a major work that has made a substantial contribution to literature in the United States—for example, explaining that Alex Haley's best-selling novel* Roots *is about his African ancestors*); and • specific examples of components of a particular culture (styles of dance, styles of song, styles of storytelling, styles of drama, stories, narratives, poems, songs) (*e.g., explaining and exemplifying how a specific style of drama is often used by a specific culture—for example, discussing Kabuki theater in Japan*). **The student exhibits no major errors or omissions.**

Score 2.0	**The student exhibits no major errors or omissions regarding the simpler details and processes, such as . . .**
	• recognizing and recalling specific terminology, events, people, and locations (*e.g., custom, tradition*); and
	• recognizing and recalling isolated details, such as . . .
	  ○ some works of art reflect the cultural heritage of the artist;
	  ○ Maya Angelou is an African American poet; and
	  ○ some cultures have a unique style of dance.
	However, the student exhibits major errors or omissions with score 3.0 elements.

Grade 1

Score 3.0	**While engaged in tasks that address the nature and influence of culture, the student demonstrates an understanding of important information, such as . . .** • specific examples of various cultures (Spanish, Irish, French, Italian, Chinese, Japanese, Russian, African) encountered in stories from literature (*e.g., explaining and exemplifying how a specific story or folktale takes place in a specific cultural setting—for example, explaining that* Aladdin and the Wonderful Lamp *by Andrew Lang takes place in Persia*); • specific examples of aspects of culture (beliefs, customs, ceremonies, traditions, social practices, moral teachings) encountered in stories from literature (*e.g., explaining and exemplifying how a specific story presents a moral teaching—for example, explaining that Aesop's fable "The Tortoise and the Hare" presents the moral "Slow and steady wins the race"*); and

Score 3.0 (continued)	• specific examples of how families express culture (dance, songs, art, stories, food) (*e.g., explaining and exemplifying how some families express their cultural heritage through food—for example, explaining that many Mexican American families will prepare traditional breakfast dishes from Mexico, such as huevos rancheros, or versions based on the original dishes from Mexico*). **The student exhibits no major errors or omissions.**

Score 2.0	**The student exhibits no major errors or omissions regarding the simpler details and processes, such as . . .**
	• recognizing and recalling specific terminology, events, people, and locations (*e.g., folktale, song*); and
	• recognizing and recalling isolated details, such as . . .
	  ◦ some cultures have different versions of the same story;
	  ◦ some stories deal with the moral teachings of a specific culture; and
	  ◦ some families express their culture through folktales.
	However, the student exhibits major errors or omissions with score 3.0 elements.

Grade K	
Score 3.0	**While engaged in tasks that address the nature and influence of culture, the student demonstrates an understanding of important information, such as . . .** • specific examples of stories from various cultures (African, European, Asian) around the world (*e.g., explaining and exemplifying how a specific story comes from a specific culture—for example, explaining that "Hansel and Gretel," adapted by the Brothers Grimm, is a fairy tale from Germany*); and • specific examples of music from various cultures (African, European, Asian) around the world (*e.g., explaining and exemplifying how a specific song or style of music comes from a specific culture—for example, explaining that mariachi bands often play music from the Jalisco region of Mexico*). **The student exhibits no major errors or omissions.**

Score 2.0	**The student exhibits no major errors or omissions regarding the simpler details and processes, such as . . .**
	• recognizing and recalling specific terminology, events, people, and locations (*e.g., story, music*); and
	• recognizing and recalling isolated details, such as . . .
	  ◦ the same story is often told and retold with each generation; and
	  ◦ some cultures have their own style of music.
	However, the student exhibits major errors or omissions with score 3.0 elements.

Economics

The Nature and Function of Economic Systems

	Grade 8	
Score 4.0	**In addition to score 3.0 performance, the student demonstrates in-depth inferences and applications that go beyond what was taught.**	
	Score 3.5	In addition to score 3.0 performance, the student demonstrates in-depth inferences and applications with partial success.
Score 3.0	**While engaged in tasks that address the nature and function of economic systems, the student demonstrates an understanding of important information, such as . . .** • characteristics of various types of economic systems (market, mixed, planned, traditional) (*e.g., explaining and exemplifying key concepts of a mixed economic system—for example, explaining that such a system has industries that are privately owned and are regulated by government agencies in areas such as consumer safety and worker safety*); and • effects of changes in the price of goods and services (impact on supply, impact on demand) (*e.g., explaining and exemplifying how changes in the price of goods and services influence the economy—for example, describing what happens to the supply of a good when demand is low due to higher prices*). **The student exhibits no major errors or omissions.**	
	Score 2.5	The student exhibits no major errors or omissions regarding the score 2.0 elements and partial knowledge of the score 3.0 elements.

Score 2.0	**The student exhibits no major errors or omissions regarding the simpler details and processes, such as . . .**
	• recognizing and recalling specific terminology, events, people, and locations (*e.g., law of demand, economic system, market economy*); and
	• recognizing and recalling isolated details, such as . . .
	  ○ an economic system is composed of people, institutions, and their relationships to resources; and
	  ○ attempts to determine how supply and demand interact began with Adam Smith's *The Wealth of Nations*, first published in 1776.
	However, the student exhibits major errors or omissions with score 3.0 elements.	

	Score 1.5	The student demonstrates partial knowledge of the score 2.0 elements but major errors or omissions regarding the score 3.0 elements.
Score 1.0	**With help, the student demonstrates partial understanding of some of the score 2.0 elements and some of the score 3.0 elements.**	
	Score 0.5	With help, the student demonstrates partial understanding of some of the score 2.0 elements but not the score 3.0 elements.
Score 0.0	**Even with help, the student demonstrates no understanding or skill.**	

Grade 7	
Score 3.0	**While engaged in tasks that address the nature and function of economic systems, the student demonstrates an understanding of important information, such as . . .** • how the price of one product is influenced by the prices of other products (prices of other products are higher, prices of other products are lower) (*e.g., explaining and exemplifying how the prices of other products can influence the price of one product—for example, describing what happens to the demand for a product when the price of other products is higher*); and • how the price of one product can influence the prices of other products (price of one product is higher, price of one product is lower) (*e.g., explaining and exemplifying how the prices of other products can be influenced by the price of one product—for example, describing what happens to the demand for other products when the price of one product is lower*). **The student exhibits no major errors or omissions.**

Score 2.0	**The student exhibits no major errors or omissions regarding the simpler details and processes, such as . . .**
	• recognizing and recalling specific terminology, events, people, and locations (*e.g., product, price, influence*); and
	• recognizing and recalling isolated details, such as . . .
	   ◦ the price of one product can be influenced by the prices of other products; and
	   ◦ the price of one product can influence the prices of other products.
	However, the student exhibits major errors or omissions with score 3.0 elements.

Grade 6	
Score 3.0	**While engaged in tasks that address the nature and function of economic systems, the student demonstrates an understanding of important information, such as . . .** • characteristics and purposes of money (saving, spending) (*e.g., explaining and exemplifying the characteristics and purposes of money—for example, describing different ways money can be used to save for retirement*). **The student exhibits no major errors or omissions.**
Score 2.0	**The student exhibits no major errors or omissions regarding the simpler details and processes, such as . . .** • recognizing and recalling specific terminology, events, people, and locations (*e.g., purchasing power, trade, saving*); and • recognizing and recalling isolated details, such as . . . ◦ money can be set aside or put in a bank. **However, the student exhibits major errors or omissions with score 3.0 elements.**
Grade 5	
Score 3.0	**While engaged in tasks that address the nature and function of economic systems, the student demonstrates an understanding of important information, such as . . .** • distinctions between money and barter (storage, division, value assignment, value comparison) (*e.g., explaining and exemplifying the key differences between money and forms of barter—for example, explaining that value assignment in a barter system can be subjective, as when one farmer values his chickens more than another farmer*). **The student exhibits no major errors or omissions.**
Score 2.0	**The student exhibits no major errors or omissions regarding the simpler details and processes, such as . . .** • recognizing and recalling specific terminology, events, people, and locations (*e.g., goods, services, barter*); and

Score 2.0 *(continued)*	• recognizing and recalling isolated details, such as . . . 　○ barter is a type of trade. **However, the student exhibits major errors or omissions with score 3.0 elements.**

Grade 4	
Score 3.0	**While engaged in tasks that address the nature and function of economic systems, the student demonstrates an understanding of important information, such as . . .** • examples of basic ways households can earn income (natural resources, capital resources, entrepreneurial resources) (*e.g., explaining and exemplifying how a household can earn money by starting a business—for example, explaining that a family can start a business selling handmade crafts to earn extra money*). **The student exhibits no major errors or omissions.**
Score 2.0	**The student exhibits no major errors or omissions regarding the simpler details and processes, such as . . .** • recognizing and recalling specific terminology, events, people, and locations (*e.g., labor, resources, household*); and • recognizing and recalling isolated details, such as . . . 　○ households can sell certain resources for income. **However, the student exhibits major errors or omissions with score 3.0 elements.**

Grade 3	
Score 3.0	Not applicable.
Score 2.0	Not applicable.

Grade 2	
Score 3.0	Not applicable.
Score 2.0	Not applicable.

Grade 1	
Score 3.0	Not applicable.
Score 2.0	Not applicable.

Grade K	
Score 3.0	Not applicable.
Score 2.0	Not applicable.

Economics Throughout the World

Grade 8	
Score 4.0	**In addition to score 3.0 performance, the student demonstrates in-depth inferences and applications that go beyond what was taught.**
	Score 3.5 — In addition to score 3.0 performance, the student demonstrates in-depth inferences and applications with partial success.
Score 3.0	**While engaged in tasks that address economics throughout the world, the student demonstrates an understanding of important information, such as . . .** • implications of various problems of scarcity (impact on governments, impact on society) (*e.g., explaining and exemplifying how a lack of funding can affect the local government—for example, describing how a local recreation program is affected if tax revenue is lower than anticipated*); • implications of governments comparing (or failing to compare) their revenues to the cost of public projects their citizens want (*e.g., explaining and exemplifying how failing to compare revenue to cost affects the local government—for example, describing how a public improvement project would be affected if available funds were used up before the project is completed*); and • implications of international trade (*e.g., explaining and exemplifying the impact of foreign trade on society in the United States—for example, describing how society in the United States is affected by dependence on foreign countries for oil*). **The student exhibits no major errors or omissions.**
	Score 2.5 — The student exhibits no major errors or omissions regarding the score 2.0 elements and partial knowledge of the score 3.0 elements.

Score 2.0	**The student exhibits no major errors or omissions regarding the simpler details and processes, such as . . .**
	• recognizing and recalling specific terminology, events, people, and locations (*e.g., scarcity, public project*); and
	• recognizing and recalling isolated details, such as . . .
	   ◦ the availability of water is often limited during a drought;
	   ◦ local government revenue often comes from sales tax; and
	   ◦ the United States relies on other countries to supply needed oil for energy.
	However, the student exhibits major errors or omissions with score 3.0 elements.

	Score 1.5 — The student demonstrates partial knowledge of the score 2.0 elements but major errors or omissions regarding the score 3.0 elements.
Score 1.0	**With help, the student demonstrates partial understanding of some of the score 2.0 elements and some of the score 3.0 elements.**
	Score 0.5 — With help, the student demonstrates partial understanding of some of the score 2.0 elements but not the score 3.0 elements.
Score 0.0	**Even with help, the student demonstrates no understanding or skill.**
Grade 7	
Score 3.0	**While engaged in tasks that address economics throughout the world, the student demonstrates an understanding of important information, such as . . .** • implications of various economic decisions in a market economy (types of goods, types of services, manufacturing locations) (*e.g., explaining and exemplifying how a specific economic decision affects a market economy—for example, discussing whether a manufacturing plant in the central area of a country would be more or less advantageous than a plant located at the edge of the country*); and

Score 3.0 (continued)	• general implications of international trade for the United States (*e.g., explaining and exemplifying the basic impact of foreign trade on society in the United States—for example, describing how a local company is affected by selling its products in a foreign country*). **The student exhibits no major errors or omissions.**

Score 2.0	**The student exhibits no major errors or omissions regarding the simpler details and processes, such as . . .**
	• recognizing and recalling specific terminology, events, people, and locations (*e.g., international trade, money exchange*); and
	• recognizing and recalling isolated details, such as . . .
	  ○ economic decisions are driven by self-interest in a market economy; and
	  ○ computers are exported by the United States.
	However, the student exhibits major errors or omissions with score 3.0 elements.

Grade 6	
Score 3.0	**While engaged in tasks that address economics throughout the world, the student demonstrates an understanding of important information, such as . . .** • general implications of economic decisions (production of resources, distribution of resources, consumption of resources) (*e.g., explaining and exemplifying basic reasons why the cost of distribution affects where a distribution center is located—for example, explaining that many national companies have several regional distribution centers and how this helps keep costs down*); • general implications of interstate commerce in the United States (*e.g., explaining and exemplifying the basic impact of interstate commerce on the student's state—for example, explaining why consumer choices are sometimes limited by the availability of goods that must be imported into the state*); and • general implications of things in the local community that have changed over time (the use of technology, the types of work members do, the means of transportation, local resources, the use of land, economic activities) (*e.g., explaining and exemplifying the basic impact of changes to the types of transportation available in the local community—for example, explaining how additional jobs are often created when new transit systems are built in a community*). **The student exhibits no major errors or omissions.**

Score 2.0	**The student exhibits no major errors or omissions regarding the simpler details and processes, such as . . .**
	• recognizing and recalling specific terminology, events, people, and locations (*e.g., interstate commerce, economic decision*); and
	• recognizing and recalling isolated details, such as . . .
	  ○ economic decisions involve weighing the costs and benefits of alternative choices;
	  ○ many states in the central United States import seafood; and
	  ○ some communities have improved their transit system to include electric rail cars.
	However, the student exhibits major errors or omissions with score 3.0 elements.

Grade 5	
Score 3.0	**While engaged in tasks that address economics throughout the world, the student demonstrates an understanding of important information, such as . . .** • examples of current industries in a state (e.g., Colorado) (*e.g., explaining and exemplifying a specific industry that currently operates within Colorado—for example, wine is produced by vineyards in Colorado*); • general history of economic growth in a state (e.g., Colorado—recessions, depressions, booms) (*e.g., explaining and exemplifying basic details about a specific time of economic growth in the history of Colorado—for example, providing basic information about the Colorado silver boom in the late 19th century*); and

Score 3.0 (continued)	• examples of different jobs throughout the state (*e.g., explaining and exemplifying how a specific job can be performed in different places throughout the state—for example, explaining that construction workers, such as carpenters and electricians, perform the same kind of work on any construction site in the state*). **The student exhibits no major errors or omissions.**
Score 2.0	**The student exhibits no major errors or omissions regarding the simpler details and processes, such as . . .** • recognizing and recalling specific terminology, events, people, and locations (*e.g., economic growth, recession*); and • recognizing and recalling isolated details, such as . . . ◦ industries are often determined by availability of local resources; ◦ a recession is a significant decline in economic activity spread across the economy; and ◦ some people work in government. **However, the student exhibits major errors or omissions with score 3.0 elements.**

Grade 4

Score 3.0	**While engaged in tasks that address economics throughout the world, the student demonstrates an understanding of important information, such as . . .** • examples of uses of revenue in the local community (*e.g., explaining and exemplifying how revenue in the community can be used for a specific purpose—for example, providing staffing for and maintenance of a community recreation center*); • examples of past industries in a state (e.g., Colorado) (*e.g., explaining and exemplifying how a specific industry may no longer be present in parts of Colorado—for example, providing basic information about why the last significant mine to operate in Leadville, the Black Cloud, ceased operation in 1999*); and • examples of different types of work throughout the state (*e.g., explaining and exemplifying how a specific type of work can be performed in different places throughout the state—for example, explaining that construction work is performed throughout the state when new homes are built*). **The student exhibits no major errors or omissions.**
Score 2.0	**The student exhibits no major errors or omissions regarding the simpler details and processes, such as . . .** • recognizing and recalling specific terminology, events, people, and locations (*e.g., technology, industry*); and • recognizing and recalling isolated details, such as . . . ◦ permit fees help provide revenue to many local communities; ◦ some industries decline over a period of time; and ◦ some types of work are available in each community throughout a state. **However, the student exhibits major errors or omissions with score 3.0 elements.**

Grade 3

Score 3.0	**While engaged in tasks that address economics throughout the world, the student demonstrates an understanding of important information, such as . . .** • examples of sources of revenue in the local community (*e.g., explaining that the government of the local community gets its revenue from a specific source—for example, receiving sales tax on gasoline*); and • examples of different jobs in the local community (*e.g., explaining that a specific job can be performed in different places in the local community—for example, explaining that firefighters can work in any of the town's fire stations*). **The student exhibits no major errors or omissions.**
Score 2.0	**The student exhibits no major errors or omissions regarding the simpler details and processes, such as . . .**

Score 2.0 *(continued)*	• recognizing and recalling specific terminology, events, people, and locations (*e.g., economic activities, use of land*); and
	• recognizing and recalling isolated details, such as . . .
	  ◦ the local government needs revenue to operate; and
	  ◦ some people work in public service.
	However, the student exhibits major errors or omissions with score 3.0 elements.

Grade 2	
Score 3.0	**While engaged in tasks that address economics throughout the world, the student demonstrates an understanding of important information, such as . . .** • examples of different types of work found in the local community (*e.g., explaining that a specific type of work can be performed in the local community—for example, explaining that medical workers perform various services at the local hospital*); and • examples of different jobs in the student's school (*e.g., explaining that a specific job can be performed at the school—for example, explaining that custodians clean the classrooms after school*). **The student exhibits no major errors or omissions.**

Score 2.0	**The student exhibits no major errors or omissions regarding the simpler details and processes, such as . . .**
	• recognizing and recalling specific terminology, events, people, and locations (*e.g., work, job*); and
	• recognizing and recalling isolated details, such as . . .
	  ◦ different types of work are performed in the local community; and
	  ◦ different jobs are performed in a school.
	However, the student exhibits major errors or omissions with score 3.0 elements.

Grade 1	
Score 3.0	Not applicable.
Score 2.0	Not applicable.
Grade K	
Score 3.0	Not applicable.
Score 2.0	Not applicable.

Personal Economics

Grade 8		
Score 4.0	**In addition to score 3.0 performance, the student demonstrates in-depth inferences and applications that go beyond what was taught.**	
	Score 3.5	In addition to score 3.0 performance, the student demonstrates in-depth inferences and applications with partial success.
Score 3.0	**While engaged in tasks that address personal economics, the student demonstrates an understanding of important information, such as . . .** • characteristics and purpose of various elements of a simple budget (mandatory expenses, discretionary expenses, variable expenses) (*e.g., explaining and exemplifying the types of expenses that would be considered mandatory versus types that would be considered discretionary—for example, explaining that "rent/mortgage" is a mandatory expense that usually does not change each month, whereas "eating out" is a discretionary expense that varies each month depending on how many times meals are eaten at a restaurant*); • strengths and weaknesses of various ways to prepare a budget (electronic spreadsheet, financial software, paper and pencil) (*e.g., explaining and exemplifying the strengths and weaknesses of preparing a budget using paper and pencil—for example, explaining that the paper-and-pencil method has more flexibility in terms of where the budget can be prepared—at the kitchen table—but can be prone to greater error because all the calculations are done by hand*); • the impact on people when they do not compare their income to their expenses (*e.g., explaining and exemplifying how failing to compare income to expenses can affect a person—for example, describing how a family is affected by not being able to pay rent when more money has been spent than earned*); and • implications of interest on loans and other debts (impact of paying minimum due on amount of time to pay off debt, impact of interest on total amount owed) (*e.g., explaining and exemplifying how the amount of monthly payment affects the amount of time it takes to pay off a debt and total amount owed—for example, explaining that paying a $75 minimum payment on a $3,000 credit card balance at 18 percent interest would take 263 months (almost 22 years) to pay off and would cost almost $4,155 in interest*). **The student exhibits no major errors or omissions.**	
	Score 2.5	The student exhibits no major errors or omissions regarding the score 2.0 elements and partial knowledge of the score 3.0 elements.

Score 2.0	**The student exhibits no major errors or omissions regarding the simpler details and processes, such as . . .**
	• recognizing and recalling specific terminology, events, people, and locations (*e.g., loan, debt, interest*); and
	• recognizing and recalling isolated details, such as . . .
	  ◦ one element of a simple budget is a section for mandatory expenses such as rent;
	  ◦ a spreadsheet can be used to prepare a budget;
	  ◦ a budget is a tool that can be used to compare income to expenses; and
	  ◦ paying just the minimum payment on a credit card will increase the time it takes to pay off the debt.
	However, the student exhibits major errors or omissions with score 3.0 elements.	

	Score 1.5	The student demonstrates partial knowledge of the score 2.0 elements but major errors or omissions regarding the score 3.0 elements.
Score 1.0	**With help, the student demonstrates partial understanding of some of the score 2.0 elements and some of the score 3.0 elements.**	

	Score 0.5	With help, the student demonstrates partial understanding of some of the score 2.0 elements but not the score 3.0 elements.
Score 0.0		**Even with help, the student demonstrates no understanding or skill.**

<table>
<tr><td colspan="3" align="center">Grade 7</td></tr>
<tr>
<td>Score 3.0</td>
<td colspan="2">
While engaged in tasks that address personal economics, the student demonstrates an understanding of important information, such as . . .

• implications of personal economic decisions (to work or not, to save or not, to invest or not) (e.g., explaining and exemplifying how failing to save can affect a person—for example, describing how a family is affected if an unexpected repair, such as a car repair, is needed and there is little or no money in the savings account); and

• reasons why people should compare their income to their expenses (overdrawing an account, avoiding debts, paying bills on time, saving for retirement) (e.g., explaining and exemplifying how there are consequences for failing to compare income to expenses—for example, explaining that a person who buys things without confirming there is enough money in his account to cover the expense might overdraw the account, which often costs more money in overdraft fees).

The student exhibits no major errors or omissions.
</td>
</tr>
<tr>
<td>Score 2.0</td>
<td colspan="2">
The student exhibits no major errors or omissions regarding the simpler details and processes, such as . . .

• recognizing and recalling specific terminology, events, people, and locations (e.g., economic decision, retirement, budget); and

• recognizing and recalling isolated details, such as . . .
  ○ investing in a retirement plan is an example of a personal economic decision; and
  ○ some people use credit cards for purchases when they don't have money in their bank account.

However, the student exhibits major errors or omissions with score 3.0 elements.
</td>
</tr>
<tr><td colspan="3" align="center">Grade 6</td></tr>
<tr>
<td>Score 3.0</td>
<td colspan="2">
While engaged in tasks that address personal economics, the student demonstrates an understanding of important information, such as . . .

• reasons why people should compare their income to the costs of goods and services they need/want (e.g., explaining and exemplifying how people need to compare their income to costs of goods and services they desire—for example, describing how a person is affected [bills paid late, overdraft charges] when money is spent on purchasing something that is wanted but not really needed); and

• reasons why people often have to choose between wants and needs (e.g., explaining and exemplifying how people sometimes need to choose between wants and needs—for example, describing how a person is affected [debt, little or no savings] when income is insufficient to cover both wants and needs).

The student exhibits no major errors or omissions.
</td>
</tr>
<tr>
<td>Score 2.0</td>
<td colspan="2">
The student exhibits no major errors or omissions regarding the simpler details and processes, such as . . .

• recognizing and recalling specific terminology, events, people, and locations (e.g., cost, want, need); and

• recognizing and recalling isolated details, such as . . .
  ○ sometimes a person cannot afford a new purchase; and
  ○ wants and needs are different.

However, the student exhibits major errors or omissions with score 3.0 elements.
</td>
</tr>
<tr><td colspan="3" align="center">Grade 5</td></tr>
<tr>
<td>Score 3.0</td>
<td colspan="2">Not applicable.</td>
</tr>
</table>

Score 2.0	Not applicable.
Grade 4	
Score 3.0	Not applicable.
Score 2.0	Not applicable.
Grade 3	
Score 3.0	Not applicable.
Score 2.0	Not applicable.
Grade 2	
Score 3.0	Not applicable.
Score 2.0	Not applicable.
Grade 1	
Score 3.0	Not applicable.
Score 2.0	Not applicable.
Grade K	
Score 3.0	Not applicable.
Score 2.0	Not applicable.

History

Significant Individuals and Events

	Grade 8	
Score 4.0	**In addition to score 3.0 performance, the student demonstrates in-depth inferences and applications that go beyond what was taught.**	
	Score 3.5	In addition to score 3.0 performance, the student demonstrates in-depth inferences and applications with partial success.
Score 3.0	**While engaged in tasks that address significant individuals and events, the student demonstrates an understanding of important information, such as . . .** • how immigration affected society in the United States in the antebellum period (1814–1864) (impact on national identity, increases in population, demographic changes) (*e.g., explaining and exemplifying ways that society in the United States was affected by immigration during the antebellum period—for example, describing how a sense of national identity was made more difficult by the increased number of immigrants from different countries*); and • implications of the conflict between religious beliefs and scientific thought during the Scientific Revolution (impact on acceptance of scientific theories, impact of science on established religious beliefs) (*e.g., explaining and exemplifying how commonly held viewpoints were influenced during the Scientific Revolution—for example, describing why Copernicus's work contradicted religious dogma accepted in his day by inferring that science could explain everything attributed to God*). **The student exhibits no major errors or omissions.**	
	Score 2.5	The student exhibits no major errors or omissions regarding the score 2.0 elements and partial knowledge of the score 3.0 elements.

Score 2.0	**The student exhibits no major errors or omissions regarding the simpler details and processes, such as . . .**
	• recognizing and recalling specific terminology, events, people, and locations (*e.g., Scientific Revolution, antebellum period, civil disobedience, woman suffrage*); and
	• recognizing and recalling isolated details, such as . . .
	   ○ the antebellum period refers to U.S. history before the Civil War; and
	   ○ the Scientific Revolution built upon the foundation of ancient Greek learning.
	However, the student exhibits major errors or omissions with score 3.0 elements.	

	Score 1.5	The student demonstrates partial knowledge of the score 2.0 elements but major errors or omissions regarding the score 3.0 elements.
Score 1.0	**With help, the student demonstrates partial understanding of some of the score 2.0 elements and some of the score 3.0 elements.**	
	Score 0.5	With help, the student demonstrates partial understanding of some of the score 2.0 elements but not the score 3.0 elements.
Score 0.0	**Even with help, the student demonstrates no understanding or skill.**	

	Grade 7
Score 3.0	While engaged in tasks that address significant individuals and events, the student demonstrates an understanding of important information, such as . . . • implications of woman suffrage in the United States (early 20th century) (*e.g., explaining and exemplifying the impact of efforts to pass and ratify the 19th Amendment—for example, describing how women have been influenced, from then until now, by individuals and groups that worked to pass and ratify the 19th Amendment*); and • implications of the African American civil rights movement (1955–1968) (*e.g., explaining and exemplifying the impact of the African American civil rights movement on society in the United States—for example, discussing how African Americans and other racial groups have been influenced by individuals and groups involved in the movement from then until now*). **The student exhibits no major errors or omissions.**

Score 2.0	The student exhibits no major errors or omissions regarding the simpler details and processes, such as . . .
	• recognizing and recalling specific terminology, events, people, and locations (*e.g., economic imperialism, nationalism, militarism*); and
	• recognizing and recalling isolated details, such as . . .
	  ○ the 19th Amendment was proposed on June 4, 1919, and ratified on August 18, 1920; and
	  ○ Martin Luther King Jr. delivered his "I Have a Dream" speech on August 28, 1963, from the steps of the Lincoln Memorial.
	However, the student exhibits major errors or omissions with score 3.0 elements.

	Grade 6
Score 3.0	While engaged in tasks that address significant individuals and events, the student demonstrates an understanding of important information, such as . . . • implications of various factors and events that contributed to the outbreak of World War I (nationalism, alliances, colonial rivalries, economic rivalries, arms races, earlier wars, assassination, rise to power of Kaiser Wilhelm II) and aftereffects of the war (*e.g., explaining and exemplifying how a specific event contributed to the outbreak of World War I and the impact of the war on a specific country—for example, describing why the rise to power of Kaiser Wilhelm II contributed to the outbreak of WWI and how Germany was affected after the war*); • implications of various factors and events that contributed to the outbreak of World War II (nationalism, alliances, competition for resources, appeasement, racism, militarism, World War I, attack on Pearl Harbor, invasion of Poland, other wars) and aftereffects of the war (*e.g., explaining and exemplifying how a specific factor contributed to the outbreak of World War II and the impact of the war on a specific country—for example, describing why the Treaty of Versailles contributed to the outbreak of World War II and how Japan was affected after the war*); and • implications of nationalist movements and other attempts by colonial countries to achieve independence after World War II (impact on other countries seeking independence, impact on citizenry) (*e.g., explaining and exemplifying how a specific country sought to achieve independence after World War II—for example, describing ways in which Mahatma Gandhi influenced the Indian people to gain independence from British rule*). **The student exhibits no major errors or omissions.**

Score 2.0	The student exhibits no major errors or omissions regarding the simpler details and processes, such as . . .
	• recognizing and recalling specific terminology, events, people, and locations (*e.g., the First World War, the Second World War, affirmative action*); and
	• recognizing and recalling isolated details, such as . . .
	  ○ Archduke Franz Ferdinand of Austria, heir to the Austro-Hungarian throne, was assassinated on June 28, 1914;
	  ○ Japan invaded China in 1937; and
	  ○ India gained independence on August 15, 1947.
	However, the student exhibits major errors or omissions with score 3.0 elements.

Grade 5	
Score 3.0	While engaged in tasks that address significant individuals and events, the student demonstrates an understanding of important information, such as . . . • basic implications of the American Revolutionary War (basic impact on America, basic impact on England, basic impact on other countries) (*e.g., explaining and exemplifying how the United States was affected by the Revolutionary War—for example, describing how the war helped unify the colonies into a new nation*); • basic implications of the American Civil War (basic impact on Northern states, basic impact on Southern states, basic impact on society in the United States) (*e.g., explaining and exemplifying how all of society in the United States was affected by the Civil War—for example, explaining that Northern and Southern casualties were all Americans*); and • general characteristics of the first explorers and settlers of a state (e.g., Colorado) (*e.g., explaining and exemplifying who the first settlers of Colorado were and where they settled—for example, explaining that former fur traders returned to the lands they trapped, as exemplified by Antoine Janis and other trappers from Fort Laramie who established a town site near Laporte along the Cache la Poudre in 1858*). **The student exhibits no major errors or omissions.**

Score 2.0	The student exhibits no major errors or omissions regarding the simpler details and processes, such as . . .
	• recognizing and recalling specific terminology, events, people, and locations (*e.g., American Revolutionary War, American Civil War, settler*); and
	• recognizing and recalling isolated details, such as . . .
	  ○ George Washington was a general in the Revolutionary War;
	  ○ Abraham Lincoln was president of the United States during the Civil War; and
	  ○ some settlers came to Colorado from the eastern states.
	However, the student exhibits major errors or omissions with score 3.0 elements.

Grade 4	
Score 3.0	While engaged in tasks that address significant individuals and events, the student demonstrates an understanding of important information, such as . . . • basic impact of major historical events in a state (e.g., Colorado) (*e.g., explaining and exemplifying how attaining statehood affected the state of Colorado—for example, explaining that the territorial government appointed by the president of the United States would be replaced by elected state officials and Colorado would join the other states as an equal member of the federal union*); and • general characteristics of a state's first inhabitants (e.g., Colorado) (*e.g., explaining and exemplifying who the first inhabitants of Colorado were and where they lived—for example, explaining that the Ute Indians were well established in the northern Colorado Plateau by AD 1500*). **The student exhibits no major errors or omissions.**

Score 2.0	The student exhibits no major errors or omissions regarding the simpler details and processes, such as . . .
	• recognizing and recalling specific terminology, events, people, and locations (*e.g., historical event, inhabitant, tourism*); and
	• recognizing and recalling isolated details, such as . . .
	  ○ Colorado attained statehood on August 1, 1876; and
	  ○ Native Americans were among Colorado's first inhabitants.
	However, the student exhibits major errors or omissions with score 3.0 elements.

Grade 3	
Score 3.0	While engaged in tasks that address significant individuals and events, the student demonstrates an understanding of important information, such as . . .

Score 3.0 (continued)	• basic impact of major historical events on people in a state (e.g., Colorado) at the time it occurred (e.g., *explaining how the 1859 gold rush affected opportunities and perceptions of Colorado—for example, explaining that the gold rush of 1859 created opportunities for wealth*); • general history of the local community (e.g., Denver, Colorado—significant dates, people who made significant contributions, basic details about key events and important milestones) (e.g., *explaining that a significant event happened in Denver during a specific year or on a specific date—for example, explaining that the Denver Pacific, Kansas Pacific, and Colorado Central Railroads reached Denver in 1870*); and • major national holidays in the United States (e.g., *explaining basic reasons why a specific holiday is celebrated on a specific date in the United States—for example, explaining that Labor Day is a United States federal holiday that takes place on the first Monday in September as a national tribute to the contributions workers have made to the strength, prosperity, and well-being of the country*). **The student exhibits no major errors or omissions.**

Score 2.0	**The student exhibits no major errors or omissions regarding the simpler details and processes, such as . . .**
	• recognizing and recalling specific terminology, events, people, and locations (*e.g., history, Presidents' Day, Fourth of July*); and
	• recognizing and recalling isolated details, such as . . .
	   ◦ the Colorado Gold Rush of 1859 brought many settlers to the Denver area;
	   ◦ Denver was named after the Kansas territorial governor James W. Denver; and
	   ◦ Presidents' Day commemorates the birthdays of American presidents George Washington and Abraham Lincoln.
	However, the student exhibits major errors or omissions with score 3.0 elements.

	**Grade 2**
Score 3.0	**While engaged in tasks that address significant individuals and events, the student demonstrates an understanding of important information, such as . . .** • examples of major state and local holidays in the United States (*e.g., explaining that a specific holiday is not commemorated in every state—for example, explaining that Patriots Day is a state holiday in Maine and Massachusetts that is celebrated on the third Monday of April*). **The student exhibits no major errors or omissions.**
Score 2.0	**The student exhibits no major errors or omissions regarding the simpler details and processes, such as . . .** • recognizing and recalling specific terminology, events, people, and locations (*e.g., state holiday, local holiday*); and • recognizing and recalling isolated details, such as . . . ◦ not every state celebrates the same holidays. **However, the student exhibits major errors or omissions with score 3.0 elements.**
	**Grade 1**
Score 3.0	**While engaged in tasks that address significant individuals and events, the student demonstrates an understanding of important information, such as . . .** • examples of major national holidays in the United States (*e.g., explaining that a specific holiday is commemorated by the entire country—for example, explaining that Thanksgiving Day is a United States federal holiday celebrated on the fourth Thursday of November*). **The student exhibits no major errors or omissions.**
Score 2.0	**The student exhibits no major errors or omissions regarding the simpler details and processes, such as . . .** • recognizing and recalling specific terminology, events, people, and locations (*e.g., national holiday, Thanksgiving Day*); and

Score 2.0 (*continued*)	• recognizing and recalling isolated details, such as . . . ◦ some holidays are celebrated by the entire country. **However, the student exhibits major errors or omissions with score 3.0 elements.**
Grade K	
Score 3.0	Not applicable.
Score 2.0	Not applicable.

Current Events and the Modern World

Grade 8		
Score 4.0	**In addition to score 3.0 performance, the student demonstrates in-depth inferences and applications that go beyond what was taught.**	
	Score 3.5	In addition to score 3.0 performance, the student demonstrates in-depth inferences and applications with partial success.
Score 3.0	**While engaged in tasks that address current events and the modern world, the student demonstrates an understanding of important information, such as . . .** • international events of 2006 (*e.g., explaining how a specific current international event affects residents where the event occurred—for example, how residents of Baghdad were affected by armed insurgents during a given time period*); • national events of 2006 (*e.g., explaining how a specific current national event affects residents where the event occurred—for example, how residents living along the border of Texas and Mexico were affected by citizens of Mexico crossing the border into the United States and plans to increase border security in the region*); • state (*e.g., Kentucky*) events of 2006 (*e.g., explaining how a specific current event in a state affects residents where the event occurred—for example, how the families of trapped miners were affected by lapses in mine safety at Darby Mine No. 1*); and • local (*e.g., Denver, Colorado*) events of 2006 (*e.g., explaining how a specific current event in a city affects residents where the event occurred—for example, how some residents were affected by technology glitches in the November 2006 Denver election*). **The student exhibits no major errors or omissions.**	
	Score 2.5	The student exhibits no major errors or omissions regarding the score 2.0 elements and partial knowledge of the score 3.0 elements.

Score 2.0	**The student exhibits no major errors or omissions regarding the simpler details and processes, such as . . .**
	• recognizing and recalling specific terminology, events, people, and locations (*e.g., Iraq, Iraq war, Sunni, Shiite*); and
	• recognizing and recalling isolated details, such as . . .
	  ◦ Sunnis and Shiites continued to fight each other in Iraq;
	  ◦ the border between Mexico and the United States spans California, Arizona, New Mexico, and Texas;
	  ◦ five miners died in an explosion at the Kentucky Darby Mine No. 1 on May 20, 2006; and
	  ◦ technical problems caused voters to stand in line for more than three hours at voting centers in downtown Denver.
	However, the student exhibits major errors or omissions with score 3.0 elements.	

	Score 1.5	The student demonstrates partial knowledge of the score 2.0 elements but major errors or omissions regarding the score 3.0 elements.
Score 1.0	**With help, the student demonstrates partial understanding of some of the score 2.0 elements and some of the score 3.0 elements.**	
	Score 0.5	With help, the student demonstrates partial understanding of some of the score 2.0 elements but not the score 3.0 elements.
Score 0.0	**Even with help, the student demonstrates no understanding or skill.**	
Grade 7		
Score 3.0	**While engaged in tasks that address current events and the modern world, the student demonstrates an understanding of important information, such as . . .**	

Score 3.0 (continued)	• international events of 2006 (*e.g., explaining how a specific current international event affects people throughout the world—for example, how people in different countries were affected by World AIDS Day*); • national events of 2006 (*e.g., explaining how a specific current national event affects people throughout the country—for example, how people in different states were affected by congressional elections*); • state (*e.g., Colorado*) events of 2006 (*e.g., explaining how a specific current event in a state affects people throughout the state—for example, how people in different Colorado cities were affected by general elections held in November*); and • local (*e.g., Denver, Colorado*) events of 2006 (*e.g., explaining how a specific current event in a city affects people throughout the city—for example, how people in different Denver neighborhoods were affected by local elections held in November*). **The student exhibits no major errors or omissions.**

Score 2.0	**The student exhibits no major errors or omissions regarding the simpler details and processes, such as . . .**
	• recognizing and recalling specific terminology, events, people, and locations (*e.g., World AIDS Day, congressional district, HIV, AIDS*); and
	• recognizing and recalling isolated details, such as . . .
	  ○ India had the largest population of HIV-infected people in the world in 2006;
	  ○ the Democratic Party regained control of both houses of Congress in 2006;
	  ○ former Denver district attorney Bill Ritter was elected governor of Colorado in 2006; and
	  ○ Denver Question 1B asked voters if they would approve creating a position of chief financial officer to improve financial oversight in Denver in 2006.
	However, the student exhibits major errors or omissions with score 3.0 elements.

Grade 6	
Score 3.0	**While engaged in tasks that address current events and the modern world, the student demonstrates an understanding of important information, such as . . .** • international events of 2006 (*e.g., explaining how a specific current international event affects people throughout the world—for example, how people in different countries were affected by Pope Benedict XVI's visit to Turkey*); • national events of 2006 (*e.g., explaining how a specific current national event affects people throughout the country—for example, how people in different states were affected by severe weather in 2006*); • state (*e.g., Colorado*) events of 2006 (*e.g., explaining how a specific current event in a state affects people throughout the state—for example, how people in different Colorado cities were affected by voting problems during the November 2006 election*); and • local (*e.g., Denver, Colorado*) events of 2006 (*e.g., explaining how a specific current event in a city affects people throughout the city—for example, how people in different Denver neighborhoods were affected by Bike to Work Day*). **The student exhibits no major errors or omissions.**

Score 2.0	**The student exhibits no major errors or omissions regarding the simpler details and processes, such as . . .**
	• recognizing and recalling specific terminology, events, people, and locations (*e.g., Election day, voting center, Istanbul, Blue Mosque*); and
	• recognizing and recalling isolated details, such as . . .
	  ○ Pope Benedict XVI prayed in Istanbul's Blue Mosque on November 30, 2006, during a four-day trip to Turkey;
	  ○ two major hurricanes, Hurricane Gordon and Hurricane Helene, formed during the 2006 Atlantic hurricane season;
	  ○ As many as 20,000 people in Colorado gave up trying to vote as new online systems for verifying voter registrations crashed repeatedly; and
	  ○ Denver encourages residents to ride bicycles to work for one day every June.
	However, the student exhibits major errors or omissions with score 3.0 elements.

	Grade 5
Score 3.0	**While engaged in tasks that address current events and the modern world, the student demonstrates an understanding of important information, such as . . .** • international events of 2006 (*e.g., explaining the basic impact of a specific current international event on residents where the event occurred—for example, explaining the basic ways in which the people of Darfur have been affected by violence in the region*); • national events of 2006 (*e.g., explaining the basic impact of a specific current national event on residents where the event occurred—for example, explaining basic ways the Midwest snowstorm on December 1, 2006, affected people living in the region*); • state (e.g., Colorado) events of 2006 (*e.g., explaining the basic impact of a specific current event in a state on residents where the event occurred—for example, explaining basic ways drivers in Colorado were affected by the addition of an express toll option for solo drivers to Interstate 25 HOV lanes*); and • local (e.g., Denver, Colorado) events of 2006 (*e.g., explaining the basic impact of a specific current event in a city on residents where the event occurred—for example, explaining basic ways Denver residents were affected by an immigration reform event on May 1, 2006*). **The student exhibits no major errors or omissions.**

Score 2.0	**The student exhibits no major errors or omissions regarding the simpler details and processes, such as . . .**
	• recognizing and recalling specific terminology, events, people, and locations (*e.g., HOV lane, Darfur, unemployment, diplomacy*); and
	• recognizing and recalling isolated details, such as . . .
	  ◦ at least 200,000 people have been killed in Darfur;
	  ◦ hundreds of flights were canceled due to a snowstorm that passed through the Midwest on December 1, 2006;
	  ◦ the multiuse, optional tolled express lane opened on I-25 between downtown Denver and U.S. Highway 36 on June 2, 2006; and
	  ◦ the immigration reform parade took place on May 1, 2006.
	However, the student exhibits major errors or omissions with score 3.0 elements.

	Grade 4
Score 3.0	**While engaged in tasks that address current events and the modern world, the student demonstrates an understanding of important information, such as . . .** • international events of 2006 (*e.g., explaining the basic details of a specific current international event—for example, a natural gas explosion in a coal mine killed eight people in Romania on January 14, 2006*); • national events of 2006 (*e.g., explaining the basic details of a specific current national event—for example, Samuel Alito was sworn in as an associate justice of the Supreme Court of the United States on January 31, 2006*); • state (e.g., Alaska) events of 2006 (*e.g., explaining the basic details of a specific current event in a state—for example, the Augustine volcano erupted twice on January 11, 2006, its first major eruption since 1986*); and • local (e.g., Denver, Colorado) events of 2006 (*e.g., explaining the basic details of a specific current event in a city—for example, the Colorado Crush, Denver's Arena Football League team, finished their season on April 21, 2006, in first place in the American Conference Central division*). **The student exhibits no major errors or omissions.**
Score 2.0	**The student exhibits no major errors or omissions regarding the simpler details and processes, such as . . .** • recognizing and recalling specific terminology, events, people, and locations (*e.g., discrimination, civic-mindedness, peaceful demonstration*); and • recognizing and recalling isolated details, such as . . . ◦ an explosion occurred in a Romanian mine in January 2006;

Score 2.0 (*continued*)	◦ a new judge was appointed to the United States Supreme Court in January 2006; ◦ a volcano erupted twice in Alaska in January 2006; and ◦ the Colorado Crush took first place in their division in 2006. **However, the student exhibits major errors or omissions with score 3.0 elements.**

Grade 3	
Score 3.0	**While engaged in tasks that address current events and the modern world, the student demonstrates an understanding of important information, such as . . .** • international events of 2006 (*e.g., explaining the basic details of a specific current international event—for example, the 2006 Winter Olympics opened in Turin, Italy, on February 10, 2006*); • national events of 2006 (*e.g., explaining the basic details of a specific current national event—for example, NASA's Mars Reconnaissance Orbiter entered orbit around Mars on March 10, 2006*); • state (*e.g., Colorado*) events of 2006 (*e.g., explaining the basic details of a specific current event in a state—for example, Bill Ritter was elected governor of Colorado on November 7, 2006*); and • local (*e.g., Pittsburgh, Pennsylvania*) events of 2006 (*e.g., explaining the basic details of a specific current event in a city—for example, the Pittsburgh Steelers won Super Bowl XL on February 5, 2006, by defeating the Seattle Seahawks*). **The student exhibits no major errors or omissions.**
Score 2.0	**The student exhibits no major errors or omissions regarding the simpler details and processes, such as . . .** • recognizing and recalling specific terminology, events, people, and locations (*e.g., community, patriotism, human rights*); and • recognizing and recalling isolated details, such as . . . ◦ the 2006 Winter Olympics took place in Turin, Italy; ◦ NASA put a satellite in orbit around Mars in 2006; ◦ Bill Ritter was elected Colorado's governor in 2006; and ◦ the Pittsburgh Steelers won the Super Bowl in 2006. **However, the student exhibits major errors or omissions with score 3.0 elements.**

Grade 2	
Score 3.0	Not applicable.
Score 2.0	Not applicable.

Grade 1	
Score 3.0	Not applicable.
Score 2.0	Not applicable.

Grade K	
Score 3.0	Not applicable.
Score 2.0	Not applicable.

Geography

Spatial Thinking and the Use of Charts, Maps, and Graphs

Grade 8		
Score 4.0	**In addition to score 3.0 performance, the student demonstrates in-depth inferences and applications that go beyond what was taught.**	
	Score 3.5	In addition to score 3.0 performance, the student demonstrates in-depth inferences and applications with partial success.
Score 3.0	**While engaged in tasks that address spatial thinking and the use of charts, maps, and graphs, the student demonstrates an understanding of important information, such as . . .** • how to use a variety of maps and globes that illustrate data sets (*e.g., explaining and exemplifying how to read and evaluate information depicted on a contour map—for example, how to determine the barometric pressure of several regions as depicted on a contour map*). **The student exhibits no major errors or omissions.**	
	Score 2.5	The student exhibits no major errors or omissions regarding the score 2.0 elements and partial knowledge of the score 3.0 elements.
Score 2.0	**The student exhibits no major errors or omissions regarding the simpler details and processes, such as . . .** • recognizing and recalling specific terminology, events, people, and locations (*e.g., population density, population distribution, population growth rate, land-use data*); and • recognizing and recalling isolated details, such as . . . ○ a contour map can show elevation of land features. **However, the student exhibits major errors or omissions with score 3.0 elements.**	
	Score 1.5	The student demonstrates partial knowledge of the score 2.0 elements but major errors or omissions regarding the score 3.0 elements.
Score 1.0	**With help, the student demonstrates partial understanding of some of the score 2.0 elements and some of the score 3.0 elements.**	
	Score 0.5	With help, the student demonstrates partial understanding of some of the score 2.0 elements but not the score 3.0 elements.
Score 0.0	**Even with help, the student demonstrates no understanding or skill.**	
Grade 7		
Score 3.0	**While engaged in tasks that address spatial thinking and the use of charts, maps, and graphs, the student demonstrates an understanding of important information, such as . . .** • how to use thematic maps that depict patterns (*e.g., explaining and exemplifying how to read and evaluate information depicted on a choropleth map—for example, how to determine margin of victory and voter turnout for the 2004 U.S. presidential election as depicted on a choropleth map*); and • how to construct various geographic representations (*e.g., explaining and exemplifying how to construct a topological map depicting historical information—for example, creating a topological map depicting the Battle of Gettysburg*). **The student exhibits no major errors or omissions.**	

Score 2.0	The student exhibits no major errors or omissions regarding the simpler details and processes, such as . . . • recognizing and recalling specific terminology, events, people, and locations (*e.g., population region, regional boundary, land-use pattern, principal meridians*); and • recognizing and recalling isolated details, such as . . . ◦ maps contain a legend of different symbols, colors, and other indicators that help describe what the map shows; and ◦ maps should have accurate boundaries to differentiate between regions. **However, the student exhibits major errors or omissions with score 3.0 elements.**

Grade 6

Score 3.0	While engaged in tasks that address spatial thinking and the use of charts, maps, and graphs, the student demonstrates an understanding of important information, such as . . . • characteristics and uses of various geographic tools (maps, satellite imagery, aerial photography) (*e.g., explaining and exemplifying how satellite imagery can be used—for example, explaining that detailed images of a volcano can be taken by a satellite orbiting the earth*); • how to construct various basic maps (topographic, road, thematic) (*e.g., explaining and exemplifying how to construct a thematic map depicting given information—for example, creating a map depicting different crops grown in several regions*); and • how to plot absolute location (latitude and longitude, alphanumeric system) (*e.g., explaining and exemplifying how to plot a given location on a map—for example, showing that Athens, Greece, can be found at 37° 58′ north latitude and 23° 43′ east longitude on a globe/map of the world*). **The student exhibits no major errors or omissions.**
Score 2.0	The student exhibits no major errors or omissions regarding the simpler details and processes, such as . . . • recognizing and recalling specific terminology, events, people, and locations (*e.g., prime meridian [Greenwich meridian], grid, major parallel, thematic map*); and • recognizing and recalling isolated details, such as . . . ◦ a geographic information system is a system for storing spatial data and associated attributes; ◦ a thematic map can be used to display various kinds of data; and ◦ the latitude and longitude of a place can be plotted on a map. **However, the student exhibits major errors or omissions with score 3.0 elements.**

Grade 5

Score 3.0	While engaged in tasks that address spatial thinking and the use of charts, maps, and graphs, the student demonstrates an understanding of important information, such as . . . • characteristics and uses of various kinds of maps (topographic, geologic, road, thematic) (*e.g., explaining and exemplifying how topographic maps are used—for example, explaining how a hiker can use a topographic map to determine the elevation of the trail being taken*); and • characteristics and uses of map grids (*e.g., explaining and exemplifying how a map grid can be used—for example, explaining how the location on a map grid can be used to help determine the direction needed to go in order to locate a historic landmark in a national park*). **The student exhibits no major errors or omissions.**
Score 2.0	The student exhibits no major errors or omissions regarding the simpler details and processes, such as . . . • recognizing and recalling specific terminology, events, people, and locations (*e.g., topographic map, geologic map, road map*); and • recognizing and recalling isolated details, such as . . . ◦ a geologic map is made for the purpose of showing subsurface geological features; and ◦ a map grid breaks a map into grid squares. **However, the student exhibits major errors or omissions with score 3.0 elements.**

	Grade 4
Score 3.0	**While engaged in tasks that address spatial thinking and the use of charts, maps, and graphs, the student demonstrates an understanding of important information, such as . . .** • characteristics and uses of various elements of maps and globes (legend, symbols, scale) (*e.g., explaining that the legend of a map has a specific purpose—for example, explaining that the legend contains symbols and descriptions needed to interpret the map*); • how to use a map of the United States (including maps of each state) to find various places discussed in history, language arts, and science (*e.g., explaining and exemplifying how to use a map to locate famous Civil War battles—for example, finding York County, where the Battle of Hanover took place, on a map of Pennsylvania*); and • how to use a globe to find various places discussed in history, language arts, and science (Great Wall of China, Roman Empire) (*e.g., explaining and exemplifying how to use a globe to locate ancient civilizations—for example, locating Egypt in the northern section of Africa on a globe*). **The student exhibits no major errors or omissions.**

Score 2.0	**The student exhibits no major errors or omissions regarding the simpler details and processes, such as . . .**
	• recognizing and recalling specific terminology, events, people, and locations (*e.g., meridian, latitude, longitude*); and
	• recognizing and recalling isolated details, such as . . .
	  ◦ a meridian is an imaginary line on the earth's surface from the North Pole to the South Pole that connects all locations with a given longitude;
	  ◦ sometimes battles are named for a nearby town; and
	  ◦ the names given to some countries have changed over time.
	However, the student exhibits major errors or omissions with score 3.0 elements.

	Grade 3
Score 3.0	**While engaged in tasks that address spatial thinking and the use of charts, maps, and graphs, the student demonstrates an understanding of important information, such as . . .** • how to use a map of the local community (locations of schools, parks, police stations, fire stations) (*e.g., explaining and exemplifying how to use a map of the local community to find a park—for example, given a starting point on the map, using the map symbol for a park to locate the closest park on the map*). **The student exhibits no major errors or omissions.**
Score 2.0	**The student exhibits no major errors or omissions regarding the simpler details and processes, such as . . .** • recognizing and recalling specific terminology, events, people, and locations (*e.g., legend, scale, equator*); and • recognizing and recalling isolated details, such as . . . ◦ police stations can be found on a map of the local community. **However, the student exhibits major errors or omissions with score 3.0 elements.**
	Grade 2
Score 3.0	**While engaged in tasks that address spatial thinking and the use of charts, maps, and graphs, the student demonstrates an understanding of important information, such as . . .** • how to use the concept of intermediate directions (northwest, northeast, southwest, southeast) (*e.g., explaining that intermediate directions can be used to find an object—for example, explaining that the next clue in a game can be found 10 steps to the southwest under a rock*); and • how to use the concept of absolute locations (*e.g., explaining that places within a community have an absolute location—for example, explaining that every building in the community has an address that can be used to locate the building*). **The student exhibits no major errors or omissions.**

Score 2.0	**The student exhibits no major errors or omissions regarding the simpler details and processes, such as . . .**
	• recognizing and recalling specific terminology, events, people, and locations (*e.g., absolute location, intermediate direction [northwest/northeast/southwest/southeast]*); and
	• recognizing and recalling isolated details, such as . . .
	    ○ northwest is between north and west; and
	    ○ the street address of the school describes an absolute location.
	However, the student exhibits major errors or omissions with score 3.0 elements.

Grade 1	
Score 3.0	**While engaged in tasks that address spatial thinking and the use of charts, maps, and graphs, the student demonstrates an understanding of important information, such as . . .** • how to use the concept of cardinal directions (north, south, east, west) (*e.g., explaining that cardinal directions can be used to find a building on a street—for example, the post office can be found by going four blocks to the north*); and • how to use the concept of relative locations (*e.g., explaining that places within a community have a relative location—for example, the location of a building can be described by relating it to something familiar that is nearby, such as the fire station being located next to the library*). **The student exhibits no major errors or omissions.**

Score 2.0	**The student exhibits no major errors or omissions regarding the simpler details and processes, such as . . .**
	• recognizing and recalling specific terminology, events, people, and locations (*e.g., relative location, cardinal direction [north/south/east/west]*); and
	• recognizing and recalling isolated details, such as . . .
	    ○ north is one of four cardinal directions; and
	    ○ "the house across the street from the police station" describes a relative location.
	However, the student exhibits major errors or omissions with score 3.0 elements.

Grade K	
Score 3.0	**While engaged in tasks that address spatial thinking and the use of charts, maps, and graphs, the student demonstrates an understanding of important information, such as . . .** • how to use directions to locate things (left, right, in front, in back) (*e.g., explaining that directions are used to find things—for example, the red ball is on the ground in front of the bush*); • how to find locations on a globe (the United States of America, continents, North Pole, South Pole) (*e.g., explaining that the countries of the world can be found on a globe—for example, the United States can be found on a globe between Canada and Mexico within the continent of North America*); and • how to use basic relative locations (near, far) (*e.g., explaining that basic relative locations can be used to describe the location of people/places/things—for example, the park is near the school*). **The student exhibits no major errors or omissions.**

Score 2.0	**The student exhibits no major errors or omissions regarding the simpler details and processes, such as . . .**
	• recognizing and recalling specific terminology, events, people, and locations (*e.g., globe, map*); and
	• recognizing and recalling isolated details, such as . . .
	    ○ directions are important to adults and children;
	    ○ globes show where places are in the world; and
	    ○ every physical object has a location.
	However, the student exhibits major errors or omissions with score 3.0 elements.

Scoring Scales for
Life Skills

Life Skills

Participation

	High School (Grades 9–12)	
Score 4.0	**In addition to score 3.0 performance, the student demonstrates in-depth inferences and applications that go beyond what was taught.**	
	Score 3.5	In addition to score 3.0 performance, the student demonstrates in-depth inferences and applications with partial success.
Score 3.0	**While engaged in classroom activities, the student meets identified expectations regarding participation, such as . . .** • asking questions for clarification (*e.g., asking "why" and "how" questions to better understand a math topic that is confusing*); • offering ideas without waiting for a question to be asked (*e.g., providing possible interpretations of a poem being discussed in a literature class*); • staying focused during whole-class activities (*e.g., taking notes of key points in order to actively participate in a discussion about the topic presented*); • staying focused during individual activities (*e.g., setting and working toward a goal as to what will be accomplished during seatwork activity*); and • being open-minded about comments and questions from peers (*e.g., honestly considering the validity of other students' opinions; providing constructive reasons for disagreeing with another student's opinion during a class discussion*). **The student exhibits no major errors or omissions.**	
	Score 2.5	The student exhibits no major errors or omissions regarding the score 2.0 elements and partial knowledge of the score 3.0 elements.
Score 2.0	**The student is successful with the simpler details and behaviors, such as . . .** • having a strategy for asking questions for clarification (*e.g., restating key points in the form of a question to check understanding of the topic; asking for key information to be repeated; asking for the definition or meaning of confusing terms*); • having a strategy for offering ideas without being called on (*e.g., locating related information from notes taken from a previous discussion or course material that has been read*); • having a strategy for staying focused during whole-class activities (*e.g., trying to anticipate the main ideas during a lecture; trying to anticipate a few questions that will be answered during a classroom discussion; establishing a participatory mood with attentive expression and posture*); • having a strategy for staying focused during individual activities (*e.g., setting a goal as to what will be accomplished during seatwork*); and • explaining what it means to be open-minded about comments and questions from peers (*e.g., explaining that part of being open-minded is refraining from criticizing another student's comments or questions without having a valid, constructive reason for the critique*). **However, the student exhibits major errors or omissions with score 3.0 elements.**	
	Score 1.5	The student demonstrates partial knowledge of the score 2.0 elements but major errors or omissions regarding the score 3.0 elements.
Score 1.0	**With help, the student demonstrates partial understanding of some of the score 2.0 elements and some of the score 3.0 elements.**	
	Score 0.5	With help, the student demonstrates partial understanding of some of the score 2.0 elements but not the score 3.0 elements.
Score 0.0	**Even with help, the student demonstrates no understanding or skill.**	

Middle School (Grades 6–8)	
Score 4.0	**In addition to score 3.0 performance, the student demonstrates in-depth inferences and applications that go beyond what was taught.**

	Score 3.5	In addition to score 3.0 performance, the student demonstrates in-depth inferences and applications with partial success.

Score 3.0	**While engaged in classroom activities, the student meets identified expectations regarding participation, such as . . .** • offering ideas without waiting for a question to be asked (*e.g., taking an active role in a classroom discussion by volunteering opinions for consideration*); • staying focused during whole-class activities (*e.g., attending to whole-class activities by taking notes*); and • staying focused during individual activities (*e.g., actively engaging in assigned seatwork*). **The student exhibits no major errors or omissions.**

	Score 2.5	The student exhibits no major errors or omissions regarding the score 2.0 elements and partial knowledge of the score 3.0 elements.

Score 2.0	**The student is successful with the simpler details and behaviors, such as . . .** • having a strategy for offering ideas without being called on (*e.g., reviewing class materials, such as the textbook, prior notes, and prior homework, before a class discussion*); • having a strategy for staying focused during whole-class activities (*e.g., setting a mood with attentive expression and posture; making information presented in class personally relevant*); and • having a strategy for staying focused during individual activities (*e.g., describing the "be here now" strategy—that is, when attention starts to drift, say, "be here now" and refocus attention on the subject with questions, summarizing, outlining, and other approaches to maintain attention as long as possible*). **However, the student exhibits major errors or omissions with score 3.0 elements.**

	Score 1.5	The student demonstrates partial knowledge of the score 2.0 elements but major errors or omissions regarding the score 3.0 elements.

Score 1.0	**With help, the student demonstrates partial understanding of some of the score 2.0 elements and some of the score 3.0 elements.**

	Score 0.5	With help, the student demonstrates partial understanding of some of the score 2.0 elements but not the score 3.0 elements.

Score 0.0	**Even with help, the student demonstrates no understanding or skill.**

Upper Elementary (Grades 3–5)	
Score 4.0	**In addition to score 3.0 performance, the student demonstrates in-depth inferences and applications that go beyond what was taught.**

	Score 3.5	In addition to score 3.0 performance, the student demonstrates in-depth inferences and applications with partial success.

Score 3.0	**While engaged in classroom activities, the student meets identified expectations regarding participation, such as . . .** • volunteering to answer general questions asked by the teacher (*e.g., volunteering to answer a question posed to the entire class regarding information in the textbook*); • raising a hand when wishing to ask a question or make a comment (*e.g., waiting for an appropriate time and then raising a hand to ask a question*); and • looking at the teacher or presenter during whole-class activities (*e.g., making periodic eye contact with the teacher/presenter during a presentation to the class*). **The student exhibits no major errors or omissions.**

	Score 2.5	The student exhibits no major errors or omissions regarding the score 2.0 elements and partial knowledge of the score 3.0 elements.
Score 2.0		**The student is successful with the simpler details and behaviors, such as . . .** • being aware of how much he volunteers to answer questions asked by the teacher (*e.g., recognizing that he volunteers to answer only those questions he is sure about*); • being aware of the extent to which she raises a hand to ask a question (*e.g., recognizing that she periodically forgets to raise a hand*); and • being aware of the extent to which he looks at the teacher during whole-class activities (*e.g., recognizing that he doesn't try to look at the teacher during whole-class activities*). **However, the student exhibits major errors or omissions with score 3.0 elements.**
	Score 1.5	The student demonstrates partial knowledge of the score 2.0 elements but major errors or omissions regarding the score 3.0 elements.
Score 1.0		**With help, the student demonstrates partial understanding of some of the score 2.0 elements and some of the score 3.0 elements.**
	Score 0.5	With help, the student demonstrates partial understanding of some of the score 2.0 elements but not the score 3.0 elements.
Score 0.0		**Even with help, the student demonstrates no understanding or skill.**
Elementary (Grades K–2)		
Score 4.0		**In addition to score 3.0 performance, the student demonstrates in-depth inferences and applications that go beyond what was taught.**
	Score 3.5	In addition to score 3.0 performance, the student demonstrates in-depth inferences and applications with partial success.
Score 3.0		**While engaged in classroom activities, the student meets identified expectations regarding participation, such as . . .** • attempting to answer direct questions asked by the teacher (*e.g., trying to answer a question when called on by the teacher*); and • waiting for an appropriate time to ask a question or make a comment (*e.g., waiting to ask a question, raising a hand, and not speaking until called on by the teacher*). **The student exhibits no major errors or omissions.**
	Score 2.5	The student exhibits no major errors or omissions regarding the score 2.0 elements and partial knowledge of the score 3.0 elements.
Score 2.0		**The student is successful with the simpler details and behaviors, such as . . .** • explaining how answering direct questions asked by the teacher might be helpful to the teacher and students (*e.g., explaining that answering direct questions can help the teacher determine what a student knows*); and • explaining how raising a hand when wishing to ask a question or make a comment is helpful to the teacher and students (*e.g., explaining that raising a hand can help the teacher pick different students so that each question is answered in turn*). **However, the student exhibits major errors or omissions with score 3.0 elements.**
	Score 1.5	The student demonstrates partial knowledge of the score 2.0 elements but major errors or omissions regarding the score 3.0 elements.
Score 1.0		**With help, the student demonstrates partial understanding of some of the score 2.0 elements and some of the score 3.0 elements.**
	Score 0.5	With help, the student demonstrates partial understanding of some of the score 2.0 elements but not the score 3.0 elements.
Score 0.0		**Even with help, the student demonstrates no understanding or skill.**

Scoring Scales for Life Skills © 2007 Marzano and Associates

Work Completion

High School (Grades 9–12)		
Score 4.0	**In addition to score 3.0 performance, the student demonstrates in-depth inferences and applications that go beyond what was taught.**	
	Score 3.5	In addition to score 3.0 performance, the student demonstrates in-depth inferences and applications with partial success.
Score 3.0	**The student meets all required expectations regarding assignments and work completion, such as . . .** • following formal written format specifications for assignments without being reminded (*e.g., following* The Chicago Manual of Style, *school format guide*); • developing and implementing comprehensive time-management plans for assignments (*e.g., determining component tasks required to complete an assignment, determining reasonable due dates for each component task, and tracking the completion of each task to help ensure completion of the assignment on time*); and • completing assignments on time and providing acceptable explanations when assignments are not handed in on time (*e.g., turning in assignments on time and complete; when assignments are not turned in on time, having a plausible explanation that meets established classroom policy regarding late assignments*). **The student exhibits no major errors or omissions.**	
	Score 2.5	The student exhibits no major errors or omissions regarding the score 2.0 elements and partial knowledge of the score 3.0 elements.
Score 2.0	**The student is successful with the simpler details and behaviors, such as . . .** • being aware of formal written format specifications for assignments (*e.g., describing the format required for a given assignment*); • developing and implementing basic time-management plans for assignments (*e.g., creating a homework organizer to track due dates for various assignments*); and • monitoring her effectiveness at turning in assignments on time (*e.g., using a chart to keep track of when assignments are turned in*). **However, the student exhibits major errors or omissions with score 3.0 elements.**	
	Score 1.5	The student demonstrates partial knowledge of the score 2.0 elements but major errors or omissions regarding the score 3.0 elements.
Score 1.0	**With help, the student demonstrates partial understanding of some of the score 2.0 elements and some of the score 3.0 elements.**	
	Score 0.5	With help, the student demonstrates partial understanding of some of the score 2.0 elements but not the score 3.0 elements.
Score 0.0	**Even with help, the student demonstrates no understanding or skill.**	
Middle School (Grades 6–8)		
Score 4.0	**In addition to score 3.0 performance, the student demonstrates in-depth inferences and applications that go beyond what was taught.**	
	Score 3.5	In addition to score 3.0 performance, the student demonstrates in-depth inferences and applications with partial success.
Score 3.0	**The student meets all required expectations regarding assignments and work completion, such as . . .** • handing in assignments that meet format requirements specified by the teacher (*e.g., handing in assignments with proper heading, margins, and citations*);	

Score 3.0 (continued)	• developing and implementing basic time-management plans for assignments (*e.g., creating a homework organizer to track due dates for various assignments*); and • completing assignments on time and providing acceptable explanations when assignments are not handed in on time (*e.g., turning in assignments on time and complete; when assignments are not turned in on time, having a plausible explanation that meets established classroom policy regarding late assignments*). **The student exhibits no major errors or omissions.**	
	Score 2.5	The student exhibits no major errors or omissions regarding the score 2.0 elements and partial knowledge of the score 3.0 elements.
Score 2.0	**The student is successful with the simpler details and behaviors, such as . . .** • being aware of format requirements for assignments (*e.g., describing the format requirements for a given assignment*); • being aware of elements of basic time-management plans (*e.g., explaining that a basic homework organizer should include the due date, description, and specific tasks for each assignment*); and • being aware of deadlines for assignments (*e.g., using a simple chart to keep track of the due date for each assignment*). **However, the student exhibits major errors or omissions with score 3.0 elements.**	
	Score 1.5	The student demonstrates partial knowledge of the score 2.0 elements but major errors or omissions regarding the score 3.0 elements.
Score 1.0	**With help, the student demonstrates partial understanding of some of the score 2.0 elements and some of the score 3.0 elements.**	
	Score 0.5	With help, the student demonstrates partial understanding of some of the score 2.0 elements but not the score 3.0 elements.
Score 0.0	**Even with help, the student demonstrates no understanding or skill.**	
Upper Elementary (Grades 3–5)		
Score 4.0	**In addition to score 3.0 performance, the student demonstrates in-depth inferences and applications that go beyond what was taught.**	
	Score 3.5	In addition to score 3.0 performance, the student demonstrates in-depth inferences and applications with partial success.
Score 3.0	**The student meets all required expectations regarding assignments and work completion, such as . . .** • bringing necessary materials to class and following rules for borrowing when necessary (*e.g., having required materials, such as pencils, notebooks, and paper, and borrowing materials occasionally only after asking permission from the teacher*); • following a small set of routine instructions for assignments (*e.g., writing name and date in the upper-right-hand corner of the paper; writing on every other line; stapling multiple pages in the upper-left-hand corner; writing legibly*); and • completing assignments on time and providing acceptable explanations when assignments are not handed in on time (*e.g., turning in assignments on time and complete; when assignments are not turned in on time, having a plausible explanation that meets established classroom policy regarding late assignments*). **The student exhibits no major errors or omissions.**	
	Score 2.5	The student exhibits no major errors or omissions regarding the score 2.0 elements and partial knowledge of the score 3.0 elements.
Score 2.0	**The student is successful with the simpler details and behaviors, such as . . .** • being aware of required class materials (*e.g., describing the materials that the student is required to bring to class each day*);	

Score 2.0 (continued)	• being aware of rules for borrowing class materials (*e.g., describing the rules established in class for borrowing materials, such as using a check-out/check-in system*); • being aware of instructions for assignments (*e.g., describing the instructions provided by the teacher for a given assignment*); and • being aware of requirements regarding turning in assignments on time (*e.g., describing requirements established by the teacher for turning in assignments on time, including when an assignment would be considered late; what would be considered an acceptable explanation for when an assignment is not handed in on time*). **However, the student exhibits major errors or omissions with score 3.0 elements.**	
	Score 1.5	The student demonstrates partial knowledge of the score 2.0 elements but major errors or omissions regarding the score 3.0 elements.
Score 1.0	**With help, the student demonstrates partial understanding of some of the score 2.0 elements and some of the score 3.0 elements.**	
	Score 0.5	With help, the student demonstrates partial understanding of some of the score 2.0 elements but not the score 3.0 elements.
Score 0.0	**Even with help, the student demonstrates no understanding or skill.**	
Elementary (Grades K–2)		
Score 4.0	**In addition to score 3.0 performance, the student demonstrates in-depth inferences and applications that go beyond what was taught.**	
	Score 3.5	In addition to score 3.0 performance, the student demonstrates in-depth inferences and applications with partial success.
Score 3.0	**The student meets all required expectations regarding assignments and work completion, such as . . .** • bringing a pencil or pen to class and following established rules for borrowing when necessary (*e.g., having a pencil or pen available for class work and borrowing materials when needed after asking the teacher's permission*); and • attempting to follow general directions for assignments (*e.g., following the teacher's directions regarding how to hand in papers after a particular assignment*). **The student exhibits no major errors or omissions.**	
	Score 2.5	The student exhibits no major errors or omissions regarding the score 2.0 elements and partial knowledge of the score 3.0 elements.
Score 2.0	**The student is successful with the simpler details and behaviors, such as . . .** • being aware of established rules for borrowing (*e.g., restating the rules established in class for borrowing materials*); and • being aware of general directions for assignments (*e.g., restating the general directions provided by the teacher for a given assignment*). **However, the student exhibits major errors or omissions with score 3.0 elements.**	
	Score 1.5	The student demonstrates partial knowledge of the score 2.0 elements but major errors or omissions regarding the score 3.0 elements.
Score 1.0	**With help, the student demonstrates partial understanding of some of the score 2.0 elements and some of the score 3.0 elements.**	
	Score 0.5	With help, the student demonstrates partial understanding of some of the score 2.0 elements but not the score 3.0 elements.
Score 0.0	**Even with help, the student demonstrates no understanding or skill.**	

Behavior

	High School (Grades 9–12)	
Score 4.0	**In addition to score 3.0 performance, the student demonstrates in-depth inferences and applications that go beyond what was taught.**	
	Score 3.5	In addition to score 3.0 performance, the student demonstrates in-depth inferences and applications with partial success.
Score 3.0	**While engaged in classroom activities, the student follows all classroom rules and procedures, such as . . .** • following routine and spontaneous classroom rules and procedures (*e.g., following the procedure for cleaning up the classroom; following a spontaneous direction by the teacher regarding how to behave during a presentation by a guest speaker*); • helping others follow classroom rules and procedures (*e.g., courteously reminding other students about established rules and procedures*); • not teasing or bullying others (*e.g., treating other students in a courteous and respectful manner; following the school's student code of conduct regarding bullying behaviors that have been established as inappropriate behavior in school*); and • helping others who are being teased or bullied (*e.g., behaving in a supportive way to students who are being bullied—for example, not engaging in group teasing—and intervening when feasible by challenging the bullying behavior directly or indirectly, or reporting the incident to a teacher*). **The student exhibits no major errors or omissions.**	
	Score 2.5	The student exhibits no major errors or omissions regarding the score 2.0 elements and partial knowledge of the score 3.0 elements.
Score 2.0	**The student is successful with the simpler details and behaviors, such as . . .** • explaining the unique contribution of each classroom rule and procedure to student learning (*e.g., explaining how each classroom rule and procedure would affect student learning if it had not been established*); • explaining the characteristics of helping others follow classroom rules and procedures (*e.g., describing what it looks like to help others follow established classroom rules and procedures*); • explaining the detrimental effects of teasing and bullying others (*e.g., describing how teasing and bullying negatively affect the self-esteem of the student being teased or bullied*); and • explaining the characteristics of helping others who are being teased or bullied (*e.g., describing what it looks like to help others who are being teased or bullied*). **However, the student exhibits major errors or omissions with score 3.0 elements.**	
	Score 1.5	The student demonstrates partial knowledge of the score 2.0 elements but major errors or omissions regarding the score 3.0 elements.
Score 1.0	**With help, the student demonstrates partial understanding of some of the score 2.0 elements and some of the score 3.0 elements.**	
	Score 0.5	With help, the student demonstrates partial understanding of some of the score 2.0 elements but not the score 3.0 elements.
Score 0.0	**Even with help, the student demonstrates no understanding or skill.**	

Middle School (Grades 6–8)		
Score 4.0	In addition to score 3.0 performance, the student demonstrates in-depth inferences and applications that go beyond what was taught.	
	Score 3.5	In addition to score 3.0 performance, the student demonstrates in-depth inferences and applications with partial success.
Score 3.0	While engaged in classroom activities, the student follows all classroom rules and procedures, such as . . . • following behavioral directions (*e.g., following a routine or spontaneous direction given by the teacher*); • helping others follow complex directions (*e.g., providing assistance to other students who might find a given set of directions confusing or too complex to follow*); and • not teasing or bullying others (*e.g., treating other students in a courteous and respectful manner; following the school's student code of conduct regarding bullying behaviors that have been established as inappropriate behavior in school*). The student exhibits no major errors or omissions.	
	Score 2.5	The student exhibits no major errors or omissions regarding the score 2.0 elements and partial knowledge of the score 3.0 elements.
Score 2.0	The student is successful with the simpler details and behaviors, such as . . . • explaining the critical features of following directions (*e.g., describing important features of following directions, such as listening to or reading every step carefully, following every step*); • explaining the characteristics of helping others follow directions (*e.g., describing what it looks like to help others follow directions*); and • explaining the characteristics of refraining from teasing and bullying others (*e.g., describing what it looks like to refrain from teasing and bullying others*). However, the student exhibits major errors or omissions with score 3.0 elements.	
	Score 1.5	The student demonstrates partial knowledge of the score 2.0 elements but major errors or omissions regarding the score 3.0 elements.
Score 1.0	With help, the student demonstrates partial understanding of some of the score 2.0 elements and some of the score 3.0 elements.	
	Score 0.5	With help, the student demonstrates partial understanding of some of the score 2.0 elements but not the score 3.0 elements.
Score 0.0	Even with help, the student demonstrates no understanding or skill.	
Upper Elementary (Grades 3–5)		
Score 4.0	In addition to score 3.0 performance, the student demonstrates in-depth inferences and applications that go beyond what was taught.	
	Score 3.5	In addition to score 3.0 performance, the student demonstrates in-depth inferences and applications with partial success.
Score 3.0	While engaged in classroom activities, the student follows all classroom rules and procedures, such as . . . • following general behavioral directions (*e.g., stopping an activity when directed by the teacher*); and • no pushing, no shoving, no name calling (*e.g., no pushing or shoving either in jest or in anger; no name calling in jest or in anger*). The student exhibits no major errors or omissions.	
	Score 2.5	The student exhibits no major errors or omissions regarding the score 2.0 elements and partial knowledge of the score 3.0 elements.

Score 2.0	**The student is successful with the simpler details and behaviors, such as . . .** • explaining the characteristics of following directions regarding behavior (*e.g., describing what it means to stop an inappropriate behavior when asked by the teacher*); and • explaining the characteristics of not pushing, shoving, or name calling (*e.g., describing what it means to push or shove other students, or to call other students names*). **However, the student exhibits major errors or omissions with score 3.0 elements.**	
	Score 1.5	The student demonstrates partial knowledge of the score 2.0 elements but major errors or omissions regarding the score 3.0 elements.
Score 1.0	**With help, the student demonstrates partial understanding of some of the score 2.0 elements and some of the score 3.0 elements.**	
	Score 0.5	With help, the student demonstrates partial understanding of some of the score 2.0 elements but not the score 3.0 elements.
Score 0.0	**Even with help, the student demonstrates no understanding or skill.**	
Elementary (Grades K–2)		
Score 4.0	**In addition to score 3.0 performance, the student demonstrates in-depth inferences and applications that go beyond what was taught.**	
	Score 3.5	In addition to score 3.0 performance, the student demonstrates in-depth inferences and applications with partial success.
Score 3.0	**While engaged in classroom activities, the student follows all classroom rules and procedures, such as . . .** • following basic directions regarding behavior (*e.g., consistently following basic directions such as lining up quickly and quietly when preparing to leave the classroom as a group*); and • keeping one's hands to oneself (*e.g., not pushing or pulling other students*). **The student exhibits no major errors or omissions.**	
	Score 2.5	The student exhibits no major errors or omissions regarding the score 2.0 elements and partial knowledge of the score 3.0 elements.
Score 2.0	**The student is successful with the simpler details and behaviors, such as . . .** • explaining why it is important to follow directions regarding behavior (*e.g., describing what could happen if directions are not followed—for example, a student who fails to keep quiet after being asked might not hear important information being told to the class*); and • explaining why it is important keep hands off someone else (*e.g., describing what could happen if students don't keep their hands to themselves—for example, another student might get hurt*). **However, the student exhibits major errors or omissions with score 3.0 elements.**	
	Score 1.5	The student demonstrates partial knowledge of the score 2.0 elements but major errors or omissions regarding the score 3.0 elements.
Score 1.0	**With help, the student demonstrates partial understanding of some of the score 2.0 elements and some of the score 3.0 elements.**	
	Score 0.5	With help, the student demonstrates partial understanding of some of the score 2.0 elements but not the score 3.0 elements.
Score 0.0	**Even with help, the student demonstrates no understanding or skill.**	

Working in Groups

High School (Grades 9–12)		
Score 4.0	**In addition to score 3.0 performance, the student demonstrates in-depth inferences and applications that go beyond what was taught.**	
	Score 3.5	In addition to score 3.0 performance, the student demonstrates in-depth inferences and applications with partial success.
Score 3.0	**While engaged in classroom activities, the student exhibits group-maintenance and interpersonal skills, such as . . .** • taking on a role—recorder, information gatherer, information synthesizer, and so on—that furthers the efforts of the group even though a different role might be preferred (*e.g., volunteering for a role no one else wants*); and • helping to solve group problems and reconcile differences among group members (*e.g., creating a positive environment by suggesting rules that encourage group members to respect each other, such as identifying inappropriate behaviors that would inhibit a cooperative environment and offering procedures to courteously address the behaviors*). **The student exhibits no major errors or omissions.**	
	Score 2.5	The student exhibits no major errors or omissions regarding the score 2.0 elements and partial knowledge of the score 3.0 elements.
Score 2.0	**The student is successful with the simpler details and behaviors, such as . . .** • being aware of roles within a group and their various functions (*e.g., describing the specific functions of each role within a group*); and • explaining the characteristics of trying to reconcile differences among group members (*e.g., describing different tactics that can be used to reconcile differences in opinion among group members, such as finding commonalities between seemingly conflicting ideas*). **However, the student exhibits major errors or omissions with score 3.0 elements.**	
	Score 1.5	The student demonstrates partial knowledge of the score 2.0 elements but major errors or omissions regarding the score 3.0 elements.
Score 1.0	**With help, the student demonstrates partial understanding of some of the score 2.0 elements and some of the score 3.0 elements.**	
	Score 0.5	With help, the student demonstrates partial understanding of some of the score 2.0 elements but not the score 3.0 elements.
Score 0.0	**Even with help, the student demonstrates no understanding or skill.**	
Middle School (Grades 6–8)		
Score 4.0	**In addition to score 3.0 performance, the student demonstrates in-depth inferences and applications that go beyond what was taught.**	
	Score 3.5	In addition to score 3.0 performance, the student demonstrates in-depth inferences and applications with partial success.
Score 3.0	**While engaged in classroom activities, the student exhibits group-maintenance and interpersonal skills, such as . . .** • helping the group stay on task (*e.g., working in a cooperative manner to establish and implement strategies to stay on task—for example, determining attainable goals as a group and tasks that each group member can complete toward fulfilling those stated goals, and monitoring completion of each task*); and • trying to understand contrary opinions expressed in the group as opposed to immediately rejecting them (*e.g., making attempts to honestly evaluate opposing opinions—for example, listing pros and cons for each viewpoint before dismissing the opinion as irrelevant*).	

Score 3.0 (continued)	The student exhibits no major errors or omissions.	
	Score 2.5	The student exhibits no major errors or omissions regarding the score 2.0 elements and partial knowledge of the score 3.0 elements.
Score 2.0	The student is successful with the simpler details and behaviors, such as . . . • explaining the characteristics of helping the group stay on task (*e.g., describing different tactics that can be used to help group members stay on task, such as allowing any group member the authority to courteously remind others when a discussion goes off topic*); and • explaining the characteristics of trying to understand contrary opinions (*e.g., describing what it looks like to consider contrary opinions—for example, evaluating the strengths and weaknesses of each opinion*). However, the student exhibits major errors or omissions with score 3.0 elements.	
	Score 1.5	The student demonstrates partial knowledge of the score 2.0 elements but major errors or omissions regarding the score 3.0 elements.
Score 1.0	With help, the student demonstrates partial understanding of some of the score 2.0 elements and some of the score 3.0 elements.	
	Score 0.5	With help, the student demonstrates partial understanding of some of the score 2.0 elements but not the score 3.0 elements.
Score 0.0	Even with help, the student demonstrates no understanding or skill.	
Upper Elementary (Grades 3–5)		
Score 4.0	In addition to score 3.0 performance, the student demonstrates in-depth inferences and applications that go beyond what was taught.	
	Score 3.5	In addition to score 3.0 performance, the student demonstrates in-depth inferences and applications with partial success.
Score 3.0	While engaged in classroom activities, the student exhibits group-maintenance and interpersonal skills, such as . . . • listening attentively to the opinions and ideas expressed by others in the group (*e.g., actively listening to others in the group—for example, asking other group members questions; maintaining an attentive posture*); and • offering suggestions that contribute to the overall goal of the group (*e.g., attempting to provide opinions and ideas that contribute to stated goals of the group*). The student exhibits no major errors or omissions.	
	Score 2.5	The student exhibits no major errors or omissions regarding the score 2.0 elements and partial knowledge of the score 3.0 elements.
Score 2.0	The student is successful with the simpler details and behaviors, such as . . . • explaining the characteristics of listening attentively to the opinions and ideas expressed by others (*e.g., describing what it looks like to be an active listener—for example, refraining from interrupting other group members; maintaining attentive expression and posture*); and • distinguishing between suggestions that contribute to the overall goal of the group and suggestions that distract from the overall goal (*e.g., describing what would happen when opinions and ideas that are not related to the topic are discussed—for example, discussing opinions and ideas that are off topic takes time away from constructive discussions that can help the group complete the assignment*). However, the student exhibits major errors or omissions with score 3.0 elements.	
	Score 1.5	The student demonstrates partial knowledge of the score 2.0 elements but major errors or omissions regarding the score 3.0 elements.

Score 1.0	With help, the student demonstrates partial understanding of some of the score 2.0 elements and some of the score 3.0 elements.	
	Score 0.5	With help, the student demonstrates partial understanding of some of the score 2.0 elements but not the score 3.0 elements.
Score 0.0	Even with help, the student demonstrates no understanding or skill.	
Elementary (Grades K–2)		
Score 4.0	In addition to score 3.0 performance, the student demonstrates in-depth inferences and applications that go beyond what was taught.	
	Score 3.5	In addition to score 3.0 performance, the student demonstrates in-depth inferences and applications with partial success.
Score 3.0	While engaged in classroom activities, the student exhibits group-maintenance and interpersonal skills, such as . . . • taking turns in group activities (*e.g., waiting for other group members to take their turn during a group activity*); and • not interrupting others in the group when they are speaking (*e.g., refraining from interrupting group members who are speaking*). **The student exhibits no major errors or omissions.**	
	Score 2.5	The student exhibits no major errors or omissions regarding the score 2.0 elements and partial knowledge of the score 3.0 elements.
Score 2.0	The student is successful with the simpler details and behaviors, such as . . . • explaining why it is important to take turns (*e.g., describing what would happen if group members don't take turns—for example, if* group m*embers don't take turns the assignment might take longer to complete than the time allowed*); and • explaining why it is important to refrain from interrupting others when they are speaking (*e.g., describing what would happen if group members don't refrain from interrupting—for example, the rest of the group might get distracted by the interruption and miss an idea that could help the group finish the assignment*). **However, the student exhibits major errors or omissions with score 3.0 elements.**	
	Score 1.5	The student demonstrates partial knowledge of the score 2.0 elements but major errors or omissions regarding the score 3.0 elements.
Score 1.0	With help, the student demonstrates partial understanding of some of the score 2.0 elements and some of the score 3.0 elements.	
	Score 0.5	With help, the student demonstrates partial understanding of some of the score 2.0 elements but not the score 3.0 elements.
Score 0.0	Even with help, the student demonstrates no understanding or skill.	

References

Ainsworth, L. (2003a). *Power standards: Identifying the standards that matter most.* Denver, CO: Advance Learning Press.

Ainsworth, L. (2003b). *Unwrapping the standards: A simple process to make standards manageable.* Denver, CO: Advance Learning Press.

Ainsworth, L., & Viegut, D. (2006). *Common formative assessments.* Thousand Oaks, CA: Corwin.

Anderson, J. R. (1983). *The architecture of cognition.* Cambridge, MA: Harvard University Press.

Black, P., & Wiliam, D. (1998). Assessment and classroom learning. *Assessment in Education, 5*(1), 7–75.

Bloom, B. S. (1976). *Human characteristics and school learning.* New York: McGraw-Hill.

Carnevale, A. P., Gainer, L. J., & Meltzer, A. S. (1990). *Workplace basics: The essential skills employers want.* San Francisco: Jossey-Bass.

Farkas, S., Friedman, W., Boese, J., & Shaw, G. (1994). *First things first: What Americans expect from public schools.* New York: Public Agenda.

Fuchs, L. S., & Fuchs, D. (1986). Effects of systematic formative evaluation: A meta-analysis. *Exceptional Children, 53*(3), 199–208.

Glaser, R., & Linn, R. (1993). Foreword. In L. Shepard, *Setting performance standards for student achievement* (pp. xiii–xiv). Stanford, CA: National Academy of Education, Stanford University.

Hattie, J. (1984). An empirical study of various indices for determining unidimensionality. *Multivariate Behavioral Research, 19,* 49–78.

Hattie, J. (1985). Methodology review: Assessing the unidimensionality of tests and items. *Applied Psychological Measurement, 9*(2), 139–164.

Kendall, J. S., & Marzano, R. J. (2000). *Content knowledge: A compendium of standards and benchmarks for K–12 education* (3rd ed.). Alexandria, VA: Association for Supervision and Curriculum Development.

Lord, F. M. (1959, June). Problems in mental test theory arising from errors of measurement. *Journal of the American Statistical Association, 54*(286), 472–479.

Marzano, R. J. (2002). *Identifying the primary instructional concepts in mathematics: A linguistic approach.* Centennial, CO: Marzano & Associates.

Marzano, R. J. (2003). *What works in schools: Translating research into action.* Alexandria, VA: Association for Supervision and Curriculum Development.

Marzano, R. J. (2004). *Workshop materials*. Centennial, CO: Marzano & Associates.

Marzano, R. J. (2006). *Classroom assessment and grading that work*. Alexandria, VA: Association for Supervision and Curriculum Development.

Marzano, R. J., Kendall, J. S., & Cicchinelli, L. F. (1998). *What Americans believe students should know: A survey of U.S. adults*. Aurora, CO: Mid-continent Regional Education Laboratory.

Marzano, R. J., Kendall, J. S., & Gaddy, B. B. (1999). *Essential knowledge: The debate over what American students should know*. Aurora, CO: Mid-continent Regional Education Laboratory.

National Commission on Excellence in Education. (1983, April). *A nation at risk: The imperative for educational reform*. Washington, DC: U.S. Government Printing Office.

National Council of Teachers of Mathematics. (2000). *Principles and standards for school mathematics*. Reston, VA: Author.

Ohio Department of Education. (2001). *Academic content standards: K–12 mathematics*. Columbus, OH: Author.

Oklahoma State Department of Education. (2005). *Pocket pass for science: Priority academic student skills: Grades 6–8*. Oklahoma City, OK: Author.

Reeves, D. B. (2002). *Holistic accountability: Serving students, schools, and community*. Thousand Oaks, CA: Corwin.

Secretary's Commission on Achieving Necessary Skills. (1991). *What work requires of schools: A SCANS report for America 2000*. Washington, DC: U.S. Department of Labor.

Wiggins, G., & McTighe, J. (1998). *Understanding by design*. Alexandria, VA: Association for Supervision and Curriculum Development.

Wiggins, G., & McTighe, J. (2005). *Understanding by design* (expanded 2nd ed.). Alexandria, VA: Association for Supervision and Curriculum Development.

About the Authors

Robert J. Marzano is President of Marzano and Associates; a Senior Scholar at Mid-continent Research for Education and Learning (McREL) in Aurora, Colorado; and an Associate Professor at Cardinal Stritch University in Milwaukee, Wisconsin. He has developed programs and practices used in K–12 classrooms that translate current research and theory in cognition into instructional methods. An internationally known trainer and speaker, Marzano has authored 26 books and more than 150 articles and chapters in books on such topics as reading and writing instruction, thinking skills, school effectiveness, restructuring, assessment, cognition, and standards implementation. Recent titles include *Classroom Instruction That Works: Research Strategies for Increasing Student Achievement* (ASCD, 2001); *Classroom Management That Works: Research-Based Strategies for Every Teacher* (ASCD, 2003); *What Works in Schools: Translating Research into Action* (ASCD, 2003); *Building Background Knowledge for Academic Achievement* (ASCD, 2004); *School Leadership That Works* (ASCD, 2005); *Classroom Assessment and Grading That Work* (ASCD, 2006); *The New Taxonomy of Educational Objectives* (Corwin, 2007); and *The Art & Science of Teaching* (ASCD, 2007). Marzano received his bachelor's degree in English from Iona College in New York; a master's degree in education in reading/language arts from Seattle University; and a doctorate in curriculum and instruction from the University of Washington. Address: 7127 S. Danube Court, Centennial, CO 80016 USA. Telephone: (303) 796-7683. E-mail: robertjmarzano@aol.com.

Mark W. Haystead is Director of Technology and Senior Data Analyst for Marzano & Associates in Centennial, Colorado. He performs and manages the company's standards evaluation work, helping schools and districts refine their standards with attention toward making them more useful for classroom teachers. Haystead has worked with schools and districts in six states. He earned a bachelor's degree in Information Technology from University of Phoenix. Address: 7127 S. Danube Court, Centennial, CO 80016 USA. Telephone: (303) 796-7683. E-mail: mhaystead@marzanoandassociates.com.